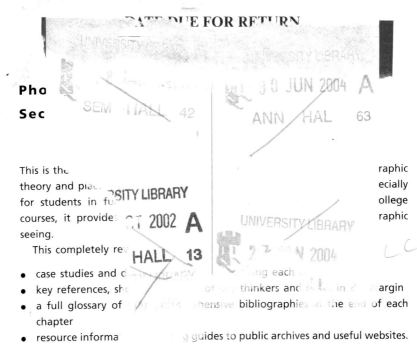
**Pho
Sec**

This is the _____ raphic
theory and pla_____ SITY LIBRARY _____ ecially
for students in fu_____ ollege
courses, it provides _____ 2002 A _____ raphic
seeing.

This completely re_____ HALL 13

- case studies and c_____ ng each
- key references, sho_____ of ____ thinkers and ____ in ____ argin
- a full glossary of _____ hensive bibliographies ____ the end of each
  chapter
- resource informa_____ guides to public archives and useful websites.

Individual chapters in __oduce major photographic theories, histories, genres and
issues, covering:

- Key debates in photographic theory and history • Documentary photography
  and photojournalism • Personal and popular photography • Photography as
  commodity culture • Photography and the human body • Photography as
  art
- Photography in the age of electronic imaging.

The text is impressively illustrated with over a hundred photographs and
images, their diversity reflecting the breadth of issues and practices covered.
They include images by Bill Brandt, Lee Friedlander, Hannah Höch, Roshini
Kempadoo, Dorothea Lange, Lee Miller, Jacob Riis, Alexander Rodchenko,
Sebastaio Salgado, Andres Serrano and Jo Spence.

The Editor: **Liz Wells** is Senior Lecturer in Media Arts in the Faculty of Arts and
Education, University of Plymouth.

Contributors: Michelle Henning, Patricia Holland, Martin Lister, Derrick Price,
Anandi Ramamurthy, Liz Wells.

Comments on the first edition:

'The first textbook to place photographic practice within the context of contemporary theory at a level suitable for undergraduate study. Liz Wells and co. have now given us the basis for a "New History of Photography". An excellent contribution to the literature.'

Howard Riley, Swansea Higher Education Institute

'This is precisely the kind of book I have been yearning to see appear for a long time. Carefully structured, it fulfills the need for a critical theory text for FE, HE and introductory college courses.'

Nicky West, University of Northumbria at Newcastle

'Been waiting years for this one. A unique overview. I will recommend it to all students and refer it to colleagues.'

Pam Isherwood, City and Islington College

'It clearly identifies key debates in photographic theory, is very user-friendly and fills a long-needed gap.'

R. W. Powell, Northumbria University at Newcastle

'Ideal for stimulating discussions on the critical use of photographic images and their evaluation. It is ideal for teaching this part of my BTEC Media and BTEC Art and Design courses.'

Ken Absalom, Gwent Tertiary College

'Well structured – each chapter is thorough and relevant. The quality of the finish is superb – lovely photos and good use of margin notes.'

Richard Swales, Roade School, Northampton

'Informed, interesting and stimulating.'

Dr J. Stokes, South Bank University

'The first edition was invaluable to myself and my fellow students. The layout with a second margin, allowed us to make notes beside key points. The footnotes and referencing chapter by chapter was very useful. The discussions of selected theories directed students to further reading in order to form their own opinions. The language is precise and clear.'

Lucy Johnson, student, Swansea Institute of Higher Education

'Most useful for students following a professional photography "pathway". . . . It will make students think about the context of images rather than as mere technical artefacts and follow current debates on the nature of photographic seeing. The glossary is especially useful. The modest cost is especially welcome.'

Sidney Ray, Westminster University

'Its major strength is that it encourages the reader to think highly of the photographic art.'

Erik Knudsen, Salford University College

Photography:
A Critical Introduction

Second Edition

EDITED BY LIZ WELLS

ROUTLEDGE · Taylor & Francis Group

London and New York

First published 1996 by Routledge
11 New Fetter Lane, London EC4P 4EE

Simultaneously published in the USA and Canada
by Routledge
29 West 35th Street, New York, NY 10001

Reprinted 1998

Second edition published 2000 by Routledge

Reprinted 2001

Routledge is an imprint of the Taylor & Francis Group

© 2000 Liz Wells and contributors

Typeset in Bembo by Florence Production Ltd,
Stoodleigh, Devon
Printed and bound in Great Britain by
Butler & Tanner Ltd, Frome, Somerset

1002153637

British Library Cataloguing in Publication Data
A catalogue record for this book is available from the
British Library

Library of Congress Cataloging in Publication Data
Photography : a critical introduction / edited by Liz
Wells. – 2nd ed.
  p. cm.
 Includes bibliographical references and index.
 1. Photography. I. Wells, Liz, 1948– .
TR145.P48 2000
770–dc21

          99–16503
          CIP

ISBN 0–415–19057–6 (hbk)
ISBN 0–415–19058–4 (pbk)

Contents

Contributors

Michelle Henning lectures in the School of Cultural Studies at the University of the West of England, Bristol, and is a multimedia artist. She has written on representations of the body in J. Arthurs and J. Grimshaw, *Women's Bodies* (Cassell 1999) and on digital images in M. Lister (ed.), *The Photographic Image in Digital Culture* (Routledge 1995).

Patricia Holland is a writer, lecturer and film-maker. She has written about popular photography in *What is a Child* (Virago 1992) and *Family Snaps* (Virago 1991), co-edited with Jo Spence. She has contributed to several readers on photography, television and cultural studies and is author of *The Television Handbook* (Routledge 1997; second edition 2000).

Martin Lister is Head of the School of Cultural Studies at the University of the West of England, Bristol. He is the editor of *The Photographic Image in Digital Culture* (Routledge 1995) and co-author of *Youth, Culture and Photography* (Macmillan 1988). He is a contributor and project director of the Interactive CD Rom *From Silver to Silicon* (ARTEC, London), and is currently working on a book on critical issues in new media.

Derrick Price is a freelance writer and researcher who has published widely on photography, film and literature. A Visiting Research Fellow at the University of the West of England, Bristol (where he was formerly Associate Dean of the Faculty of Art, Media and Design), he is a Director of the Bristol-based research group, Creative Urban Space Projects (CUSP).

Anandi Ramamurthy is Senior Lecturer in the Department of Historical and Critical Studies, University of Central Lancashire. Her Ph.D. research was on 'The representation of African and Asian people in British advertising (1881–1990)'. She curated the exhibition *Black Markets* (Manchester, Cornerhouse). Publications include 'Landscapes of Order and Imperial Control: the representation of plantation production in late nineteenth and early twentieth century tea advertising' *Space and Culture* (forthcoming).

Liz Wells is Senior Lecturer in Media Arts at the Faculty of Arts and Education, University of Plymouth. She has researched, taught and published widely, including editing *Camerawork* (Issues 31 and 32). She edited *Viewfindings, Women Photographers: 'Landscape' and Environment* (1994) and curated the related exhibition, and co-edited *Shifting Horizons* (2000). She is currently developing a *Photo Reader* for Routledge.

Editor's preface

This book aims to remedy the absence of a good, coherent introduction to issues in photography theory, and results from the frustrations of teaching without the benefit of a succinct introductory textbook. There are a number of published histories of photography which define the field according to various agendas, although almost invariably with an emphasis upon great photographers, historically and now. Fewer publications critically engage with debates about the nature of photographic seeing. Most are collections of essays pitched at a level that assumes familiarity with contemporary cultural issues and debates which students new to this field of enquiry may not yet have.

The genesis of this book was complex. The first edition resulted initially from a discussion between myself and Rebecca Barden of Routledge, in which she solicited suggestions for publications which would support the current curriculum. Responding subsequently to her invitation to put forward a developed book proposal, two factors were immediately clear: first, that the attempt to be relatively comprehensive could best be tackled through a collective approach. Thus, a team of writers was assembled right from the start of the project. Second, it quickly became apparent that the project was, in effect, impossible. Photography is ubiquitous. As a result, there are no clear boundaries. It follows that there cannot be precise agreement as to what a 'comprehensive' introduction and overview should encompass, prioritise or exclude. After much consideration, we focused on issues and areas of practice which, given our experience as lecturers in a number of different university institutions, we know feature frequently. That we worked to a large extent in relation to an established curriculum did not mean that the project has been either straightforward or easy. On the contrary, the intention to introduce and explore issues reasonably fully, taking account of what critics have had to say on various aspects of photographic practices, involved investigating and drawing upon a wide and diverse range of resources.

The overall response to the first edition has been extremely positive. Comments included some useful suggestions, many of which we have been able to incorporate within this second, revised edition. A number of readers noted lack of specific address to the body in photography which, by the late 1990s, was a central focus of discussion. These debates are engaged in a new chapter

(chapter 5), commissioned for this edition. This chapter, taken as a whole, stands as an example of the range of debates that may become engaged when the content or subject matter of images is taken as a starting point. In this respect it contrasts in particular with chapters 2 and 6, in which the focus is on a specific genre, or an arena, of practice.

As editor, researching this book led to further questions, as well as to engaging discoveries. The tension between looking, thinking, investigation and discovery is one of the pleasures of academic research. Revising the book has offered an opportunity to clarify through adjusting the organisation of some of the contents (lecturers revising reading lists might like to note that section and page numbers have changed). More significantly, writing at the end of the twentieth century and in anticipation of the publication of the second edition in the twenty-first century has provoked speculation as to how developments in the 1970s, 1980s and 1990s, which seemed not so far distant historically when this project was first conceptualised (c. 1992) may appear retrospectively from the perspective of the new millennium.

This book aims to be relevant, and of interest, to students of photography, graphics, fine art, art and design history, journalism, media studies, communication and cultural studies. We hope that it proves both useful and enjoyable.

Acknowledgements

This book could not have been produced without the support of a number of people. First and foremost I should like to thank Michelle Henning, Patricia Holland, Martin Lister, Derrick Price and Anandi Ramamurthy, without whom the book would not have been possible. The project has been a difficult one but nonetheless a happy one, due to the quality of the team which I have had the good fortune to be in a position to assemble. I should like to thank Rebecca Barden, Moira Taylor and others at Routledge for their support.

I should like to thank Deborah Roland, Department of Learning Resources, The London Institute: LCP, where I was Senior Lecturer in Film- and Photo-related Theory at the time of developing this book; also colleagues and students who, in some instances without realising, contributed to the final shaping. I should also like to thank staff at various archives, including MOMA, New York and CCP, Tucson, for their help in introducing me to their study collections. Many people have read and commented on the first edition of this book, and offered advice on this new edition. Needless to state, the book could not have been further developed without this extensive feedback for which we are all very grateful.

Liz Wells
September 2000

Illustration acknowledgements

We are indebted to the people and archives below for permission to reproduce photographs. Every effort has been made to trace copyright-holders but in a few cases this has not been possible. Any omissions brought to our attention will be remedied in future editions.

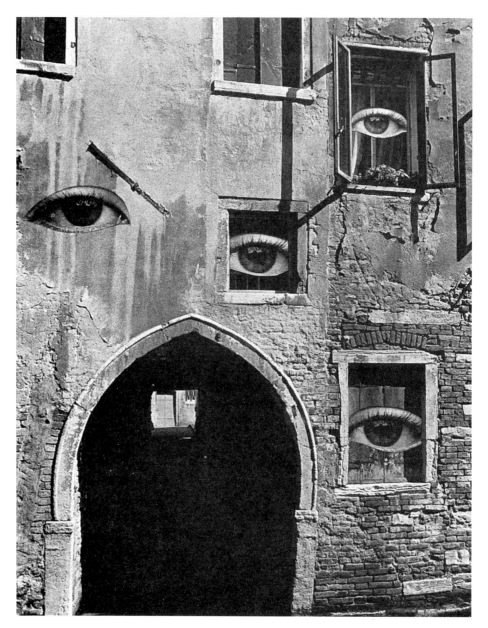

Patricia Townsend, *Critical Observations*, 1988

Introduction

LIZ WELLS

Introduction

THE PURPOSE OF THIS BOOK

The purpose of this book is to introduce and offer an overview of conceptual issues relating to photography and to ways of thinking about photographs. It considers the photograph as an artefact used in a range of different ways and circumstances, and photography as a set of practices which take place in particular contexts. Thus it is essentially about *reading* photographic images rather than about their making. The primary purpose is to introduce key debates, and to indicate sources and resources so students (and other readers) can further develop particular lines of enquiry. The book centrally examines British debates and developments but within a broader, international context. We refer to developments in other parts of Europe and in North America. The perspective is informed by the British base of the team of writers, particularly showing the influence of cultural studies within British academia in the 1990s. Our writing thus reflects a specific point of departure and context for debates. There is no chronological history. Rather, we discuss past attitudes and understandings, technological limitations, and sociopolitical contexts through focus on issues pertinent to contemporary practices. In other words, we consider how ideas about photography have developed in relation to the specific focus, or field of practice, which forms the theme of each chapter. We cannot render theory easy, but we can contribute to clarifying key issues by pointing to ways in which debates have been framed.

Why study theory? As will become clear, theory informs practice. Essentially there are two choices. You can disregard theoretical debates, taking no account of ways in which images become meaningful, thereby limiting critical understanding and, if you are a photographer, restricting the depth of understanding supporting your own work. The alternative is to engage consciously with questions of photographic meaning in order to develop critical perceptions which can be brought to bear upon photographic practices, historically and now, or upon your own photography.

HOW TO USE THIS BOOK

This book introduces a range of debates pertaining to specific fields of photographic practice. We identify key reading, and other resources, in order to illuminate critical debates about photography itself, and to place such debates in relation to broader theoretical and critical discussions. Our aim is to mediate such discussions, indicating key intellectual influences within the debates and alerting you to core reading and other resources. In some instances, our recommendations are highly directive. Thus, we summarise and appraise different critical positions, and point to books and articles in which these positions have been outlined. In most cases the literature which we discuss offers clear priorities and quite explicit points of view in relation to photographic cultures. One part of our task is to draw attention to implicit, underlying assumptions which inform the theoretical stances adopted.

Since the purpose of the book is to introduce issues and ideas which may not yet be familiar, design elements have been incorporated to help. Some chapters include specific case studies, and summary diagrams, which are separated from the main flow of text. This is so that they can be seen in relation to the main argument, but also considered relatively autonomously. Likewise, photographs are sometimes used to illustrate points of discussion. However, images may also be viewed as a specific line of development within each chapter. In order to facilitate visual connections we have limited the range of topics or genres in each chapter. Thus, for instance, in chapter 2, on documentary practices, we concentrate primarily upon street photography. Comparison of images of similar content should help you to see some of the ways in which forms and styles of documentary have changed over time. It should be added that, in order to keep the size (and price) of the book reasonably manageable, we have used fewer photographs than is really desirable in a book about photography. Furthermore, the book has no colour, which means that we have been limited to black and white images. On occasions, especially in examples of advertising in chapter 4, when the original was in colour we have offered a brief description. However, you will need to use other visual sources, books and archives, alongside this book, in order to pursue visual analysis in proper detail.

Throughout the book there is a margin for notes. Key references to core reading, and also to archive sources, appear in the margin so you can follow up the issues and ideas which have been introduced. All references are summarised in a consolidated bibliography at the end of each of the chapters. The margins are also used for technical definitions and for mini-biographies of key theorists. At the end of the book, we include a list of the principal magazines and journals published in English; also archives in Britain which are open to the public (and some suggestions for seeking out archives internationally). There is also a glossary of terms frequently used within the theoretical debates. Terms which may be new to you are printed in bold on their first occurrence in each chapter to remind you that a glossary definition is available.

The book is divided into seven chapters, each of which may be read separately, although there are points of connection between them. We have indicated some of these linkages between chapters, but it is up to you to think them through in detail. A summary of the principal content of each chapter follows at the end of this introduction. This will help you to map your route through the book.

The book cannot be fully comprehensive. Photographic practices are diverse, and it is not possible to focus upon every possible issue and field of activity of interest, historically and now. Furthermore, since the book is reliant on the existence of other source material to which it acts as a guide, it is largely restricted to issues and debates which have been already documented and discussed. Some areas of practice have not had the full focus they might be deemed to deserve. For example, there are many collections of fashion photographs, and there have been numerous articles and books written in recent years on questions of gender, representation, fashion, style and popular culture. But there has been relatively little *critical* writing on fashion photography. This is an omission which we could not rectify here. Thus, fashion photography forms one section of the more general chapter on commodity culture rather than attracting a chapter to itself. Likewise, a number of more technical practices within medical and scientific imaging fall beyond the scope of this book because relevant philosophical and critical writing to date is insufficiently developed.

To some extent the chapters seem quite different from one another. There are a number of reasons for this, of which the first – and most obvious – is that each is written by a different author, and writers each have their own style. The specific tasks allotted to each chapter, and the material included, also lead to different approaches. Two chapters, concerning photography in relation to commodity culture and to digital imaging, both broadly concentrate upon the contemporary. The chapter on the body in photography takes image content as the starting point for discussion. Three chapters, in appraising the specific fields of documentary, photography as Art, and personal photography, are more obviously historical in their approach. Each takes it as axiomatic that the exploration of the history of debates and practices is a means to better understanding how we have arrived at present ways of thinking and operating.

Finally, of course, writing is not interest-free. You should not take the discussion in any of the chapters as representing everything that could be said on its subject. Aside from the limitations of length, authors have their own priorities. Each chapter is written from a considered viewpoint, and each of the authors has studied their subject in depth over many years. As a result of their expertise, and their broader political and social affiliations, they have arrived at particular conclusions. These contribute to determining which issues and examples they have selected for central focus and, indeed, the way they have structured the exposition and argument in their chapter. Whilst each offers you the opportunity to consider key issues and debates, you should not view them as either comprehensive or objectively 'true'. Rather, you should see the book as a guide to what is at stake within particular debates, bearing in mind that the writer, too, has something at stake. You should also remember that this is essentially only an introduction to issues and ideas.

CHAPTER BY CHAPTER

● In chapter 1 we introduce key debates relating to photography and, most particularly, identify some of the positions within these debates taken by established theorists. The chapter focuses initially on a number of debates which have characterised theoretical and critical discussions of the photograph and of photographic practices starting with the interrelation between aesthetics and technologies. We then summarise and discuss historical accounts of photography. Finally we consider sites of practice, institutions and the audience for photography. Central to the chapter is a case study of various ways in which one single image, Dorothea Lange's *Migrant Mother*, has been discussed. It acts as a model of how particular attitudes and assumptions can be illuminated through considering a specific example. The chapter is designed as a foundation for discussions, many of which will be picked up again for more detailed examination later in the book.

● Chapter 2 focuses upon the documentary role of the camera, especially in relation to recording everyday life. There is also some discussion of travel photography and of photojournalism, especially the expanding journalistic role for photography in the early twentieth century. Claims have been made for the authenticity or 'truth' of photography used within surveys or viewed as evidence. The chapter considers disputes that have arisen in relation to such claims in the nineteenth century, in the early twentieth century – especially in the 1920s and 1930s when the term 'documentary' was coined – and in relation to contemporary practices in documentary and reportage.

The chapter is concerned throughout with the multiple discourses through which the nature of photography and its social project has been constructed and understood. By concentrating on particular periods it offers a critical history of documentary which problematises and clarifies the relationship of a specific form of representation to other debates and movements.

● Chapter 3 focuses upon the popular and the personal, developing an historical overview of leisure and domestic uses of photography as a medium through which individual lives and fantasies have been recorded. Particular attention is paid to the family album, which both documents social histories and stands as a talisman of personal experience. The chapter also considers the strategies by which a mass market for photography was constructed, in particular by Kodak. Finally the chapter comments upon recent research on the family photograph, considering what is concealed, as much as what is revealed, in family relationships, gender and sexuality. Attention throughout is drawn to the role of women as photographers and keepers of the photograph album.

In keeping with the style of this book, this chapter signals key texts and further reading. However, the history of popular photography to date has attracted less critical attention than has been directed to other fields of photographic practice; for instance, documentary. In contrast to other parts of the book, this chapter draws upon original research and little-known materials.

● Chapter 4 continues the focus upon everyday uses of photography through considering advertising and commodity culture. Photography is a cultural tool which is itself a commodity as well as a key expressive medium used to promote commercial interests. These links are examined through a series of case studies offering examples of analysis of the single image – tourism, fashion and the exotic – and Benetton as an example of strategic self-publicity. Within commodity culture, that which is specific to photography interacts extensively with broader political and cultural issues. Thus we note references both to commercial photography and, more generally, to questions of the politics of representation, paying particular attention to gender and ethnicity. The chapter employs semiotics within the context of socio-economic analysis to point to ways in which photography is implicated in the concealing of international social and economic relations.

● Chapter 5 focuses upon the photographic body, discussing the extent to which the body image came under scrutiny at the end of the twentieth century. Here a history of attitudes to photography and the body is traced, noting ways in which the photograph has been taken to embody social difference. Taking as its starting point the proposal that there is a crisis of confidence in the body consequent upon new technological developments along with a crisis of representation of the body, the chapter explores questions of desire, pornography, the grotesque and images of the dead, in relation to different modes of representing the body familiar from media imagery as well as within art history.

● Chapter 6 considers photographic practices in relation to Art, discussing claims made for the status of photography as a fine art practice, historically and now. The chapter is organised chronologically in three historical sections: the nineteenth century, modern art movements, and the late twentieth century. This historical division is intended not as a sort of chart of progress so much as a method of identifying different moments and shifting terms of reference relating to photography as an Art practice. Attention is paid to current forms of work and to themes which feature frequently in contemporary practice including questions of gender, ethnicity and identity. The principal concern is to trace the shifting terms of debate as to the status of the photograph as Art and to map historical changes in the situation of the photographic within the museum and art gallery.

● Chapter 7 explores photography and digital imaging. New means of electronic and digital imaging are emerging within societies that are undergoing significant economic, technological and political change. How can these developments be understood? How are these technologies being used? What effect will they have on the historically established practices of photography? The chapter is based on two key ideas. First, amidst dramatic developments in electronic communications and digital image technologies, it no longer seems possible to take the cultural dominance of the photographic for granted. Second, given that the photographic image has shaped the way the world is seen and represented, it is clear that the history of photographic codes, practices and uses will contribute to shaping new media.

Given the very contemporary nature of this chapter it is, inevitably, more speculative than other sections of the book. The range of relevant further reading references is also more restricted, certainly in relation to cultural theory and digitalisation. However, as is clearly argued in the chapter, old debates persist through new technological developments. The unease associated with the idea of manipulation of the image indicates the extent to which, in terms of commonsense ideologies, the photograph is viewed as relating directly and unproblematically to (what is conceptualised as) external reality. It is suggested that the introduction of (relatively) cheap and accessible photo-manipulation software programs has brought discussion of realism once again into central focus.

CHAPTER 1

Thinking about photography

Debates, historically and now

DERRICK PRICE

LIZ WELLS

A knowledge of photography is just as important as that of the alphabet. The illiterate of the future will be ignorant of the use of camera and pen alike.

László Moholy-Nagy 1923

Thinking about photography
Debates, historically and now

INTRODUCTION

This chapter introduces and discusses key writings on photography. The references are to relatively recent publications, and to current debates about photography; however, these books often refer back to earlier writings, so a history of changing ideas can be discerned. This history focuses on photography itself as well as considering photography alongside art history and theory, and cultural history and theory more generally.

The chapter is in four sections: Aesthetics and technologies, Contemporary debates, Histories of photography, and Photography and social history. The principal aim is to locate writings about photography both in terms of its own history, as a specific medium and set of practices, and in relation to broader historical, theoretical and political considerations. Thus we introduce and consider some of the different approaches – and difficulties – which emerge in relation to the project of theorising photography.

E.H. Carr has observed that history is a construct consequent upon the questions asked by the historian (Carr 1964). Thus, he suggests, histories tell us as much about the historian as about the period or subject under interrogation. Furthermore, the historian's selection and organisation of material is to some extent predetermined by the purpose and intellectual parameters of any particular project. Such parameters reflect the interests of the historian, who nearly always has to take account of institutional constraints (for instance, the expectation that a publication will be made from research findings within a set period of time). Projects are also framed by underpinning ideological and political assumptions and priorities.

Such observations are obviously pertinent when considering the history of photography. They are also relevant to investigating ways in which photography has been implicated in the construction of history. As the French cultural critic, Roland Barthes, has pointed out, the nineteenth century gave us both history and photography. He distinguishes between *history* which he describes as 'memory fabricated according to positive formulas', and *the photograph* defined as 'but fugitive testimony' (Barthes 1984: 93). It is attitudes to photography, its contexts, usages and critiques of its nature that we explore in this chapter.

AESTHETICS AND TECHNOLOGIES

The impact of new technologies

Photography emerged as part of a cluster of technical inventions and innovations around the middle of the nineteenth century (including inventions in the electrical industries and new discoveries in optics and chemistry). Hailed as a great technological invention it immediately became the subject of debates concerning its **aesthetic** status and social uses.

The excitement generated by the announcement, or marketing, of innovations tends to distract us from the fact that technologies are researched and developed in human societies. New machinery is normally presented as the agent of social change, not as the outcome of a desire for such change, i.e. as a cause rather than a consequence of culture. However, it can be argued that particular cultures invest in and develop new machines and technologies in order to satisfy previously foreseen social needs. Photography is one such example. A number of theorists have identified precursors of photography in the late eighteenth century. For instance, an expanding middle-class demand for portraiture which outstripped available (painted) means led to the development of the mechanical Physiognotrace[1] and to the practice of silhouette cutting (Freund 1980). Geoffrey Batchen also points out that photography had been a 'widespread social imperative' long before Daguerre and Fox Talbot's official announcements in 1839. He lists twenty-four names of people who had 'felt the hitherto strange and unfamiliar desire to have images formed by light spontaneously fix themselves' from as early as 1782 (Batchen 1990: 9). Since most of the necessary elements of technological knowledge were in place well before 1839, the significant question is not so much who invented photography but rather why it became an active field of research and discovery at that particular point in time (Punt 1995).

1 For definitions see Gordon Baldwin (1991) *Looking at Photographs: A Guide to Technical Terms*, California: The J Paul Getty Museum and London: British Museum Press.

Once a technology exists, it may become adapted and introduced into social use in a variety of both foreseen and unforeseen ways. As cultural theorist Raymond Williams has argued, there is nothing in a technology itself which determines its cultural location or usage (Williams 1974). If technology is viewed as determining cultural uses, much remains to be explained. Not the least of this is the extent to which people subvert technologies and resist or invent new uses which had never originally been intended or envisaged. In addition, new technologies become incorporated within established relations of production and consumption, contributing to articulating – but not causing – shifts and changes in such relations and patterns of behaviour.

Art or technology?

Central to the nineteenth-century debate about the nature of photography as a new technology was the question as to how far it could be considered as Art. It was celebrated for its putative ability to produce accurate images of what was in front of its lens; images which were seen as being mechanically produced and thus free of the selective discriminations of the human eye and hand. On precisely the same grounds, the medium was often regarded as falling outside the realm of art, as its assumed power of accurate, dispassionate recording appeared to displace the artist's compositional creativity.

Writing on the Salon of 1859, the French poet Charles Baudelaire attacked those who confused photography with art and were excited by the new discovery, seeing in it the possibility of the exact delineation of nature. Fox Talbot had defined photography as 'the pencil of nature'. Indeed, in referring to his images as photogenic *drawing*, he seems to have been claiming photography to be just as much a useful art as it was a chemistry. But some caution is appropriate, as drawing was perceived differently then. If drawing was viewed as primarily functional, rather than creative, then Talbot was welcoming the photograph as a substitute for the informational sketch. Indeed, debates concerning the status of photography as art took place in periodicals throughout the nineteenth century. The French journal, *La Lumière*, published writings on photography both as a science and as an art.[2] Baudelaire linked 'the invasion of photography and the great industrial madness of today' and asserted that 'if photography is allowed to deputize for art in some of art's activities, it will not be long before it has supplanted or corrupted art altogether' (Baudelaire 1859: 297). In his view photography's only function was to support intellectual enquiry:

> Photography must, therefore, return to its true duty which is that of handmaid of the arts and sciences, but their very humble handmaid, like printing and shorthand, which have neither created nor supplemented literature. Let photography quickly enrich the traveller's album and restore to his eyes the precision his memory may lack; let it adorn the library of the naturalist, magnify

2 Lemagny and Rouille (1987: 44) point out that the subtitle for the journal was 'Review of photography: fine arts-heliography-sciences, non-political magazine published every Saturday'.

microscopic insects, even strengthen, with a few facts, the hypotheses of the astronomer; let it, in short, be the secretary and record-keeper of whomsoever needs absolute material accuracy for professional reasons.

(Baudelaire 1859: 297)

'Absolute material accuracy' was seen as the hallmark of photography, because most people at the time accepted that the medium rendered a complete and faithful image of its subjects. Moreover, the nineteenth-century desire to explore, record and catalogue human experience, both home and abroad, encouraged people to emphasise photography as a method of naturalistic documentation. Baudelaire, who was among the more prominent French critics of the time, not only accepts its veracity but adds: 'if once it be allowed to impinge on the sphere of the intangible and the imaginary, on anything that has value solely because man adds something to it from his soul, then woe betide us!' (1859: 297). Here he is opposing industry (seen as mechanical, soulless and repetitive) with art, which he considered to be the most important sphere of existential life. Thus Baudelaire is evoking the irrational, the spiritual and the imaginary as an antidote to the positivist interest in measurement and statistical accuracy which, as we have noted, characterised much nineteenth-century investigation. From this point of view the mechanical nature of the camera militated against its use for anything other than mundane purposes.

Photographers responded to criticisms of this kind in two main ways: either they accepted that photography was something different from Art and sought to discover what the intrinsic properties of the medium were; or they pointed out that photography was more than a mechanical form of image-making, that it could be worked on and contrived so as to produce pictures which in some ways resembled paintings. 'Pictorial' photography, from the 1850s onwards, sought to overcome the problems of photography by careful arrangement of all the elements of the composition and by reducing the signifiers of technological production within the photograph. For example, they ensured that the image was out of focus, slightly blurred and fuzzy; they made pictures of allegorical subjects, including religious scenes; and those who worked with the gum bichromate process scratched and marked their prints in an effort to imitate something of the appearance of a canvas.

In the other camp were those photographers who celebrated the qualities of **straight photography** and did not want to treat the medium as a kind of monochrome painting. They were interested in photography's ability to provide apparently accurate records of the visual world and tried to give their images the formal status and finish of paintings while concentrating their attention on its intrinsic qualities.

Most of these photographs were displayed on gallery walls – this was a world of exhibition salons, juries, competitions and medals. In the journals

See chapter 6 for discussion of Pictorialism as a specific photographic movement.

straight photography
Emphasis upon direct documentary typical of the Modern period in American photography.

of the time (which already included the *British Journal of Photography*), tips about technique coexisted with articles on the rules of composition. If the photographs aspired to be Art, their makers aspired to be artists, and they emulated the characteristic institutions of the art world. However, away from the salon, in the high streets of most towns, jobbing photographers earned a living by making simple photographic portraits of people, many of whom could not have afforded any other record of their own appearance. This did not please the painters:

> The cheap portrait painter, whose efforts were principally devoted to giving a strongly marked diagram of the face, in the shortest possible time and at the lowest possible price, has been to a great extent superseded. Even those who are better entitled to take the rank of artists have been greatly interfered with. The rapidity of execution, dispensing with the fatigue and trouble of rigorous sittings, together with the supposed certainty of accuracy in likeness in photography, incline many persons to try their luck in Daguerreotype, a Talbotype, Heliotype, or some method of sun or light-painting, instead of trusting to what is considered the greater uncertainty of artistic skill.
>
> (Howard 1853: 154)

The industrial process, so despised by Baudelaire and other like-minded critics, is here seen as offering mechanical accuracy combined with a degree of quality control. Photography thus begins to emerge as the most commonly used and important means of communication for the industrial age.[3]

Writing at about the same time as Baudelaire, Lady Elizabeth Eastlake agreed that photography was not an art but emphasised this as its strength.[4] She argued that:

> She is made for the present age, in which the desire for art resides in a small minority, but the craving, or rather the necessity for cheap, prompt, and correct facts in the public at large. Photography is the purveyor of such knowledge to the world. She is the sworn witness of everything presented to her view . . . (her studies are 'facts') . . . facts which are neither the province of art nor of description, but of that new form of communication between man and man – neither letter, message, nor picture – which now happily fills the space between them.
>
> (Eastlake 1857: 93)

In this account, photography is not so much concerned with the development of a new aesthetic as with the construction of new kinds of knowledge as the carrier of 'facts'. These facts are connected to new forms of communication for which there is a demand among all social groups; they are neither arcane nor specialist, but belong in the sphere of everyday life. In this respect,

3 For an interesting account of debates and discourses on realism and photography in the nineteenth century see Jennifer Green-Lewis (1996) *Framing the Victorians, Photography and the Culture of Realism*, Ithaca and London: Cornell University Press.

4 Lady Eastlake, a photographer in her own right, was married to Sir Charles Eastlake, first President of the London Photographic Society (later the Royal Photographic Society).

Eastlake is one of the first writers to argue that photography is a democratic means of representation and that the new facts will be available to everyone.

Photography does not merely transmit these facts, it creates them, but Eastlake sees photography as the 'sworn witness' of the appearance of things. This juridical phrase strikingly captures what, for many years, was considered to be the inevitable function of photography – that it showed the world without contrivance or prejudice. For Eastlake, such facts came from the recording without selection of whatever was before the lens. It is photography's inability to choose and select the objects within the frame that locates it in a factual world and prevents it from becoming Art:

> Every form which is traced by light is the impress of one great moment, or one hour, or one age in the great passage of time. Though the faces of our children may not be modelled and rounded with that truth and beauty which art attains, yet *minor* things – the very shoes of the one, the inseparable toy of the other – are given with a strength of identity which art does not even seek.
>
> (Eastlake 1857: 94; emphasis in original)

The old hierarchies of Art have broken down. Photography bears witness to the passage of time, but it cannot make statements as to the importance of things at any time, nor is it concerned with 'truth and beauty' or with teasing out what underlies appearances. Rather, it voraciously records anything in view; in other words it is firmly in the realm of the contingent.

Photography, then, is concerned with facts that are 'necessary', but may also be contingent, may draw our attention to what formerly went unnoticed or ignored. Writing within fifteen years of its invention Eastlake points to the many social uses to which photography has already been put:

> photography has become a household word and a household want; it is used alike by art and science, by love, business and justice; is found in the most sumptuous saloon and the dingiest attic – in the solitude of the Highland cottage, and in the glare of the London gin palace – in the pocket of the detective, in the cell of the convict, in the folio of the painter and architect, among the papers and patterns of the mill owner and manufacturer and on the cold breast of the battle field.
>
> (Eastlake 1857: 81)

For Eastlake, photography is ubiquitous and classless; it is a popular means of communication. Of course, it was not true that people of all classes and conditions could commission photographs as a necessary 'household want' – she anticipates that state by several decades, during which time the use of photography was also spreading from its original practitioners (relatively affluent people who saw themselves as experimenters or hobbyists) to those who undertook it as a business and began to extend the repertoire of conventions of the 'correct' way to photograph people and scenes.

Eastlake's facts are produced, she claims, by a new form of communication, which she is unable to define very clearly. But for all her vagueness, she does identify an important constituent in the making of modernity: the rise of previously unknown forms of communication which had a dislocating effect on traditional technologies and practices. She is writing at an historical moment marked by a cluster of technical inventions and changes and she places photography at the centre of them. The notion that the camera should aspire to the status of the printing press – a mechanical tool which exercises no effect upon the medium which it supports – is here seriously challenged. For Eastlake calmly accepts that photography is not Art, but hints at the displacing effect the medium will have on the old structures of Art. Photography, she says, bears witness to the passage of time, but it cannot select or order the relative importance of things at any time. It does not tease out what underlies appearances, but records voraciously whatever is in its view. By the first decade of the twentieth century the Pictorialists had all but retreated from the field and it was the qualities of straight photography that were subsequently prized. Moreover, modernism argued for a photography that was in opposition to the traditional claims of Art.

The photograph as document

In Britain, as elsewhere, the idea of documentary has underpinned most photographic practices since the 1930s. The terminology is indicative: the *Oxford English Dictionary* definition of 'documentary' is 'to document or record'. The simultaneous 'it was there' (the pro-photographic event) and 'I was there' (the photographer) effect of the photographic record of people and circumstances contributes to the authority of the photographic image. Photographic aesthetics commonly accord with the dominant modes and traditions of Western two-dimensional art, including perspective and the idea of a vanishing point. Indeed, as a number of critics have suggested, photography not only echoes post-Renaissance painterly conventions, but also achieves visual renderings of scenes and situations with what seems to be a higher degree of accuracy than was possible in painting. Photography can, in this respect, be seen as effectively substituting for the **representational** task previously accorded to painting. In addition, as **Walter Benjamin** argued in 1936, changes brought about by the introduction of mechanical means of reproduction which produced and circulated multiple copies of an image shifted attitudes to Art (Benjamin 1970). Formerly unique objects, located in a particular place, lost their singularity as they became accessible to many people in diverse places. Lost too was the 'aura' that was attached to a work of Art which was now open to many different readings and interpretations. For Benjamin, photography was therefore inherently more democratic. Yet established attitudes persist. In Western art the artist is accorded the status of someone

Walter Benjamin
(1892–1940)
Born in Berlin, Benjamin studied philosophy and literature in a number of German universities. In the 1920s he met the playwright, Bertolt Brecht, who exercised a decisive influence on his work. Fleeing the Nazis in 1940, Benjamin found himself trapped in occupied France and committed suicide on the Spanish border. During the 1970s his work began to be translated into English and exercised a great critical influence. His critical essays on Brecht were published in English under the title *Understanding Brecht* in 1973. Benjamin was an influential figure in the exploration of the nature of modernity through essays such as his study of Baudelaire, published as *Charles Baudelaire: A Lyric Poet in the Era of High Capitalism* (London: Verso, 1973). He is acclaimed as one of the major thinkers of the twentieth century, particularly for his historically situated interrogations of modern culture. Two highly important essays for the student of photography are 'A Short History of Photography' (1931) and 'The Work of Art in the Age of Mechanical Reproduction' (1936). The latter essay and 'Theses on the Philosophy of History' are frequently drawn upon in discussion of the cultural implications of new technological developments.

endowed with particular sensitivities and vision. That the photographer as artist, viewed as a special kind of seer, chose to make a particular photograph lends extra authority and credibility to the picture.

In the twentieth century, photography continued to be ascribed the task of 'realistically' reproducing impressions of actuality. Writing after the Second World War in Europe, German critic, Siegfried Kracauer and French critic, André Bazin, both stressed the ontological relation of the photograph to reality (Bazin 1967; Kracauer 1960). Walter Benjamin was among those who had disputed the efficacy of the photograph in this respect, arguing that the reproduction of the surface appearance of places tells us little about the socio-political circumstances which influence and circumscribe actual human experience (**Benjamin 1931**).

WALTER BENJAMIN (1931) 'A Small History of Photography' in (1979) **One Way Street**, London: New Left Books.

The photograph, technically and aesthetically, has a unique and distinctive relation with that which is/was in front of the camera. Analogical theories of the photograph have been abandoned; we no longer believe that the photograph directly replicates circumstances. But it remains the case that, technologically, the chemically produced image is an indexical effect caused by a particular conjuncture of circumstances (including subject-matter, framing, light, characteristics of the lens, chemical properties and darkroom decisions). This basis in the observable lends a sense of authenticity to the photograph. Italian **semiotician**, Umberto Eco, has commented that the photograph reproduces the conditions of optical perception, but only some of them (see Eco in Burgin 1982). That the photograph appears iconic not only contributes an aura of authenticity, it also seems reassuringly familiar. The articulation of familiar-looking subjects through established aesthetic conventions further fuels realist notions associated with photography. Thus philosophical, technical and aesthetic issues – along with the role accorded to the artist – all feature within **ontological** debates relating to the photograph.

In recent years, developments in computer-based image production and the possibilities of digitalisation and reworking of the photographic image have increasingly called into question the idea of documentary realism. The authority attributed to the photograph is at stake. That this has led to a reopening of debates about 'photographic truth' in itself shows that, in everyday parlance, photographs are still viewed as realistic.

Photography and the modern

See chapter 7 for further discussion.

Photography was born into a critical age, and much of the discussion of the medium has been concerned to define it and to distinguish it from other practices. There has never, at any one time, been a single object, practice or form that is *photography*; rather, it has always consisted of different kinds of work and types of image which in turn served different material and social uses. Yet discussion of the nature of the medium has often been either reductionist – looking for an *essence* which transcends its social or aesthetic forms – or highly descriptive and not theorised.

Photography was a major carrier and shaper of **modernism**. Not only did it *dislocate* time and space, but it also undermined the linear structure of conventional narrative. Modern photography, in the first half of the twentieth century, offered a particular *way of seeing*. To some extent this idea is as old as the medium itself. But it took on a particular form in the 1920s and 1930s when both the putative political power of photography and its status as the most important modern form of communication were at their height. Modernism aimed to produce a new kind of world and new kinds of human beings to people it. The old world would be put under the spotlight of modern technology and the old evasions and concealments revealed. The photo-eye was seen as revelatory, dragging 'facts', however distasteful or deleterious to those in power, into the light of day. As a number of photographers in Europe and North America stressed, albeit somewhat differently, another of its functions was to show us the world as it had never been seen before. Here, the stress on form in *photographic seeing* typical of American modern photography parallels the stress on photography as a particular kind of vision in European movements of the 1920s. Our vision will be changed because we can see the world from unfamiliar viewpoints, for instance, through a microscope, from the top of high buildings, from under the sea. Moreover, photography validated our experience of 'being there', which is not merely one of visiting an unfamiliar place, but of capturing the authentic experience *of* a strange place. Photographs are records and documents which pin down the changing world of appearance.

European modernism, with its contempt for the aesthetic forms of the past and its celebration of the machine, endorsed photography's claim to be the most important form of representation. Moholy-Nagy, writing in the 1920s, argued that now our vision will be corrected and the weight of the old cultural forms removed from our shoulders:

> Everyone will be compelled to see that which is optically true, is explicable in its own terms, is objective, before he can arrive at any possible subjective position. This will abolish that pictorial and imaginative association pattern which has remained unsuperseded for centuries and which has been stamped upon our vision by great individual painters.
>
> (Moholy-Nagy 1967: 28)

A world cleansed of traditional forms and hierarchies of values would be established, one in which we would be free to see clearly without the distorting aesthetics of the past. This new world had already been named by Paul Strand in describing American photographic practice, which he saw as indigenous, and viewed as being as revolutionary as the skyscraper. As he put it in a famous article in the last issue of *Camerawork*:

> America has been expressed in terms of America without the outside influence of Paris art schools or their dilute offspring here . . .

[photography] found its highest esthetic achievement in America, where a small group of men and women worked with honest and sincere purpose, some instinctively and a few consciously, but without any background of photographic or graphic formulae much less any cut and dried ideas of what is Art and what isn't: this innocence was their real strength. Everything they wanted to say had to be worked out by their own experiments: it was born of actual living. In the same way the creators of our skyscrapers had to face the similar circumstances of no precedent and it was through that very necessity of evolving a new form, both in architecture and photography that the resulting expression was vitalised.

(Strand 1917: 220)

Here, in a distinctively American formulation, photography is seen as having been developed outside history. Strand is claiming that a new frontier of vision was established by hard work and a kind of innocence, that it was a product of human experience rather than of cultural inheritance.

The postmodern

There are several strands within the notion of the **postmodern** which are pertinent to photography. First, there is a philosophical argument that defines postmodernism as marking the collapse of overarching narratives and witnessing the end of history. Second, there is the notion of the centrality of the simulacrum in which the endless production, reproduction and circulation of signs has rendered trivial the distinction between 'original' and 'copy', thereby, some fifty years later, achieving the democratisation and loss of 'aura' that Benjamin had discussed. The camera has, of course, been centrally implicated in this. Finally, there is the idea that what marks this period is the endless creation, circulation, distribution and exchange of signs.

Writing as early as 1859, the American jurist and writer, Oliver Wendell Holmes, considered the power of photography to change our relationship to original, single and remarkable works:

There is only one Coliseum or Pantheon; but how many millions of potential negatives have they shed – representatives of billions of pictures – since they were erected! Matter in large masses must always be fixed and dear; form is cheap and transportable. We have got the fruit of creation now and need not trouble ourselves with the core. Every conceivable object of Nature and Art will soon scale off its surface for us. We will hunt all curious, beautiful grand objects, as they hunt the cattle in South America, for their *skins*, and leave the carcasses as of little worth.

(Holmes 1859: 60)

While this is a percipient remark, Holmes did not go far enough. He did conceive of some essential difference between originals and copies.

Nevertheless, he realised that the mass trade in images would change our relationship to originals; making them, indeed, little more than the source of representation.

In a world overwhelmed by signs, what status is there for photography's celebrated ability to reproduce the real appearance of things? Fredric Jameson argues that photography is:

> renouncing reference as such in order to elaborate an autonomous vision which has no external equivalent. Internal differentiation now stands as the mark and moment of a decisive displacement in which the older relationship of image to reference is superseded by an inner or interiorized one . . . the attention of the viewer is now engaged by a differential opposition within the image itself, so that he or she has little energy left over for intentness to that older 'likeness' or 'matching' operation which compared the image to some putative thing outside.
>
> (Jameson 1991: 179)

He is among a number of contemporary critics who argue that photography has given up attempting to provide depictions of things which have an autonomous existence outside the image and that we spectators no longer possess the psychic energy needed to compare the photograph with objects, persons or events in the world external to the frame of the camera. A simulacrum is a copy for which there is no original; it is, as it were, a copy in its own right. Thus, in postmodernity it may be that the photograph has no referent in the wider world and can be understood or critiqued only in terms of its own internal aesthetic organisation. Yet, as Roland Barthes argued, the photograph is always and necessarily *of* something (Barthes 1984: 28).

So what are we to make of a photography which does not traffic in multiple images but, rather, is constructed for the gallery? Cultural theorist, Rosalind Krauss, has described photography's relationship to the world of aesthetic distinction and judgement in the following terms:

> Within the aesthetic universe of differentiation – which is to say; 'this is good, this is bad, this, in its absolute originality, is different from that' – within this universe photography raises the specter of nondifferentiation at the level of qualitative difference and introduces instead the condition of a merely quantitative array of difference, as in series. The possibility of aesthetic difference is collapsed from within and the originality that is dependent on this idea of difference collapses with it.
>
> (Krauss 1981: 21)

This 'collapse of difference', however, has had an enormous effect on painting and sculpture, for photography's failure of singularity undermined the very ground on which the aesthetic rules that validated originality was established.

Multiple, reproducible, repetitive images destabilised the very notion of 'originality' and blurred the difference between original and copy. The 'great masters' approach to the analysis of images becomes increasingly irrelevant, for in the world of the simulacrum what is called into question is the originality of authorship, the uniqueness of the art object and the nature of self-expression.

CONTEMPORARY DEBATES

What is theory?

> The role of any theory is to explain. But as recent critical debate has taught us, systems of discourse are themselves implicated in real social and political relationships of power. Explanations inevitably privilege one set of interests over others, and today few of those engaged in critical work would claim to speak from a neutral or objective place. Theoreticians now aspire less to the erection of alternative global systems and more to the questioning and challenging of existing patterns of cultural power. In the current climate, any smooth and unambiguous unity of theory is likely to arouse suspicion. The most insidious explanations are those which see no need to explain themselves.
>
> (Ferguson 1992: 5)

All discussions of photographs rest upon some notion of the nature of the photograph and how it acquires meaning. The issue is not whether theory is in play but, rather, whether theory is acknowledged. Two strands of theoretical discussion have featured in recent debates about photography: first, theoretical approaches premised on the relationship of the image to reality; second, those which stress the importance of the interpretation of the image by focusing upon the reading, rather than the taking, of photographic representations. In so far as there has been crossover between these two strands, this is found in the recent interest in the contexts and uses of photographs.

'Theory' refers to a coherent set of understandings about a particular issue which have been, or potentially can be, *appropriately* verified. It emerges from the quest for explanation, offers a system of explanation and reflects specific intellectual and cultural circumstances. Theoretical developments occur within established paradigms, or manners of thinking, which frame and structure the academic imagination. On the whole, modern Western philosophy, from the eighteenth century onwards, has stressed rational thought and posited a distinction between subjective experience and the objective, observable or external. One consequence of this has been positivist approaches to research both in the sciences and the social sciences and, as we have already indicated, photography has been centrally implicated within the empirical as a recording tool. Positivism has not only influenced uses of photography; it has also framed attitudes towards the status of the photograph.

Academic interrogation of photography employs a range of different types of theoretical understandings: scientific, social scientific and aesthetic. Historically, there has been a marked difference between scientific expectations of theory, and the role of theory within the humanities. Debates within the social sciences have occupied an intellectual space which has drawn upon both scientific models *and* the humanities. In the early/mid-twentieth century, literary criticism centred upon a canon of key texts deemed worthy of study. Similarly, art history was devoted to a core line of works of 'great' artists, and much time was given to discussion of their subject-matter, techniques, and the provenance of the image. The academic framework was one of sustaining a particular set of critical standards and, perhaps, extending the canon by advocating the inclusion of new or newly rediscovered works. A number of major exhibitions and publications on photography have taken this as their model, offering exposition of the work of selected photographers as 'masters' in the field. This approach, in literature, art history and aesthetic philosophy, has been critiqued for its esoteric basis. It has also been criticised for reflecting white, male interests and, indeed, for blinkering the academic from a range of potential alternative visual and other pleasures. For instance, within photography the fascination of domestic or popular imagery, in its own right as well as within social history, was long overlooked, largely because such images do not necessarily accord with the aesthetic expectations of the medium and because they tend to be anonymous.

A more systematic critical approach, associated with mainland European intellectual debates, penetrated the Anglo-American tradition in some areas of·the humanities, especially philosophy and literary studies, in the 1970s. The parallel influence on visual studies came slightly later. This impact was most pronounced in the relatively new – and therefore receptive – discipline of film studies. But there was also a significant displacement of older, established preoccupations and methods within art history and criticism, from which emerged what has come to be termed *new art history*. Increasingly, methodologically more eclectic visual cultural studies have superseded the more limited focus of traditional art history and aesthetic philosophy.

Photography theory

One of the central difficulties in the establishment of photography theory, and of priorities within debates relating to the photographic image, is that photography lies at the cusp of the scientific, the social scientific and the humanities. Thus, contemporary ontological debates relating to the photograph are divergent. One approach centres on analysis of the rhetoric of the image in relation to looking, and the desire to look. This is premised on models of visual communication which draw upon linguistics and, in particular,

psychoanalysis. This approach locates photographic imagery within broader **poststructuralist** concerns to understand meaning-producing processes.

In introducing the collection of essays, *Thinking Photography*, artist/critic Victor Burgin distinguishes between photography theory and criticism (**Burgin 1982**). This distinction is crucial. Up until the 1980s 'photography theory' within education had been taken to refer to technologies and techniques as in optics, colour temperature, optimum developer heat, etc. 'Theory' related to the craft base of photography. Burgin argues that photography theory must be interdisciplinary and must engage not only with techniques but, more particularly, with processes of signification. He also comments that, as yet, photography theory does not exist in any adequately developed form. Rather, we have photography criticism which, as currently practised, is evaluative and normative, authoritative and opinionated, reflecting what he terms an 'uneasy and contradictory amalgam' of Romantic, Realist and Modernist aesthetic theories and traditions. He suggests that photography history, as written up until the 1980s, reflects the same ideological positions and assumptions; that is to say, it uncritically accepts the dominant paradigms of aesthetic theory. Burgin warns against confusing photography theory with a general theory of culture, arguing for the specificity of the still, photographic image.

In relation to this, as we have already seen, a number of critics have focused on the realist properties of the image. Film critic André Bazin, in the 1950s, in his key essay on the subject, emphasised the truth-to-appearances characteristics of the photographic (Bazin 1967). Albeit within wider-ranging terms, **Susan Sontag**, in her 1970s series of essays collected as *On Photography*, also discussed photographs as traces of reality and interrogated photography in terms of the extent to which the image reproduces reality. Similarly, Roland Barthes emphasised the referential characteristics of the photograph in his final book *Camera Lucida* (**Barthes 1984**).

Critical reflections on realism

Photographing is essentially an act of non-intervention.

(Sontag 1979: 11)

Because of the disjunction between the thinking, seeing photographer and the camera that is the instrument of recording, the viewer finds it more difficult than with other visual artifacts to attribute creativity to any photographer.

(Price 1994: 4)

In philosophical terms, any concern with truth-to-appearances or traces of reality presupposes 'reality' as a given, external entity. Notions of the photograph as empirical proof, or the photograph as witness offering descriptive testimony, ultimately rest upon the view of reality as external to the human individual and objectively appraisable. If reality is somehow there, present, external, and

VICTOR BURGIN (ed.) (1982) **Thinking Photography**, London: Macmillan. A collection of eight essays, including three by Burgin himself, which, although varying in theoretical stance and focus, all aim to contribute to developing a materially grounded analysis of photographic practices.

SUSAN SONTAG (1979) **On Photography**, Harmondsworth: Penguin. A collection of six essays on various aspects of photography which, despite seeming slightly out of date in its concern with realism, still offers many key insights. Her programme on photography, *It's Stolen Your Face*, produced for the BBC in 1978, is based on this collection.

ROLAND BARTHES (1984) **Camera Lucida**, London: Fontana. First published in French in 1980 as *La Chambre Claire*. In this, his final book, Barthes offers a quite complex, rhetorical, but nonetheless interesting and significant set of comments on how we respond to photographs.

available for objective recording, then the extent to which the photograph offers accurate reference, and the significance of the desire to take photographs or to look at images of particular places or events, become pertinent.

Susan Sontag defines the photograph as a 'trace' directly stencilled off reality, like a footprint or a death mask. *On Photography* offers a series of interconnected essays, essentially based on a realist view of photography. Her concern is with the extent to which the image adequately represents the moment of actuality from which it is taken. She emphasises the idea of the photograph as a means of freezing a moment in time. If the photograph misleads the viewer, it is because the photographer has not found an adequate means of conveying what he or she wishes to communicate about a particular set of circumstances. Her focus is on the photograph as document, as a report, or as evidence of activities such as tourism. She also comments that the use of a camera satisfies the work ethic and stands in when we are unsure of our responses to unfamiliar circumstances, but can also reduce travel and other experiences to a search for the photogenic. Sontag is also concerned to point out the ethics of the relationship between the photographer as reporter and the person, place or circumstances recorded. The photographer, especially the photojournalist, is relatively powerful within this relationship, and thus may be seen as predatory. She points out that the language of military manoeuvre – 'load', 'shoot' – is central to photographic practices. Given this relative power, in her view it is even more important to emphasise the necessity of accurate reporting or relating of events. Photographs are not necessarily sentimental, or candid; they may be used for a variety of purposes including policing or incrimination.

Sontag's discussion veers between the reasons for taking photographs and the uses to which they are put. It is marked by a sense of the elusiveness of the photo-image itself. She notes our reluctance to tear up photos of relatives, and the rejection of politicians through symbolically burning images. She describes photographs as relics of people as they once were, suggesting that the still camera embalms (by contrast with the movie camera, which savours mobility). Thus she draws attention to the fascination of looking at photographs in terms of what we think they may reveal of that which we cannot otherwise have any sense of knowing, characterising photographs as a catalogue of acquired images which stand in for memories. Photographs can also, she suggests, give us an unearned sense of understanding things, past and present, having both the potential to move us emotionally, but also the possibility of holding us at a distance through aestheticising images of events. Photographs can also exhaust experiences, using up the beautiful through rendering it into cliché. For instance, she notes that sunsets may now look corny, too much like photographs of sunsets. Throughout, however, we have the sense that meaning may be sought within the photograph, providing it has been well composed and therefore accurately traces a relic of a person, place or event.

In her book *The Photograph: A Strange, Confined Space* (1994), American critic Mary Price argues that the meaning of the photographic image is primarily determined through associated verbal description and the context in which the photograph is *used*. By contrast with Sontag's emphasis on the relation between the image and its source in the actual historical world, Price starts from questions of viewing and the context of reception. Thus, she suggests, in principle there is no single meaning for a photograph, but rather an emergent meaning, within which the subject-matter of the image is but one element. Her analysis is practical in its approach. She takes a number of specific examples, aiming to demonstrate the extent to which usage and contextualisation determine meaning.

Realist theories of photography can take a number of different starting points: first, the photograph itself as an aesthetic artefact; second, the institutions of photography and the position and behaviour of photographers; third, the viewer or audience and the context in which the image is used, encountered, consumed. The particular starting point organises investigative priorities. For instance, ethical questions relating to who has the right to represent whom are central when considering the photographer and institutions such as the press.

Sontag takes a particular position within debates about realism, stressing the referential nature of the photographic image both in terms of its iconic properties and in terms of its **indexical** nature. For Sontag, the fact that a photograph exists testifies to the actuality of how something, someone or somewhere once appeared. Max Kozloff has challenged Sontag's conceptual model, criticising her proposition that the photograph 'traces' reality, and arguing instead for a view of the photograph as 'witness' with all the possibilities of misunderstanding, partial information or false testament that the term 'witness' may be taken to imply (Kozloff 1987: 237). In his collection of essays, *Photography and Fascination*, Kozloff starts from the question of the enticement of the photograph. He concludes that:

> Though infested with many bewildering anomalies, photographs are considered our best arbiters between our visual perceptions and the memory of them. It is not only their apparent 'objectivity' that grants photographs their high status in this regard, but our belief that in them, fugitive sensation has been laid to rest. The presence of photographs reveals how circumscribed we are in the throes of sensing. We perceive and interpret the outer world through a set of incredibly fine internal receptors. But we are incapable, by ourselves, of grasping or tweezing out any permanent, sharable figment of it. Practically speaking, we ritually verify what is there, and are disposed to call it reality. But, with photographs, we have concrete proof that we have not been hallucinating all our lives.
>
> (Kozloff 1979: 101)

However the relation between the image and the social world is conceptualised, it is worth noting that the authority which emanates from the sense of authenticity or 'truth to actuality' conferred by photography is a fundamental element within photographic language and aesthetics. This authority, founded in realism, has come to be taken for granted in the interpretation of images made through the lens. It is precisely this which sets lens-based imagery apart from other media of visual communication. Again, to quote Kozloff, 'A main distinction between a painting and a photograph is that the painting alludes to its content, whereas the photograph summons it, from wherever and whenever, to us' (1987: 236). The photographic is distinct from the **autographic**, or from the digital, in that it seems to emanate directly from the external. Inherent within the photographic is the particular requirement for the physical presence of the referent. This has led to photographs (along with film and video) being viewed as realist in ways that, say, technical drawing or portrait painting are not (although they are also based upon observation). That this is the case needs to be clearly acknowledged and addressed, in order to develop theory adequate and specific to photography.

Reading the image

> It is seeing which establishes our place in the surrounding world, we explain that world with words, but words can never undo the fact that we are surrounded by it. The relationship between what we see and what we know is never settled.
>
> (Berger 1972: 7)

Two key theoretical developments, semiotics and psychoanalysis, have significantly contributed to changes within the humanities and both have figured in debates relating to the constitution of photographic meaning. **Semiology**, or semiotics, the idea of a science of signs, originates from comments in Ferdinand de Saussure's *General Theory of Linguistics* (1916) but was not further developed until after the Second World War. Essentially, semiology proposed the systematic analysis of cultural behaviour. At its extremes it aimed at establishing an empirically verifiable method of analysis of human communication systems. Thus, **codes** of dress, music, advertising – and other forms of communication – are conceptualised as logical systems. The focus is upon clues which together constitute a *text* ready for reading and interpretation. The key limitation of semiology as first proposed, with its focus upon systems of signification, was that it failed to address how particular *readers* of signs interpreted communications, made them meaningful to themselves within their specific context of experience. It is currently common to use the term 'semiology' to refer to the earlier, relatively inflexible approach based upon structuralist linguistics, and to use 'semiotics' to indicate later, more fluid models, incorporating psychoanalysis, wherein the focus is more upon meaning-producing processes than upon textual systems. Social semiotics, taking account of questions of interpretation and context, inflects the emphasis specifically towards cultural artefacts and social behaviour.

Italian semiotician Umberto Eco specifically discusses the codification of the photograph as text (Eco, 'Critique of the Image' in Burgin 1982). He argues that, despite the appearance of resemblance between the image and its referent, the iconic sign is, nonetheless, like other sign systems, 'completely arbitrary, conventional and unmotivated'. Thus he focuses on the conventions of perception and the cultural understandings which inform interpretation. He offers a ten-point summary of the range of codes implicated in photographic communication. The codes are presented with relatively little elaboration, and with no ascription of hierarchy within the overall model. This thus stands as a starting point for exploring the potential of complex semiotics as a mode of analysis of the photographic.

Roland Barthes is known for his contribution to the semiological analysis of visual culture, in particular from his early work, *Mythologies*. Working inductively from his observations of differing cultural phenomena, he proposed that everyday culture can be analysed in terms of language of communication (visual and verbal) and integrally associated myths or culturally specific discourses. The central objective of this early work was the development of all-encompassing models of analysis of meaning-production processes. This was conceptualised both generally and in terms which could take account of particular cultural characteristics. Thus, for example, his analysis of the codification of a short story *S/Z* (1970) was intended to identify, test and demonstrate the explanatory potential of a set of five codes which, he was then suggesting, were potentially applicable to a range of storytelling media (the novel, film, oral narratives). This is the point at which his work is most characterised by strict **structuralist** methodology. Later works, including *The Pleasure of the Text* (1973) and *Camera Lucida* (1984), are no longer primarily text-focused and less strictly 'scientific' (i.e. seeking to objectively classify significatory phenomena) in their approach. These works take more account of the individual reader, of processes of interpretation, of psychoanalytic factors, and of what we might term cultural 'slippages' – thereby implicitly accepting a degree of unpredictability in human agency or response.

Camera Lucida is motivated by an ontological desire to understand the nature of the photograph 'in itself'. In semiotic terms, the photograph is disorderly because its ubiquity renders it unclassifiable: 'photography evades us' (Barthes 1984: 4). The style of writing is narrative and rhetorical, the tone is personal: he starts from discussion of himself as reader of the photographic image, asking why photos move him emotionally. In Part One he develops a commentary upon the nature and impact of the photograph using examples from documentary and photojournalism. In Part Two he focuses upon his own family photographs, particularly images of his mother – some

Roland Barthes
(1915–1980) Studied French Literature and Classics at the University of Paris, and taught French abroad in Rumania and Egypt before returning to Paris for a research post in sociology and semiotics. He taught a course on the sociology of signs, symbols and collective representations at the *École Pratique des Hautes Études*, and became known for his contribution to the development of semiology, the science of signs, first proposed by linguist Ferdinand de Saussure in 1916 but not fully explored until after the Second World War. Barthes' publications include *Mythologies* (1957), *Elements of Semiology* (1964), *The Empire of Signs* (1970) and *Image, Music, Text* (1977), which includes his well-known essay on 'The Rhetoric of the Image'. *Camera Lucida*, originally titled *La Chambre Claire* (1980), was his last work, and the only publication devoted entirely to photography.

of which date from 'history'; that is, a time before his birth – in order to contemplate more subjective meanings (this discussion is not illustrated). However, the objective is not to do with specific genres. For instance, there is no discussion of commercial imagery; nor of fine art uses of the medium. His purpose is essentialist in that he seeks to define that which is specific to the photograph as a means of representation. He is not concerned with the taker of a photograph (the photographer or, as he terms it, 'operator') and the act of taking but, rather, with the act of looking (the spectator) and with the 'target' of the photograph; that is, the object or person represented within the 'spectrum' of the photograph. Thus he observes that the knowing portraitee adopts a pose which anticipates the representational image, and takes account of the fact that this piece of paper will outlast the actual person who is the subject of the portrait becoming the 'flat death', which both exposes that which has been and precedes actual death.

Barthes concludes that it is 'reference' rather than Art, or communication, which is fundamental to photography. Central to his exploration is the contention that, unlike in any other medium, in photography the referent uniquely sticks to the image. In painting, for instance, it is not necessary for the referent to be present. Painting can be achieved from memory, photography cannot. From this emerges the time-specific characteristic of the photograph. It deals with *what was*, regardless of whether the terms or conditions continue to obtain. For Barthes photography is never about the present, although the act of looking occurs in the present. In addition, the photograph is indescribable: words cannot substitute for the weight or impact of the resemblance of the image. The photograph is always about looking, and seeing. Furthermore, the photograph itself – that is, the chemically treated and processed paper – is invisible. It is not *it* that we see. Rather, through it we see that which is represented. (This, he suggests, is one source of the difficulty in analysing photography ontologically.)

What, then, is the attraction of certain (but never all) photographs for the spectator? As writer-lecturer Philip Stokes has pointed out in relation to the potentially boring experience of looking at other people's family albums, 'in every dreary litany there is an instant when a window opens onto a scene of fascination that stops the eye and seizes the mind, filling it with questions or simply joy' (Stokes 1992: 194). Why do some images arrest attention, animating the viewer, while others fail to 'speak' to the particular spectator? Barthes proposes that photographs arrest attention when they encompass a duality of elements – two (or more) discontinuous, and not logically connected, elements which form the 'puzzle' (our term, not his) of the image. Here he distinguishes between *studium*, general enthusiasm for images and, indeed, the polite interest which may be expressed when confronted with any particular photograph, and the *punctum* (prick, sting or wound) which arrests attention. Previously, in an essay entitled 'The Third Meaning', he had suggested that photographs encompass the obvious and the obtuse, implying play of meaning within the photograph as text (Barthes 1977). This leads him to explore why, when so many images are noted as a matter of routine, only some images make an impact on us. Here, again, he makes a detailed distinction between the photograph which captures attention through 'shouting' or because of the *shock* of revelation of subject-matter (for instance, a particularly startling photojournalistic image), and the punctum of recognition which transcends mere surprise, or rarity value, to inflict a poignancy of recognition for the particular spectator. This, he proposes, emanates more often from some detail within the image which stands out, rather than from the unity of the content as a whole. He sees this effect as essentially a product of the photograph itself. This, we would suggest, limits his discussion. The noticing of detail is also a consequence of the particular spectator's history and interests – even a relatively insignificant detail might offer a key point of focus for a person. In other words, the poignancy or joy of recognition is founded in the act of engagement, the act of looking at a particular image, the relation between the spectator and the photograph.

Barthes goes on to suggest that the photograph in itself, through being contingent upon its referent, is outside meaning. In this sense he views it as 'a message without a code' (to use a phrase drawn from his earlier essay on the rhetoric of the image). Thus he suggests that it is the fact of social observation which is immediate rather than the photograph. For Barthes photography is at its most powerful not because of what it can reveal, but because it is, as he terms it, 'pensive'. It thinks. Of course Barthes does know that a photograph is not a thinking subject: the photograph itself is an inanimate piece of paper. The photographer thinks, the portraitee poses, and the spectator may respond reflectively. Animation occurs only through the act of looking.

Barthes' precise use of words (which, in the French, offers careful nuancing but, in translation, may seem over-precious), and the personal tone, to some extent obscure the general argument which is more **phenomenological** than semiotic in its method. His discussion is useful in reminding us of the essential contingency of the photograph. Like Sontag, he draws attention to its referential characteristics; unlike Sontag, who relates this to a range of practices, he defines this as that which characterises the medium, but it does not necessarily follow from this that it is a representation without a code. On the contrary, it is impossible to contemplate the image without operationalising a range of aesthetic and cultural codes. Ultimately, he also takes relatively little account of the specificity of the spectator and the reasons and context of looking. Despite his emphasis upon looking, and seeing, he focuses centrally on the image as text rather than upon the relation between image and spectatorship. This does limit his ontological conclusions.

Photography reconsidered

The individual as spectator, the reception and usage of photographs, and the nature of processes whereby photographs become meaningful subjectively and collectively have remained central to contemporary debates. Here the influence of psychoanalysis has to be taken into account alongside semiotics, together with the concerns of **social history**.

Psychoanalysis, founded in **Freud**'s investigations of the human psyche (from the 1880s onwards), centres upon the individual in ways which are now taken for granted but which, at the time, reflected certain revolutionary strands of political and philosophical thought. For political theorists the individual became viewed as the basic social unit; also, someone expected to take personal responsibility for social and economic survival. Philosophers such as Nietzsche, regarded by many as the father figure of individualism, emphasised personal moral responsibility, engaging, in particular, with what he conceptualised as the enslaving influence of Christianity. Individualism is a taken-for-granted feature of twentieth-century Western experience. We talk of the individual consumer, individual professional responsibilities, individual responsibilities within the family, and so on. Yet this emphasis is relatively new. Psychoanalytic understandings of individual subjective responses to social experience have offered new models of insight into human behaviour in ways which have been challenging academically (as well as offering therapeutic means of coming to terms with personal trauma).

Published in the context of a series on communications and culture, Victor Burgin's *Thinking Photography* (1982) focuses on debates within the theory, practice and criticism of photography. The book's authors set out to challenge the notion of the autonomous creative artist, to question the idea of documentary 'truth' and to interrogate the notion of purely visual languages. The intention is to situate photography within broader theoretical debates and understandings pertaining to meaning and communication, visual culture and the politics of representation.[5] The history of theories of art as they relate to – or 'position' – photography is also a key theme. The eight essays (including three by Burgin himself), while they vary in their theoretical stance and critical style, share 'the project of developing a materialist analysis of photography'. What Burgin is concerned with is photography 'considered as a practice of *signification*'; that is, specific materials worked on for specified purposes within a particular social and historical context. Semiotics is one starting point for this theoretical project, but, as Burgin states, semiotics is not sufficient to account for 'the complex articulations of the moments of institution, text, distribution and consumption of photography' (Burgin 1982: 2).

In effect, this collection of essays traces a particular trajectory through Left debates of the 1970s, centring on questions of class, revolutionary struggle and the role of the artist, through semiotics, to questions of realism, to psychoanalysis and spectatorship. (Questions of gender are addressed,

Sigmund Freud (1856–1939) Freud's copious writings and his work with patients form the basis of the discipline of psychoanalysis, used both as a therapeutic method and as a tool to understand interpersonal relations and cultural activities. Psychoanalysis has irrevocably changed the way we understand the world and ourselves. Possibly Freud's most important contribution to modern thought is the concept of the unconscious, which insists that human action always derives from mental processes of which we cannot be aware. Many photographers have used the ideas of Freud as the basis of their work.

5 At this time Burgin lectured in photography at the Polytechnic of Central London (now the University of Westminster). His other publications include *Between* (1986), *The End of Art Theory* (1986), and *Formations of Fantasy* (co-edited 1989). He is now based at the University of California.

although, notably, no essays by women theorists are included.) The book posits two key theoretical starting points: materialist analysis, as represented in the reprinting of Frankfurt School theorist Walter Benjamin's essay on 'The Author as Producer' (first published in German in 1966) and the semiotic, represented in Italian semiotician Umberto Eco's essay, 'Critique of the Image'. The other central historical reference is that of Russian Futurism and the **Formalist–Constructivist** theoretical debates which followed.

Classic Marxist models of artistic production are addressed, critically, in the penultimate essay of the book, 'Making Strange: The Shattered Mirror', by Simon Watney. Focusing on seeing, vision and the social nature of perception, Watney discusses various 1920s/1930s manifestations – in Russian aesthetic debates and in Brecht – of the proposal that through alienation, or 'making strange', new ways of 'seeing', politically and aesthetically, may be forged. The subtitle, 'The Shattered Mirror', refers to the rupturing of any notion of the photograph as a mirror or transparent recorder of reality. (It does not carry the psychoanalytic implications which, as we shall see, characterise Burgin's contributions.) The essay situates ideas of defamiliarisation in relation to past practices in order to reflect upon modern European and American work which he exemplifies, briefly, through reference to French photographer Atget; Bauhaus theorist-photographer Moholy-Nagy; and American documentarian Berenice Abbott. He argues that the project of defamiliarisation in photography rested upon acceptance of the fallacy of the transparency of the photograph. In other words, if we relinquish realist theories of the photograph, the problem of employing effective techniques for defamiliarisation dissolves.

Semiotics, in conjunction with psychoanalysis, informs Burgin's own three essays which, respectively, develop a series of related points about: the nature of the photograph as conceptualised in the context of new art theory; the experience of 'looking at photographs' from the point of view of the spectator; and exploring the psychological nature of the pleasurable response to the image. Thus he is concerned to trace links between the image, interpretation and ideological discourses. The model is most fully developed in 'Photography, Phantasy, Function', wherein the main part of the essay draws upon Freud to discuss psychological aspects of the act of looking, noting that looking is not indifferent. Thus he draws our attention to the voyeuristic and fetishistic *investment* in looking, arguing that to look is to become sutured within ideological discourse(s). He further argues that the photograph, like the fetish, is the result of an isolated fragment or frozen moment, and describes the fetishistic nature of the photograph as one source of its fascination.

At the time of its publication this collection of essays provoked markedly differing critical responses. For instance, writing in *Creative Camera* (1982), Ian Jeffrey largely dismissed what he described as an unfortunate new line of development in photography analysis on the grounds that:

History, dialectical or otherwise, is a department in which the Burgin squad is under-rehearsed. History is often invoked but not much practiced, and I am left with the sense here of an endless drawing up of rules for a game which is never played.

(Jeffrey 1982: 724)

Conversely, Stevie Bezencenet in the same issue of *Creative Camera* welcomed the attempt to move beyond the traditional analysis of photography – from the three standpoints of the technical, artistic and social – towards a more complex theoretical comprehension of the medium, noting that, as a publication, it had emerged from contemporary debates and suggesting that:

The practising of theory and theorising of practice are becoming united in the development of a materialist analysis of photography. This is a process which will lead us into the disciplines of linguistics, sociology, Marxism, art history and psychoanalysis, so that we may return to a study of the production of images, with a better understanding of their social operations.

(Bezencenet 1982b: 727)

Theory, criticism, practice

What has all this got to do with making photographs? Visual methods of communication are, of course, embedded in particular cultural circumstances and therefore reflect specific assumptions and expectations. For instance, as has been argued, given the nineteenth-century desire for empirical evidence, photography was hailed for its apparent ability to represent events accurately. This desire or expectation persists in fields such as photojournalism. Furthermore, theoretical concepts interact. For instance, criteria based upon established visual aesthetics inform the assessment of what makes a 'good' photograph, photojournalistic or otherwise. Similarly, questions of representation pertaining to, for example, gender or race, which have contributed to the challenge to the canon within literary studies and art history, are relevant to photography.

The key point is that theoretical assumptions founded in varying academic fields, from the scientific to the philosophic and the aesthetic, intersect to inform both the making and the interpretation of visual imagery. One consequence of the postmodern is a change in type of theoretical endeavour and, consequently, a change in style of publications concerning photography which, in recent years, have become more eclectic in their theoretical sources and less all-embracing in terms of questions posed and projects pursued. Books of essays on a diversity of subjects, adopting a range of differing theoretical concerns and conjunctions, are increasingly common.

Yet, in common with other fields of the arts, photography criticism still tends to be normative, evaluating work in relation to established and accepted traditions and practices. At its worst, criticism masks personal opinion, dressed

33

up as objective or authoritative with the aim of impressing, for example, the readers of review articles in order to generate their respect and support for the reviewer. At its best, criticism helps to locate particular work in relation to specific debates about practice through elucidating appreciation of the effect, meaning, context and import of the imagery under question.

In order to think about photographic communication, we need to take account of communication theory in broad terms as well as focusing specifically on photographs as a particular type of visual sign, produced and used in specific, but differing, contexts. The photograph, therefore, might be conceptualised as a site of intersection of various orders of theoretical understanding relating to its production, publication and consumption or reading. Central to the project of theorising photography is the issue of the relation between that which particularly characterises the photographic (which, as we have seen, is its referential qualities), and theoretical discourses which pertain to the making and reading of the image but whose purchase is broader, for instance, aesthetic theory or sexual politics. What is crucially at stake is how we think about the tension between the referential characteristics of the photograph and the contexts of usage and interpretation.

The key characteristic of photography – as opposed to digital imaging – is its ultimate dependence upon, and therefore reference to, a physical person or object present at the moment of making the original exposure. This physical presence is the origin or source of the possibility of an image and, consequently, the image stands as an index of the once physical presence. It is this indexical status which is the source of the authority of the image and, thus, of central theoretical debates relating to realism and 'truth'. Photography theory cannot rest simply on optics and chemistry (or, indeed, the binary mathematical systems which underpin digital imaging). Given the ubiquity of photographic practices, a twofold problem emerges: first, to analyse ways in which clusters of theoretical discourses intersect, or acquire priority, in particular fields of practice; and second, to define and analyse that which is peculiar to photography. If we take Barthes' final words on the subject, it is primarily its referential characteristic which variously lends it particular credibility, force or significance. If we start from the greater diversity of positions – semiotic, psychoanalytic and social-historical – outlined in Burgin's edited collection, then the focus must be upon the political and **ideological**. The project of theorising photography thus relies upon the development of complex models of analysis which can take account of these rather different starting points.

Within this conceptual approach it is not the objective presence of the image which is at stake, but rather the force field within which it generates meaning. This contrasts with semiological stress on systems of signification. In effect we are invited to consider not only the text, its production and its reading, but also to take account of the social relations within which meaning is produced and operates.[6] Here, the semblance of the real underpins

6 For a good general discussion of questions of representation, semiotics and discursive practices see Stuart Hall (1997) 'The Work of Representation', Chapter 1 in Stuart Hall (ed.) (1997) **Representation, Cultural Representations and Signifying Practices**, London: Sage/Open University.

processes of interpretation. Photography is reassuringly familiar, not least because it seems to reproduce that which we see, or might see. In so far as visual representations contribute to constructing and reaffirming our sense of identity, this familiarity, and the apparent realism of the photographic image, render it a particularly powerful discursive force.

CASE STUDY: *Image analysis: the example of* Migrant Mother

In 1936 the documentary photographer, Dorothea Lange, was working for a government-run project known as the Farm Security Administration (FSA). Lange has recounted the story of how she stopped one night on the road – although she was already exhausted by the work of the day – to investigate a group of people who were employed to pick peas. In less than a quarter of an hour she was back˙on the road having taken several shots of the woman with her children. One of these photographs, *Migrant Mother* (figure 1.1), became the most reproduced image in the history of photography and is known to many people who could not name its author.

In the subsequent sixty years this photograph has been used and contextualised in a number of ways. This, not only as a photograph; it has appeared on a USA postage stamp (illustrating the decade of the 1930s) and has acted as a source for cartoons. The picture has had a history beyond its original context within the FSA and it is regularly referred to as one of the world's greatest news photographs. Many critics have commented on this, noting various moments of appropriation of the image.

A number of differing approaches may be used to analyse photographs. Each model reflects its own particular concerns and priorities. For instance, any single photograph might be:

- viewed primarily as social or historical evidence
- investigated in relation to the intentions of the photographer and the particular context of its making
- related to politics and ideology
- assessed through reference to process and technique
- considered in terms of aesthetics and traditions of representation in art
- discussed in relation to class, race and gender
- analysed through reference to psychoanalysis
- decoded as a semiotic text.

Here we take the example of Dorothea Lange's *Migrant Mother* in order to illustrate and comment upon some of the ways in which this photograph has been discussed, and to draw attention to assumptions which underpin particular remarks about it.

See, for instance, Martha Rosler's celebrated essay 'In, around, and afterthoughts (on documentary photography)' (reprinted variously), or the opening section of Judith Fryer Davidov (1998) *Women's Camera Work*, Durham and London: Duke University Press.

Commonly, discussion of images draws upon two or three analytic approaches. For instance, those concerned with the status of a photograph as evidence may also be interested in the intentions of the photographer and the context of making; semiotic analysis makes reference to aesthetic coding and to cultural contexts.

In order to avoid emphasising artificial boundaries between academic disciplines, and to demonstrate the extent to which we operate in an interdisciplinary manner, this case study is organised under a series of headings which allow us to indicate the range of concerns that may be implicated simultaneously in particular writing about a photograph.

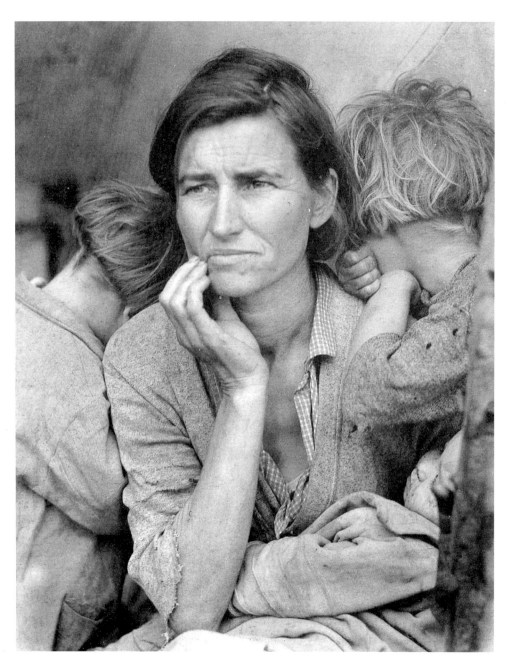

1.1 Dorothea Lange, *Migrant Mother*, 1936

The photograph as testament

Given that Lange took a number of shots of the woman and children, why is it this image which has become so famous? A number of critics have commented upon this:

> The woman is used purely as subject. She is appropriated within a symbolic framework of significance as declared and determined by Lange. Indeed, the other images taken by Lange at this 'session' add to the sense of construction and direction. They remain distant, though, and lack the compelling presence which Lange achieves in the Migrant Mother image. In this Lange creates a highly charged emotional text dependent upon her use of children and the mother. The central position of the mother, the absence of the father, the direction of the mother's 'look', all add to the emotional and sentimental register through which the image works. The woman is viewed as a symbol larger than the actuality in which she exists. As Lange admitted, she wasn't interested in 'her name or her history'.
>
> (Clarke 1997: 153)

Lange made five exposures of the woman and children in a tent (see figures 1.2–1.5). One image was selected for publication and this became one of the most famous photographs of the twentieth century. We can see that this image excludes literal detail (reference to the whole tent and the woodlands beyond, or to domestic objects) which might anchor the image to a particular place and time.

That the image was in accordance with the intentions of the photographer, and, indeed, of the FSA project is confirmed by Roy Stryker, director of the project, in an interview:

> STRYKER: I still think it's a great picture. I think it's one of America's great pictures . . .
> Interviewer: Would you want to say anything about what that picture means to you personally?
> STRYKER: I can, in two words. Mother and child. What more do I need to say? A great, great, great picture of the mother and child. She happens to be badly dressed. It was bad conditions. But she's still a mother and she had children. We'd found a wonderful family.
>
> (Stryker 1972: 154)

Clearly the potential for the image to transcend its particular location and socio-economic context was recognised by those involved in this project. In this sense, the image reflects a humanitarian notion of universal similarities in the condition of humankind. Many critics have noted this, for instance:

> For Lange, a compelling photograph presented an engaging human drama that addressed questions larger than the immediate subject. Her subjects gained importance from external value systems. . . . 'We were after the

Looking at the picture alongside the others allows us to explore the criteria by which photographers select shape and organise images, and to consider why none of the other images could have acquired the same status in terms of documentary aesthetics and its iconic status.

Clarke does not discuss the specific history and context of the making of the image, or of its immediate use. By excluding detail, Lange made it possible for the picture to be seen as a universal symbol of motherhood, poverty and survival. Clarke seems to go along with this. His approach emphasises the notion of the good photograph, but the criteria whereby an image might be considered 'good' are taken for granted. Emotional empathy is clearly one element, but this is assumed rather than treated as something for critical discussion.

Stryker's emphasis on the drama of the photograph reflects his drive to use pictures for emotional impact.

1.2–1.5 *Migrant Mother*, alternative versions

truth', she wrote, 'not just making effective pictures'. She was concerned with the human condition, and the value of a fact was measured in terms of its own consequences. . . . Today, the subjects of Lange's picture are, as Therese Heyman has observed, 'figures in history whose hardship the present viewer is incapable of healing – symbols of timeless sorrow'.

(Tucker 1984: 50–51)

Indeed, this picture was included in the exhibition, 'Family of Man' (organised by the American curator, Edward Steichen, in 1955 as a sort of indirect response to the Second World War).[7] The exhibition set out to emphasise all

7 *Family of Man,* facsimile catalogue, page 151.

38

that humanity has in common. Roland Barthes commented on the 'ambiguous myth' of community whereby diversity between peoples and cultures was brought into focus in order to forge a sense of unity from this pluralism (Barthes 1973).

The photographer's account

In an essay written almost thirty years after the event, entitled 'The Assignment I'll Never Forget', Dorothea Lange gave us her story of how she made the photograph.

> I saw and approached the hungry and desperate mother, as if drawn by a magnet. I do not remember how I explained my presence or my camera to her, but I do remember she asked me no questions. I made five exposures, working closer and closer from the same direction. I did not ask her name or her history. She told me her age, that she was thirty-two. She said that they had been living on frozen vegetables from the surrounding fields, and birds that the children killed. She had just sold the tires from her car to buy food. There she sat in that lean-to tent with her children huddled around her, and seemed to know that my pictures might help her, and so she helped me. There was a sort of equality about it.
>
> (Lange 1960: 264)

In relation to the alleged 'equality' between the photographer and her subject it is worth noting that in 1978, the 'Migrant Mother' herself, Florence Thompson, was tracked down to their trailer home in Modesto, California. One of the twentieth century's most familiar and telling images was recuperated as an ordinary, aged woman who was poor in a humdrum way and no longer able to function as an icon of nobility and sadness in the face of destitution.

Her image has appeared in many forms and in many settings, and has been multiply copied millions of times. She was a most familiar figure, but not until fifty years after the event did she get to comment on it publicly. She told United Press that she was proud to be the subject of the photograph, but that she had never made a penny out of it and that it had done her no good (Rosler 1989).

Genre and usage

The FSA project was essentially documentary. However, control of the repro-duction of images did not lie in the hands of the photographers. As photo-historian, Naomi Rosenblum notes, the FSA in effect acted as a photo agency supplying pictures for photojournalistic use:

> In common with other government agencies that embraced photographic projects, the F.S.A. supplied prints for reproduction in the daily and periodical press. In that project photographers were given shooting scripts from which to work, did not own their negatives, and had no control

Here Tucker is taking a critical stance, discussing the impact of the picture in terms both of culture and ideology and of the reception of the image, acknowledging differences between now and then.

Note also that she credits her source. This allows us to find the original context of the Heyman quote to check whether we agree with Tucker's interpretation. Crediting sources is a part of good academic practice, as it acknowledges previous critical contributions and helps the reader to find further information.

This essay by Barthes is included in his early collection, *Mythologies*. He draws our attention to, and questions, the fundamental premise of the exhibition. See general discussion of Barthes (pp. 28–30).

The fact that Lange's story was reprinted in a major collection suggests that a photographer's account is of particular interest in considering the image. The intention of the photographer and her memory of the occasion are in some way assumed to add to our appreciation of the image and our understanding of its significance. We have to ask ourselves, sixty years on, why this should be relevant to our reading of the image now, in different circumstances.

For discussion of the concept of documentary see chapter 1, pp. 17–18 and chapter 2, esp. section 2, pp. 89–99.

over how the pictures might be cropped, arranged, and captioned. Their position was similar to that of photojournalists working for the commercial press – a situation that both Evans and Lange found particularly distasteful.

(Rosenblum 1997: 366–369)

One of the central principles of the documentary aesthetic was that a photograph should be untouched, so that its veracity, its genuineness, might be maintained. Even minor violations of this principle were frowned upon:

> Lange's great *Migrant Mother* photograph had always bothered her a little. Just at the instant that she had taken the picture, a hand had reached out to draw the tent flap back a bit further and the photograph had caught a disembodied thumb in the foreground. That thumb had worried Lange. So, when she prepared the picture for *American Exodus*, the thumb was retouched out of the negative.
>
> This was a simple technique that she had employed hundreds of times during her career as a portrait photographer. For Stryker it was a lapse of taste. He was quite bitter over the incident.

(Hurley 1972: 142)

Image in context

The FSA project was a response to the economic crisis of 1929 and the ensuing economic depression of the 1930s together with the collapse of sharecropping agriculture in a number of the south-west states of the USA. It aimed to document and record statistically the position of the rural poor, but the photographers it employed eschewed a mere photography of record in favour of works that stressed the depiction of human destitution and distress. Such images had a clear political purpose, but one that has been criticised for individualising what were collective problems with potentially collective solutions. Abigail Solomon-Godeau:

> Commenting on the works of Dorothea Lange, the film maker Pare Lorentz noted the following: "She has selected with an unerring eye. You do not find in her portrait gallery the bindle-stiffs, the drifters, the tramps, the unfortunate, the aimless dregs of a country." In other words, the appeal made to the viewer was premised on the assertion that the victims of the Depression were to be judged as the deserving poor, and thus the claim for redress hinged on individual misfortune rather than on systematic failure in the political, economic, and social spheres.

(Solomon-Godeau 1991: 179)

Here Solomon-Godeau is concerned with the political implications of that to which the image testifies.

In this account, the significance of the question of who retains control of the image rests upon an unspoken notion of the integrity of the image in terms of its original composition. For those concerned with a notion of documentary authenticity, there are ethical implications relating to the use of images. These ideas are not brought into question here. If, however, we take the more contemporary view that photographic meaning shifts according to usage or, indeed, that the photograph, once in circulation, stands apart from its maker, this is less a matter of concern.

This quote reminds us of rules that functioned as indicators of authenticity. It seems to be concerned with realism. However, implicit within this is a very literal notion of realism viewed as pictures true to appearance. A number of critics, among whom Brecht and Benjamin were prominent, have argued that realism goes beyond a mere matter of appearances and, indeed, that the photograph, in its apparent literal veracity, is limited in its ability to convey information about socio-economic and political relations.

In analysing this quote, we want to ask whether Lorentz is accurate in his comment – are there examples of photographs by Lange which might contradict his view? (Several other photographs by Lange are included in Andrea Fisher (1987).) Furthermore, do we agree with Solomon-Godeau's interpretation of his comment? Finally, what distinction is being made here between 'individual misfortune' and 'systematic failure' and what political positions underpin each of these phrases?

Image-text

The image is titled *Migrant Mother*. This caption, together with the formal organisation of the photograph, are key elements of its appeal. Yet in *A Concise History of Photography* by Helmut and Alison Gernsheim, published in 1965, the same picture is captioned *Seasonal Farm Labourer's Family*, a title which seems less potent since it implies the presence of a working father. The original title and date are given by Andrea Fisher as 'Destitute pea pickers in California, a 32 year old mother of seven children. February 1936'.

Aesthetics and art history

Western aesthetic philosophy is concerned to examine principles of taste and systems for the appreciation of that which is deemed beautiful. Thus the aesthetics of photography have been concerned with formal matters such as composition, subject-matter, and the organisation of pictorial elements within the frame. It has also encompassed questions of technique – sharpness of image, exposure values, print quality, etc. Karin Becker Ohrn tells us that:

> Many of Lange's prints were poor. She made them according to no formula, and they varied widely in density, making it a challenge to print them.
>
> (Ohrn 1980: 228)

These failures of technique were unimportant when the photographs were reproduced in books and journals, but towards the end of her life, Lange presented her work in a number of major exhibitions, and this required careful technical work to take place:

> The prints were processed to archival standards and placed on white mounts. The final result was superb; the print quality was commended by several reviewers of the exhibition.
>
> (ibid.)

The context of viewing is also influential. Naomi Rosenblum comments:

> The images were transformed into photographic works of art when they were exhibited under the auspices of the Museum of Modern Art. For the first time, photographs made to document social conditions were accorded the kind of recognition formerly reserved for aesthetically conceived camera images.
>
> (Rosenblum 1997: 369)

If the photograph is in a book or magazine concerned with social conditions, its status as evidence is foregrounded. Lange's photographs were published by the FSA in 1939 as a book titled *An American Exodus: A Record of Human Erosion*. The title directs the reader to consider the group of photographs sociologically; the focus is upon the implications of the content. By contrast, when exhibited in the art gallery the context invites us to look at the picture in

---

Titles contribute to holding the meaning of pictures, to limiting the potential range of interpretations or responses on the part of the audience or reader. Examining – or imagining – alternative titles for an image can help us understand how the title lends resonance to the picture.

This concern with print quality is often seen as excessively formal, privileging matters of technique at the expense of content, meaning and context. However, different contexts require differing levels of attention to print quality. While a mediocre print may be adequate for newspapers given their low-quality reproduction, gallery exhibition demands high-quality visual resolution. Shift in usage of the image required a different degree of precision.

In traditional art history, questions of genre, form and technique, as well as subject-matter deemed appropriate for artistic expression, are central. When photographs are re-appropriated within the gallery context, specific art-historical traditions associated with them come into play, becoming, as it were, laid over the picture.

aesthetic and symbolic terms. For instance, art historians have observed that Lange's photograph is related – in terms of both subject-matter and framing – to the many paintings of the Madonna and Child in Western art.

As gendered image

A number of feminist photo-historians have looked at the FSA in terms of the participation of women photographers and the gendering of the image. Lange has been cast as 'mother' of documentary. Thus, for instance, Andrea Fisher in *Let us Now Praise Famous Women* discusses her contribution:

> Dorothea Lange became a key figure in securing the humanism of documentary. She was repeatedly represented in popular journals as the 'mother' of documentary: the little woman who would cut through ideas by evoking personal feeling. Through her pathos for destitute rural migrants, the New Deal's programs of rural reform might be legitimized, not as power, but as the exercise of care. Her place in the construction of documentary rhetoric was thus crucially different but every bit as important as Walker Evans', more widely recognized as the paradigmatic figure of documentary. Where Evans was thought of as the guarantor of honest observation, with his flat-lit frontal shots, Lange was lauded as the keeper of documentary's compassion.
>
> (Fisher 1987: 131)

Fisher argues that Stryker over-edited the FSA work and in so doing obscured the work and the role played by women in the project. She particularly argues that representations of femininity played a crucial role in the rhetoric of the FSA photographs, both in terms of the gender of the photographer and subject-matter.

In hailing Lange as the 'Mother', Stryker placed her as the mirror of immutable motherhood that many of her photographs would subsequently suggest. Her consuming empathy for her subjects became synonymous with her subjects' caring for their children. Though only a fraction of her images conformed to the transcendent ideal of mother and child, it was the image of the Migrant Mother which soared to the status of icon, and became the hall-mark of Lange herself:

Here Fisher draws attention to the centrality of 'motherhood', a concept which was brought under scrutiny in feminist critiques of the 1970s.

> The naming of Lange as 'Mother' folded across the reading of her images. It not only prioritized certain images, but became intimately embedded in the sense that could be made of them.
>
> (Fisher 1987: 140–141)

Photography critic John Roberts has summarised her argument thus:

> Fisher argues that one of the principal ideological props of the way FSA photographs were used to construct an American community under threat was the image of the maternal. She cites Dorothea Lange's *Migrant Mother*

(1937) as a primary example of this, one of the most reproduced photographs of the period, so much so in fact that it could be said to stand in iconically *for* the Depression. For Fisher the way the image was cropped and contextualised reveals how much the image of a damaged femininity came to symbolise the crisis of community for the American public. Anxious and in obvious poverty, the woman holds on to her two children, suggesting the power of maternal values to overcome the most dire of circumstances. Here is a woman who has lost everything, yet heroically, stoically keeps her family together. Here in essence was what the magazine editors were waiting for: an image of tragedy AND resistance. That this image became so successful reflects how great a part gender played in the symbolic management of the Depression.

(Roberts 1998: 85)

Fisher herself offers a slightly different account:

The incessant picturing of women with their children was never prioritized by Stryker for his photographers; *it was not a conscious political device.* But perhaps it arose, like the whole of Stryker's enterprise, as part of that widely felt nostalgia for a mythic American past: an American essence as natural as the land, and so located in an immutable rural family. But only for an urban audience could the land achieve this mythic status, and the rural mother the status of universal touchstone. Perhaps, too, that desire for lost plenitude found in the image of the Mother its most appropriate analogue.

(Fisher 1987: 138; our emphasis)

Here, questions of gender are seen as interrelating with other sets of ideas about Americanness. Fisher points to the power of this interaction.

Reading the photograph

As we have noted, the 1960s and 1970s witnessed a shift in photography theory whereby images became viewed as complexly coded artefacts to be read as cultural, psychoanalytic and ideological signs. For Barthes, in his later writings, specifically *Camera Lucida*, the photograph *signifies* reality, rather than reflecting or representing it. The emphasis is upon what the viewer as 'reader' of the image takes as the principal cues and clues for use as the basis of interpretation.

In reading photographs we may choose to concentrate on the formal qualities of the image; for example, its arrangement within the frame, or the dispositions, stances and gestures of its subjects. Alternatively, or additionally, we may seek to locate the work within the history of image-making, noting similarities and differences from other works of the same kind. Or we may want to explore the way in which the image may be examined from the standpoint of a number of disciplines or discourses which exist outside the photographic.

Questions of gender have been discussed both in relation to the photographer and to the content of the image as a particular representation of, in this instance, maternity. But Roberts takes this up in terms which contain overtones of conspiracy, seeing the gendering in terms of political rhetoric. When we look back to Fisher herself we find a different emphasis. This illustrates, once again, the importance of checking original sources. As we see, Roberts has imposed a specific inflection on Fisher's original research.

Semiotics focuses on the formal components of the image, emphasising the centrality of sign systems. Sign systems are viewed as largely conventional; that is, primarily consequent not upon 'natural' relations between images and that to which they refer but upon cultural understandings. For American semiotician C S. Pierce, signs may be iconic (based upon resemblance to that represented), indexical (based upon a trace or indicator, for instance, smoke indicates fire) or symbolic (based upon conventional associations). Chemically produced photographs incorporate all three constituents: images resemble the person or place or object re-presented; they are indexical in that the subject had to be present for the photograph to be made, which means that the image is essentially a 'trace'; and images circulate in specific cultural contexts within which differing symbolic meanings and values may adhere.

Freudian theory has been acknowledged in Western academia, especially in the latter part of the twentieth century. Within photography criticism, two influential ideas derived from psychoanalytic theory have been that of the function of the gaze, and of analysis of the way in which what might be thought of as 'abstractions' may be inscribed upon the body – literally embodied. These ideas form the background to Pultz's discussion of how we look at this image. Note that in this instance it is the interrelation of gender and of aesthetics which is woven into his analysis. However, we might ask whether Pultz believes Lange's reference to the virgin and child was conscious on her part.

John Pultz begins his analysis of *Migrant Mother* by referring to these ideas in the context of a reading of the gestural system at work within the image. He then moves to consider the woman's body within the tradition of painting; and concludes by commenting on the gendered nature of the space within which the image is set:

> *Migrant Mother* . . . centers on the female body, the body that is socially constructed through the gaze, and has the quality 'to be looked at'. In *Migrant Mother*, Lange builds a narrative around a woman and her three children, centered on the single gesture of an upraised arm. As the two older children turn their heads away from the photographer (out of shame or shyness?) and an infant child sleeps, the mother alone remains awake and vigilant. Her arm is upraised, not to support her head but to finger her chin in tentative thought. The picture is created around certain notions of the female body, including the idea of the nurturing mother. Lange drew on traditional, such as Renaissance depictions of the Virgin and Child and the secularised versions of these that began to appear in the mid nineteenth century with the rise of the Victorian cult of domesticity. Moreover, even though *Migrant Mother* was made in a public space, the close cropping of the image creates within the frame itself a protected, interior, feminised space.

> (Pultz 1995: 93)

Image as icon

Halla Beloff wants to grant the image an iconic status that takes it out of the realm of representation altogether:

> Such is the power of the camera that we can easily think of photographs as having a kind of independent reality. Dorothea Lange's *Migrant Mother* is a picture that has entered Western consciousness. She is not a mere representation.

> (Beloff 1985: 15)

'Icon' here refers not so much to the verisimilitude of the image but to the symbolic value invested in it.

Part of the iconic power of the work derives from its multiple appearances over the years, in many contexts and forms. For instance, in 1964 it appeared on the cover of the Hispanic magazine, *Bohemia Venezolana*, and in 1973 was referenced in *Black Panther* magazine (figures 1.6 and 1.7). Paula Rabinowitz comments on this aspect of the photograph in the following terms:

> I do not need to remind my readers of the power of images – a power that includes their ability to exceed the original impulse of their creation. For instance, the troubling story of Lange's 'Migrant Mother', told and retold, offers with acute poignancy an example of discourse as repository of meaning – the photograph as much as its checkered history includes a woman and her children, a photographer, a government bureau, popular magazines, museums, scholars, and a changing public – an image and tale

1.6 (left) Reference to 'Migrant Mother', *Bohemia Venezolana*
1.7 (right) Reference to 'Migrant Mother', *Black Panther* magazine

composed, revised, circulated, and reissued in various venues until whatever reality its subject first possessed has been drained away and the image become icon.

(Rabinowitz 1994: 86)

In summary, critical writings appropriate and 're-frame' images in relation to particular sets of concerns. This image has attracted extensive discussion from a range of perspectives, reflecting many differing concerns. Our procedure here was to seek out, select and analyse specific quotes as examples of different 'takes' on the picture.

Here, there is a notion of photographs as containing 'reality' – a commodity that, as it were, leaches out over time, so that the initial complexity gives way to the merely iconic. Do we agree with this? Or does the image continue to be 'troubling'?

See chapter 4 for further examples of analysis of specific images.

HISTORIES OF PHOTOGRAPHY

Inventions – the name by which we call devices that seem fundamentally new – are almost always born out of a process that is more like farming than magic. From a complex ecology of ideas and circumstance that includes the condition of the intellectual soil, the political climate, the state of technical competence, and the sophistication of the seed, the suggestion of new possibilities arises.

(Szarkowski 1989: 11)

Typically, histories of photography offer a series of histories of photographers illustrated with examples from their work. In the twentieth century, in common with other areas of the arts, such as painting or the novel, there has been a tendency to conflate the history of the subject with the work of particular practitioners. The central purpose of this opening section is to compare key books, published in English in recent years, most of which are variously titled *The History . . .* or *A Concise History. . . .*

What is the story of photography? It was invented in 1839, or so we have commonly been led to believe, but this apparently simple statement masks a complex set of factors. It is true that it was in 1839 that both Fox Talbot in England and Daguerre in France announced the processes whereby they had succeeded in making and fixing a photo-graphic image. But the idea of photography long precedes that date.

To a large extent the history of photography prior to 1938, when **Beaumont Newhall** first published his commentary, then entitled *Photography, A Short Critical History*, has been represented as a history of techniques. The focus was not on what sort of images were made, but on *how* they were made. This approach is to some extent reflected in museum collections wherein it is the instruments of photography which are prioritised for display, with photographs acting as examples of particular printing methods, detailed in accompanying descriptions. The subject-matter of such photographs (and associated aesthetic and social implications), if acknowledged at all, is presented as being of secondary importance.

So, was the story of photography always an account of changing technologies? Martin Gasser suggests that this history is more complicated (Gasser 1992). Considering German, French, British and American publications written between 1839 and 1939, he identifies three emphases: first, what is termed 'the priority debate'; second, histories of the development of photography written primarily as handbooks detailing methods and techniques and also potential uses for photography; third, histories of the photograph as image. It is worth noting that it is the proliferation of material in the second of these categories which has led to the false assumption that the first hundred years of publication were largely devoted to technologies and techniques. Aside from any other consideration, a number of the papers published in the early years of photography made assertions about the intrinsic nature of the medium and speculated on its potential uses.

Which founding father?

Before considering histories of the photograph as *image*, the priority debate deserves brief comment. This debate is concerned with who first achieved the fixing of the photographic image. A number of historical accounts exist whose primary purpose is to argue – usually through a combination of biography and discussion of photographic techniques – that someone other than Fox Talbot in Britain or Daguerre in France 'invented' photography. These two men were the first to announce their findings publicly (in the appropriate scientific journals of the time, in Britain and France) in 1839. But it

BEAUMONT NEWHALL (1982)
The History of Photography, New York: MOMA, fifth edition, revised and enlarged. This remains a key text, although, as a number of critics have commented, it is limited in its compass by its foundations in the MOMA collection which is primarily American in orientation and idiosyncratic in its holdings, having been built up over the years according to the interests and tastes of its particular curators.

Key archives in Britain for equipment and techniques:
- The National Museum of Photography, Film and Television, Bradford
- The Fox Talbot Museum, Lacock, Wiltshire (National Trust)

is also clear, from contemporary correspondence, that Fox Talbot was not alone in Britain in his experimentation. Similarly, in France, Nicephore Nièpce was responsible in the early 1820s for key discoveries leading up to the **daguerreotype**. As every history of early photography emphasises, the challenge did not lie with the development of camera and lens technology. The principle of concentrating light through a small hole in order to create reflection on the wall of a dark chamber was known to Aristotle (384–322 BC). The photographic camera was based on the camera obscura, described as early as the tenth century AD, of which the first illustration was published in 1545. The problem which preoccupied experimentation in the late eighteenth and early nineteenth centuries was how to fix the image once it had been obtained.

The credit for discovering practical chemical processes lies with no single person. As historian Helmut Gernsheim remarks in relation to the daguerreotype, 'though to Nièpce goes the credit of having devised the first photographic process, and of having invented the earliest photo-engraving method, it was left to his partner Daguerre to make photography practicable as distinct from possible' (**Gernsheim and Gernsheim 1969: 41**).

Nor, indeed, does the credit lie with any particular nation, although, as Gasser reminds us, the ascription of credit has always had nationalistic overtones with, for example, the French, keen to downgrade British claims (1839 was within a generation of the Battle of Trafalgar). Likewise, strenuous rewritings of history allowed the German photo-historian, Stenger, writing in the 1930s during the ascendance of Hitler, to claim German experiments of the eighteenth century as fundamental for photography. Re-examining the prehistory, Mary Warner Marien urges caution in two respects: first, she warns against too uncritical an acceptance of the work of early photo-historians. She notes the extent to which the burgeoning of research in the field since the Second World War has both uncovered new findings and suggested new ways of thinking about previously known facts within the history of photography; recent research represents only the beginning of a much needed archaeology of early photography. In addition, she emphasises the broader historical context of political, technological and cultural change within which photography developed. The overall point is that, in considering the origins of photography, a stance which is both cautious and critical should be adopted (Warner Marien 1991).

The photograph as image

While earlier writing on photography had not exclusively focused on technology and techniques, since the Second World War art-historical concerns have become more central, together with a new stress on connoisseurship of the photograph as a privileged object. A number of the books which we now take as key texts on the history of photography were first written as exhibition catalogues for works collected and shown in institutions. For

daguerreotype Photographic image made by the process launched by Louis-Jacques-Mandé Daguerre in France in 1839. It is a positive image on a metal plate with a mirror-like silvered surface, characterised by very fine detail. Each one is unique and fragile and needs to be protected by a padded case. It became the dominant portrait mode for the first decades of photography, especially in the United States.

HELMUT AND ALISON GERNSHEIM (1969) **The History of Photography from the Earliest Use of the Camera Obscura in the Eleventh Century up to 1914**, 2 vols, London and New York (first edition, 1955). One of the two classic histories. It is interesting to compare later editions with the first edition in order to see how their interests and research developed.

instance, Beaumont Newhall's *The History of Photography* stems from a catalogue written to accompany 'Photography 1839–1937' at the Museum of Modern Art (MOMA) in New York in 1937. The broader context for the introduction of art-historical methods and concerns into photography collection and exhibition includes the development of art history as an academic discipline and, more particularly, the increasing influence of art criticism within modern art in the first half of the twentieth century. Here it is relevant to remember the emphasis upon **Art** as a set of special practices which informed **modernist** thinking. A central feature of modernist criticism was that of maintaining a clear distinction between high and low culture, a differentiation which was equally evident in the writings of some Marxist critics as it was among conservative critics. If photographs were to take their place in the gallery, they inevitably became caught up within more general intellectual trends and discourses.

Since the Second World War, then, the predominant approach to writing the history of photography has been to focus on the photograph as image. Two classic histories, still consulted, are Beaumont Newhall's *The History of Photography* (now in its fifth, revised edition); and Helmut and Alison Gernsheim's *History of Photography*, which, as we have seen, was organised in its earliest form in relation to developing technologies but has subsequently been rewritten to take fuller account of photographs as specific types of image. It is worth pausing to consider and compare these two publications; together they established a specific canon for the history of photography which has been the basis for further development – or taken as a starting point for challenge – ever since.[8]

Educated as an art historian, and appointed on to the library staff at New York's Museum of Modern Art, Newhall was invited to research its first major photography exhibition. His historical overview, which formed the principal essay in the exhibition catalogue, described changing techniques, but also included comments on specific photographers and particular periods of aesthetic development. Newhall was one of the first to introduce aesthetic judgements into the discussion of photographs, but, at this stage, as he has noted himself, he avoided the identification of artists, thereby refusing MOMA's expectations of what an exhibition catalogue should be. It was only in the third edition of his *History of Photography* that emphasis on photographers and an account of the work of practitioners emerges. In this edition he also, for the first time, introduced chapters on straight photography, documentary and 'instant vision', thereby acknowledging characteristics specific to photography. The third edition thus represents the beginning of an engagement with the idea of photography theory as distinct from art theory.[9]

Similarly, it is only in later editions that Helmut Gernsheim refocuses the history to comment more extensively upon particular practitioners. His contribution to the history, developed in collaboration with Alison Gernsheim, was founded in the study of their collection of nineteenth-century photographs.[10]

8 We are indebted to insights and observations offered by Deborah Roland in her unpublished postgraduate diploma dissertation *Two Histories of Photography* (London Institute, 1995).

9 All editions are credited to Newhall, but a number of commentators have noted the research contribution of his wife, Nancy Newhall.

10 The Gernsheim collection is now at the University of Texas in Austin.

The full title of their research, first published in 1955 and dedicated to Beaumont Newhall, is *The History of Photography from the Earliest Use of the Camera Obscura in the Eleventh Century up to 1914*. The second edition, in 1969, was divided into two volumes, with considerably more emphasis on illustration than previously. The third, revised edition appeared in the 1980s, by then under the single authorship of Helmut Gernsheim (since the death of his wife). The first volume of *The History of Photography* focuses on the origins of photography in France, America, Great Britain and Germany.[11] A chapter on Italy was added later, in the third edition, which was published in 1982. A summary version of the research was published in 1965 as *A Concise History of Photography*, offering a shorter, and thus easier entry into his work. This version includes a brief, and highly selective, discussion of modern photography up to the 1950s. (For purposes of studying the nineteenth century, the two-volume edition which is in large format, with good quality picture reproduction, is recommended for the detail of observation and the range of imagery.)

Both Newhall and Gernsheim focus upon Western Europe and the United States (with no comment, for instance, on Soviet Russia or South America). The key difference between Newhall and Gernsheim lies in Gernsheim's relative concentration on the nineteenth century, and his greater emphasis on technical aspects of photography. His study is more lengthy and less literary in approach than Newhall's. This may reflect the origins of Newhall's essay as an exhibition catalogue, which meant that he had to take account of the problem of succinct communication to a diverse audience. Further differences may stem from nationality: Newhall was American; Gernsheim was born in Germany but was naturalised British. As has already been noted, they were working in relation to particular archive collections, the former drawing upon the collection at MOMA with, inevitably, a central focus upon developments in America, as well as upon the research in Europe conducted prior to the 1937 exhibition. The Gernsheim collection focused on the nineteenth century, and was centred upon British photography.

Both historians proceed to a greater or lesser extent by way of discussion of great photographers. Gernsheim notes that their collection was organised not only in files about photographic processes, apparatus, exhibitions, but also folders on important photographers (see **Hill and Cooper 1992**). Newhall, as an art historian, was accustomed to emphasis on the contribution of the individual artist, and by the fifth edition of his work, the contribution of individual photographers and the authority of their work is clearly a priority. This has the effect of raising the profile of certain 'masters' of photography, thereby defining a canon, or authoritative list, of great practitioners. To quote lecturer and critic, Stevie Bezencenet:

> The complex detail of Gernsheim's history and the simple linear
> progression that Newhall presents do not allow us to comprehend
> just how these histories have been constructed. We are locked into a

11 The chapter is in fact entitled 'The Daguerreotype in German-Speaking Countries'. He refers to what is now known as Germany and Austria, although in the mid-nineteenth century, Germany had not yet been united, so technically, these were developments in Prussia, Bavaria and elsewhere.

VICKI GOLDBERG (ed.) (1981) **Photography in Print**, Albuquerque: University of New Mexico Press

PAUL HILL AND THOMAS COOPER (1992) **Dialogue with Photography**, Manchester: Cornerhouse Publications

NATHAN LYONS (1966) **Photographers on Photography**, Englewood Cliffs: Prentice-Hall

CHRISTOPHER PHILLIPS (ed.) (1989) **Photography in the Modern Era**, New York: Metropolitan Museum/Aperture limited and traditional perception of a medium developing from one *Master* to another, marginally influenced by technical factors and with a minimal relation to anything else: the key site of analysis becomes the qualities of the individual photograph.

(Bezencenet 1982a: 485)

The canonisation of photographers as artists, in line with the emphasis on individual practitioners in other art fields in the Modern period, characterises many contemporary publications. For instance, Photo Poche publish a three-part 'history' organised as brief biographies with comments on photographers, accompanied by one image selected from their lifetime's work. Similarly, *The Photography Book*, published by Phaidon, includes 500 photographs by 500 different photographers (presented alphabetically by surname). Such collections offer useful starting points for identifying the style of particular photographers, but the socio-historical contextualisation is strictly limited. By selecting known practitioners, rather than sets of ideas or types of practice, such books have the effect of reinforcing the canon of acclaimed photographers and marginalising practices which cannot be illustrated through reference to specific names.

History in focus

There are several consequences of canonisation: first, changing attitudes to photography as a set of practices have tended to become obscured behind the eulogisation of particular photographers, their photographs and their contribution. Second, the focus (led by male historians) has been upon male photographers, with the consequence that the participation of women has been overlooked or obscured. Third, there has been relatively extensive discussion of professional and serious commercial practices, but relatively few accounts of popular photography or of more specialist areas of practice, such as architecture or medicine. Fourth, as has already been mentioned, photography history has tended to prioritise aesthetic concerns over broader and more diverse forms of involvement of photography in all aspects of social experience, including personal photography, publishing and everyday portraiture.

Other contemporary histories, published in English and selected for comment here, reflect or engage with these problems to a greater or lesser degree. **Peter Turner**'s *History of Photography* is perhaps the most aware of potential limitations, and most explicitly sets out to transcend them. His range is broader than the other histories, and includes fashion photography and advertising within its compass. Sections are organised primarily in terms of discussion of particular practices rather than technologies or practitioners, although, perhaps inevitably, there is some focus on particular photographers, through the selection of photographs as illustration and through identification of leading exponents. This book, with reasonably sized reproductions of photographs (including some colour reproduction) makes pleasurable

PETER TURNER (1987) **History of Photography**, London: Hamlyn. Includes chapters on particular fields of practice such as fashion and advertising.

reading. Concentrating on images, **Graham Clarke** explores how we understand a photograph through a brief introductory historical overview of practices in terms of genres: landscape, the city, the portrait, the body, documentary, fine art, and photographic manipulations. **Naomi Rosenblum**'s *A World History of Photography* offers an excellent, clearly written account which is thorough and markedly international in its compass. The device of including three separate sections on technical history allows her to focus on images and movements in the main body of the text, which is extensively illustrated.

Mark Haworth-Booth's discussion of *Photography: An Independent Art* offers an eminently readable account of the development of the photography archive at the Victoria and Albert Museum in London. While focusing upon images in that particular collection, his discussion is informed and informative about more general developments in photography as both art and technology. Likewise, **Ian Jeffrey**'s account *Photography, A Concise History* is purposeful and generally clearly written. This book set out to be a radical reappraisal of the history of photography as written to date, although Stevie Bezencenet has argued that it was less than successful in its re-evaluation on the grounds that to produce a history of photography now requires a diversity of academic approaches (Bezencenet 1982b). She also notes that Jeffrey offers another history overwhelmingly concerned with male practitioners, making the point that, however radical his declared intentions, his work mirrors the established formula of a chronological account of changes and focuses on dominant modes of photography and particular practitioners.

Lemagny and Rouille's account is of interest to the English reader, for its central starting point is within French culture which, in effect, recentres France within photography history. While discussion of photography in Britain is more limited than in some of the other accounts, the references to Europe as a whole are more comprehensive. This book is an edited collection. Despite the editors' stated intention of holding a balance between discussion of photography as a field in itself, and discussion of the broader context within which it functions, some chapters succeed in being more analytic than others. While expressing strong criticisms, in reviewing the book, Warner Marien suggests that its strengths lie in two chapters on photography as art, and she adds that in general this collection takes more account of contemporary theoretical ideas than do most works of this kind (Warner Marien 1988). Likewise, **Michel Frizot**'s *A New History of Photography* is written from a French perspective, as indicated, for instance, in its emphasis in early chapters on the spread of the daguerreotype. Organised chronologically, it offers groups of images juxtaposed with specific thematic discussions which range from the technical to particular fields of practice.

The year 1989 saw the publication of two major historical overviews, both designed to accompany retrospective exhibitions celebrating 150 years of photography. The title of Mike Weaver's *The Art of Photography* (1989) reflects

GRAHAM CLARKE (1997) **The Photograph**, Oxford: Oxford University Press

NAOMI ROSENBLUM (1997) **A World History of Photography** (third edition), New York, London, and Paris: Abbeville Press. Previous editions, 1984, 1989

MARK HAWORTH-BOOTH (1997) **Photography: An Independent Art**, London: V&A publications. Haworth-Booth is Curator of Photography at the V&A. This book was published to coincide with the establishment, in May 1998, of a permanent photography gallery at the V&A for showing works from the museum's collection.

IAN JEFFREY (1981) **Photography, A Concise History**, London: Thames and Hudson

JEAN-CLAUDE LEMAGNY AND ANDRÉ ROUILLE (1987) **A History of Photography**, Cambridge: Cambridge University Press

MICHEL FRIZOT (ed.) (1998) **A New History of Photography**, Cologne. Konemann

JOHN SZARKOWSKI (1989) **Photography Until Now**, New York: MOMA. Published to coincide with the exhibition of the same name on the occasion of the 150 years' celebration

the location of this exhibition at the Royal Academy in Piccadilly, London. This was the first ever exhibition of photographs to be held there and, as such, both the show and the accompanying publication emphasise the image as art and the status of the photographer as artist. Similarly, **John Szarkowski**'s *Photography Until Now* (1989) – which accompanied the MOMA celebration of 150 years of photography – in relying primarily on the MOMA collection reinforces the American canon (which includes a number of European photographers). Szarkowski trained both as an art historian and as a photographer before working in the MOMA collection for thirty years. His interests centred upon the formal and technical properties which distinguish photographs from other visual media, and in the status of the unauthored or vernacular photograph. However, the production values of both of these publications are high, which makes each a useful source for visual reference and research.

If you are coming to the story of photography for the first time, Rosenblum offers a good, clearly written starting point for engaging with this history. Alternatively, Szarkowski and Jeffrey complement one another in taking America, or Europe, as central starting points. Indeed, Szarkowski specifically comments on the difference in the situation of photography in the US, as opposed to Europe, at the turn of the century. He suggests that American (he specifies 'Yankee') photographers were more inclined towards reportage than their European counterparts, having invested less in claims for the status of the photograph as art, since America lacked the depth of artistic tradition that was central to post-Renaissance Europe.

Each of the histories reviewed above reflects, to a greater or lesser degree, an established selection of photographers and their images. The 'great masters' approach has been challenged variously. Anne Tucker, in *The Woman's Eye* (1973) was among the first to draw attention to the considerable participation of women as photographers historically. As the title implies, she suggests that what we see photographically – that is, subject-matter and treatment – to some extent reflects gender. This question of gender has been pursued by **Val Williams** in her discussion of British women's participation in a range of practices, including the local (studio) and the domestic (the family album), and, like Peter Turner, her historical account takes stock of commercial practices. Likewise, Jeanne Montoussamy-Ashe (1985) reinstates black women into the history of American photography, noting, for instance, documentation for the 1866 Houston city directory which lists 'col' against the name of a female photographic printer. (Some women are also listed in D. Willis Thomas' *Black Photographers* bio-bibliography (1985), again American.) In all instances, what is at stake is to note the presence of women within a particular field and to consider ways in which gender, positively or negatively, contributed to constructing or limiting the roles played. By contrast, Constance Sullivan's *Woman Photographers* (1990), considering European (including British) and American examples, has stressed women's participation as artists, arguing that women's

VAL WILLIAMS (1986) **Women Photographers: The Other Observers, 1900 to the Present**, London: Virago. Revised edition (1991) **The Other Observers: Women Photographers from 1900 to the Present**

NAOMI ROSENBLUM (1994) **A History of Women Photographers**, New York, London and Paris: Abbeville Press work historically has demonstrated equivalent aesthetic values to those which characterise the work of their better-known male contemporaries, while often bringing different subject-matter into focus. This book is particularly useful for its quality reproduction of images. But the fundamental point is that each author focuses on putting women back into the picture even if, ultimately, they challenge the canon rather than canonisation.

PHOTOGRAPHY AND SOCIAL HISTORY

Social history and photography

Further challenge to the dominance of the 'great masters' history of photography has come from re-interrogation of the status and significance of popular photography. By 'popular' we refer to personal photography, or to photographs which may have been commissioned from professional photographers, but were intended for personal use.[12] The term also extends to include postcards exchanged between individuals, and pictures made to record events or membership of clubs and societies. The high street portrait studio is also a legacy of Victorian photography, and was by no means confined to major cities (see chapter 3). Such studios were often family enterprises, or were run by women photographers.

The contribution of particular photographers, and the economic circumstances within which Victorian and Edwardian photography was pursued, has become a focus of much recent research. But one of the points about reviewing popular photography and rethinking its significance is that concern with the authoring of images is related to questions of provenance (establishing where and when a photograph was taken) rather than to questions of artistic significance. This is because popular photography is increasingly used as social-historical evidence. Personal albums, and other materials, are viewed as a form of visual anthropology and are catalogued within a number of archives, of differing scale and thematic concern. Public museums and libraries may have photographic collections within their local or regional archive; and there are many independent collections.[13] Such rich collections offer myriad research possibilities. They also contribute to the fast-expanding 'Heritage' industry in Britain wherein photographs play a high profile as 'evidence' from the past. As such, they are displayed, or used as reference for the design of reconstructions of buildings or machinery, or republished as postcards.

The photograph as testament

Photographs are commonly used as evidence. They are among the material marshalled by the historian in order to investigate the past. Over the past thirty years they have become a major source of information by which we picture or imagine the nineteenth century. Historians have for the most part had an uneasy relationship with the medium, as their professional training

12 Travelling photographers were common prior to Kodak's introduction of the Box Brownie and the consequent more widespread ownership of cameras.

13 See the Royal Photographic Society (1977) *Directory of British Photographic Collections*, London: Heinemann.

did not introduce them to an analysis of visual images. It was television that first raided the many photographic archives for images of historical interest; this necessarily led to some difficulties, not least of which was that of an archive used in a general way to illustrate commentary, with scant regard for the purposes for which the photographs were made. The social historian may be interested in changing modes of dress, or agricultural and industrial machinery. Photographs are used as evidence of such changes, which means that the detailing of the source and date of the photograph – that is, its *provenance* – becomes especially important. Hence we come across titles of publications such as 'The Camera as Historian' or 'The Camera as Witness'.[14]

Popular education also led to a growth in the use of photographs for the analysis of local or community history.[15] There are a number of reasons why people are interested in using old photographs: some have an ethnographic curiosity about the kinds of clothes or tools that were common at a particular period, while others are fascinated by the characteristic stance and gait of workers in particular trades. Social and labour historians who wanted to gain some idea of ordinary life and work in the Victorian era have also been drawn to the examination of visual material; not merely for the information provided by photographs, but also to begin to recognise in the faces and stances of the subjects something of the real people in the scenes that have been the subject of so many accounts and narratives.

Photography was used throughout the nineteenth century in the service of political and industrial change. One motivation for early landscape photography was governmental employment of photographers for civil and military mapping purposes. For instance, the British government employed photographers for a military survey of the Highlands of Scotland in order to help quell anti-English rebellion (Christian 1990). Similarly, in America, early landscape photography in the West was often commercial in origin: Carleton Watkins' employers included the California State Geological Survey and the Pacific railroads (Snyder 1994). These photographs, along with others made for less systematic purposes, are used as a form of social-historical evidence. Examples range widely: for instance, Alison Gernsheim uses photographs as a basis for a survey of changing fashions (Gernsheim 1981). The status of the photograph as evidence is not questioned. Likewise, books based on past photojournalism are common.[16] Such books purport to present the past 'as it was', taking for granted that this is what photographs do. As is asserted on the inside cover of one such book presenting pictures of Britain and Ireland, 'More than words, more than paintings or prints, old photographs convey an immediate, undistorted impression of the past' (Minto 1970).

Such use of photographs reflects a broader set of academic assumptions. Until recently, British historical, scientific and social scientific method was characterised by empiricism. The nineteenth century was a period of extensive technological and social change, characterised by faith in progress and

14 Tagg remarks on the publication in London as early as 1916 of a handbook entitled *The Camera as Historian* aimed at those who used the camera for survey and record societies.

15 See 'The Pencil of History' in Patrice Petro (ed.) *Fugitive Images*, Bloomington: Indiana University Press, 1995.

16 There are too many examples to enumerate, but many draw upon pictures from the *Illustrated London News* or *Picture Post*.

'Modernity'. Modernity refers to a complex set of developments relating to industrial change, which include the increasing concentration of people in towns and cities, geographical mobility consequent upon the invention of the steam engine and the spread of railway networks, and economic faith in technological progress. In Britain, France and elsewhere, such changes were underpinned economically through imperialism (which made available raw materials and cheap labour from other parts of the world) and through the low pay and poor working conditions experienced by industrial and agrarian labour at home. All these factors contributed to the increasingly public and urban nature of modern life, with the increasing separation of the aristocracy (in Britain), the professional and entrepreneurial middle class, and the workers.

Photography not only developed in the Victorian era but was also implicitly caught up in nineteenth-century interests and attitudes. The Victorians invested considerable faith in the power of the camera to record, classify and witness. This meant that the camera was also entrusted with delineating social appearance, classifying the face of criminality and lunacy, offering racial and social stereotypes. In one of few histories to investigate the photograph neither primarily as image nor as technology, **Alan Thomas** in *The Expanding Eye* considers ways in which early uses of photography reflect and reinforce nineteenth-century concerns. Centred upon Victorian Britain, his account focuses on the popularisation of photography both in terms of *uses* of photographs (it is one of the first accounts to give a whole chapter to photography as family chronicler) and in terms of representation of the everyday. Thus he includes discussion of personal uses of photography in, for instance, the family album; portraiture (including theatre portraits); and photographs which investigate rural and urban working and living conditions. Likewise, **Mary Warner Marien** critically considers the history of the idea of photography, its cultural impact and implications, including discussion of the photograph within mass culture.

One of the consequences of extensive social change was a series of social surveys, which were designed to try to understand further how different social groups responded to the changing times and sought explanation through the quantitative assembly of information. In 1851 The Great Exhibition celebrated industrial and technological achievement. In that same year, the British Census recorded differences in work status and living circumstances.[17] The motivation for the Victorian survey was not simply academic. Also in 1851 Henry Mayhew published his *London Labour and London Poor*. This first survey of living conditions was illustrated with wood engravings based upon photographs, and therefore stands as an early example of the photograph being used as documentation. It became common for authenticity to be stressed through using such phrases as 'drawn from an original photograph'. The photographic image was already being mobilised as witness.

ALAN THOMAS (1978) **The Expanding Eye**, London: Croom Helm

MARY WARNER MARIEN (1997) **Photography and Its Critics, A Cultural History, 1839–1900**, Cambridge: Cambridge University Press

17 It is interesting to note that in 1851, fifty-one people recorded themselves by occupation as photographers, and in 1961 there were 2879 (Gernsheim and Gernsheim 1969: 234).

Categorical photography

John Tagg has written extensively on the uses of photography within power relations, noting that photographs became implicated in surveillance very early on. He employs the genealogical method typical of the work of French philosopher, **Michel Foucault**. In *The Burden of Representation* Tagg traces intersecting ways in which photography was involved in maintaining social class hierarchies through delineation of, for instance, prisoners or the poor. He insists on the need to trace the complex relations between representation, knowledge and ideology in terms which take account of fundamental class interests at stake. In his essay 'The Currency of the Photograph' (Burgin 1982) Tagg focuses on what he terms 'the prerequisites of realism'. His title metaphorically references the notion of the photograph as symbolic exchange, while simultaneously referring to the values implicated in such an exchange. Thus he discusses the relationship of the photograph to reality, the constitution of photographic meaning, the social utility of photographs, and the institutional frameworks within which they are produced and consumed.

Likewise, recent reappraisals of uses of photography within social anthropology, and within the records of colonial travellers implicated in European imperialism, have drawn attention to the political and ideological implications of using photography to define social types viewed as different or **Other**. As a number of critics have variously observed, such definitional uses of the image contribute to legitimating colonial rule (**Edwards 1992**). Furthermore, as Sarah Graham-Brown has argued, there is a complex interplay between imperialism and patriarchy, within which women become particular sorts of exoticised victims of the stereotyping of the colonial Other (Graham-Brown 1988).

In his 'The Archive and the Body' (1986), photographer and critic Allan Sekula traces the attempts of Victorian men of science to delineate, record and classify particular 'types' of human being (Sekula 1991). They used physiognomy and phrenology to show that it was possible to read from the surface of the body the inner delineation and moral character of the subject being studied. They employed the developing science of statistics in order to demonstrate that science – aided by one of its new tools, the seemingly impartial eye of the camera – would reveal and systematically record the varieties of criminal faces.

Sekula is, in this complex article, particularly interested in photography's relation to police procedures, but mad people and native peoples from other cultures were similarly subjected to processes of measurement and scientific appraisal. In 1869 T.H. Huxley was asked to make a photographic record of people from a number of races:

> Huxley . . . was asked . . . by the Colonial Office to devise
> instructions for the 'formation of a series of photographs of the

JOHN TAGG (1988) **The Burden of Representation: Essays on Photographies and Histories**, London: Macmillan

Michel Foucault (1926–1984) One of the most influential of French philosophers of recent times. He enjoyed a distinguished career as a scholar and academic which culminated in his appointment as Professor in the History of Systems of Thought at the College de France. In the 1960s Foucault rejected humanism and philosophies of consciousness and set about the construction of a new kind of critical theory. His concerns were with the way in which specific social institutions and practices construct the objects and forms of knowledge and help to determine our human subjectivity. Some key works in this project are, in English translation: *The Order of Things: An Archeology of the Human Sciences* (1970); *The Archeology of Knowledge* (1972); *The Birth of the Clinic* (1973); *Discipline and Punish* (1977); *The History of Sexuality* (1978).

ELIZABETH EDWARDS (ed.) (1992) **Photography and Anthropology**, New Haven: Yale University Press. An impressive collection of essays on the subject which takes advantage of access to key archives including the Pitt River Museum, Oxford, where Edwards is Curator of Photography.

[See chapter 5, pp. 220–4.]

various races of men comprehended within the British Empire'. The system he conceived called for unclothed subjects to be photographed full- and half-length, frontally and in profile, standing in each exposure beside a clearly marked measuring stick. Such photographs reproduced the hierarchical structures of domination and subordination inherent in the institutions of colonialism.

(Pultz 1995: 25)

But a number of further issues beg attention in considering surveillance, social survey and other 'mapping' usages of photography. In referring to the photograph as 'fugitive testimony', Barthes draws our attention to the fleeting nature of the moment captured in the photograph and the extent to which contemporary experience (we are looking back with eyes informed by circumstances and ways of thinking of the 1990s), along with limited knowledge of the specific context within which – and purpose for which – the photograph was taken, make the image an unreliable witness. Photography is involved in the construction of history. But when photographs are presented as 'evidence' of past events and circumstances, a set of assumptions about their accuracy as documents is being made. Such assumptions are usually acknowledged through statements of provenance: dates, sources, and so on. But this is to ignore wider questions relating to visual communication and ways in which we interpret photographs.

In recent years, photography has been used by those who want to construct history around the notion of 'popular memory'. Here the photographs are often of a personal nature, through which communities might begin the process of establishing their own non-formal history; accounts which might well challenge or be oppositional to more official versions. One problem with this is that photographs have often been treated as though they really were a source of disinterested facts, rather than as densely coded cultural objects:

Ultimately, then, when photographs are uncritically presented as historical documents, they are transformed into aesthetic objects. Accordingly, the pretence to historical understanding remains although that understanding has been replaced by aesthetic experience.

(Sekula 1991: 123)

The history of photography is to a large extent shaped by the characteristic ways in which photographs have been collected, stored, used and displayed. With the passage of time the original motive for the making of a photograph may disappear, leaving it accessible to being 're-framed' within new contexts.

Institutions and contexts

Let us assume that a photograph of a homeless, unemployed man, published in a 1930s magazine to advance some philanthropic cause, is shown, massively enlarged, on the walls of a gallery fifty years after it was first made. Originally tied to the page with a caption and an explanatory text, it now stands alone as some kind of Art object. How are we to read such an image? As an example of a genre? For its technical qualities? As part of the *oeuvre* of a distinguished practitioner? As a work of Art, or as an historical object which conveys specific information or exemplifies 'pastness'? Do we try to make sense of it in terms of its distance from our own lives, or because there are many similarities to prevailing conditions? Do we try to read through the image some notion of human nature, of how, regardless of political context or the specificity of time, it would feel to be destitute and suffering? Or do we see it merely as a *photograph*, one among many and to be distinguished in terms of its formal, aesthetic qualities rather than its relationship to a world outside itself?

The very ubiquity of the medium has meant that photographs have always circulated in contexts for which they were not made. It is also important to remember that there is no single, intrinsic, aboriginal meaning locked up within them. Rather, there are many ways in which photographs can be read and understood, but in 'reading' photographs we rely on many contextual clues which lie outside the photography itself. We rarely encounter photographs in their original state, for we normally see them on hoardings, in magazines and newspapers, as book covers, on the walls of galleries or on the sides of buses. Their social meanings are already indicated to us and they are designed into a space, often accompanied by a text that gives us the preferred readings of their producers and allows us to make sense of what might otherwise be puzzling or ambiguous images. Indeed, commercial uses of photography, especially in advertising, often play on the multiple possible connotations that are provoked by the image.

One determinant of the way in which we understand photographs, then, is the context within which we view them, and key institutions shape the nature of photography by the way they provide this context. This approach to understanding photography was particularly influential in Britain in the 1970s and 1980s and was central to the concerns of a number of magazines at that time, pre-eminently *Ten/8* and *Camerawork* (**Evans 1997**). As was argued, photographs are weak at the level of imminent meaning and depend for their decoding on text, surrounding, organisation, and so on. Although collections of photographs have always been assembled, photography's ambiguous status with regard to Art has often meant that they were not displayed in museums as objects in themselves, but rather, used as a source of supplementary information to some more valued objects.

The museum

Douglas Crimp has argued that the entry of photographs into the privileged space of the museum stripped them of the multiple potential meanings with which they are invested. They were removed from the many realms

JESSICA EVANS (ed.) (1997) **The Camerawork Essays**, London: Rivers Oram. Includes fifteen essays originally printed in *Camerawork* between 1976 and 1985.

DOUGLAS CRIMP (1995) **On the Museum's Ruins**, Cambridge, MA: MIT Press. A collection of key essays originally published in *October* and other journals.

within which they made sense, in order to stress their status as separate objects – as *photographs*. Crimp is particularly interested in the work of the Museum of Modern Art, New York, in transforming photographs into objects of merely aesthetic attention. He is not alone in drawing attention to the way in which MOMA embraced photographs as art objects, brought them into the privileged space of the gallery and surrounded them with the apparatus of scholarship, appreciation and connoisseurship formerly reserved for paintings and sculptures.

But Crimp also examined the practice of the New York Public Library which, becoming aware of the number of photographs it possessed and of their historic and financial value, created a Department of Photography. They scoured all sections of the huge library for a trawl of photographs, which were removed from multitudinous subject areas and reclassified as photographs, often under the individual photographer.[18] Crimp comments of photography that:

> Thus ghettoized it will no longer primarily be *useful* within other discursive practices; it will no longer serve the purposes of information, documentation, evidence, illustration, reportage. The formerly plural field of photography will henceforth be reduced to the single, all-encompassing *aesthetic*.
>
> (Crimp 1995: 75)

What is lost in this process is the ability of photography to create information and knowledge through its interaction with other discourses. Photographs, doomed to the visual solitude of the art object, lose their plurality and their ability to traverse fields of meaning. They are treated as though they are unique and singular, rather than as the kind of industrial object – capable of being multiply reproduced – that constitutes their real existence.

The archive

Allan Sekula, in his article 'Reading an Archive' (1991), draws our attention to the power of the photographic archive. There are, of course, many different kinds of archive, from those held in museums to commercial or historical collections or family albums. They are found in libraries, commercial firms, museums and private collections. What they have in common is the fact that they heap together images of very different kinds and impose upon them a homogeneity that is a product of their very existence within an archive. The unity of an archive, he argues, is imposed by ownership of the objects themselves and of the principles of classification and organisation by which they are structured.[19]

Photographs of many kinds, which may have been taken for different – perhaps even antagonistic – purposes, are brought together: 'in an archive, the possibility of meaning is "liberated" from the actual contingencies of use. But this liberation is also a loss, an *abstraction* from the complexity and richness of

18 Likewise, the V&A collection of photographs was established through bringing together photographs from a number of different sections of the museum. For an introduction to this international collection see Mark Haworth-Booth (1997) **Photography: An Independent Art**, London: V&A Publications.

19 See Chrissie Iles and Russell Roberts (eds) (1997) *In Visible Light*, Oxford: Museum of Modern Art. This exhibition catalogue includes four key essays on photography and classification in art, science and the everyday.

use, a loss of context' (Sekula 1991: 116). But archives play an important function in the creation of knowledge. Characteristically, an archive seeks to grow; it aspires to completeness and through this process of mass acquisition a kind of knowledge emerges:

> And so archives are contradictory in character. Within their confines meaning is liberated from use, and yet at a more general level an empiricist model of truth prevails. Pictures are atomized, isolated in one way and homogenized in another.
>
> (Sekula 1991: 118)

But if serious historians have sometimes neglected to read photographs in the complex way they deserve, the heritage industry has used photography as a central tool in its attempt to reconstruct the past as a site of tourist pleasure. Here, photography becomes a direct way through which our experience of the past is structured.

Many critics have been worried by, or contemptuous of, the touristic use of historical materials and of the function of the visual. For example, Donald Horne claims that photography is an essential part of the tourist experience because it allows us to convert the places we visit into signs which we can then possess. Photography, he suggests:

> offers us the joys of possession: by taking photographs of famous sites and then, at home, putting them into albums or showing them as slides, we gain some kind of possession of them. For some of us this can be the main reason for our tourism. Between them, the camera and tourism are two of the uniquely modern ways of defining reality.
>
> (Horne 1984: 12)

Similarly, Robert Hewison argues:

> Heritage is gradually effacing history, by substituting an image of the past for its reality. At a time when Britain is obsessed by the past, we have a fading sense of continuity and change, which is being replaced by a fragmented and piecemeal idea of the past constructed out of costume drama on television, re-enactments of civil war battles and mendacious celebrations of events such as the Glorious Revolution, which was neither glorious nor a revolution.
>
> (Hewison, in Corner and Harvey 1990: 175)

JOHN CORNER AND SYLVIA HARVEY (1990) 'Heritage in Britain', **Ten/8**: 36

JOHN TAYLOR (1994) **A Dream of England: Landscape, Photography and the Tourist's Imagination**, Manchester: Manchester University Press

Now the archive is raided not for photographs as aesthetic objects, but for photographs as signifiers of past times. Blown up from their original proportions, sepia-toned and mounted on walls, photographs retain their implicit claim to authenticity. As cultural critics, including **John Corner** and **Sylvia Harvey**, have argued, we are now looking at the past in new ways and this kind of commodification of the image raises complex questions about how history is constructed and photographs employed to visualise the past. The

relation between past and present, and the assumptions we make about photographs as sources of evidence of past times and events, are brought into particular focus in Chapter 2, on documentary, and Chapter 3, on personal photography.

BIBLIOGRAPHY

KEY TEXTS

Barthes, Roland (1984) *Camera Lucida*, London: Fontana
Burgin, Victor (ed.) (1982) *Thinking Photography*, London: Macmillan
Clarke, Graham (1997) *The Photograph*, Oxford: Oxford University Press
Corner, John and Harvey, Sylvia (1990) 'Heritage in Britain', *Ten/8* 36
Crimp, Douglas (1995) *On the Museum's Ruins*, Cambridge, MA: MIT Press
Edwards, Elizabeth (ed.) (1992) *Photography and Anthropology*, New Haven: Yale University Press
Evans, Jessica (ed.) (1997) *The Camerawork Essays*, London: Rivers Oram Press
Frizot, Michel (ed.) (1998) *A New History of Photography*, Cologne: Könemann (originally published in French, 1994)
Gernsheim, Helmut and Gernsheim, Alison (1969) *The History of Photography from the Earliest Use of the Camera Obscura in the Eleventh Century up to 1914*, 2 vols, London and New York: McGraw-Hill (first edition, 1955)
Goldberg, Vicki (ed.) (1981) *Photography in Print*, Albuquerque: University of New Mexico
Haworth-Booth, Mark (1997) *Photography: An Independent Art*, London: V&A Publications.
Hill, Paul and Cooper, Thomas (1992) *Dialogue with Photography*, Manchester: Cornerhouse Publications
Jeffrey, Ian (1981) *Photography, A Concise History*, London: Thames and Hudson
Lemagny, Jean-Claude and Rouille, André (1987) *A History of Photography*, Cambridge: Cambridge University Press
Lyons, Nathan (1966) *Photographers on Photography*, Englewood Cliffs: Prentice Hall
Newhall, Beaumont (1982) *The History of Photography*, New York: MOMA, fifth edition, revised and enlarged (first edition, 1937)
Phillips, Christopher (ed.) (1989) *Photography in the Modern Era*, New York: Metropolitan Museum/Aperture
Rosenblum, Naomi (1994) *A History of Women Photographers*, New York, London, and Paris: Abbeville Press
—— (1997) *A World History of Photography* New York, London, and Paris: Abbeville Press, third edition (previous editions, 1984, 1989)
Sontag, Susan (1979) *On Photography*, Harmondsworth: Penguin
Szarkowski, John (1989) *Photography Until Now*, New York: MOMA
Tagg, John (1988) *The Burden of Representation: Essays on Photographies and Histories*, London: Macmillan
Taylor, John (1994) *A Dream of England: Landscape, Photography and the Tourist's Imagination*, Manchester: Manchester University Press
Thomas, Alan (1978) *The Expanding Eye*, London: Croom Helm
Turner, Peter (1987) *History of Photography*, London: Hamlyn
Williams, Val (1986) *Women Photographers: The Other Observers, 1900 to the Present*, London: Virago (revised edition 1991, *The Other Observers: Women Photographers from 1900 to the Present*)

OTHER REFERENCES

Barthes, Roland (1973) *Mythologies*, London: Granada (first published 1957)

—— (1977) 'The Rhetoric of the Image' and 'The Third Meaning' in *Image, Music, Text*, London: Fontana

Batchen, Geoffrey (1990) 'Burning with Desire: The Birth and Death of Photography', *Afterimage*, January

Baudelaire, Charles (1859) 'The Salon of 1859', reprinted in P.E. Charvet (ed.) (1992) *Baudelaire, Selected Writings on Art and Artists*, Harmondsworth: Penguin

Bazin, André (1967) 'The Ontology of the Photographic Image' in *What is Cinema?* Volume 1, Berkeley, Los Angeles, and London: University of California Press

Beloff, Halla (1985) *Camera Culture*, Oxford: Blackwell

Benjamin, Walter (1931) 'A Small History of Photography' in (1979) *One Way Street*, London: New Left Books

—— (1970) 'The Work of Art in an Age of Mechanical Reproduction' in Hannah Arendt (ed.) *Illuminations*, London: Fontana (first published 1936)

Berger, John (1972) *Ways of Seeing*, Harmondsworth: Penguin

Bezencenet, Stevie (1982a) 'What is a History of Photography?', *Creative Camera* 208, April

—— (1982b) 'Thinking Photography', *Creative Camera* 215, November

Bolton, Richard (ed.) (1989) *The Contest of Meaning*, Cambridge, MA: MIT Press

Burgin, Victor (1986) 'Re-Reading *Camera Lucida*' in *The End of Art Theory*, London: Macmillan

Carr, E.H. (1964) *What is History?*, Harmondsworth: Penguin

Christian, J. (1990) 'Paul Sandby and the Military Survey of Scotland' in N. Alfrey and J. Daniels (eds) *Mapping the Landscape*, University of Nottingham

Corner, John and Harvey, Sylvia (eds) (1991) *Enterprise and Heritage*, London: Routledge

Delpire, Robert and Frizot, Michel (1989) *Histoire de Voir*, Paris: Photo Poche

Eastlake, Lady Elizabeth (1857) 'Photography', *Quarterly Review*, April, reprinted in Newhall, Beaumont (ed.) (1980) *Photography: Essays and Images*, London: Secker and Warburg

Ferguson, Russell (1992) 'A Box of Tools: Theory and Practice' in R. Ferguson, W. Olander, M. Tucker and K. Fiss (eds) *Discourses: Conversations in Postmodernism, Art and Culture*, Cambridge, MA: MIT Press

Fisher, Andrea (1987) *Let Us Now Praise Famous Women*, London: Pandora

Freund, Gisele (1980) *Photography and Society*, London: Gordon Fraser

Gasser, Martin (1992) 'Histories of Photography 1839–1939', *History of Photography* 16(1), Spring

Gernsheim, Alison (1981) *Victorian and Edwardian Fashion, A Photographic Survey*, New York: Dover (originally published 1963, revised edition)

Gernsheim, Helmut and Gernsheim, Alison (1965) *A Concise History of Photography*, London: Thames and Hudson

Graham-Brown, Sarah (1988) *Images of Women: The Portrayal of Women in Photography of the Middle East 1860–1950*, London: Quartet Books

Green-Lewis, Jennifer (1996) *Framing the Victorians, Photography and the Culture of Realism*, Ithaca and London: Cornell University Press

Hall, Stuart (ed.) (1997) *Representation, Cultural Representations and Signifying Practices*, London: Sage/Open University

Haworth-Booth, Mark (1997) *Photography: An Independent Art*, London: V&A

Heron, Liz and Williams, Val (1996) *Illuminations: Women Writing on Photography from the 1850s to the Present*, London and New York: I.B. Tauris

Hewison, Robert (1987) *The Heritage Industry*, London: Methuen

Holmes, Oliver Wendell (1859) 'The Stereoscope and the Stereograph', *Atlantic Monthly* 3, reprinted in B. Newhall (ed.) (1980) *Photography: Essays and Images*, London: Secker and Warburg

Horne, Donald (1984) *The Great Museum: The Re-presentation of History*, London: Verso

Howard, F. (1853) 'Photography Applied to Fine Art', *Journal of the Photographic Society*, London

Hurley, Jack (1972) *Portrait of a Decade: Roy Stryker and the Development of Documentary Photography in the Thirties*, Baton Rouge: Louisiana State University Press

Iles, Chrissie and Roberts, Russell (eds) (1997) *In Visible Light*, Oxford; Museum of Modern Art

Jameson, Fredric (1991) *Postmodernism, Or, the Cultural Logic of Late Capitalism*, London: Verso

Jeffrey, Ian (1982) 'Some Sacred Sites', *Creative Camera* 215, November

Kozloff, Max (1979) *Photography and Fascination*, USA New Hampshire: Addison House

—— (1987) *The Privileged Eye*, Albuquerque: University of New Mexico Press

Kracauer, Siegfried (1960) 'Photography', Chapter 1 of *Theory of Film*, Oxford: Oxford University Press

Krauss, Rosalind (1981) 'A Note on Photography and the Simulacral', *October*, Winter, reprinted in Carol Squiers (ed.) (1991) *The Critical Image*, Seattle: Bay Press/London: Lawrence and Wishart

Lange, Dorothea (1960) 'The Assignment I'll Never Forget' in Beaumont Newhall, (ed.) (1980) *Photography: Essays and Images*, London: Secker and Warburg

Minto, C.S. (1970) *Victorian and Edwardian Scotland from Old Photographs*, London: Batsford

Moholy-Nagy, Lazlo (1967) *Painting, Photography, Film*, London: Lund Humphries

Montoussamy-Ashe, Jeanne (1985) *Viewfinders: Black Women Photographers*, New York: Dodd, Mead

Ohrn, Karen Becker (1980) *Dorothea Lange and the Documentary Tradition*, Baton Rouge: Louisiana State University Press

Phaidon (1997) *The Photography Book*, London: Phaidon

Price, Mary (1994) *The Photograph: A Strange, Confined Space*, Stanford, CA: Stanford University Press

Pultz, John (1995) *The Body and the Lens: Photography 1839 to the Present*, New York: Harry N. Abrams, Inc

Punt, Michael (1995) 'The Elephant, the Spaceship and the White Cockatoo: An Archeology of Digital Photography' in Martin Lister (ed.) *The Photographic Image in Digital Culture*, London: Routledge

Rabinowitz, Paula (1994) *They Must be Represented: The Politics of Documentary*, London: Verso

Roberts, John (1998) *The Art of Interruption: Realism, Photography and the Everyday*, Manchester: Manchester University Press

Rosler, Martha (1989) 'In, Around and Afterthoughts (on Documentary Photography)' in Richard Bolton (ed.) *The Contest of Meaning: Critical Histories of Photography*, Cambridge, MA: MIT Press

Sekula, Allan (1986) 'The Archive and the Body', *October* 39, reprinted in Richard Bolton (ed.) (1989) *The Contest of Meaning*, Cambridge, MA: MIT Press

—— (1991) 'Reading an Archive' in Brian Wallis and Marcia Tucker (eds) *Blasted Allegories*, Cambridge, MA: MIT Press

Snyder, Joel (1994) 'Territorial Photography' in W.J.T. Mitchell (ed.) *Landscape and Power*, London: University of Chicago Press

Solomon-Godeau, Abigail (1991) *Photography at the Dock: Essays on Photographic History, Institutions and Practices*, Minneapolis: University of Minnesota Press

Squiers, Carol (ed.) (1990) *The Critical Image*, London: Lawrence and Wishart

Stokes, Philip (1992) 'The Family Photograph Album: So Great a Cloud of Witnesses' in Graham Clarke (ed.) *The Portrait in Photography*, London: Reaktion Books

Strand, Paul (1917) 'Photography', *Camera Work* 49/50, reprinted in B. Newhall (1982)

—— (1980) *Photography: Essays and Images*, London: Secker and Warburg

Stryker, Roy (1972) interview, reprinted in Peninah R. Petruck (ed.) (1979) *The Camera Viewed: Writings on Twentieth-Century Photography*, New York: E.P. Dutton

Sullivan, Constance (1990) *Woman Photographers*, London: Virago

Thomas, Deborah Willis (1985) *Black Photographers 1840–1940: An Illustrated Bio-Bibliography*, New York: Garland

Tucker, Anne (1973) *The Woman's Eye*, New York: Knopf

—— (1984) 'Photographic Facts and Thirties America' in David Featherstone (ed.) *Observations: Essays on Documentary Photography*, Carmel, CA: Friends of Photography

Warner Marien, Mary (1988) 'Another History of Photography', *Afterimage*, October: 4–5

—— (1991) 'Toward a New Prehistory of Photography' in Daniel P. Younger (ed.) *Multiple Views*, Albuquerque: University of New Mexico Press

—— (1997) *Photography and Its Critics, A Cultural History, 1839–1900*, Cambridge: Cambridge University Press

Weaver, Mike (1989) *The Art of Photography*, London: Royal Academy of Art

Williams, Raymond (1974) *Television, Technology and Cultural Form*, London: Fontana

CHAPTER 2

Surveyors and surveyed

Photography out and about

DERRICK PRICE

2.1 Sebastaio Salgado, *Sao Paulo Construction*, 1996
Brazilian-born, Salgado is one of the most important contemporary photographers. He has photographed
workers, the poor and the dispossessed around the world

Surveyors and surveyed
Photography out and about

INTRODUCTION

Within a decade or two of its invention, photography was used to chronicle wars, to survey remote regions of the world and to make scientific observations. Life on the streets of great cities was recorded, but so were the monuments of Egypt and Syria, the vast ranges of the Himalayas, the USA railroad as it moved West, the fishing village of Whitby and the architecture of Paris. Pornographic images were soon in circulation, as were charity shots of the poor and homeless. **Montage** techniques were used to produce pictures of fairies, ghosts and elves. Less sensationally, the dead were recorded as they lay in their coffins (photography was hailed as an excellent substitute for the death mask), while all the living seemed appropriate subjects for the camera's **gaze**.

In this chapter we examine some of the ways photography has been used in order to bring us images of the wider world. Although we look briefly at some aspects of travel and war photography, we are essentially concerned with documentary photographs and with the history through which 'documentary' was shaped and developed. It was to grow into a movement with many practitioners throughout the world but, in order to look closely at the nature of its origins and development, we have concentrated on the British experience. So closely is that related to documentary projects in the USA, however, that we have also taken examples from that country.

montage or **photomontage**
The use of two or more originals, perhaps also including written text, to make a combined image. A montaged image may be imaginative, artistic, comic or deliberately satirical.

67

Documentary realism as expressed in film, photography and literature was of importance in the development of cultural politics and social investigation in both countries.

This approach allows us to explore the connections between documentary, social investigation, modes of **representation** and forms of reportage at particular times. In this sense the chapter is centrally concerned with questions of history, but it does not offer a chronicle of the great practitioners of documentary photography. Indeed, so all-pervasive has been documentary, and its associated forms, that such a chronicle would need to include many of the major figures in the history of photography. Particular photographers are discussed in order to illustrate some aspect of the documentary project, rather than to provide a description of the nature of their work.

We begin by noting photography's inexhaustible ability to provide us with pictures of the world; images which we are asked to accept as faithful to the real appearance of things. We want to examine the medium's putative capability to furnish us with accurate transcriptions of reality; an ability once thought to be guaranteed by the technology itself. Later this naive view was challenged and, as we shall see, the relationship of photography to reality was problematised and contested.

From the 1970s, a stream of critical work has rejected the notion that acts of looking and recording can ever be neutral, disinterested or innocent, but has seen them as containing and expressing relations of power and control. To examine this we need to consider why, and under what conditions, certain groups became the object of the camera's gaze, as well as to investigate the ways in which they were represented.

SURVEYS AND SOCIAL FACTS

Photography and imperialism

Despite the physical difficulties of transporting large, unwieldy cameras and portable darkrooms, photographers covered the world in search of images of historic sites, sacred places and curious peoples. Photography grew up in the days of Empire and became an important adjunct of imperialism, for it returned to the Western spectator images of native peoples which frequently confirmed prevailing views of them as primitive, bizarre, barbaric or simply picturesque.

As Robert Hershkowitz has put it:

Photographic images, particularly from the late 1850s onward, reinforced the attitude(s) of mind which lay behind the imperialist approach to international politics, the positivist, materialist approach to the natural world and a belief in progress through advancing technological development.

(Hershkowitz 1980: 7)

These photographs were often regarded as offering amusing or fascinating glimpses of other societies, but they were also thought to be instructive or educative, for, within the evolutionary theories of the day, they were considered to reveal something of people at an earlier stage of development. In consequence, the images were also invested with a certain kind of poignancy, for, at the height of industrialism in the USA and Europe, it seemed clear that many of the communities recorded by the photographers of Empire were doomed to disappear.

James R. Ryan has argued that photography:

> with its detail, ubiquity and currency across a range of institutional sites – played a significant role within the construction of the imaginative geography of Empire, creating a parallel Empire within a range of discourses including science, art, commerce and government.
>
> (Ryan 1997: 26)

The photograph functioned in complex ways which transcended any simple representation of reality:

> Despite claims for its accuracy and trustworthiness, however, photography did not so much record the real as signify and construct it. Through various rhetorical and pictorial devices, from ideas of the picturesque to schemes of scientific classification, and different visual themes, from landscapes to 'racial types', photographers represented the imaginative geographies of Empire. Indeed, as a practice of representation, photography did more than merely familiarise Victorians with foreign views: it enabled them symbolically to travel through, explore and even possess those spaces.
>
> (Ryan 1997: 214)

But Ryan also investigates the range of work which collectively produced the geography of imperialism and he looks at a number of individuals, places and activities – from African explorers, travellers in India, commercial photographers, military campaigns and the study of racial types – all of which helped to construct an archive of the the achievements of the Victorian colonial and imperial project.

The Victorian passion for classification extended to whole peoples, who were categorised and ranked according to 'anthropological type'. Those who were subjected to the coloniser's gaze were often seen as merely representative of racial or social groups, and were usually posed so as to embody particular kinds of dress, social roles and material cultures.

Peter Quartermaine, in his discussion of the photographs of Johannes Lindt of the native peoples of Australia and New Guinea, comments that:

> These people were photographed as 'other': the white settler population was interested in learning *about* them, a quasi-scientific

attitude which presupposed a controlling position. The photographic images produced by Australian photographers sold to a metropolitan and international consumer market. Such prints doubly privileged the purchasers since, although reflecting their own aesthetic (natives clothed and posed with decorative artifacts), they also supposedly granted direct access to the culture depicted; their use as raw evidence by anthropologists and ethnographers certainly assumed this.

(Quartermaine 1992: 85)

The concept of **the Other** is of central importance to this argument. The phrase is used in feminist, **psychoanalytic** theory to indicate that men construct women as 'the Other'; that is, as an opposite, in reaction to which their own maleness can be defined. Similarly, European culture was defined *against* 'the Other' of colonised peoples: 'Photography is here no mere handmaid of empire, but a shaping dimension of it: formal imperial power structures institutionalised the attitudes and assumptions necessarily entailed in viewing another individual as a subject for photography' (Quartermaine 1992: 85).

We must remember that, unlike the body of painting and engravings of 'exotic' peoples that had been popular Victorian subjects, photography claimed to be able to create objective, 'scientific' records which were free from the bias of human imagination. Carefully contrived and constructed photographs were consumed as though they were unmediated images and offered a neutral reflection of the world. They were, however, far from being transparent and dispassionate images of the world, for, as Jill Lloyd puts it: 'both photography as a medium and anthropology as a discipline masked their ideological standpoints and connotative potential with the appearance of scientific objectivity' (Lloyd 1985: 13).

The public appetite for images of native peoples was accompanied by a demand for photographs of historic sites, many of which were familiar from paintings and engravings, but which were given a new authenticity by the camera. It is difficult now to gain any idea of just how many travel photographs were made and sold, but the market in them was certainly vast. In addition to the beautifully mounted and bound albums that are now preserved in archives and museums, the new commercial photography firms that were established in the years after 1850 sold thousands of cheap postcards and single prints. For example, in 1865 the London Stereoscopic Company sold half a million pictures, many of them scenes from foreign places. At the same time we see the emergence of the professional travel photographer of whom Francis Frith is probably the best known. In addition to his own work, he established a company bearing his name that was to become the largest publisher of photographs in its time. The camera and travel became linked together and, as tourism slowly developed into a mass industry, photography functioned both to set the scene in advance of a trip and to provide a record of the journey when it was over. Soon there were few places in the world that had

2.2 William Thomas, *Mrs Lewis Waller with a Kaffir Boy*, 1903
The relationship between coloniser and colonised is sharply focused in this portrait of Mrs Waller and her African servant

not been surveyed by the camera and few people who had not been subjected to the photo-eye; wildernesses gave up their seclusion as surely as cities yielded their secret places to the new image-makers.

It has frequently been argued that photography has been used as a way of consuming the world in a manner that gives us power over it; a way that allows us to discipline and naturalise what might otherwise seem strange or frightening:

To photograph is in some ways to appropriate the object being photographed. It is a power/knowledge relationship. To have visual knowledge of an object is in part to have power, even if only momentarily over it. Photography tames the object of the gaze, the most striking examples being of exotic cultures. In the USA the railway companies did much to create 'Indian' attractions to be photographed, carefully selecting those tribes with a particularly 'picturesque and ancient' appearance.

(Urry 1990: 139)

While photography produced a particular kind of knowledge it was also seen by many of its practitioners as a form of entertainment, and not all photographers went abroad with educational aims. For example, Burton Holmes made his debut in 1890 with a slides and anecdote show, 'Through Europe with a Kodak', which he delivered to the Chicago Camera Club.

In order to distinguish his performance from lectures, Holmes invented the word 'travelogue'. In pursuit of material he went around the world six times and gave over 8,000 illustrated talks. Holmes was so successful an entertainer and entrepreneur of photography that he was said to have grossed $5 million in fifty-three years.

The camera at war

While Burton Holmes was coining a name for a new kind of photographic show, other people travelled with graver purposes. War plays an important part in the story of photography and today most people's understanding of the nature of war comes from photographic images rather than literary accounts. It was, however, the highly critical reports of the London *Times* reporter, William Russell, on the progress of the Crimean War that led to Roger Fenton being sent to take photographs that would reassure the public. Fenton used the newly invented wet **collodion** process to produce more than 350 photographs which did, indeed, show scenes of calm and disciplined order. He produced a number of handsome albums with original photographs 'tipped in', but his images were also used as the basis of illustrations in the *Illustrated London News*.

Fenton spent only a short time in the Crimea and his work did little to reveal the hardships or horrors of war. The American Civil War (1861–1865) was the first to be photographed extensively throughout its duration, and in which photography was seen not only as providing realistic images of the struggle, but also as 'news'. In this sense, it also provided one of the foundation stones for the development of photojournalism. Michael L. Carlebach comments that:

Two weekly newspapers that were established in America in the years just preceding the Civil War made photographs and other visual materials equal partners of the printed word in the reporting

collodion This process, known as wet collodion (or Ambrotype), invented by English photographer Frederick Scott Archer in 1851, increased the speed of photography as the glass plate was treated and exposed while still 'wet' (i.e. gummy) but it had the drawback of involving bulky equipment. It became one of the major processes until the invention in the 1870s of gelatin-coated plates known as dry plates.

of news. These new publications would provide the public, or at least the northern public, with accurate and timely illustrations of the war. The pictures they published, many based on photographs, offered vivid, graphic and reliable glimpses into all aspects of the conflict. For the first time, Americans would see through the eyes of a score of photographers, exactly what was going on at the front.

(Carlebach 1992: 63)

But, as Carlebach makes plain, these significant images were not the most numerous of the photographs produced in the war. A boom was experienced by photographic studios trying to deal with the demand for portraits of those who were going into battle. In addition, photographs of the commanders of the Federal army were turned out in their hundreds; purchased by people anxious to support the cause and made the subject of a special tax.

The most important photographer of the Civil War was Matthew Brady. Already celebrated for his portraits, 'Brady of Broadway' produced photographs that showed scenes of action, together with shots of the dead on the battlefield, and more tranquil views of soldiers relaxing at their camps. Brady put teams of photographers into the field of battle, including Alexander Gardner, Timothy O'Sullivan and George Barnard, and published this work under his own imprint. Alan Trachtenberg describes his function in the following terms:

'Brady's pictures' did not mean pictures made by Brady himself but those he displayed or published. . . . Organiser of one of several corps of private photographers, collector of images made by others, a kind of archivist or curator of the entire photographic campaign of the war, Brady played many roles, swarmed with ambiguities, in the war.

(Trachtenberg 1989: 72)

Since Brady's time, no war or violent conflict has lacked its photographic record and interpreters. For example, hundreds of thousands of images of the First World War were made, most of which have been rendered anonymous by the system of classification and archiving that was subsequently employed. Despite the sheer number of photographs of that conflict, there is little work that really gives us a sense of the nature of trench warfare, and the poetry, films and paintings of the time are often more moving and revealing.

Photography was considerably more important as a means of depicting the Spanish Civil War (1936–1939). The many illustrated journals of the day carried photographs and these images were influential in shaping people's view of the war. The single most famous photograph was Robert Capa's *Death of a Loyalist Soldier* which later became the subject of speculation as to its authenticity. Capa was also one of the photographers of the Second

World War whose work became very familiar to the public, along with that of Bert Hardy, W. Eugene Smith, Carl Mydans and *Life* photographer David Douglas Duncan, who went on to produce heroic images of American soldiers in Korea and Vietnam.

The Second World War (1939–1945) blurred the distinction between combatant and civilian and, thereafter, war photographers concentrated as much attention on those caught up in conflict as on the soldiers themselves. This is, of course, also true for violent conflict which is not defined as a 'war', as in Cyprus or Northern Ireland.

Jorge Lewinski has commented that:

> It is only in the post-war period, starting with the Korean war, that the immediacy of war photographs begins to have a significant effect. Since then, a stream of authentic images has overwhelmed us with cumulative power. The images from Korea, Cyprus, Israel, the Congo, Biafra and Vietnam have left their indelible mark on our imaginations.
>
> (Lewinski 1978: 12)

Certainly, it is often said that the stream of images revealing the death, injury and sorrows of the people of Vietnam was a major factor in the public's eventual repugnance for that war. In the sophisticated photographic work of the time the themes of martial conflict and civilian anguish are intertwined. An excellent example is given in the work of Philip Jones Griffiths, who produced one of the most important photographic records of the war (Griffiths 1971).

War has been seen as an important subject for photography for a number of reasons: the photographer might reveal scenes and actions which would not otherwise come to the attention of the public; war inevitably throws up scenes of great emotional force which can best be captured by the camera; it has a dark psychic fascination for us, which coexists with our feelings of revulsion. The person who has most mused on this ambivalence is the English photographer, Don McCullin, who has documented many wars and violent uprisings since the early 1960s.

Documentary photography

Photographs by travellers and scenes of war became photographic genres in their own right, and they are sometimes difficult to distinguish from the kind of photograph with which we are most interested in this chapter – the documentary.

Since documentary has been described as a form, a genre, a tradition, a style, a movement and a practice, it is not useful to try to offer a single definition of the word. John Grierson coined it in 1926 to describe the kind of cinema that he wanted to replace what he saw as the dream factory of Hollywood, and it quickly gained currency within photography. The word had an imperialist tendency, and rather different kinds of photography were soon being subsumed within it. Some nineteenth-century photographers had regarded their work as 'documents', but many more were innocent of the fact that they were documentary photographers. Indeed, **Abigail Solomon-Godeau** (1991) has pointed out that in the nineteenth century almost all photography was what would later be described as 'documentary'.

But, if most photographs are a *kind* of documentary, how can we make distinctions between them? Historians and critics have frequently drawn attention to the difficulty of defining documentary which cannot be recognised as possessing a unique style, method or body of techniques. One answer to the question is to define documentary in terms of its connection with particular kinds of social investigation. Karin Becker Ohrn argues:

> The cluster of characteristics defining the documentary style incorporates all aspects of the making and use of photographs. Although not rigid, these characteristics serve as referents for comparing photographers working within . . . the documentary tradition − a tradition that includes aspects of journalism, art, education, sociology and history. Primarily, documentary was thought of as having a goal beyond the production of a fine print. The photographer's goal was to bring the attention of an audience to the subject of his or her work and, in many cases, to pave the way for social change.
>
> (Ohrn 1980: 36)

Our concern in this chapter will be to unpick some of the components of this tradition and examine ways in which we can distinguish documentary from other kinds of **straight photography**. Certainly the nature of an image itself is not enough to classify a particular photograph as in some essential way 'documentary'; rather we need to look at the contexts, practices, institutional forms within which the work is set. Documentary work may be seen to belong to the history of a particular kind of social investigation, although it employed its own forms, conventions and tropes. **Martha Rosler** (1989) tells us that to understand it we need to look to history, and she characterises documentary as 'a practice with a past'. A past, we might add, which, despite changing technologies, practices and fashions, was always concerned to claim for documentary a special relationship to real life and a singular status with regard to notions of truth and authenticity. In looking at this past we will present an account of some of the theoretical, cultural and historical elements that are necessary in order to examine critically the history of documentary. The first of these is its implicit claim that it offers us a disinterested and true picture of the world.

Documentary and authenticity

Perhaps the simplest and most obvious test of authenticity in the kind of photography that claims to be an unmediated transcription of reality is to

ABIGAIL SOLOMON-GODEAU (1991) **Photography at the Dock**, Minneapolis: University of Minnesota Press

straight photography
Emphasis upon direct documentary typical of the Modern period in American photography.

MARTHA ROSLER (1989) 'In, Around and Afterthoughts (on Documentary Photography)' in R. Bolton (ed.) **The Contest of Meaning: Critical Histories of Photography**, Cambridge, MA: The MIT Press ask whether what is in front of the lens to be photographed has been tampered with, set up or altered by the photographer.

Early in its history photography had been presented with many cases of fraud, as, for example, when the French photographer E. Appert published his book *Les Crimes de la Commune* in 1871. This purported to be a record of the vile behaviour of those who took part in the rising of the Paris Commune and was received with relish by many bourgeois commentators of the time. It consists, for the most part, of crudely montaged and retouched photographs, but was convincing enough for a public who were confident that the camera could not lie. It would, however, be incorrect to deduce that in the nineteenth century only outright deception was commented upon. Many sophisticated arguments about the ability of photographs to be true to appearances were rehearsed at that time. Indeed the Victorians were to stage a dramatic debate on the relationship between truth and representation in the public trial of Dr Barnardo.

In 1876 the philanthropist Dr T.J. Barnardo appeared at a public hearing charged with deceiving the public. His detractors claimed, and Barnardo finally conceded, that he had misled the public in his use of 'before and after' photographs of the orphans in his care. He had produced a series of cards which purported to reveal the transformative power of his project: one card was of dirty, ragged children lounging about against a background of urban decay; a second card showed one of these children cleaned up and neatly dressed, undertaking some useful task. Dr Barnardo used child models for these cards and one, Katie Smith, is pictured in several of them, posing as a crossing-sweeper or a match-seller. At the hearing Barnardo agreed that Katie had never sold matches, but he pointed out that she was a child of the streets who might well have ended up as a beggar and that, in any case, she represented the appearance and state of a match–girl in an honest manner. Moreover, Katie could easily have stumbled into that kind of life had she not been saved by his mission.

As a result of the public hearing Barnardo gave up using photographs in this way, but his case raises questions that were to recur throughout the next century. Why should we trust the camera to be true-to-appearances? What is the relationship between the accurate portrayal of a single case and a general truth about the nature of things? Cannot something arranged or set up offer us an authentic insight into the nature of things? It was questions of this kind that were rehearsed, long after Barnardo, in the furore that broke out over a photograph made in the USA.

In 1936 the American photographer Arthur Rothstein photographed a steer's skull that had been bleached by the sun and left lying on the earth. A simple still life, then, but one that was clearly intended to exemplify the contemporary crisis in agriculture. Rothstein took two photographs of this object, the most famous of which shows it resting on cracked, baked, water-less earth. The second, however, revealed it as resting on the less symbolically charged ground of a stretch of grass. The photographer acknowledged that he had moved the skull a few metres in order to obtain a more dramatic pictorial effect. When the presence of these two rather different images was discovered there was an outcry from Republican politicians, who claimed that the public had a right to see photographs that were objectively true rather than those that had been manipulated for purposes of rhetoric or propaganda. Two kinds of truth were in play; for, while the right-wing politicians demanded a truth at the denotative level, the photographer, like Dr Barnardo, laid claim to a greater truth at the connotative level. Nevertheless, Rothstein was at pains to draw attention to the smallness of his intervention in the 'real' state of things and would certainly have subscribed to the view that the authentic could only be guaranteed by a relatively unmediated representation of things as they are.

When it became plain that the technologies of photography were not automatic transcribers of the world, other questions about the nature of authenticity began to be raised and other guarantors of photography's fidelity were advanced. Among these was the notion that we need to trust, not the mechanical properties of the camera, but the personal integrity of the photographer. Increasingly the 'reality' revealed by the camera's lens was regarded as being to some extent a product of the personality, sensitivity or creativity of the photographer. The camera would provide not the objective facts that were craved by positivism, but accounts of the world in which 'truth' was achieved through the power of the image-maker. Thus, photographer and historian, Tim Gidal sums up the qualities needed by a photojournalist:

> The genuine reporter – and by this we mean the rare phenomenon
> of the passionately committed photojournalist – personally
> experiences what he captures on film: laughter and tears, joy and
> sorrow, tragedy and comedy. It is only through his subjective
> experience of the objective facts that the photoreporter can become
> a witness to his time. His alertness and his gift of observation
> distinguish his work from that of others – not as an artist, but related
> to the artist by virtue of this talent of creative observation.
>
> (Gidal 1973: 6)

The photographer, on this account, is both gifted with a particular acuity of vision and acts as a kind of 'exemplary sufferer' on our behalf; an artist who, in his or her person, becomes a guarantor of the accuracy of the image. It is, of course, a major step to argue that authenticity is not certified by the medium itself, but is only validated through the personal qualities and professional practices of the photographer.

Victorian surveys and investigations

One reason why the veracity of the camera was readily accepted in the nineteenth century was that photographs appeared to confirm ideas about the world that had been the subject of other artistic and cultural forms. The camera reinforced journalistic and literary accounts of aspects of social life which had rarely been seen or experienced by middle-class people. Moreover, we may argue that Victorian actuality photographs were regarded as 'authentic' precisely because they were images of the poor and the dispossessed; people whose lives had about them (to the middle-class spectator) an air of being simple, real and untrammelled by the overt complexity of middle-class existence. 'Real', here, takes on a class inflection which it was not to lose in documentary work for many years as photography established itself as an important component in an extensive series of projects to investigate and record the lives of the poor. Photography's subjects were those that had already been the topic of examination in reports, surveys, philanthropy and literature. It established itself as part of a tradition of enquiry into the health, housing, education, economic condition and moral state of the poor. Enquiries emanated from government departments, newspapers, independent scholars, medical practitioners, religious leaders and philanthropic bodies. The discourses of these enquiries overlapped, from popular newspapers through statistical surveys and scholarly works to official boards of enquiry. The apparently impartial eye of the camera added to the Victorian passion for the accumulation of statistical detail, painstaking observation and careful classification.

Photography also became a mode of surveying the unknown. Gradually those mysterious and threatening city streets were being visually inspected and hauled into the light of day in much the same way as the wild places and strange peoples of the earth were being recorded by map-makers, artists, scientists and photographers. Describing the anonymous photographers of the day, the historian **Alan Thomas** comments that:

ALAN THOMAS (1978) **The Expanding Eye: Photography and the Nineteenth Century Mind**, London: Croom Helm

> They entered the back streets, it appears, in the same spirit as expeditionary cameramen journeying in strange lands, for one of the commonest documentary photographs of the century shows a line of back street dwellers, generally women and children, with perhaps a man lurking in the rear, who are ranged across the middle of the composition, gazing expectantly into the camera. From the 1860s to the end of the century, and from every great city comes this photograph; it always seems worth looking at because of the candid directness with which the subjects give themselves to the camera – like those foreign aboriginals photographed for the first time by expeditionary photographers.
>
> (Thomas 1978: 136)

The city was seen as dangerous, but also as obscure, crowded with secrets and containing districts that were inaccessible to respectable folk. It was to such areas that the inspectors of city life and labour had to journey in order to illuminate them.

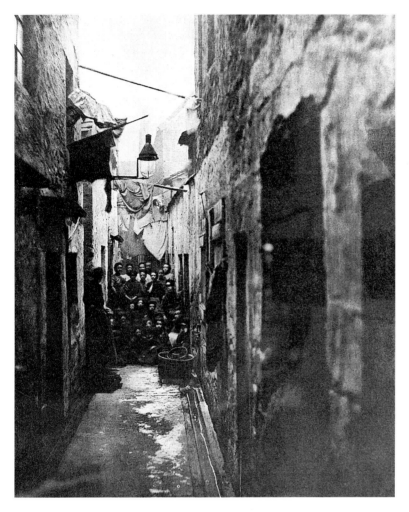

2.3 Thomas Annan, *Close No 118 High Street*, 1868
One of Annan's evocative studies of the Glasgow slums. The inhabitants of Close No 118 huddle together as they are recorded for posterity

In the United States the new newspapers consciously elevated the reporter to the position of adventurer in the obscure areas of the city. The American historian Alan Trachtenberg comments that:

> Exploration of forbidden and menacing spaces emerged in the 1890s as a leading mode of the dailies, making spectacles of the 'nether side of New York' or 'the other half'. The reporter appeared now often as a performer, one who had ventured into alien streets and

habitations, perhaps in disguise, and returned with a tale, a personal story of the dark underside of the city.

(Trachtenberg 1982: 126)

If the professional reporter journeyed to the dark places of the city an army of amateur photographers snapped away in the more salubrious areas. But here the all-pervading quality of photography began to be seen as undesirable, and by the 1880s the takers of snapshots had been defined as a public nuisance. In London, licences were required to film in many places, while the photographic press carried articles deploring the activities of those who photographed respectable people without their specific consent.

Codes of conduct were beginning to emerge and a range of permissible and impermissible subjects was being informally drawn up. If the photographers were middle class, the posed *anonymous* subjects were likely to be poor or working class. What distinguished documentary photographers within this ferment of picture-making was that they worked with some notion of improving or ameliorating the lot of their subjects. But this, in turn, led to some curious social interactions. To illustrate this point it is worth looking at the work of the photographer who is generally taken to be the first of the American documentary photographers, Jacob Riis.

Riis in the New York slums

Danish-born Jacob Riis emigrated to the USA in the 1860s. He worked as a police reporter firstly for *Tribune* and later for the *Evening Sun* and began to concentrate on reporting the conditions of life in the East Side slums of New York City. Like many philanthropists and reporters before him, Riis was frustrated by his inability to convince people of the nature of the poverty, overcrowding, sweated labour and sheer misery that existed at the heart of a prosperous city. When he read an advertisement for an early kind of flash gun which would enable photographs to be taken indoors, he decided to use photography as an 'objective' witness to the way of life he had already described in his prose pieces. He cooperated originally with jobbing photographers, none of whom proved satisfactory, so he reluctantly decided to undertake the task himself.

He produced a picture of social conditions in the area that is of considerable interest despite the lack of formal aesthetic qualities in his images. In a typical Riis picture a crude flash of light in an otherwise dark room illuminates a scene of woeful overcrowding, with ragged people huddled on wooden benches or asleep on the floor. Others show garment-workers at their trade and, of course, children sleeping in doorways or labouring alongside their parents in tiny rooms.

Riis worked at a time when the conventions of documentary photography had yet to be established, and he certainly wasted no time by seeking the cooperation of his subjects. Not only was he anxious to reveal the

2.4 Jacob Riis, *Lodgers in a Crowded Tenement* – 'five cents a spot'*, 1880s
A typical scene of poverty and overcrowding is revealed in the harsh light of Riis' flash gun

appalling social conditions of the area, but he sometimes cooperated with the police to bring prosecutions against landlords. His way of working might be described as direct and muscular and, in his autobiography *The Making of an American*, Riis cheerfully describes how he set about obtaining his images of the dispossessed:

> It is not too much to say that our party carried terror wherever it went. The flashlight of those days was contained in cartridges fired from a revolver. The spectacle of half a dozen strange men invading a house in the midnight hour armed with big pistols which they shot off recklessly was hardly reassuring, however sugary our speech, and it was not to be wondered at if the tenants bolted through windows and down fire-escapes wherever we went.
>
> (Riis 1918: 268)

81

Twice he set houses on fire in pursuit of his vigorous art and there is surely something chilling about the notion of the poor leaping from windows to evade the philanthropic documentarist. Perhaps inevitably, his photographs provide us with ethnographic detail of material life and social conditions rather than more complex subjective readings of the nature of poverty and destitution. Work of that kind was left to his successors, but Riis is important as a forerunner, and as a figure who directly connected photography to the journalistic enterprise. He was in no doubt of the power of photography to be a witness to the true nature of things. Describing a case of gross overcrowding, he writes:

> When the report was submitted to the Health Board the next day, it did not make much of an impression – these things rarely do, put in mere words – until my negatives, still dripping from the dark-room, came to re-enforce them. From them there was no appeal. It was not the only instance of the kind by a good many. Neither the landlord's protests nor the tenant's plea 'went' in the face of the camera's evidence, and I was satisfied.
>
> (Riis 1918: 273)

'Mere words' were to give way, in Riis' opinion, to the irrefutable veracity of the camera, and he saw his contribution as being that of bringing evidence to bear on what might otherwise be problematic. But he would not have seen his own personal vision as being of importance: the facts would speak for themselves and the people of the slums had been converted, through the documentary gaze, into 'facts'.

Complex and difficult lives are simplified into iconic statements of social deprivation. Riis captured his photographs as if he were shooting game; he inscribed 'objectivity' into his images by refusing to allow his subjects to negotiate in any way the manner in which they might be recorded. Sally Stein has commented perceptively on this:

> We can indeed marvel at the consistency of Riis's photography in which so few of the exposures presented a subject sufficiently composed to return the glance of the photographer. That he rejected those rare photographs in which the subject did happen to look back suggests how premeditated the effect was. . . . The averted gaze, the appearance of unconsciousness or stupefaction, were only a few of the recurring features which gave Riis's pictorial documents stylistic unity and ideological coherence in relation to the text.
>
> (Stein 1983: 14)

A history of documentary could be structured around an account of the association between photographer and subject, and of the power relationships that are mediated between them. In the ostensible interest of revealing (and subsequently ameliorating) harsh conditions of life, photographers often rendered those they recorded into passive sufferers of poverty, rather than active agents in their own lives.

Social travels and disguises

In Britain, too, the new journalism encouraged forays into the underworld, connecting the poor with crime, delinquency and hopelessness. Reporters went in search of the nether region of the city; a place that was, of course, constituted as both a physical and a psychic space. Sometimes they went in disguise, pretending to be identical to the subjects of their studies, as James Greenwood did in 1866 to report on homeless men for his 'night in the workhouse' which was serialised in the *Pall Mall Gazette*.

The overt purpose of such masquerades was to pass unnoticed by those they were examining, so that they might share a common experience and avoid being treated as outsiders. Inevitably, though, these disguises inspired in readers a sense of vicarious danger or disgust. Social reformers, philanthropists and statisticians had reported on the state of the poor on innumerable occasions, but their work did not have the immediacy of the new journalism.

The taste for first hand accounts, and a journalism based around interviews with participants in events, was developed in the United States and took a rather different character in the more formal press of Victorian England. Nevertheless, it created a narrative form which was structured around descriptions of scenes and people: accounts which were relatively free of moralising and which depended for their authenticity on the testimony of an individual journalist. In other words, it created a literary form to which the camera was an ideal adjunct, and many reports were carried in the new periodicals of the day.

The new journalism of the 1890s coexisted with a group of writers who, drawing on the wider movement of naturalism, produced novels which took the lives of the poor as their subject-matter. Out of the popular novels and journalism of the time came accounts of low life, full of ostensibly authentic detail which was reinforced by the use of argot and slang. Other investigators concentrated on describing the conditions of work and housing and presented a picture of people enduring lives of great hardship with patience and docility.

Constituted as 'the Other', workers, poor, lumpen proletariat, criminals, all were often ill-distinguished in the middle-class mind, despite the efforts of people such as the social observer and writer, Henry Mayhew, to provide detailed typologies of the 'labouring poor'. Mayhew's approach to his investigations – a mixture of interview, statistics and descriptive writing – was to be one of the dominant modes through which working people were surveyed. Nor is it any accident that his monumental study of London life was illustrated with engravings that were based on photographs (Mayhew 1861).

Photographing workers

In the last decades of the nineteenth century a number of significant British photographers recorded the life of the poor in great cities: John Thomson and Paul Martin in London, and Thomas Annan in Glasgow are three examples. Working several decades before Jacob Riis, they were influenced by the studies of the poor being carried out in literature and by philanthropists and social investigators. John Thomson directly cites the work of James Greenwood, the journalist, and Mayhew's monumental study, *London Labour and the London Poor*. Thomson is anxious to demonstrate that photography was a guarantor of authenticity and that his studies transcended the casual illustration of idiosyncratic types. He asserts that he is:

> bringing to bear the precision of photography in the illustration of our subject. The unquestionable accuracy of this testimony will enable us to present true types of the London Poor and shield us from the accusation of either underrating or exaggerating individual peculiarities of appearance.
>
> (Thomson 1877: n.p.)

Thomson may also have been attempting to distinguish his work from the staged productions of other photographers. In the 1860s and 1870s the poor were so potent a subject that notable photographers, such as Oscar Gustav Rejlander, created artistic studies of ragged street children. These were much admired and, indeed, were used by Dr Barnardo to justify his own practices.

This preoccupation with the poor was not matched by a similar concern with capturing images of the world of work. Photography came into existence at a dynamic period in the development of capitalism, a time of technical innovation and of major engineering feats. Little of this energy is represented in the photographic archives; nor is the sheer drudgery of work and the army of labourers who carried it out made visible. Where there are shots of workers they tend to be inadvertently caught in a corner of the frame, or deliberately placed so as to give a sense of scale to some major building or engineering scheme. Rob Powell has commented:

> Very few photographs of workers in the time of Brunel exist, and indeed the catalogue of the British worker in 19th century photography – insofar as it can be gathered at all – is a history of exceptions. If real justice were to be done to this yawning absence, images of workers would be represented in the photographic history books by a long series of blank pages.
>
> (Powell 1985: 32)

There are many reasons for the absence of portraits of workers, not least that photographers tended not to live in the sites where industrial work was carried out. Moreover, notions of what made a good subject for a photograph were determined by convention, and also by such factors as the subjects

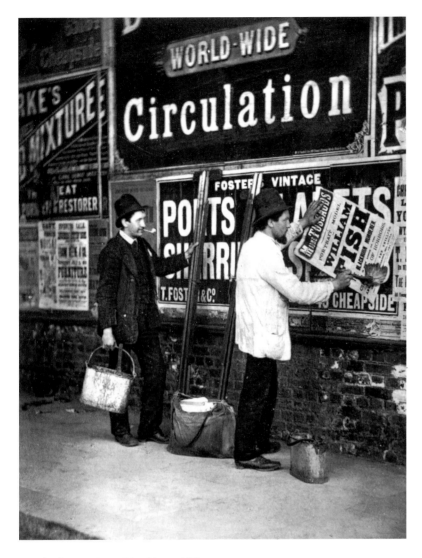

2.5 John Thomson, Street Advertising, c. 1877
Thomson was perhaps the first person to record systematically the street life, characters and traders of a great city

set by the juries of photographic competitions. In the 1890s many clubs established 'street characters' or 'city trades' as subjects for competition, but they would have been very unlikely to establish categories based on industrial labour or domestic work.

Once again one can trace some continuities of practice with older forms of representation. In the 1870s a group of British artists provided illustrations of scenes drawn from the life of the poor for the weekly magazine, *The Graphic*.

2.6 Frank Meadow Sutcliffe, A Fish Stall, c. 1882
Sutcliffe's long study of Whitby, Yorkshire, yielded hundreds of photographs that reveal the pattern of work and leisure in a Victorian fishing village

These illustrations then acted as reference material for large oil paintings which were shown in galleries. Commenting on these artists, Julian Treuherz has noted that, throughout Victoria's reign, the poor were depicted within the sphere of social problems. He also draws our attention to the importance of literary sources in determining subject-matter for paintings – for example, Thomas Hood's poem *The Song of the Shirt* led to the seamstress becoming 'the most commonly depicted subject in Victorian painting' (Treuherz 1987: 26).

Photographers were deeply influenced by these conventional subjects and ways of treating the poor, and there are some examples of sustained and careful recording of working life. For example, Frank Meadow Sutcliffe diligently documented the village of Whitby as both a fishing village and a holiday resort over a long period of time. This work drew on the picturesque qualities of much of the labour involved, but also added new qualities of directness and close observation.

But such detailed, long studies were rare, and confined to one or two trades. Other workers passed without any great notice; of the vast army of clerks and domestic workers there is scarcely a sign, and those photographs of workers that do exist are usually of male labourers engaged in heavy, manual tasks. There are few images of women carrying out any kind of work and they are absent from the ranks of manual labourers. Indeed, if it were not for the curious obsession of Arthur Munby,[1] women manual workers would have disappeared with scarcely a trace (Hudson 1972). Of course, some documentary photographers were able to undertake sustained studies of labour, as did Lewis Hine in the United States from the turn of the century. Hine was a most committed and subtle photographer of people at work and was dedicated to the cause of using his images in the service of social reform. His output spans the time from Jacob Riis to the Farm Security Administration project of the 1930s. An excellent account of the work of Lewis Hine is given in **Trachtenberg**'s *Reading American Photographs* (1989).[2]

DISCUSSION: Illustrated magazines

In the nineteenth century, magazines that told stories with the help of pictures were extremely popular. The *Illustrated London News* sold 26,000 copies of its first issue in 1842, and by 1863 had a weekly print run of 310,000. The illustrations were in the form of wood engravings which were produced with machine-like speed and precision through the use of a complex division of technical and artistic labour. The magazine claimed for itself a civilising mission rather than a concern for profit, but not all its competitors took such a high tone. *The Pictorial Times*, for example, was considerably less staid, but its general standards of drawing and production were low. Of more interest was *The Graphic*, which was founded in 1869 with the intention of using professional artists as illustrators of its copy, and it aimed for greater frankness and a more realist approach than its competitors.

Nor was this a particularly British movement, for these magazines had their counterparts in Germany, France and the United States. These illustrated magazines were to be radically changed by the coming of photography, but the photographic revolution was not immediately matched with a transformation in the means of reproduction. Not until 1880 was the half-tone process used to reproduce a photograph directly in the *Daily Graphic*, and it took decades for the process to be refined and widely accepted. Photography in this period celebrated its ability to scour the world for images, but it was powerless to put these images into general circulation. However, so potent was the idea that photography was an objectively true medium that publishers made it clear that particular illustrations (albeit copied and possibly edited by an artist) were based on photographs.

1 Arthur Joseph Munby (1828–1910)
Munby was a barrister and minor poet who is now best known for his diaries and notebooks which tell us something about the fashionable and artistic life of the time, and also reveal his obsession with working women. In a number of tours, he sought out women working in coalmining, fishing and farming and commissioned local photographers to make portraits of them. A collection of these photographs at Trinity College, Cambridge, provides an invaluable historical resource for anyone exploring the way in which labour has been depicted. Munby did not confine his passion to organising these pictures; he also secretly married his maidservant, Hannah Cullwick, and they lived together for many years. The standard work on Munby is Derek Hudson's *Munby: Man of Two Worlds*, London: John Murray, 1972.

ALAN TRACHTENBERG (1989) **Reading American Photographs**, New York: Hill and Wang

2 For an account of the connections between photography and other kinds of social investigation in the nineteenth and twentieth centuries see Derrick Price, 'Photographing the Poor and the Working Class', **Framework** 22(22), Autumn 1983.

The development of documentary photography in the 1930s also owed much to the fact that there were many outlets through which such work could be shown. These magazines, which were based on the extensive use of photographs to tell stories, constitute the start of the modern movement of photojournalism. They include *Look* and *Life* in the USA, *Vu* in France, and *Illustrated* and *Picture Post* in Britain. There was also a host of new or revitalised publications in Germany where the movement began and most of the rhetorical devices of presentation were established; devices which emphasised the role of picture editors and designers in creating powerful stories through the juxtaposition of image and text. Many of the German *Illustrirte* disappeared after Hitler came to power in 1933 and the editors and photographers who had worked for them went into exile, taking their skills with them to their adopted countries. Stefan Lorant moved to Britain where he persuaded Edward Hulton to found a new magazine, *Picture Post*, which was to become (under the editorship of Tom Hopkinson, who succeeded Lorant) the most important publication of its kind in Britain. *Picture Post* attempted to make visible the whole of society: to show the toffs at Ascot, the clerks in their pin-stripe suits and bowler hats streaming across London Bridge, the housewife out shopping, the unemployed man lounging on the street corner. Its first few issues of 1938 carried stories on 10 Downing Street ('The House from Which the Empire is Governed'), actors in rehearsal, painters in their studios, soldiers in training, surgeons in an operating theatre and life on a lighthouse – together with people in the street, in pubs and on buses, débutantes at a London club, down-and-outs at the Salvation Army, portraits of the men who built the *Queen Elizabeth*, a history of the corset and images of an old favourite – London by night.

Picture Post drew together the disparate strands of documentary and gave them a coherence and purpose which they had not formerly possessed. It developed the photo-essay – an organised and integrated series of photographs which was as important as the written text – into a dynamic way of telling stories, so that the latent narrative power of documentary photographs was released through creative techniques of editing and layout.

Soon after *Picture Post* began, Britain was at war, and the confrontational politics of the 1930s gave way to a sense of common purpose and an attempt to forge national unity. The magazine both reflected and helped to create this project and for the duration of the war it helped to articulate a sense of communality within the British people (Hall 1972).

The magazine was determinedly populist and provided readers with a conspectus of the everyday, inviting them to treat routine and commonplace aspects of life as worthy of attention. This celebration of ordinary life was intermingled with news stories set in other countries and an attempt to show the extraordinary diversity of human existence. *Picture Post* also used the camera as a kind of character in its own right and recognised that we would be interested in how images were made. It showed us how 'candid camera' shots of the Café Royal were achieved using a camera concealed in a briefcase, explained how a model is made up so as to look beautiful, and gave us a shot of a photographer robing for the operating theatre session. This stress on the capturing of images rendered the camera less awe-inspiring than it might otherwise have been and, together with the conventions of page layouts and picture formats, called up a particular kind of rather quiet, simple photograph – one which sometimes cleverly resembled a snapshot and did not aim to connote complex messages.

In 1936 a new kind of illustrated magazine began in the USA. *Life* spread large format pictures over several pages, condoned flash, but would not at first allow the use of the newly developed 35mm cameras. *Life* was important for its size, technical slickness and for the fact that it routinised the production of photo-essays in a sophisticated way. The magazine was distant from the prevailing political ferment of the day and saw its mission in a soft-centred concern to capture images from around the world. Henry Luce had introduced *Fortune* in 1930, but *Life* was quickly to outstrip it in sales and income. Financially successful and technically resourceful, it was the most influential magazine of its day and, together with *Look*, dominated the market well into the 1950s.

During the next decade, though, the world of the illustrated magazine slowly crumbled. *Picture Post* ceased publication in 1958, *Look* and *Life* in 1972. Many people have offered explanations for the decline of these periodicals, citing, for example, the influence of television on sales and advertising revenue. The latter was also under threat from the free colour supplements that were introduced by newspapers. These were crowded with photographs, but were primarily designed to increase advertising revenue. Although interesting documentary photographs continued to be made, they were no longer part of a coherent movement of photojournalism.

THE CONSTRUCTION OF DOCUMENTARY

During the 1930s the paradigmatic form of documentary was produced: one which cast its subjects within a 'social problem' framework, and which argued for a politics of reform, and social education. Treating photographs produced much earlier as 'documentary' was not a simple act of labelling, but meant that we were invited to reconsider this work within the framework of the 1930s documentary project.

Photography in the 1930s was influenced by a number of factors. Technically the development of new, lightweight 35 mm cameras made new camera angles possible. There was a growth in the number of illustrated magazines and, within these, an increasingly sophisticated approach to the role of photo editors and the construction of photo-essays. Not least, there was a new and vast public with a hunger to see images drawn from real life. The documentary movement was, of course, largely discussed in relation to the cinema, and there is no doubt that John Grierson was an important figure in determining the nature of its aesthetic and political project. Grierson wanted to see a society of people who had received an appropriate education for citizenship; they would not aspire to be intellectuals, but would be trained so that they could make rational decisions about the society in which they lived, on the basis of the available information. Documentary was a tool of education which would militate against the foolish distractions offered by Hollywood and anchor people in a rational world of work and social obligation. It would offer, in an exciting form, facts about the social order which everyone would need in order to play a part in modern society. But how would documentary function in order to achieve these objectives? In an influential book on documentary, **William Stott** (1973) writes:

WILLIAM STOTT (1973)
**Documentary Expression
and Thirties America**,
London: Oxford University Press

> This is how documentary works. . . . It defies comment; it imposes its meaning. It confronts us, the audience, with empirical evidence of such nature as to render dispute impossible and interpretation superfluous. All emphasis is on the evidence; the facts themselves speak . . . since just the fact matters, it can be transmitted in any plausible medium. . . . The heart of documentary is not form or style or medium, but always content.
>
> (Stott 1973: 14)

The putative power of the camera to be an unmediated form of communication is here applied to a genre which is now held to be able to transcend the discursive structures of any particular form: imposing rather than creating meaning; disempowering the reader or spectator from any acts of interpretation *vis-à-vis* the text. Documentary, on this definition, becomes a kind of ideologically charged common sense which is inaccessible to critical engagement. It is a fascinating definition because it spells out, forty years after the time, what lies at the heart of 1930s notions of documentary. There was an assumption that the world was productive of facts and that those facts could be communicated to others in a transparent way, free of the complex codes through which narratives are structured. The main component of what we might think of as 'the documentary gaze' is precisely described in the notion that 'the facts . . . speak'. Workers and the poor were caught in the documentary gaze; a gaze that transformed them into facts, facts that precisely could not be challenged, but which imposed meaning at a single stroke.

Picturing ourselves

In the 1930s a plethora of conventional and novel means of investigation were employed by a variety of people. In addition to formal reports based on statistical investigation, there were varieties of journalistic reportage, travel books, diaries, films, photographs and newsreels. All involved some way of entering into the life of the people, of trying to understand the nature of particular communities and of reporting back to an audience situated geographically and socially elsewhere. Those photographers, writers, film-makers and intellectuals who undertook the journey to meet the workers did so from a variety of motives and from different political standpoints, but most found it a difficult trip. Some gazed on the workers as though they were the inhabitants of a strange land; others sought to keep a 'proper' distance from the subjects of their research. Some went with cameras, and many of those who did not went (as it were) with the metaphor of the camera – with the documentary gaze. This notion of a disinterested gaze fitted well with other attempts to look at ordinary life through objective eyes. For example, in 1937 the small magazine *Fact* published an editorial telling its readers of a new venture:

> It is nothing less than to begin a social and anthropological survey of typical parts of Britain. You have read, no doubt, plenty of statistical and economic accounts of this or that area or this and that industry. But have you ever considered the place in which you live and the trade in which you work with the impartial and distant eye of an anthropologist?
>
> (*Fact* 1937: n.p.)

There were several other organisations which set out to undertake an anthropological survey of British life in the 1930s. The best known is *Mass Observation*, founded in 1936 by Tom Harrison and Charles Madge. Harrison was an anthropologist newly returned from Borneo, and Madge a poet. What these projects have in common with the documentary movement is the sense that the world could no longer be taken for granted and understood; that ordinary day-to-day lives needed to be made strange by being examined with the supposedly 'impartial' eye of the social scientist.

Mass Observation recruited many respondents who, through the use of diaries and formal reports, would scrutinise and record their own day-to-day actions and behaviour, together with that of other people. The organisation was particularly interested in examining what happened on buses, in pubs, at the seaside and other areas where collective behaviour in public places could be observed. And their respondents were expected to distance themselves from ordinary life in order to observe and record those things that might otherwise escape notice as being uninterestingly ordinary. The diaries and notes were sent to a central point where they were analysed and edited in order to provide material for the production of books describing how people behaved in everyday life. Clearly, in all this there was an assumption that 'we' had no adequate sense of our social selves; that we needed to survey the very taken-for-granted parts of our lives that consti-tuted ordinary existence. The apparent fragmentation of the society, the political instability, the vast desire for change, the desolation of many working-class communities – all this might be resolved if only we could get a clear idea of who 'we' were.

Mass Observation used respondents, editors, painters and photographers in its attempt to build up an accurate picture of everyday life. Photographers adopted a range of techniques in order to capture their subjects; while some sought cooperation, most were concerned not to be observed and to work without the knowledge of the photographed.

One characteristic response of photographers to the political and moral debates of the time was to see themselves as part of the camera, merely recording what was in front of them. Bert Hardy, who worked his way up from being a delivery boy to becoming a major photographer on *Picture Post*, described his practice in *Camerawork*: 'I didn't think of it politically. I was never a political animal. I mean the journalists had that sort of job to do. I think I just photographed what I saw. I never angled anything' (Hardy 1977: 9).

However, Humphrey Spender (in a later issue of the same journal) comments on the work he did in Bolton for *Mass Observation* and makes clear his desire to work voyeuristically:

> My main anxiety, purpose, was to become invisible and to make my equipment invisible, which is one of the reasons I carried around an absolute minimum of equipment. . . . Summing up the relics of feelings toward *Mass Observation* I think I can remember the main enemy being boredom and tedium and embarrassment.
>
> (Spender 1978: 7)

Working for a number of magazines and newspapers as well as for *Mass Observation*, Humphrey Spender brought back many of the pictures of working-class life which were later thought to be exemplary images of the time. In one account of this work he described his procedure as allowing 'things to speak for themselves and not to impose any kind of theory'. The difficulty of his journey was that:

> I had to be an invisible spy – an impossibility which I didn't particularly enjoy trying to achieve . . . I was somebody from another planet intruding on another way of life. . . . A constant feature of taking the kind of photograph we're talking about – even when people were unaware that they were actually being photographed – was a feeling that I was exploiting the people I was photographing, even when . . . the aim explicitly was to help them.
>
> (Spender 1978: 16)

Spender's description of himself as an alien and a spy is a dramatic way of emphasising social distance, and in his account of his own feelings he points up the fact that 'our way of life' might also be seen as distinct and separate 'ways of life'. The notion of the workers as productive of useful facts gives way to a consideration of the subjects of representation as potentially

2.7 Humphrey Spender, *Men Greeting in a Pub*, Worktown Series, 1937
This carefully composed, gentle and humorous photograph reveals the influence of both realist photography and Surrealism on Spender's work

exploited by the encounter. Spender worked for *Mass Observation*, but his photographs also appeared in the *Daily Mirror* and in *Picture Post*, and by the 1930s the market for actuality photographs had grown to very large proportions. While the styles and approaches of photographers differed one from another, it is also possible to see continuities and influences from the past as well as gender differences in the way in which documentary photographers carried out their work. Val Williams has argued that women photographers did not adopt

> candid photography as exemplified in the discreet, detached
> observation of photographers like Frank Meadow Sutcliffe and Paul
> Martin. Both Sutcliffe and Martin had pictured the world as full
> of vitality, as a kaleidoscopic spectacle of trades and crafts and
> distinguishing costume. . . . The style which they evolved affected
> the production of British documentary photography enormously, and
> reverberated through to *Picture Post* and beyond. For many of those

who later took up photojournalism – a hybrid of press, candid and documentary photography – the stance became obligatory, particularly for war photographers working from the late thirties onwards. It indicated not only a kind of political detachment, allowing photographers to see themselves as reporters rather than participants, but also a particular machismo.

(Williams 1986: 25)

Williams describes women photographers as using the medium for 'diverse and often very personal reasons' while 'women documentarists usually set out to record rather than to captivate and the avoidance of the dramatic and the candid was a primary influence upon each of them' (Williams 1986: 26).

Together with these gender differences of approach we might also consider uses of the medium which were influenced by considerations of social class. We have seen that the documentary movement was part of a reformist political project and we should remember that, politically, the documentary movement was concerned with the promulgation of liberal social values rather than with the revolutionary politics to which so many people in the 1930s subscribed. Closely associated with this is the charge that the political project implicit in much documentary work was unlikely to succeed given that documentary can, at best, show suffering, degradation, despair, but can do nothing to illuminate the causes of these woes. Power and causality are difficult to express through the camera eye, as are collective struggle and resistance. Martha Rosler has critiqued this political stance in the following terms:

> In contrast to the pure sensationalism of much of the journalistic attention to working-class, immigrant and slum life, the meliorism of Riis, Lewis Hine, and others involved in social work propagandizing argued through the presentation of images combined with other forms of discourse, for the rectification of wrongs. It did not perceive those wrongs as fundamental to the social system that tolerated them – the assumption that they were tolerated rather than *bred* marks a basic fallacy of social work.

(Rosler 1989: 304)

The Farm Security Administration (FSA)

The function of documentary in the service of radical politics was affected not only by the beliefs of individual photographers, but also by the uses for which pictures were commissioned; the professional practices through which they were produced, and the source of the finance that made them possible. In this respect the Farm Security Administration project is of considerable interest.

This was a government agency established in 1935 as part of the Roosevelt administration's attempt to rebuild the economy of the United States. A young social scientist, Roy Stryker, was appointed to head the photography section of the FSA. His main responsibility was to provide contemporary images to illustrate and support the written accounts of conditions in agriculture that were published in official reports.

This enterprise became the most important example of a major state-funded documentary project in the world and many of its participants have entered into the pantheon of 'great photographers': Walker Evans, Dorothea Lange, Russell Lee, Arthur Rothstein, Ben Shahn, Marion Post Walcott. We saw in chapter 1 how Dorothea Lange's *Migrant Mother* became an iconic work but many other photographs from the project have been reproduced extensively on book jackets, as illustrations, on gallery walls, even in advertisements. They are often described in histories of photography as having revealed the human face of Depression Day America.

Their initial task, however, was to show America at work and to provide images of workers rather than the displaced poor. Once on the road, though, the photographers were free from the constraints of Washington and often returned very different kinds of photographs to those which were expected. On some accounts their genius as visual artists allowed them to go beyond the mundane business of recording labour and to penetrate to the secret heart of things. In fact, among the many thousands of negatives of the project there are very many which concern themselves with human toil.

But the huge archive has been used as a resource from which some photographs have been selected more often than others, so that our social and political sense of the project is constructed from the editing that has taken place over the years. In some ways this body of work does present us with an apparently coherent critique of American life. The most famous photographs are those of the sharecroppers of the south-west and their migration west out of the 'dustbowl' to the orange groves and fruit farms of California in search of work as itinerant labourers. This is a familiar story and was the subject of one of the most celebrated 'social' novels and movies of the time, John Steinbeck's *The Grapes of Wrath*.

Through the interest shown in them by photographers, writers and painters, these people were to become emblematic of the US Depression. What we remember about them is that the winds eroded their fields, destroying their livelihood, and that they were forced, though desperately poor, to travel long distances to try to find work in the low-wage fruit and cotton fields. The FSA photographs are almost always of individuals and families, and often show them as weary and defenceless. They evoke images of strain, of mental fatigue, but they also tease out the bonds of affection and connection between people, especially between mothers and children. And, of course, they show people on the road, moving out; their possessions packed away, their furniture roped to the tops of cars or heaped on to a rickety truck. In these images the solid elements of domestic life are often dissolved and relocated in strange, outdoor spaces. Objects do service as

2.8 Arthur Rothstein, *Dust Storm*, 1936
One of the original FSA photographers, Rothstein contributed many striking images to the archive

carriers of emotion; objects that are stranded, dislocated, treasured though cheap. For instance, Russell Lee shows us a harmonium upright, ready to be played, out in a field, all by itself, surrounded by mud. Walker Evans records a roughly piled grave of loose earth topped with the impermanent and unstable memorial of a dinner plate. Nothing appears to be anchored or solid, instead dust is everywhere; a friable earth is heaped against the walls of houses, has shawled over the gas pumps and the Coca-Cola signs, and is etched into the lines of faces and hands.

These documentary photographs, like all others, are densely constructed works which use certain techniques and forms to produce a desired response in the spectator. They do contain 'facts' in a simple sense: a woman wears a dress made from a flour sack, a family lives under a hastily constructed tent of twigs and tarpaulin. There is, in other words, plenty of evidence of poverty indicated by the traditional markers of lack of material prosperity. But, in their more complex versions, they are photographs of the (literally) dispossessed, carefully constructed to produce a meaning that transcends what is shown.

These people were not chosen merely for their 'representative' qualities: they are not simple icons of dispossession. Although they are anonymous subjects of the camera, their singularity is often stressed and their individual gestures carefully recorded. This is emphasised by the closeness of the camera and the informal stances people are allowed to take up in front of it. We feel that we are not in the presence of representatives of a class, but of ordinary people, much like us, who have fallen on hard times and are doing the best they can in the circumstances. Poverty and misery thus cease to be possessions of particular social groups living at a particular time in determinate conditions, and become a kind of dislocation or breakdown into which any one of us might stumble. In other words, we are asked to accept that we can make immediate connections between this body of work and our own life and condition; but also that these are photographs which sum up the specific experience of the migrant workers in the USA. We are invited to accept that these are 'honest' images drawn from life, but are also the product of extraordinarily gifted photographers. Some of the central contradictions of the social project of documentary photography are revealed here, for these photographs are treated as historical, but timeless; densely coded, but transparent; highly specific, but universal. And these various readings militated against the idea that the photographs should have been immediately accessible as evidence against the social and political system.

Of course, many people in the 1930s did see poverty and dispossession as consequences of the prevailing social system and this belief gave rise to a vibrant left oppositional practice of radical theatre, film and photography. Workers' film and photo leagues were established in both Britain and the USA and opened up the medium of photography so that workers could make their own records of their lives and struggles. This was an important principle, but there is little evidence that the results challenged the nature of documentary reportage or established new kinds of image-making. Perhaps more interesting were groups who saw questions of representation as a central part of political struggle and developed an alternative photographic practice. Their intention was not to reveal how things looked in the 'real world', but to disrupt the surface appearance of the image in order to construct new meanings out of the old pictorial elements. This practice was elaborated by the painter, sculptor and photographer, Alexander Rodchenko in the USSR and by German Dadaists at the end of the First World War. Working against the central tenets of documentary, these artists argued that, in order to arrive at the meaning that lies below the surface of a photograph, it was necessary to contrive and manipulate the image. John Heartfield's incisive, politically charged photomontages, which developed from his work with the Berlin Dadaists, are the best-known constructions of this kind.

Documentary meaning and form

We have so naturalised the idea of documentary as residing within particular texts, forms and traditions (as being *immanent* to texts), that those marginal forms – drama documentary, **staged** reconstructions and the like – are fiercely fought over. It is, perhaps, more useful to pursue questions of the *production* of documentary: the characteristic forms that were used to make 'documents' of this kind. Stott's notion that documentary 'imposes meaning' at a single stroke, before which the spectator is speechless and disarmed, fractures into the examination of particular forms within their institutional and historical settings; clusters of social, cultural, political and technological changes which together create the 'meaning' of documentary. But it is a meaning that is constantly changing, for, while the documentary gaze was anchored in facts and validated particular kinds of enquiry, the practice of documentary was and is problematic. In photography, a series of conventions and practices evolved to mark 'documentary' from other kinds of work. These included, for example, printing the whole of the image with a black border around it to demonstrate that everything the camera recorded was shown to the viewer. At another time, scenes lit by flash were deemed illegitimate, as only the natural light that fell on the scene should be used. A kind of rudimentary technical ethic of documentary work emerged which 'guaranteed' the authenticity of the photograph. Much of the progress of studio-based photography, whether for commercial purposes or as **Art**, was made by suppressing the contingent within the photographic frame and designing the scene so that all aspects of the image were controlled and carefully placed. We have already observed that any attempt to arrange and structure the location by a documentary photographer would be regarded as illegitimate behaviour, yet the aesthetic demand for well-composed shots remained.

Documentary photographers, too, took considerable pains to control the nature of a scene without making any obvious change to it. Thus, the celebrated French photographer Henri Cartier-Bresson lay in wait for all the messy contingency of the world to compose itself into an image which he judged to be both productive of visual information and aesthetically pleasing. This he called 'the decisive moment', a formal flash of time when all the right elements were in place before the scene fell back into its quotidian disorder. Increasingly, documentary turned away from attempting to record what would formerly have been seen as its major subjects. Instead, it began to concentrate on exploring cultural life and popular experience, and this often led to representations that celebrated the transitory or the fragmentary. The endeavour to make great statements gave way to the recording of little, dislocated moments which merely insinuated that some greater meaning might be at stake (Cartier-Bresson 1952). Cartier-Bresson's work is sometimes regarded as documentary, but he is often seen as working outside the constraints of labels of this kind. As photographer and theorist **Allan Sekula** has pointed out, 'Documentary is thought to be art when it transcends its

staged photography refers to the creating of a scene for the camera (as in staging within theatre).

ALLAN SEKULA (1978) 'Dismantling Modernism, Reinventing Documentary (Notes on the Politics of Representation)' in J. Liebling (ed.) **Photography: Current Perspectives**, Rochester, New York: Light Impressions Co reference to the world, when the work can be regarded, first and foremost, as an act of self-expression on the part of the artist' (Sekula 1978: 236).

The problem then becomes how we define 'reference to the world' and how documentary photographers can demonstrate their fidelity to the social world. To have to engage with particular conventions, technical processes and rhetorical forms in order to authenticate documentary undermines the notion of the objective camera and with it, one might imagine, any claim of documentary to be any more truthful to appearances than other forms of representation. But both the test of truth and the nature of documentary photography was changing rapidly in the decades after 1950. The social-democratic political project that underpinned 1930s documentary had lost its radical edge by the 1950s and had, indeed, in Britain, become the ground on which a postwar political consensus was built.

DOCUMENTARY SINCE THE SECOND WORLD WAR

The archetypal documentary project was concerned to draw the attention of an audience to particular subjects, often with a view to changing the existing social or political situation. To achieve this goal, documentary photographs were rarely seen as single, independent images. They were usually accompanied by or incorporated into written texts. Within this context the images functioned both to provide information about the nature of things and to confirm the authenticity of a written account. Individual photographers were rarely credited for their work in magazines, and photographs were treated as though they were anonymous productions. The postwar consumer boom, exemplified in the introduction of television and the growth of car ownership, produced a very different society to that of the 1930s. In commenting on this new social scene some photographers in the United States produced work that was to transform the nature of documentary photography.

In his collection *The Americans*, Robert Frank presented his own version of American life in which he eschewed the usual subjects of documentary investigation and presented us instead with cool and ironic images of the fleeting moments of ordinary life. Significantly enough, the introduction to the book was written by the Beat writer, Jack Kerouac, who said: 'After seeing these pictures you end up finally not knowing any more whether a juke box is sadder than a coffin' (Frank 1959: 5).

Born in Switzerland, Robert Frank brought an outsider's eye to bear on the USA of the 1950s. He went on the road with a camera, an old car and a Guggenheim scholarship and photographed not only juke-boxes and coffins, but cowboys, long empty roads, tract houses on lonely fields, flags and bikers, drive-in movies and barbers' chairs. Frank caught America at the point where commonplace life was about to be turned into myth; where even the banal and the prosaic was soon to be commodified into spectacle.

2.9 Helen Levitt, *New York*, 1942
Levitt photographed New York as a place of community and neighbourhood as in this wartime shot of children playing cheerfully in a setting of urban squalor

People in these photographs were not constituted as 'poor' or 'workers' or, indeed, as any kind of active agents. They existed as spectators, gazing out at some invisible scene: other people, the road ahead, a movie screen, a parade going by. In these closed, watchful faces we could read no significant facts, and if we had a sense of 'being there', it was as a witness to nothing of any great importance. Frank refused a documentary project which saw life as productive of weighty events that the photographer might chronicle and analyse. He seems to be saying that none of the many scenes that happen in the world are invested with any special meaning, although some may be made distinctive by the act of being photographed. Coffins are no sadder than juke-boxes because an old hierarchy of importance has been abolished; hereafter the subject-matter of documentary is both dispersed and expanded to include whatever engages or fascinates the photographer. Facts now matter less than appearances. The old documentary project gives way to a heterogeneous practice which explores the world in terms of particular subjectivities, identities and pleasures.

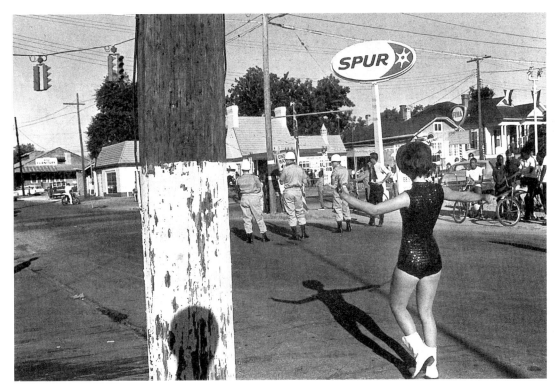

2.10 Lee Friedlander, *1 Lafayette, Louisiana*, 1970
In the 1970s, Friedlander was one of the major 'new' documentarists. His images are intricate, ambiguous, sometimes difficult to read, and tell us something about the complexity of modern life

Frank was not alone in offering new, less monumental images of America in the 1950s. Around the same time William Klein was photographing New York in a manner that stressed the disorder and randomness of life in great cities. Halla Beloff comments on them in the following terms:

> It is the truth value of American street photographs . . . that gives them their special artistic and psychological interest. Their style and their subject matter in a state of consonance, they randomly sample their subject matter. They show fragments, *randomly* set out, *arbitrarily* cut off, with *bizarre* juxtapositions, and these epithets invite us to move from the photographs to the culture and people in them.
>
> (Beloff 1985: 99)

In Klein's crowded streets the point of photographic interest may lie in a half-concealed detail somewhere in the background of a shot. His city is restless, crowded, neurotic and alienating, and was to become one dominant version of how cities were perceived and represented by later commentators.

A different version of life in a big city was offered by some British photographers. For example, Roger Mayne's photographs of street life in West London provided a portrait of the lives of people in a particular place that was relaxed, incisive, intimate and very different from earlier British documentary work (Mayne 1986).

Documentary was changing and apparently presenting new subject-matter or old themes treated in new ways. Often called 'subjective' documentary, this work was very influential in both the USA and Britain. It liberated documentary from the political project with which it had formerly been associated, and allowed photographers to move away from both the traditional subjects of documentary and the conventions of documentary representation. Now, Lee Friedlander could make a series of photographs full of visual ambiguity and allow his own silhouette to fall across his subjects to celebrate his shadowy presence on the scene. Gradually, there was an extension of the subjects which were deemed suitable for documentary. For example, Tony Ray-Jones' *A Day Off: An English Journal* (1974) attempted to cover a spectrum of social class in looking at the English at play, from Glyndebourne and Eton to Butlins and Brighton's Palace Pier. In the 1930s, perhaps the most famous photographer of British life, Bill Brandt, had compared photographs of rich and poor; for example, putting maids and mistresses into a double-page spread so that we could observe difference and privilege. By the 1960s, however, photographers were concerned to offer more personal versions of the nature of social existence.

Theory and the critique of documentary

Perhaps the single most important influence on British documentary after 1970 came from the new ways in which photography was theorised and the functions it was considered to be able to play in cultural politics. **Semiological** analysis treated films and photographs as *texts* in order to investigate the components of sign systems through which meaning is structured and encoded within a work. The point of concern was not whether the work adequately revealed or reflected a pre-existing reality, but the way particular signifying systems imposed order and created particular sets of meaning. Inscribed within the photograph, then, was not some little likeness to reality, but a complex set of technical and cultural forms which needed to be decoded. Far from being innocent transcriptions of the real, photographs were treated as complex material objects with the ability to create, articulate and sustain meaning. Using theoretical tools which often derived from Film Studies or Literary Studies, critics began to explore the way in which photography functioned as a signifying system. One of the characteristics of photography is, as we have seen, the fact that it appears to have a special relationship to reality. We speak of *taking* photographs rather than *making* them, because the marks of their **construction** are not immediately visible; they have the appearance of having come about as a function

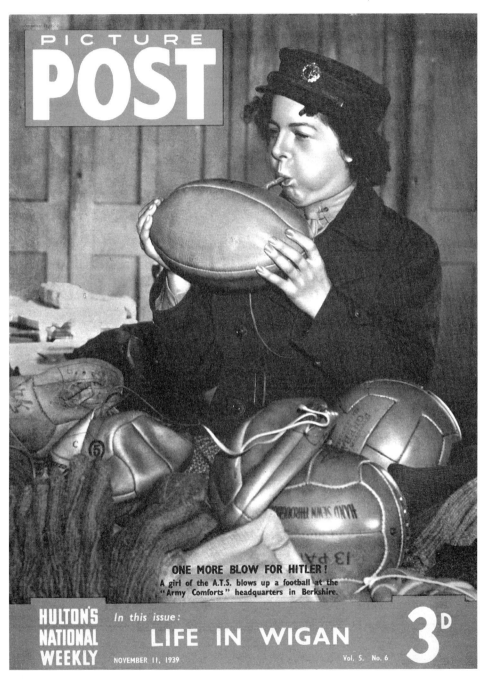

PICTURE POST

ONE MORE BLOW FOR HITLER !
A girl of the A.T.S. blows up a football at the
"Army Comforts" headquarters in Berkshire.

HULTON'S NATIONAL WEEKLY *In this issue:* **LIFE IN WIGAN** **3**D

NOVEMBER 11, 1939 Vol. 5. No. 6

2.11 *Picture Post* continued to exercise an influence after its demise in 1958. Its characteristic
layout was imitated by many later magazines. But the days of the photo-essay were numbered,
and in the 1960s/70s realist photographers broke free of the constraints of this kind of organised
narrative.

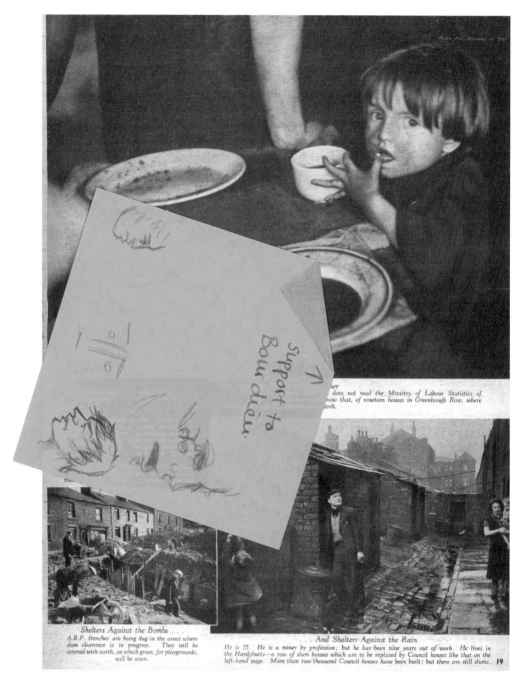

... does not read the Ministry of Labour Statistics of
... now that, of nineteen houses in Greenhough Row, where
... work.

Shelters Against the Bombs . . .

A.R.P. trenches are being dug in the areas where
slum clearance is in progress. They will be
covered with earth, on which grass, for playgrounds,
will be sown.

. . . And Shelters Against the Rain

He is 27. He is a miner by profession; but he has been nine years out of work. He lives in
the Hardybutts—a row of slum houses which are to be replaced by Council houses like that on the
left-hand page. More than two thousand Council houses have been built; but there are still slums. **19**

2.11 (Continued)

EVERYDAY LIFE IN WIGAN : *An Evening Class*
Wiganers are passionately keen on education. There are eight Evening Institutes for further education of children. Adults can find classes in an immense variety of subjects. There are also classes for unemployed.

A Talk on Tactics in the Changing Room
James Sullivan, who came to the town from Cardiff, has been Wigan's full back at the Northern Union game for 17 seasons, kicking 100 goals a season. He is now the captain and a local hero.

In the Card-room of a Big Cotton Mill
The card-room is the room into which cotton emerges in thread form. Blacking-out has meant big problems in such rooms as this, which cover a vast area and have all-glass roofs.

A.R.P. Drill at Whelley Central Elementary School
Mr. J. Dean, the head master, has organised his boys well. 210 of them march in orderly files to the shelters with their masters, in two minutes. Inside are benches made by the masters in the school workshop.

Where Wigan Lads and Lasses go for an Evening's Entertainment
Popular centre for dancing is the Empress Hall. Dancing, as a rule, goes on every evening from 7.30 to 10.30. Hall holds 500. Price is 6d. a head ; 1s. on Saturdays.

20

local comedian, Tom Moss, is the greatest attraction; prices from 6d. to 1s. 3d., 6d. to 2s. on Saturdays. There is a greyhound racing track; 6d. admission, 6d. the enclosure. And, above all there are the Rugby League matches, at the Wigan Ground, Central Park, admission 1s. to 3s. 6d. This game has drawn over 40,000 people at Wigan. The greatest personality is Jimmie Sullivan, the Wigan full-back, who has played for the team for 18 years and kicked a hundred goals every season. Rugby League, which is faster than the Rugby Union game, is played thirteen-a-side and there are many differences in the rules. In this country, it is played almost entirely in Lancashire and Yorkshire. Wigan has been one of the most enterprising clubs in the Rugby League. It has not only brought many players from South Africa, Australia and New Zealand, but has also brought a team manager from Australia namely Mr. Harry Sunderland.

If you haven't any money to spend in Wigan, you can go to the library and read the papers, or take out one of the valuable collection of 100,000 books. You can have a swim in the Corporation Baths for 4d. (a popular pastime; 143,487 people used the bath during last year). Or you can attend an evening class in such subjects as first aid, physical training, dress making and needlework, languages, musical appreciation, speech training and drama, debating and history.

The most important week in the year is Wakes Week, which falls at the beginning of August. The place to go, of course, is Blackpool. Miners

2.11 (Continued)

2.12 Edith Tudor Hart, *Poverty in London*, c. 1930
German-born Edith Tudor Hart photographed workers in London, Tyneside and South Wales in the 1930s. She worked with a reforming zeal and a sympathetic attention to the plight of the poor[3]

3 In the 1970s, magazines such as *Camerawork* and *Ten.8* re-appraised the documentary movement and displayed the work of photographers such as Edith Tudor Hart who had been half forgotten.

of the world itself rather than as carefully fabricated cultural objects. As spectators we are positioned as the eye of the camera and we gaze upon an apparently natural and unmediated scene. Our acts of looking were no longer considered to be disinterestedly innocent, but were analysed in order to distinguish the kinds of psychic pleasure and relations of power that are invested in the process. The concept of power at play in this analysis owes much to the work of the French philosopher, **Michel Foucault**. (See also note p. 56.)

Power is not seen by Foucault as a force held by a particular social group which enables them to coerce another, but is located within all parts of the social system. Power resides in all aspects of a knowledge system: in the construction of archives, the codification of information and the communication chains through which knowledge is disseminated. Nor is 'truth' a special kind of knowledge which allows us to escape the pervasive reach of power: truth and power are also intertwined. Each society has constructed its own 'regime of truth', elaborating frameworks, institutions and discourses which validate particular procedures and permit us to distinguish true from false statements.

Power, on this account, flows through the processes of science; through discourses, and the apparently trivial encounters of everyday life. Nor is power an abstract force which is only occasionally employed in order to enforce obedience, but, within a disciplinary society, it is inscribed on the body through the processes whereby the body is objectified as a source of knowledge. Photography's obsessive concern to record, catalogue, explore, reveal, compare and measure the human body was one way in which it could be seen to be an important form within the disciplinary process.

In his collection of essays *The Burden of Representation* (1988), **John Tagg** analyses the vast increase in the *power* of photography in the latter half of the nineteenth century and traces the 'complicity' of photography in the articulation of particular kinds of surveillance and observation. Documentary is seen as part of the process of examination described by Foucault as 'a procedure of objectification and subjection', in which ordinary lives are turned into accounts – into writing or, for that matter, into photographs. Such an analysis of the function of documentary clearly cast considerable doubts on the reformist social and political project with which it had been identified for so long. Its overt or implicit use as a means of surveillance and control was now being stressed, rather than its ability to reveal the nature of suffering or destitution in the service of social reform. Photography is seen as being complicit in the discourses which function to exert social control. 'Documentation' cannot act to reveal inequalities in social life, for there can be no document that is merely a transcription of reality. Rather, as part of a discursive system, it constructs the reality that it purports to reveal. But this is not a random creation, for it is created within the ideological positions framed by the discourses which are themselves part of the system of power. Cultural critic Julian Stallabrass has commented on Tagg's analysis in the following terms:

> Tagg presents 'documentary' – which includes documentary photography – as 'a liberal, corporatist plan to negotiate economic, political and cultural crises through a linked programme of structural reforms, relief measures, and a cultural intervention aimed at restructuring the order of discourse, appropriating dissent, and rescuing the threatened bonds of social consent'. In this retrospective view which entirely discounts the beliefs of those individuals

JOHN TAGG (1988) **The Burden of Representation: Essays on Photographies and Histories**, London: Macmillan

107

involved – including some who were committed to overthrowing capitalism – the complex and diverse currents of documentary photography serve the conspiracy by which the system survives.

(Stallabrass 1997: 136)

Many critics in the 1970s and 1980s, anxious to understand the political functions of modes of representation or to employ photography within cultural politics, attempted to recover, celebrate or recuperate earlier theoretical positions and political strategies. This signalled a return to earlier debates which questioned the power of documentary to be a form through which radical social and political change might be achieved. In his important essay written in 1931, **Walter Benjamin** (see note p. 17) quotes Bertolt Brecht:

WALTER BENJAMIN (1972) 'A Short History of Photography', **Screen** 13(1), Spring. Originally published in **Die Literarische Welt**, 18 and 25 September, and 2 October 1931

less than at any time does a simple reproduction of reality tell us anything about reality. A photograph of the Krupp works or GEC yields almost nothing about these institutions. Reality proper has slipped into the functional. The reification of human relationships, the factory, let's say, no longer reveals these relationships. Therefore something has actually to be constructed, something artificial, something set up.

(Benjamin 1972: 24)

Here Brecht is calling for a photographic practice that would be in sharp contrast to the documentary project, whose practitioners, as we have seen, were often concerned to let things 'speak for themselves' and were confident that things *could* speak for themselves. The dominance of documentary in the 1930s would have obscured any attempt to ground a radical photographic practice in artifice and construction. By the 1970s, however, there was a perception by some groups that the old documentary forms were inadequate to express, let alone help to change, the prevailing conditions of social, political and personal life.

Cultural politics and everyday life

Documentary was grounded in the recording and delineation of commonplace life, but the idea of 'ordinary, everyday life' was itself now to be problematised. Rather than being seen simply as a method of recording, photography begins to be regarded as a means through which we can express and articulate our own particularity and difference. We can move, as Don Slater has put it, from being consumers of images to becoming active producers:

the camera as an *active* mass tool of representation is a vehicle for documenting one's conditions (of living, working and sociality; for creating alternative representations of oneself and one's sex, class, age-group, race, etc; of gaining power of analysis and visual literacy)

2.13 Roshini Kempadoo, *Women of the UK Asian Women's Centre, Handsworth, Birmingham,*
1990 In this image, Roshini Kempadoo has used a documentary style that reminds us of a family photograph, in
order to portray a group who have not usually been the subject of a public photograph

over one's image; of presenting arguments and demands; of
stimulating action; of experiencing visual pleasure as a producer, not
consumer of images; of relating to, by objectifying, one's personal
and political environment.

(Slater 1983: 246)

If we can actively work on 'representations of ourselves', it seems that
documentary, with its historic weight of practice and ostensible claim to
transparency, might not be the perfect photographic form by which this could
be achieved. Documentary began to be deserted in favour of contrivance
and artifice. Work of this kind came from community groups and feminist
collectives, and was to be found in certain kinds of gallery practice. For
example, the community group Hackney Flashers used their photographic
project to politicise activities and concepts such as motherhood, housework

and child-care. They used a variety of montage techniques, together with text and slogans, to overcome the perceived limitations of documentary photography, a limitation that was outlined by Angela Kelly when making her 1979 selection of feminist photographs:

> The 'analytical' approach sees conventional documentary as problematic in the sense that the medium itself is a complex signifying process. Photographic images are presented as constructs and the viewer is forced to read the system of signs and to become aware of being actively involved in the process of the creation of meaning. This approach stands in opposition to the notion of the photograph as a transparent 'window on the world'.
>
> (Kelly 1979: 42)

Kelly makes it clear that she does not endorse the documentary project, which she considers to confirm, at least implicitly, photography's claim to be 'true to appearances'. Similarly, more than a decade later, Tessa Boffin and Jean Fraser introduced their book of lesbian photography with an explanation that, since sexuality is socially constructed, documentary realism might be an inappropriate form for its representation:

> Lesbianism exists in a complex relation to many other identities; concerns with sexuality intersect with those of race, class and the body . . . we looked for work which concentrated on constructed, staged or self-consciously manipulated imagery which might mirror the socially constructed nature of sexuality. We have not included much documentary work as the realism of documentary has often been used ideologically to reinforce notions of naturalness. We do not want this book to claim a natural status for lesbianism but rather to celebrate that there is no natural sexuality at all.
>
> (Boffin and Fraser 1991: 10)

Photography is used in projects of this kind in order to explore subjectivity, but, while working-class life has been surveyed through documentary, it seems that gender, race and sexuality have been analysed in terms of other kinds of photographic discourses and practices – those which stress a Brechtian concern with construction and fabrication in photography. Called into question was the ability of realist practices adequately to unmask the nature of the prevailing social conditions or to explore the social and political nature of our subjective lives. John Roberts has suggested that the movement away from documentary is associated with the 'downgrading of class within cultural politics' and a retreat from class politics itself. Rather than simply endorse the documentary movement, however, he argues:

> There can be no representation of class subjectivities without the photographer intervening *in* the process of the production of

meaning. Whether you are studio-based or working with conventional documentary images then, work on the representation of class cannot proceed without a recognition of those symbolic processes that shape and determine the construction of class identity.

(Roberts 1993: 13)

Of course, there were documentary photographers who were still concerned to represent the nature of work and the lives of working people in a style that owes a great deal to classic forms of documentary photography. For example, in very different ways, the work of Chris Killip, Nick Hedges and the Exit Photography Group (Nicholas Battye, Chris Steele-Perkins and Paul Trevor) during the 1970s and 1980s were all recognisably in the tradition of documentary, although they were more concerned with exploring class subjectivity than with aspiring to discover the 'facts' of working-class life.

Documentary in the age of postmodernism

All over the world people continue to make documentary photographs, which are shown in journals, books and newspapers, but the practice has become largely dislocated from its former social and political project. The pragmatics of the practice has changed so that, for example, documentary photographers no longer have access to a number of magazines from which they can gain commissions. More importantly 'documentary realism' is itself under attack and few people now see the still camera as a vital means of revealing unacceptable truths. The postwar development of a consumer culture displaced photography from its more traditional functions and sent out images in vast numbers to sell goods. In the 1980s and 1990s, postmodernists questioned the nature of 'originals' and 'copies', and regarded images as transmutable objects that are involved in endless, complex acts of circulation and exchange. Such objects have no necessary context, so that documentary photographs of the 1930s unemployed might be massively enlarged and used as part of the decor of restaurants; images of the dispossessed could be used to sell jeans, while the homeless of earlier generations might find themselves presented as picturesque urban characters on gallery walls.

In this world, documentary photographers are certainly not tied to the political project that was espoused by the movements of the 1930s; nor are the codes that seemed to authenticate documentary photographs necessarily employed. Traditionally, for example, documentary photographs were in black and white. Originally a necessary condition for the reproduction of their photographs, it became a guarantor of the integrity of an image for many photographers. The suppression of colour made it possible to control the aesthetic qualities of the picture and helped to structure its connotative meaning. Now colour is freely used by most British documentary photographers for projects from industrial landscapes or new technologies to the

2.14 Nick Hedges, *Packing Department, Lock Factory, Willenhall*, from *Born to Work*, 1982
Nick Hedges made a documentary study of factory life in Britain in the 1980s and many of the images disrupt our expectations of the image of 'the worker'

social life of teenage girls. Nor are documentary photographs now only to be seen, incorporated with text, as part of a magazine article, for photographers employ their work in a variety of media from books and television to gallery walls. In other words, they take part in the endless circulation of images that is a distinguishing feature of postmodernism.

Postmodernist movements existed at many levels, from serious philosophical reflection to particular kinds of surface style and fashions. Linking them all was a concern with the nature of images and their circulation; an elision between high and popular culture; a scepticism about the nature of 'the real' or 'the authentic' (for the 'simulacrum' was held to have taken over from the original); and a suggestion that the discourses which once bounded and structured knowledge (such as history or science) had broken down. Under these conditions, what future might there be for documentary; is it a practice that has run out of history?

In this context it is useful to look at the output of practising photographers whose work is of a kind that would formerly have been labelled 'documentary'. A good example is the 1990s exhibition and book by Martin Parr, *Small World*, which has a commentary by Simon Winchester (Parr 1995). Parr returns us to the world of travel photography, for his images were taken in several places around the world. Like any good Victorian photographer, he visits Egypt and the Far East, Switzerland and Rome. What he returned with, however, are not carefully composed shots of temples and pyramids, nor artfully posed portraits of picturesque native peoples, but images of other tourists; those who form part of the movement of mass tourism. Photographed in rich colour, the tourists struggle with maps, follow the raised umbrellas of guides, buy beads in Goa, take photographs and pose for photographs.

What connects the world in this exhibition is the multiple presence of the camera. Images are intertwined with what would once have been called the 'original' object; signs have broken loose from their former anchorages and float freely around a world that has been constituted as a site of spectacle. Can we consider work of this kind, with its multiple references to other images and its unwillingness to make authoritative statements, to be documentary? Certainly it fulfils the minimal condition of documentary: that it provide an account of events that have their own existence outside the frame of the photograph or the confines of the studio walls. We are no longer asked to accept that such images are impartial or disinterested; instead we inhabit a space between scepticism, pleasure and trust, from which we can read documentary images in more complex ways.

BIBLIOGRAPHY

KEY TEXTS

Benjamin, W. (1972) 'A Short History of Photography', *Screen* 13(1) (Originally published in 1931.)

Price, D. (1983) 'Photographing the Poor and the Working Class', *Framework* 22(22), Autumn

Rosler, M. (1989) 'In, Around and Afterthoughts (on Documentary Photography)' in R. Bolton (ed.) *The Contest of Meaning: Critical Histories of Photography*, Cambridge, MA: The MIT Press

Sekula, A. (1978) 'Dismantling Modernism, Reinventing Documentary (Notes on the Politics of Representation)' in J. Liebling (ed.) *Photography: Current Perspectives*, Rochester, New York: Light Impressions Co

Solomon-Godeau, A. (1991) 'Who is Speaking Thus?', *Photography at the Dock*, Minneapolis: University of Minnesota Press

Stott, W. (1973) *Documentary Expression and Thirties America*, London: Oxford University Press

Tagg, J. (1988) *The Burden of Representation: Essays on Photographies and Histories*, London: Macmillan

Thomas, A. (1978) *The Expanding Eye: Photography and the Nineteenth Century Mind*, London: Croom Helm

Trachtenberg, A. (1989) *Reading American Photographs*, New York: Hill and Wang

OTHER REFERENCES

Agee, J. and Evans, W. (1939) *Let Us Now Praise Famous Men*, New York: Random House

Beloff, H. (1985) *Camera Culture*, Oxford: Blackwell

Boffin, T. and Fraser, J. (1991) *Stolen Glances: Lesbians Take Photographs*, London: Pandora Press

Carlebach, M.L. (1992) *The Origins of Photojournalism in America*, Washington DC: Smithsonian Institute

Cartier-Bresson, H. (1952) *The Decisive Moment*, New York: Simon and Schuster

Frank, R. (1959) *The Americans*, New York: Grove Press

Gidal, T.N. (1973) *Modern Photojournalism*, New York: Collier Books

Griffiths, P.J. (1971) *Vietnam Inc.*, New York: Macmillan

Hall, S. (1972) 'The Social Eye of **Picture Post**', *Cultural Studies* 2, CCCS, Birmingham

Hardy, B. (1977) 'Bert Hardy', *Camerawork* 8

Hershkowitz, R. (1980) *The British Photographer Abroad: The First Thirty Years*, London: Robert Hershkowitz Ltd

Hudson, D. (1972) *Munby, Man of Two Worlds*, London: John Murray

Isherwood, C. (1939) *Goodbye to Berlin*, Harmondsworth: Penguin Books

Jameson, S. (1937) 'Writing in Revolt', *Fact* 4

Kelly, A. (1979) 'Feminism and Photography' in P. Hill, A. Kelly and J. Tagg *Three Perspectives on Photography*, London: ACGB

Lewinski, J. (1978) *The Camera at War*, London: W.H. Allen

Lloyd, J. (1985) 'Old Photographs, Vanished Peoples and Stolen Potatoes', *Art Monthly* 83, February

Mayhew, H. (1861) *London Labour and the London Poor*, reprinted 1967, London: Frank Cass

Mayne, R. (1986) *The Street Photographs of Roger Mayne*, London: V&A Museum

Ohrn, K.B. (1980) *Dorothea Lange and the Documentary Tradition*, Baton Rouge: Louisiana State University Press

Parr, M. (1995) *Small World: A Global Photographic Project, 1987–1994*, Stockport: Dewi Lewis Publishing

Powell, R. (1985) *Photography and the Making of History: Brunel's Kingdom*, Bristol: Watershed Media Centre

Quartermaine, P. (1992) 'Johannes Lindt: Photographer of Australia and New Guinea' in M. Gidley (ed.) *Representing Others: White Views of Indigenous Peoples*, Exeter: University of Exeter Press

Ray-Jones, T. (1974) *A Day Off: An English Journal*, London: Thames and Hudson

Riis, J.A. (1918) *The Making of an American*, New York: Macmillan

Roberts, J. (1993) *Renegotiations: Class, Modernity and Photography*, Norwich: Norwich Gallery, Norfolk Institute of Art and Design

Ryan, James R. (1997) *Picturing Empire: Photography and the Visualisation of the British Empire*, London: Reaction Books

Slater, D. (1983) 'Marketing Mass Photography' in H. Davis and P. Walton (eds) *Language, Image, Media*, Oxford: Blackwell

Spender, H. (1978) 'Humphrey Spender: M. O. Photographer', *Camerawork* 11

Stallabrass, J. (1997) 'Sebastiano Salgado and Fine Art Photojournalism', *New Left Review* 223

Stein, S. (1983) 'Making Connections with the Camera: Photography and Social Mobility in the Career of Jacob Riis', *Afterimage* 10(10)

Thomson, J. (1877) *Street Life in London*, n.p.n.

Trachtenberg, A. (1982) *The Incorporation of America*, New York: Hill and Wang

Treuherz, J. (1987) *Hard Times: Social Realism in Victorian Art*, London: Lund Humphries

Urry, J. (1990) *The Tourist Gaze: Leisure and Travel in Contemporary Societies*, London: Sage

Williams, V. (1986) *Women Photographers: The Other Observers*, London: Virago (Revised edition 1991, *The Other Observers: Women Photographers from 1900 to the Present*.)

CHAPTER 3

'Sweet it is to scan . . .'

Personal photographs and popular photography

PATRICIA HOLLAND

3.1 Studio photograph of Lily Peapell in peasant dress on roller skates, *c.* 1912

'When amid life's surging battle
Reverie its solace lends
Sweet it is to scan the faces –
Picture faces – of old friends

. . .

Some have passed the mystic
   portals
Where the usher Death presides
Some to distant climes have
   wandered
Borne on Time's relentless
   tides;
Some, perchance, to paths
   unholy;
Some to deeds without a name
But the faces in the album
Are for aye and aye the same.

. . .

Picture faces! Oh what volumes
Of unwritten life ye hold:
Youthful faces! pure, sweet
   faces!
Dearly prized as we grow old'

M.C. DUNCAN
Frontispiece to Richard Penlake
*Home Portraits for Amateur
Photographers* (1899)

'Sweet it is to scan . . .'

Personal photographs and popular photography

INTRODUCTION

The doggerel, couched in the language of late Victorian sentiment, with its yearning for purity and sense of the closeness of death, fronted a book of advice for 'amateur photographers' just at the time when home photography was undergoing a dramatic transformation. The crafted work of the 'amateur' or hobbyist, whose proliferating equipment involved tripods, black cloths, glass plate negatives, special backdrops, darkrooms and a cocktail of chemicals, was giving way to an instant push-button affair, in which the film could be sent off for processing and no special skills were required. By 1899 George Eastman had already marketed his revolutionary hand-held Kodak with the slogan 'You press the button, we do the rest' and was about to launch the 'Box Brownie' – the camera he claimed that everyone could afford and was easy enough for children to use.

But the history of personal photography is more than a simple story of technological development. The desire to scan the picture faces of old friends has been expressed in a multitude of different ways over the last century and a half. Social and cultural changes are intertwined with the history of photographic techniques and practices, as are the interpretive meanings we bring to the pictures. This chapter will outline that history, in which taking pictures is both a leisure pursuit and an increasingly flexible medium for the construction of ordinary people's accounts of their lives and **fantasies**. The history of the medium and the separate history of the **discourse** of which photography forms a part, interact with the **social and economic history** of an era. We will begin in the 1840s, imagining how it must have been when, for the first time, people could hold in their hands the marvel of a photographic likeness. The final section of the chapter will start from the other end, as it were, and will look back from where we stand today, finding ways to make sense of personal pictures from the recent and distant past. The meanings brought by the browser in the album both meet up with, and part company from, the external realities of the historical world, particularly when pictures are associated with major trauma or historical displacement.[1]

We have chosen to speak here of 'private' or 'personal' pictures rather than the more usual 'family' pictures, because our private lives cover so much more than our family lives. The equation between 'the family' and private experience is too easily made and excludes too much.[2] The evolution of private photography has indeed been family based but that link is historically contingent, not, as is often assumed, the consequence of 'natural' necessity. Even in 1899 it was the picture faces of 'old friends' that were apostrophised in M.C. Duncan's verse. The point has been made by writers such as Terry Dennett, who compare family albums to other sorts of albums that record the lives of clubs, political groups and other networks of support and obligation (**Spence and Holland 1991: 72**).

That private photography has become *family* photography is itself an indication of the domestication of everyday life and the expansion of 'the family' as the pivot of a century-long shift to a consumer-led, home-based economy. Personal photography has evolved as part of the interleaving of leisure and the domestic, whose development runs parallel to the history of photography itself.

In Britain and the West, the gradual expansion of domesticity from the respectable middle classes through to all but the very poorest has drawn women, children and finally even men into the 'charmed circle of home'.[3] Such activities as child-care, the preparation of meals and work on improving the house and garden have come to be seen as pleasures rather than duties, and the family has become the main resource for close relationships and

1 Literary theorist Shoshanna Felman and psychoanalyst Dori Laub discuss the significance of certain family photographs for survivors of the Holocaust in *Testimony* (1992), which deals with memory and the possibility of witness.

2 See Michèle Barrett and Mary McIntosh (1982) for a development of this argument.

JO SPENCE AND PATRICIA HOLLAND (eds) (1991) **Family Snaps: The Meanings of Domestic Photography**, London: Virago

3 For an account of the evolution of 'domesticity' as a concept and a way of living, see Hall (1979) and Davidoff and Hall (1976).

expressive emotion. Now, at the beginning of the twenty-first century, taking snapshots is among a plethora of leisure pursuits which underpin that specific form of family life. However, photography occupies a peculiar place among those activities, as pictures are themselves carriers of meanings and interpretations. They record and reflect on daily activities, delicately holding within the innocent-seeming image much that is intimate. Here are M.C. Duncan's 'volumes of unwritten life' for which we must scan beyond the edges of the frame.

Personal photographs are embedded in the lives of those who own or make use of them. Even when they are professionally taken, there is a contract between photographer and subject quite different from other types of photography. Personal pictures are made specifically to portray the individual or the group to which they belong *as they would wish to be seen* and as they have chosen to show themselves to one another. Even so, the conventions of the group inevitably overrule the preferences of individual members. Children, especially, have very little say over how they are pictured, and this discrepancy is the source of many of the conflicting emotions analysed by recent writers on family photography.

The photographs we keep for ourselves – not always in family albums – are treasured less for their quality than for their *context*, and for the part they play in confirming and challenging the identity and history of their users. In this discussion it will be useful to distinguish between *users* and *readers* of personal pictures, whether family snaps, school photos or the portraits in the high street photographer's window.[4] Users bring to the images a wealth of surrounding knowledge. Their own private pictures are part of the complex network of memories and meanings with which they make sense of their daily lives. For readers, on the other hand, a hazy snapshot or a smiling portrait from the 1950s is a mysterious text whose meanings must be teased out in an act of decoding or historical detective work. Users of personal pictures have access to the world in which they make sense; readers must translate those private meanings into a more public realm. Private photographs, taken alone, are a 'restricted code' in the sense described by Basil Bernstein, dependent for their specific meanings on knowledge of the rich soil of meanings that holds them in place (Bernstein 1971). Wrenched from that context, they appear thin and ephemeral, offering little in the way of either aesthetic pleasure or historical documentation. But, although such ghostly hints of other lives may tempt the reader to engage in the detective project and to construct stories from these tentative clues, the empirical historian would do well to treat them with extreme caution. The peculiar fascination of personal photographs comes from this contrast between an almost unbearable richness and the inconsequentiality and triviality of the medium. Roland Barthes, writing on photography and memory, could not bear to reproduce the snapshot of his recently deceased mother, even though it gave rise to his essay (**Barthes 1982**).

4 The distinction between users and readers derives from Basil Bernstein's analysis of elaborated and restricted codes. A restricted code is one that depends on its context to be understood (see Bernstein 1971: 76–77). See also Eco (1979).

ROLAND BARTHES (1982)
Camera Lucida, London: Jonathan Cape

BRIAN COE AND PAUL GATES (1977) **The Snapshot Photograph: The Rise of Popular Photography 1888–1939**, London: Ash and Grant

COLIN FORD (1989) **The Story of Popular Photography**, Bradford: Century Hutchinson Ltd/National Museum of Photography, Film and Television

AUDREY LINKMAN AND CAROLINE WARHURST (1982) **Family Albums**, Manchester: Manchester Polytechnic. A fully illustrated exhibition catalogue with an introduction

AUDREY LINKMAN (1993) **The Victorians: Photographic Portraits**, London: Tauris Parke Books

SUE ISHERWOOD (1988) **The Family Album**, London: Broadcasting Support Services

JO SPENCE (1987) **Putting Myself in the Picture**, London: Camden Press, (1995) **Cultural Sniping**, London: Routledge

VAL WILLIAMS (1986) **Women Photographers: The Other Observers 1900 to the Present**, London: Virago

JOHN TAGG (1988) **The Burden of Representation: Essays on Photographies and Histories**, London: Macmillan, especially chapter 1, 'A Democracy of the Image: Photographic Portraiture and Commodity Production'

Private pictures, offering up so little to the critic and art historian, have tended to feature in histories of photography chiefly as examples of technological improvement. Historians have noted the increasing lightness of cameras, the invention of roll film and similar developments (**Coe and Gates 1977**; **Ford 1989**). Until very recently, twentieth-century snapshots have been ignored, seen as slight and unimportant, of poor quality and of value only to those who make use of them. However, over the last twenty years or so, personal pictures have become the centre of a new sort of interest as the study of history itself has changed, and as working photographers, particularly women, have re-evaluated photographic practice. A concern with local and family histories, women's history, the history of everyday life and history from below has given a new interest to personal pictures as historical documents (**Linkman and Warhurst 1982**; **Linkman 1993**; Drake and Finnegan 1994). When scrutinised under the detective's magnifying glass, private pictures offer up many public meanings, some superficial, some historically illuminating. They tell us about the style of crinoline fashionable in the 1860s and about the donkeys used by beach photographers in the 1910s. But they also display public **ideologies** – stories and ideas about how things are and how they ought to be (**Isherwood 1988**).

Historically, personal pictures are deeply unreliable, but it is in this very unreliability that their interest lies. It has led to to a new set of questions – for whom are these pictures? who sees them? to whom do they communicate? In making an effort to *reread* private pictures, there has been a move to revalue the undervalued and to bring into public discourse meanings which have hitherto been concealed in the most secret parts of the private sphere. Writers, photographers and curators (Jo Spence, Sue Isherwood and Val Williams among them), while drawing attention to the importance of this most popular of the uses of photography, have insisted that the *privacy* of the meanings should not be dispersed (Spence and Holland 1991; **Spence 1987, 1995**; **Williams 1986**).

The increasing self-consciousness of the modern world has been explored and reworked in many different ways since the mid-nineteenth century. It has been argued that photography is itself a central feature of modernity – not just in its modernist moment, when photographers such as Rodchenko and Moholy-Nagy indulged in formalist abstractions and celebrations of machine culture – but as a *technology*, contributing to the control of the external world with its mechanical eye and potential for scientific neutrality (**Tagg 1988**; Slater 1995a).

Personal photography has played a different but equally important role in the **modernisation** of Western culture. It has developed as a medium through which individuals confirm and explore their **identity**, that sense of self-identity which is an indispensable feature of a modern sensibility – for in Western urban culture it is as *individuals* that people have come to experience themselves, independently of their role as family members or as occupying a recognised social position. The twentieth-century consumer-led economy has shifted these new individuals away from a culture based on work and self-discipline to one based on libidinous gratification which encourages us all to *identify* our pleasures in order to develop and refine them. In a parallel move, the century of Freud has become an age of inwardness and self-scrutiny. These changes are reflected in the images we produce of ourselves and the way we have made use of them. Scanning personal pictures has become part of that act of self-contemplation (Spence and Martin in Spence and Holland 1991; Spence 1987; Spence 1995).

Despite the intensity of such a project, in one of those many paradoxes that makes its study so fascinating, private photography insists on being a *non-serious* practice. Cuthbert Bede, writing in 1855 in the facetiously punning style enjoyed by the mid-nineteenth century, reminded his readers that photography was 'essentially a *light* subject and should be treated in a light manner' (Bede 1855). And so it has continued over its history, seeking the playful and celebrating the trivial. Personal photography sets out to be photography without pretensions, and that is how we intend to approach it. In the spirit of much recent work by feminist writers on women's culture (for example, Geraghty 1991), we will not be arguing that these forms of photography should be captured for '**Art**' or 'high culture', but that what is needed is to understand them on their own terms.

IN AND BEYOND THE CHARMED CIRCLE OF HOME

The public and the private in personal photography

From its beginnings in the 1840s, home-based popular photography was balanced by photography that looked outwards. During the nineteenth century, images of the strange and exotic were treated as marvels which enhanced the comfortable home and became part of home entertainment, as television is today. But in some family albums, kept by prosperous patriarchs up to the turn of the century, we can see how the middle-class home, even as it became increasingly protected from political and economic life, depended on the world outside. The feminine domesticity of the extended family was visibly sustained by masculine adventure, both military and entrepreneurial. The two sides of popular photography have remained, but the Imperial aspiration of this vision, and the celebration of commerce and military adventure of the Victorian era, have since been replaced by a tamer record of travel and tourism. The copious albums preserved by Sir Arnold Wilson dramatically illustrate the point. Sir Arnold was a well-connected army officer serving in India and Persia in the early years of the twentieth century. He worked with the Anglo-Persian Oil Company in the 1920s and became a Conservative MP in the 1930s. His family albums cover a period from 1870 to 1920, recording holiday trips, afternoons in the vicarage garden and regimental postings. Set-piece photographs of India and the Middle East

3.2a From the album of Sir Arnold Wilson (No. 3 Persian scenes), 1909

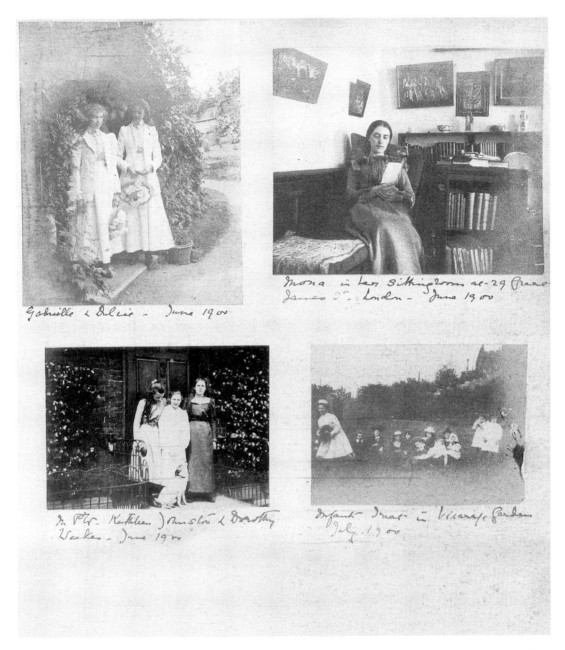

3.2b From the album of Sir Arnold Wilson (No. 7), 1900

are juxtaposed with gentle family groups and intimate portraits in the gardens and drawing-rooms of the family's homes at Leighton Park Estate and in the countryside near Rochdale. In India the regimental tug-of-war team and the local Gurkha regiment present themselves proudly to the camera. In the Middle East, British officers pose one by one with local sheikhs. Tourism overlaps with colonial rule as spectacular views of the Himalayan hill station at Muree are followed by annotated pages showing the complex decoration of local mosques. In the Persian album, alongside the purchased images of silversmiths and weavers at work, Sir Arnold included pictures of executioners and torturers demonstrating their craft.

Discussing the colonialist imagery of advertising at the turn of the century, Anne McClintock argues that 'the cult of domesticity became indispensable to the consolidation of British imperial identity' (Robertson *et al.* 1994: 133). The starkness of the contrast in Sir Arnold Wilson's albums makes visible the tensions on which domestic photography has continued to be based. They look inwards at an increasingly privatised and protected domestic haven and outwards at a world of political violence, re-presented as spectacular and exotic. The pictures in Sir Arnold's albums present this outside world with great confidence, gazing with the eyes of those who would control it and claim to civilise it. As the twentieth century progressed, and as photography became available to the ruled as well as the rulers, the politics of the world beyond the family group has come to be **repressed** in the domestic image. The *consequences* of colonial domination and the ever possible presence of violence must be read beyond the limits of the frame (Hall 1991: 152).

Beyond the domestic

From the very early days to the unflagging popularity of posters and post-cards in the twentieth century, popular photography has continued to include purchased pictures of unknown people and places. William Henry Fox Talbot, who first developed a negative/positive **calotype** process in Britain in 1839, hastened to patent his invention and turn it to financial advantage. In 1843 he set up the first printing workshop to reproduce photographs for sale. His book, *The Pencil of Nature*, was the first to be photographically illustrated.

Within twenty years there was a thriving industry in photographic prints, which included impressive landscapes, views and still lives. If Sir Arnold Wilson's turn-of-the-century collection carries the confidence of those who seek to control what they see, these pictures marketed from the 1850s onwards had the more modest aim of entertainment. However, what John Urry described as 'the tourist **gaze**' (Urry 1990) itself ensures a separation between the one who does the looking, assumed to be familiar and like 'us', and that which is looked at, assumed to be different and strange. A taste for the exotic was already well established in the mid-nineteenth century and photography gave it a new boost. Francis Frith set up a highly profitable company which produced saleable photographs of parts of the world which

calotype Photographic print made by the process launched by William Henry Fox Talbot in England in 1840. It involved the exposure of sensitised paper in the camera from which, after processing, positive paper prints could be made. Not much used in England in the early days because it was protected by Fox Talbot's own patents, but its use was developed in Scotland, especially by David Octavius Hill and Robert Adamson.

up till that time had only been seen through the eyes of artists or the imaginative descriptions of travellers. From 1856 he made three expeditions to the bible lands of the Middle East and *The Times* called his resulting photographs 'the most important ever published' (Macdonald 1979). His photographers travelled the length of the British Isles and at the height of his business his firm claimed to have one million available prints, including photographs of every city, town and beauty spot in Britain. By the later years of the nineteenth century, photographs of parts of the world, impressive because of their distance, their strangeness or the difficulty experienced in reaching them – from the high Alps to remote areas of China and Japan – were published as prints, lantern slides and stereoscopic views.

The coming of photography gave rise to a new set of dilemmas around the production of the exotic. On the one hand it displayed images of hitherto unknown and remarkable places and people, but at the same time it had to be recognised that these were *real* places and people. The veneer of exoticism may be confirmed or challenged by the photograph itself. We should not forget that photography was also developing in those very places that seemed exotic to the untravelled British. By the end of the nineteenth century in China, Japan and Taiwan, local photographers were making pictures for local use. Pictures which would be seen as exotica in Britain are someone else's family photos.

Popular photography has rarely been a medium of record. Foreign views exaggerated the exotic and the strange, and a fashion developed for the quaint and the traditional (for example, George Washington Wilson's pictures of gnarled old Scottish fishermen and other local types). With hindsight this fashion can be seen as the beginnings of a heritage industry in which the imagery was threaded through with nostalgia brought about by photography itself, already capturing a disappearing past. Groups such as the Society for Photographing Relics of Old London set up in 1875 contributed to an archive of the past which itself became part of a tourist view of the world (**Taylor 1994**).

Middle-class artistic travellers came to deplore 'vulgar' sightseers turning up with their cameras, who, they claimed, ruined the very views they had come to discover. From the turn of the century, a new generation of tourists took their cameras in search of natural beauties previously only seen on postcards and in travelogues. At first they went by train or bicycle, but by the 1930s many were travelling by car. Some were satisfied to picnic in the fields, but increasing numbers sought out the famous beauty spots. With each wave of visitors the possibility of an undiscovered rural scene or an unspoilt village seemed to become ever more elusive. A photograph was a nostalgic compensation for the loss of a world that appeared to be uncorrupted by industry and urbanisation. By the late twentieth century, that historical world itself had been preserved and packaged. The heritage industry and the tourist trade between them had provided renovated antique buildings and tidied up picturesque views that are ready-made photo opportunities. 'Viewpoints'

JOHN TAYLOR (1994) **A Dream of England: Landscape, Photography and the Tourist's Imagination**, Manchester: Manchester University Press

3.3 'The photographic craze', *Amateur Photographer*, 10 June 1887

are now clearly marked on roads and maps. Taking a picture is an intrinsic part of the tourist experience and 'places of interest' dominate the albums of many a modest traveller just as they did those of Sir Arnold Wilson.

Fiction and fantasy

Fiction and fantasy have long been more attractive than the mundanities of everyday life, and this was certainly true of one of the most popular of nineteenth-century domestic media, the stereoscopic view. From 1854 the London Stereoscopic Company produced double pictures which gave a 3D effect when peered at through a binocular viewer. This could be a small hand-held affair or a grand piece of drawing-room furniture. By 1858 there were 100,000 different views on offer and the company's slogan was 'No home without a stereoscope'.

Many stereoscopic scenes exploited the Victorians' love of theatrical tableaux and aimed for a style and subject-matter suited to the taste of their middle-brow purchasers. Such 'stereoscopic trash' outraged the proponents of photography as art. The Photographic Society (later to become Royal), founded in 1853 to protect artistic standards, deplored the debasement of the medium. In 1858 its journal fumed,

> To see that noble instrument prostituted as it is by those sentimental 'Weddings', 'Christenings', 'Distressed Sempstresses', 'Crinolines' and 'Ghosts' is enough to disgust anyone of refined taste. We are sorry to say that recently some slides have been published which are, to say the least, questionable in point of view of delicacy.
>
> (Scharf 1974)

128

3.4 Stereoscopic slide from the late nineteenth century

Sentiment, jokes, horror, melodrama and material which verged on pornography – this was the stuff of nineteenth-century photographic entertainment. Some stereoscopes even came with a locked drawer for a gentleman to keep his risqué pictures away from his family. In those days before the cinema, magic lantern shows were also popular. Impressive views could be watched in a darkened room, enhanced by exciting optical effects – from a sunset over the Alps to lifelike thunderstorms (Chanan 1996). The making of personal portraits was part of this popular aesthetic, firmly embedded in commercial practices.

Portraits and albums

Louis-Jacques-Mandé Daguerre's invention of positive images on silvered metal, each one unique, was, from the 1840s, the dominant format for personal portraits. Enterprising **daguerreotypists** learned the new skills and tried to interest customers in towns across Europe and the New World. In those very early days, sittings for fifteen to twenty minutes in as bright a sunlight as possible led to extreme discomfort for the sitter and some fairly unflattering pictures which could be difficult to discern on the highly reflective surface. Even so, within a few years, huge numbers of people of middling income wanted their portraits taken, and 'daguerreomania' had taken hold. Photographic 'glasshouses' – so called because of the wide expanse of window

daguerreotype Photographic image made by the process launched by Louis-Jacques-Mandé Daguerre in France in 1839. It is a positive image on a metal plate with a mirror-like silvered surface, characterised by very fine detail. Each one is unique and fragile and needs to be protected by a padded case. It became the dominant portrait mode for the first decades of photography, especially in the United States.

needed to maximise daylight – were established in the urban centres across Europe and the United States. In Britain, Antoine Claudet had a 'temple of photography' designed by Sir Charles Barry, who built the Houses of Parliament. In Leicester Square there was a 'Panopticon of science and art' with a room 54 feet long (approximately 16.5 metres) 'enabling family groups of 18 persons to be taken at once', which also offered lessons in daguerreotyping and studios for hire. Studio portraitists introduced painted backdrops so that the customers, whatever their social standing, could choose to place themselves within dignified parklands, seascapes, conservatories or palm houses. Many were extremely successful: Richard Beard was said to be photography's first millionaire (Macdonald 1979; Tagg 1988; Ford 1989; **Kenyon 1992: 11–12**).

The 'cheap and common establishments' in the less fashionable parts of town got a bad name for aggressive touting for trade. Someone stood outside shouting, 'Have your picture taken', and virtually 'dragging customers in by the collar' (Werge 1890: 202). Most of these early portraits were carefully posed and touched up so as to produce as flattering an image as possible under difficult circumstances. A headrest kept that most important feature, the face, static for the still lengthy exposures needed, or else the posing individual was asked to lean on a table or a mock-classical pillar which also served decorative and symbolic functions. The head resting on the hand achieved the popular Victorian soulful look, as well as helping the sitter to keep still. Smiles were difficult to sustain under such circumstances: the modern ubiquitous snapshot smile should be seen as a technological achievement as well as a change in social mores.

Every innovation was hailed as spreading photography more widely across the classes. 'Such portraits are to be found in everybody's hands', wrote André-Adolphe Disdéri, who had invented the '*carte-de-visite*' in 1854 (Lamagny and Rouille 1987: 38). Named after the leisured classes' 'visiting cards', these were small paper prints mounted on the photographer's own decorated card. Several poses could be produced on a single negative so that the process was speeded up and multiple copies were easily available. This was the first attempt at a form of mass production of popular photographs, and certainly class differences were far less visible in such pictures than they were in everyday life. Shopkeepers, minor officials and small traders all took themselves and their children to pose stiffly in their best clothes in front of one of these early cameras.

A craze for collecting *cartes-de-visite* of the famous developed. Some of the earliest photographic albums were not 'family albums' at all, but handsomely bound volumes filled with pictures of royalty, celebrities and politicians. As pressure increased on middle-class women to make their lives within the confines of the home environment, useless but suitably decorative hobbies such as collecting *cartes-de-visite* fitted in well with other genteel activities such as sketching and pressing flowers (Davidoff and Hall 1976; Warner 1992).

DAVE KENYON (1992) **Inside Amateur Photography**, London: Batsford

carte-de-visite A small paper print (2½ × 4⅛″) mounted on a card with the photographer's details on the reverse. This way of producing photographs for sale was developed by André-Adolphe Disdéri in France in 1854. Eight or more images were made on the same glass negative by a special camera with several lenses and a moving plate-holder. The prints were then cut up to size. Such prints could be produced in very large numbers.

3.5 Earliest known daguerrotype of a photographer at work. Jabez Hogg photographs Mr Johnson, *c.* 1843

Queen Victoria's family was itself presented as a model of the new respectable domesticity, but published photographs of the Royal Family remained strictly formal. When the celebrated photographer Roger Fenton was invited to photograph the Queen's children dressing up and presenting tableaux, the pictures were felt to lack dignity and were never released to the public (Hannavy 1975). Even so, it was the more relaxed picture of Princess Alexandra giving her daughter Louise a piggyback that became the best-selling *carte-de-visite*. Among their many hobbies and pastimes, women members of the Royal Family took up photography themselves, and Queen Victoria's and later Queen Alexandra's own copious albums were filled with views of family picnics and hunting parties (Williams 1986: 75).

Home photography was not for public display, but for fun with friends. In 1855 Cuthbert Bede described, for the benefit of 'all the light-hearted friends of light painting', many such social activities, including 'visiting country houses and calotyping all the eligible daughters' (Bede 1855: 44).

The light-hearted uses of photographs, part of the Victorian fascination for fads and fancies, included mounting dainty miniatures into brooches and lockets, decorating jewel cases, or even setting them into the spines of a fan. A Victorian album was itself a series of visual novelties, with the portraits often cut up and arranged in decorative shapes and incorporating drawings and other scrapbook items. Mary Queen of Scots going to her execution was a favourite. And there were the mottoes: 'Love me, love my dog' heads a page of pets squatting smugly on their cushions. The interest is not just in the individual pictures but in the arrangement as a decorative collection.[5]

The family-based albums of the nineteenth century are those of prosperous dynasties whose members had both the leisure and the money to take up photography, as well as to buy commercially produced pictures. The life of the Helm family, in their spacious mansion in Walthamstow, elegantly photographed by James Helm and preserved in a set of albums put together in the early 1860s, demonstrates not so much the luxury and overt enjoyment of a free-spending leisure class, but the decency and quiet respectability of the middle-class suburb (H. Cunningham in **Thompson 1990**). The group is large and diverse, with aunts and other relatives and friends as regular members, in striking contrast to today's pictures of tight-knit families in which parents and young children predominate. The leisurely lifestyle included croquet on the lawn, amateur dramatics, young men posing with their musical instruments and dignified ladies in layered crinolines taking tea. These are scenes from everyday life, carefully organised and staged in the tableau manner. In the 1840s, Fox Talbot had written, 'when a group of persons has been artistically arranged and trained by a little practice to maintain an absolute immobility for a few seconds of time, many delightful pictures are easily obtained. I have observed that family groups are especial favourites' (Ford 1989). The tableau was a pleasing artistic picture as much as a family record. Pictures such as these were marking out the evolving domestic sensibility of the nineteenth century, which made the home environment the centre of decent living. It was a model which the lower-middle and working classes were to emulate in the coming century.

If the home was becoming a site of leisure, the creation of the 'hobbyist', and its more elevated relative the 'amateur', meant that leisure time could be used both for scientific experiment and the creation of works of art. Although one aspect of the evolution of domesticity meant that 'the feminine ideal was to be weak and childlike' (Davidoff in Thompson 1990: 84), women could become home-based hobbyists. 'Photography is the science for amateurs, equally adapted for ladies and gentlemen, which cannot be said of the generality of sciences', wrote Bede. Among the most celebrated photographers of the nineteenth century were comfortably off women with plenty of leisure and domestic help, who made use of their family and immediate surroundings as raw material for their photographic works, rather than as family record. Julia Margaret Cameron's misty portraits and visions of cupids and angels

5 It is relatively new for photographic historians to recognise the album's importance as a complete entity. Collectors have frequently purchased an album simply to remove one or two remarkable prints. Curator Pam Roberts of the Royal Photographic Society is preserving and cataloguing albums in their own right. She makes the point that the way photographs have been selected and put together is an important part of the personal meaning of the pictures in an album.

F.M.L. THOMPSON (ed.) (1990) **The Cambridge Social History of Britain 1750–1850**, Vol. 2, **People and Their Environment**, Cambridge: Cambridge University Press

3.6 A page from the album of R. Foley Onslow, *c.* 1860

A PHOTOGRAPHIC POSITIVE.

LADY MOTHER (loquitur) "I SHALL FEEL OBLIGED TO YOU, MR. SQUILLS, IF YOU WOULD REMOVE THESE STAINS FROM MY DAUGHTER'S FACE. I CANNOT PERSUADE HER TO BE SUFFICIENTLY CAREFUL WITH HER PHOTOGRAPHIC CHEMICALS AND SHE HAS HAD A MISFOR: ·TUNE WITH HER NITRATE OF SILVER. UNLESS YOU CAN DO SOMETHING FOR HER, SHE WILL NOT BE FIT TO BE SEEN AT LADY MAYFAIR'S TO·NIGHT. "

LONDON. PUBLISHED BY T. MC'LEAN.

3.7 Illustration from Cuthbert Bede, *Photographic Pleasures*, 1855 embraced and transcended Victorian romanticism. Working-class women were needed as servants and helpers to service the middle-class domestic haven. Indeed, Julia Margaret Cameron's own favourite model was her assistant and maid, Mary Hillier (Mavor 1996). There were women working portraitists, too. John Werge remembers a 'Miss Wigley from London' who came to his home town in the North of England to practise daguerreotyping as early as the mid-1840s (Werge 1890).

Informality and intimacy

The repertoire of personal imagery was changing. There had been an elegiac tone to much Victorian personal photography, evoked by the solemnity of middle-class portraiture and by the awareness that so many died young. Death was a central part of family life, and memorial pictures of the dead and dying were common. Babies who had died were dressed in their best and photographed in their mother's arms (Williams 1994). By the end of the century the emphasis was changing to a more present celebration of life and a taste for informality.

Photographic portraits had long been valued not only for their likeness to the sitter but also for the apparent escape from convention and the greater naturalness offered by the mechanical process. Bede had written that a calotype is a step beyond a painted portrait, for a painting has 'the artist's conventional face, his conventional attitude, his conventional background' (Bede 1855: 45). In 1899 Richard Penlake advised amateur photographers how to avoid 'perfect' pictures like those of a celebrity, who is so carefully made up and posed as to seem like a wax model, or of royalty, in which the very best pose is selected from many exposures and even then 'so worked up that scarcely a single part of the original negative prints at all' (Penlake 1899: 16).

Penlake also offered advice on tricks and optical effects, such as making double images – so that the sitter magically appears twice in the same picture – and **montaging** photographed heads on to caricatured bodies, but with the coming of hand-held cameras such conceits were on the way out. Albums of the 1880s, compared with those of the 1860s, show a much more relaxed style and closeness to the subjects. The movement and visual interest was now in the picture itself rather than in the decoration and arrangement of the pictures on the page. On one page in Sir Arnold Wilson's album, girls and boys in sailor suits and boaters are trying out a bicycle. They are 'captured' with their back to the camera, in mid-conversation with each other, pointing their own hand-held cameras and playing up to the camera, in a sequence of images which have much in common with the new 'candid' work by photographers Paul Martin and Frank Meadow Sutcliffe. 'Detective cameras' were now all the rage. They were tiny, unobtrusive or concealed so that pictures could be taken without the knowledge of the subject. For the first time there was the opportunity to take a different sort of personal

montage or
photomontage The use of
two or more originals, perhaps
also including written text, to
make a combined image. A
montaged image may be
imaginative, artistic, comic or
deliberately satirical.

picture, one where the contract between photographer and subject is brought into question. Secret observation was not always welcome to the observed. One local paper wrote in 1893:

> Several decent young men are forming themselves into a Vigilance Association with the purpose of thrashing cads with cameras who go around seaside places taking pictures of ladies emerging from the deep in the mournful garments peculiar to the British female bather . . . I wish the new society stout cudgels and much success.
>
> (Coe and Gates 1977: 18)

The working classes picture themselves

From the mid-nineteenth century the middle classes began to move to the new suburbs. Behind their privet hedges they protected themselves from the grime of industry and the potential immorality of the streets. But a large proportion of the working classes remained confined to the inner cities, in areas that were filthy and unhygienic. Their homes were not places of pleasurable relaxation and they could rarely afford the cost of representing themselves through photography. Although we twenty-first-century seekers for the past may look at the family of Sir Arnold Wilson and see them as they would like to be seen, the image of the working classes which we have inherited has been produced either by those, like Oscar Rejlander, who aestheticised and sentimentalised it, or those, like Thomas Annan, who documented it for the benefit of various official projects. Middle-class concern frequently took the form of outrage at the state of the less salubrious areas, often describing the people who lived there as distasteful, smelly and unhealthy like their dwellings. Photographer Willie Swift, who published *Leeds Slumdom* in 1897, turned his pictures into lantern slides and 'with the help of my daughters who sang suitable solos for us, we went up and down showing the dark places of the city, helping to create that healthy public opinion which eventually demanded clearance of the places shown' (Tagg 1988: 225).

Against this background, middle-class intervention became the context for another kind of personal photograph, often valued by those it represents although not necessarily made for their sake. Following the Education Acts of 1870 and 1893 which introduced universal schooling, some of the earliest photographs kept by working-class families are those depicting their children ranked behind wooden desks. In 1891 and 1893 respectively, the Church Lads' Brigade and the Boys' Brigade were launched to tidy up disorderly youngsters and get them off the streets. Photographs of clubs and bands present a disciplined image, modelled on those produced by the likes of Arnold Wilson and his regiment out in the hill stations of Muree.

However, the shortening of the working week and the coming of the Saturday day off led to new sporting and leisure activities, which working-

3.8 Pupils at St Mary's School, Moss Lane, Manchester, c. 1910

class people could organise for themselves and which they were beginning to record for their own pleasure. Modest photographs from the 1890s onwards show the cycling group, the football supporters and, above all, the trip to the seaside, made possible by the expanding railway network. Opportunist photographers were now on hand for trippers who wanted their picture taken. Long before the **polaroid**, the **tintype** (or **ferrotype**) could produce an instant metal positive for little boys with buckets and spades, toddlers perched on the photographer's donkey, and young women holding up their voluminous skirts as they paddle in the shallows. Photographers working in the new postcard format were ready with cheeky devices: 'The subject's head would join a monstrously fat body holding countless bottles of beer, or he would sit in a wooden aeroplane among painted stars' (Parr and Stasiak 1986: 13).

Not surprisingly, many of the poorer people continued to choose studio portraits where dignified or exotic backdrops would remove them from their pokey homes. However, when the travelling photographer came by to set up his equipment in a local street, all the children of the neighbourhood ran after him to get their picture taken. 'Do not take too much notice of how they are taken', wrote Edward and May Bond's mother when she sent

polaroid The Polaroid land camera, producing instant black and white positives, was first marketed in 1947, but produced poor-quality images. Polaroid instant colour prints and slides were launched in 1963.

tintype (or **ferrotype**) Tintypes, instant positive images on enamelled iron plates, were produced from 1852 to around 1946. As one of the cheapest methods, they were especially favoured by seaside photographers.

3.9 Edward and May Bond taken by a street photographer outside their home in Manchester, c. 1912

such a picture to her eldest son, 'for they look a bit untidy but I did not know they were having their likenesses taken, but I thought I would buy one to let you have a look at their dear little faces' (figures 3.9 and 3.10).

By 1910 postcard sales were averaging 860 million per year (Pryce 1994: 143). As well as the usual repertoire of views, royalty, celebrities and tableaux, travelling photographers would set up their stall at a fair or a local beauty spot and offer to put *your* picture on a postcard. When people couldn't afford the threepence (1.5p) or so for a picture, clubs were set up to pay in instalments. These jobbing photographers came from a class background similar

138

3.10 Studio photograph of Edward and May Bond, c. 1910

to those whom they served. Photography was fast becoming a medium in which working-class people could present themselves to each other.

Enterprising postcard photographers would visit local collieries, docks or mills, often producing the only photographic record of such workplaces that exist. Others specialised in local events, such as strikes, lockouts or disasters. In 1910, John Leach, a local Whitehaven photographer, put together a montage of 124 of those killed in the appalling explosion and fire in the Wellington pit, as a memorial for the traumatised local community (Hiley 1983). Pictures of festivities were especially important to local people. At

3.11 Holiday postcard from a Blackpool studio, 1910

3.12 Mobile sales tent for Bailey's photographers, Bournemouth, c. 1910

the Manchester Whit Walks, 'the working class was on display and they knew it' (Linkman and Warhurst 1982). Children who were untidy or had no clean clothes were kept well out of sight by their parents, and such pictures gave a very different impression of life in the inner city from the documentarist's view of picturesque misery. Photographs made for the benefit

3.13 Black Country chain-makers, postcard, 7 August 1911

of the photographer, whether as artist or concerned reporter, stand in striking contrast to those made for the eyes of the people whom they represent.

Kodak and the mass market

It was not until George Eastman, an American photographic plate manufacturer, successfully produced sensitised paper in 1884, and followed it up with his hand-held camera in 1888, that the paraphernalia of tripods and glass plates could finally be put aside and home photography for all became a possibility. Eastman was an entrepreneur who sought to dominate the world market with a camera simple enough to be used by anyone. His crucial move was the separation of the *taking* of an image from the other stages involved in making a photograph. The smelly and difficult business of processing and printing was placed, conveniently out of sight, in the factory. The leisure activity for the home was supported by mass production and an army of employees – mostly women.

Simultaneously, photography was both domesticated and industrialised. The celebrated Kodak camera, marketed in 1888, was a lumpish wooden box with a hole at one end for the lens. When all the exposures had been made, and they amounted to about a hundred on a single film, the whole thing was sent back to the Eastman factory for processing and reloading.

141

The slogan 'You press the button, we do the rest' was to form the basis of personal photography for the next century.

Don Slater has argued that this drastic simplification amounted to depriving the new users of photography both of skills they might have put to more radical effect and a practical understanding of how photography creates meanings: 'Being separated from a knowledge of process, we have no sense of photography as manipulation, as a form of action, as a making sense through the manipulation of tools of representation and meaning' (Slater 1991: 54). However, looking back from the beginning of the twenty-first century, such an analysis underestimates the scale on which a *new* skill was introduced at the end of the nineteenth. Selecting, framing and achieving the content of a photographic image was now a possibility for those who would not otherwise have had either the time, the money or the inclination to engage in the complex processes of amateur photography. Don Slater's arguments also disregard Bede's reminder that personal photography is a *light* art. Photographic manipulation had long been part of the games people played with their cameras. Producing joke pictures and clowning in front of the lens are activities which have turned taking pictures into a pastime that secures friendship and insists on interaction between photographer and subject. This *is* collaboration in 'manipulating the tools of representation and meaning', even when it's just for fun.

In the twentieth century, the more individualist activities which the full photographic process demands have become part of the 'amateur photography' movement. Amateur photography has been a more masculine pastime, scornful of the snapshot's cheery refusal to concern itself with the complexities of the medium. Serious amateur practice has retained its fascination with technology and its striving for aesthetic control. It has its own magazines, competitions and standards, and its long-lived aspiration to the sort of pictorialism fashionable among artist-photographers at the turn of the century.

Eastman's commercial operations rapidly reached from Rochester, New York to Harrow in Middlesex, and across the world. Developments rapidly followed each other. Daylight loading, where the celluloid film came in light-tight cartons, was an advance that meant there was no longer a need to send the whole camera back to the factory. 'Anybody can use it. Everybody will use it' ran the publicity, listing some of those possible users:

> *Travellers and tourists:* Use it to obtain a picturesque diary of their travels. . . . *Bicyclists and boating men:* Can carry it where a larger camera would be too burdensome. . . . *Ocean travellers:* Use it to photograph their fellow passengers on the steamship deck. . . . *Sportsmen and camping parties:* Use it to recall pleasant times spent in camp and wilderness . . . and *Lovers of fine animals:* use it to photograph their pets.
>
> (Coe and Gates 1977: 18)

The theme was looking outwards. The new photographer should make the most of new facilities for travelling – the train and the bicycle – and point their camera at the picturesque and the unusual.

Looking inwards towards the domestic and creating an exclusive record of your family was a parallel message, directed largely at the women of the middle classes. The new technology was *gendered*. Its simplicity of operation indicated that the woman of the house could use it, while the chemicals and other technical paraphernalia could be left to the men. And what activity could be more suitable for a woman than to photograph her children. 'Do you think baby will be quiet long enough to take her picture mama?' asks a cartoon-style advertisement from 1889, as a mother lines up her camera on her toddler, 'The Kodak will catch her whether she moves or not. It is as quick as a wink.' The prosperity of those late decades had brought women a new sense of independence. The passive 'angel in the house' was being superseded by the 'new woman', and those who took up their cameras were not just housebound mothers. 'Thousands of Birmingham girls are scattered about the holiday resorts of Britain this month, and a very large percentage of them are armed with cameras', wrote *Photographic News* in September 1905. 'It is as much a feminine as a masculine hobby these days, perhaps more so' (Coe and Gates 1977: 28).

The Kodak girl, her smart but comfortable black and white striped dress always blowing in some breeze or other, was introduced in 1910, and she continued to balance her camera casually in her hand in Kodak advertisements over the next thirty years. Variously drawn by many well-known artists, adapting to changing fashions in skirt length and hairstyle, she was seen perched on a rock pointing out to sea, or on a jetty watching the yachts come in, or picturing the children romping on the beach, always urging purchasers to 'Save your happy memories with a Kodak'. As time went on, even the cameras were feminised. In the late 1920s, Kodaks were produced in fashion colours – pinks, blues and greens – and 'Vanity Kodaks' came with a matching lipstick, mirror and compact holder.

The 'Box Brownie', launched in 1900, cost five shillings, a quarter of an average week's wages, which brought it into the reach of all but the poorest.[6] Now the advertisements were directed at children, too. The Brownie was a camera for little folk and could, the advertisements claimed, 'be operated by any school boy or girl'. Like the other Kodaks, it was not only easy to use but was guaranteed to be successful. However inept the operator, its pictures will come out. Brownie albums were provided, with spaces ready prepared for slotting in a sequence of the snapshots.

Photography was not the only medium to shift from small-scale craft production to industrial production for a mass market in the last decades of the nineteenth century. Universal literacy, new printing techniques and the entrepreneurial ambitions of such men as Northcliffe and Rothermere meant that popular newspapers were launched for an unprecedentedly large readership.

6 Kenyon (1992) has a detailed discussion of income relative to price of cameras and film.

Few memories are so pleasant as the memories of
your holidays. And yet, you allow those memories
to slip away! How little you remember, even of
your happiest times! Don't let this year's holiday
be forgotten—take a Kodak and save your happi-
ness. Make Kodak snapshots of every happy
scene. The little pictures will keep your holiday
alive—they will carry you back again and again to
sunshine and freedom; they will enable you to chat
once more with your jolly companions, and to enjoy another hearty laugh over
the fun you had. Remember, you can learn to use a Kodak in half-an-hour.

The only holiday that lasts
forever is the holiday with a

Kodak

Ask your nearest Kodak dealer to show you the latest models.
Kodak Ltd., Kingsway, London, W.C. 2.

3.14 Kodak advertisement, 1920

The advertising industry was rapidly establishing itself, since the mass production of all sorts of goods for domestic consumption required wider and more innovative marketing. Photography was at the centre of these developments and was to become the heart of the intensely visual popular culture of the twentieth century. After the *Daily Illustrated Mirror* (today's *Daily Mirror*) was launched in 1903 as the first newspaper to use photographic illustrations, the popular press came to depend on photography as an indispensable part of *news* reporting, and even more importantly, as central to their *entertainment* role (Holland 1997). Celebrity and royalty pictures, which in the mid-nineteenth century found their way into *carte-de-visite* albums, were now to be found in newspapers and later in the burgeoning consumer magazines. From the latter half of the twentieth century, the coming of full-colour printing, first in magazines, then in newspapers, has meant that the whole range of fashion, gardening, cooking, travel and tourism, celebrities and music have been part of a light-hearted environment of high-quality photographic imagery which we now take for granted. Popular photography is all around us and it exerts its influence on contemporary private photography.

Back in the early years of the century the new domestic photographers had fewer models to imitate. As municipal housing became available for the less well-off, the working classes were beginning to follow the familial ideal established – and indeed enforced – by the Victorian middle classes (Davidoff in Thompson 1990: 106). With the coming of gas lighting and piped water, working-class homes were both more comfortable and more consciously 'respectable'. The elaborately furnished and scrupulously protected front parlour was 'not for relaxation, but a controlled and formal social environment' (Daunton in Thompson 1990: 207). As the lifestyles of the different classes grew closer together, the snapshot style could indicate a casual and informal mode which gave a democratic veneer to social divisions. Val Williams describes the relaxed pictures of the little Princesses, Margaret and Elizabeth, taken in the 1930s, as a studied model to which the whole nation could aspire (Williams 1986: 72). The poorer the community, the less directly are their daily activities reflected in the pictures they keep. Those who lived in the inner city tenements remained anxious to record the formality and dignity of their life, not its more distressing moments.

With the coming of the First World War there was a boom in camera sales, reaching its peak in 1917 as families bought cameras to record soldiers leaving for the war (Coe and Gates 1977: 34). Portraits of young men in uniform, many of whom never returned, make a poignant moment in most twentieth-century family collections. The increase in working-class incomes paradoxically brought about by the war meant that, by 1916, the *Kodak Trade Circular* could advise retailers that

> the people of the working class could be looked on as a likely buyer
> ... it may even be said that they are better able to appreciate the

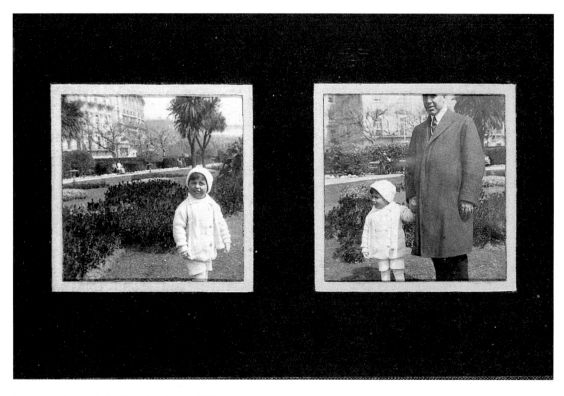

3.15 A page from a Kodak 'Brownie' album, c. 1900

Kodak than some of the people who usually buy it. The craftsman
who works a high speed tool and who has to work to very fine
measurements is just the right type of man to admire the mechanical
excellence of the Kodak – . . . If your shop is near a working class
neighbourhood, think this over.

(Coe 1989: 69)

The supersnap in Kodaland

Following each of the major upheavals of the twentieth century, 'the family'
was reasserted as a force for reconstruction and social cohesion. During the
Second World War, for a brief period, popular photography included high-
quality photojournalism developed by *Picture Post*, which concerned itself
with the 'home front', with public life and communal responsibility as well
as with military campaigns; but in the postwar period, just as in the years
following the First World War, a reconstructed economy was based on
domestic consumption and the domestic ideal. This required, in particular,
women's willing return to the home to become the pivot of family life,

relinquishing their public presence in the workplace and revaluing the ideal of a private sphere where political forces appear irrelevant. Twentieth-century family photography, with its resolute insistence on the creation of *happy* memories, has determinedly reflected this mood, in which politics and world affairs, even the most disruptive, are pushed to the background of public consciousness (Taylor 1994: 141).

Despite the depression, it was during the inter-war years of the 1920s and 1930s that a home-based family idyll took hold in the mock Tudor, semi-detached suburbs of English towns. Here the rising working class found for the first time 'such homes of which thousands have only dreamed' (Holland 1991). The stiff front parlour became a living room designed for leisure use and rigid gender and age divisions gave way to companionate marriage and demonstrative parenting (Davidoff in Thompson 1990: 116). The domestic ideal, built up over the nineteenth century as a space that would be calmer and morally superior to the turbulent world outside, was being narrowed down to a much smaller family, made up of two parents and their younger children, who aimed to lead a pleasurable rather than dutiful life. A state of

147

mind was coming about in which the satisfaction of each *individual's* desire for comfort and satisfaction would not seem incompatible with the mutual obligations demanded by family groups. The increasing relaxation and informality appearing in family snapshots echoed that change.

The image of the child became the central icon of family life. By the 1930s the two- or three-child family was the norm, which meant that individual attention could be given to each child and there was more time for birthday celebrations, Christmas trees and the snapshots which accompany these ceremonies. The domestic camera was confirmed as a ritualised element in joint celebrations (Musello 1979). As well as the visible markers for home-centred values, children signified the aspirational optimism of a century dominated by the newly prosperous working and lower-middle classes, whose horizons seemed to be ever widening. The modest pictures of the period between the wars give off a sense of hope, a belief in progress and in the possibility of a comfortable life for all.

Despite the ideology of 'home' as a warm, familial centre, most collections of personal pictures are, in fact, dominated by time spent *away* from the home. As well as becoming closer and more inward-looking, the family was also becoming *mobile* (Slater 1995b: 132). The gradual spread of motor-car ownership meant that holidays and days out could be more private, enjoyed by the couple or the young family or the noisy, gregarious group. The domestication of the *un*familiar, by capturing it on film, has remained one of the most important uses of snapshot cameras since Kodak's first appeal to tourists and travellers. A site is not a sight until we've snapped it and made it ours, often by placing a familiar face – whether travelling companion or family member – in an unfamiliar place. Many of Kodak's early advertisements addressed themselves to those who set out in search of the impressive and the educational, but these adult activities take second place to trips and holidays which have become an indispensable element of family pleasures. Sightseeing may be for adults alone, but the centre of Kodak's advertising, from the Kodak girl on the windswept British beach to the sun-saturated images from the Costa del Sol, has been the child-centred family holiday.

In the second half of the century, increasing prosperity, together with the introduction of package tours and the establishment of an energetic tourist industry, meant that overseas holidays have gradually become the norm. But, while personal collections became filled with photos of Mum, Dad and the kids in ever more distant locations, pictures of *home*-based daily life emerged in *commercial* imagery. The expansion of packaged foods and branded goods brought new outlets for visual images which showed what a happily consuming family *should* be like. Commercial photographers studied how to create ever more convincing pictures of appetising food consumed by ecstatic and grateful youngsters and of well-groomed mothers delighting in their newly technologised kitchens. Such images, perfected for advertisements and

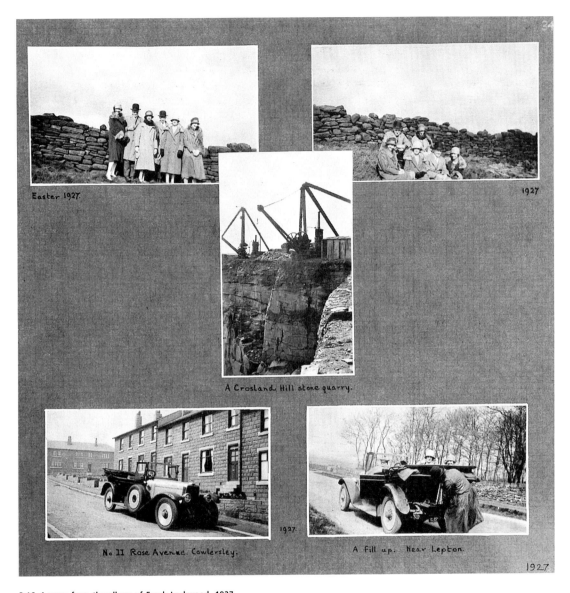

Easter 1927.

1927

A Crosland Hill stone quarry.

No. 11 Rose Avenue. Cowlersley.

1927.

A fill up. Near Lepton.

1927

3.16 A page from the album of Frank Lockwood, 1927
Frank Lockwood was a Birmingham watercolourist and designer for Cadbury Brothers

promotional design, were routinely delivered to the breakfast table on corn-flakes packages and baby food jars, and greeted shoppers with their serried ranks on the shelves of the early supermarkets. The 1960s burst into commercial colour as the burgeoning products for domestic use were promoted by advertising-based supplements to the Sunday papers and an expanding range of consumer magazines which drew on the new, high-quality colour printing techniques (Crawley 1989). The lush photography on their feature pages came to cover every aspect of domestic life – from *Home and Garden* to *Mother and Baby* (Holland 1992). Snapshots and consumer imagery were fast becoming two sides of the same coin.

In 1963 Kodak produced 'a complete new system of snapshot photography' when it brought out its 'Instamatic' series of small reliable cameras (Ford 1989: 141). It was the result of ten years of research which sought to make snapshooting even easier. Cheap colour printing and faster film stocks made it increasingly possible for home photographers to emulate the sophisticated images they were seeing all around them. Snapshot photographs now came in 'bright, beautiful colours and subtle shades – like life', in the words of a Kodak advertisement from 1969. Once more, women were the target purchasers. Unlike the 'male jewellery' of massive lenses and proliferating accessories, the 'Instamatic' removed the technological mystique. Cartridge loading and fixed focus made it so simple that 'even Mum could use it'. Advertisements encouraged a wider range of subject-matter and ever more casual and informal pictures, catching 'the moment as it happens'. Automatic built-in flash meant that colour pictures could be taken indoors, in dull weather or in the rain. 'Memories are made of this', was the slogan. Through hundreds of glowing, full-colour pictures, a couple could now confidently record every precious moment, from the birth of their first baby to their grandchildren and beyond. The last quarter of the twentieth century became the age of the 'supersnap in Kodaland'.

Those are the words of Jennifer Ransom Carter, advertising photographer for Kodak Ltd from 1970 to 1984. She produced many of those joyful images which offer themselves in advertisements and on print wallets for snapshooters to emulate. She 'tried to get pictures which were as close as possible to those that people would have liked to take for themselves'. In Majorca she photographed holiday-makers as well as models. Promotional pictures 'had to have a universal appeal, so that people would say "*I* want to take a picture like that . . .". We aimed to tread a line between reality and unreality as we produced a professional interpretation of the family snap.'[7] And, of course, the pictures people want to keep are those that record the 'happy memories', not the messy reality. It is hardly surprising that family collections include annual pictures of Christmas dinners and birthday teas, but hardly any of the daily meal or the act of peeling the potatoes or washing up. No children's party is complete without snapshots, but crying, bullying or sulky children are definitely not for posterity.

7 Information from conversations with Jennifer Ransom Carter.

As Leonore Davidoff has pointed out, as the family became more inward-looking, it came to contain 'the most immediate experience of love and hate, power and dependence, interpersonal attention and interpersonal violence that most people would experience in their lifetime' (Davidoff in Thompson 1990: 129). It was that gap between the enrichment and proliferation of ideal images of family life and the complexity of its lived reality which led to the damning critiques of the 1970s, particularly from the youthful and energetic women's movement. Unhappy childhoods, broken families, child abuse, disgruntled teenagers and the persistence of poverty are only a few of the all too common experiences *not* recorded in domestic pictures. The family image came to be seen as riven with fractures and contradictions. Divided, individualised, hypocritical, it was argued that 'the family' itself was coming up against its limits.

Many commentators have stressed the cohesive function of family photography, but the increasing use of snapshots to celebrate time out and time off has meant that fun in Kodaland, seeking individual pleasures, may well be at odds with family obligations. A hint of disruption hovers nervously just below the surface of so many personal pictures. Holidays are a time for throwing off constraints, a time of sexual adventure and illicit indulgence, and in the snapshots many such moments are for ever preserved. Pictures of leisure activities increasingly include the **carnivalesque** – cross-dressing for the last-night party, sidling up to the Greek waiter, the club outing when everyone was impossibly drunk, the risqué nude image. Just as Mediterranean food and street cafés have spilled back on to previously drab British streets, the holiday mood of these snapshots remains as a reproach to dutiful lifestyles. Local pubs now cover their walls with beery pictures which verge on the lewd, where skirts are raised, the wrong husbands kiss the wrong wives, and family values are playfully – and sometimes really – put to the test.

PATHS UNHOLY AND DEEDS WITHOUT A NAME?

Twentieth-century contemplations

Giving an account of twentieth-century personal photography is a complex task. Nineteenth-century pictures are beyond living memory. They can be treated on their own terms – as documents, as aesthetic creations or as someone else's story.[8] Twentieth-century pictures are part of our lived experience and hint at meanings which are tantalisingly within our grasp. Almost everyone has their own collection of pictures – sometimes in albums, sometimes organised in packets or drawers, sometimes just scattered around in a disorderly fashion but impossible to throw away. Every collection is different, every example unique. It is no longer enough to outline a social history of such images, since any history must now include interpretations and contextual information brought by their owners and users.[9] These pictures do not stand alone but are enriched by memory, conversation, anecdote and whispered

8 Marianne Hirsch refers to our relationship with pictures of our ancestors as 'postmemory'. This is different from memory, but also different from our reactions to pictures of completely unknown people (Hirsch 1997).

9 At the Documentary Photography Archive, Manchester, curator Audrey Linkman creates a context for the collection of about 70,000 photographs copied from local family albums by supporting them with detailed information about the subject and the photographer.

scandal. They are truly personal because they are part of the accumulated history of people currently alive, who know all too well that memories are not exclusively happy ones. Above all, they include pictures of oneself as a child and at earlier periods of one's life, pictures which carry a burden of significance that only their subjects can comprehend. It is hardly surprising that collections of such photographs hold great personal importance. In an American study of people's 'most cherished objects', many respondents broke down when describing those pictures they felt they could never part with (Csikszentmihalyi and Rochberg-Halton 1992: 68), and yet for writer Teshome Gabriel, a snapshot of himself as a young man, given to him by his mother when he returned to his birthplace in Ethiopia after an absence of thirty-two years, proved to be an 'intolerable gift' (Gabriel 1995). Because photography in all its forms holds the past before our eyes with unprecedented verisimilitude, a sense of the recent past, including one's own, is more vividly present to those now living than to any previous generation. Yet no photograph can give a clear and straightforward insight into the past. Personal photography, as we have seen, has a history of its own which meets up with and overlaps with social history but needs to be explored on its own terms. While many individuals bring to their personal collection the sort of emotional investment shown by those elderly Americans in the 'cherished objects' study, these are their responses as *users* of the images. To make sense of pictures which are not our own, we must change gear to become *readers* of the pictures and engage in a textual and **semiotic** exploration, paying attention to cultural as well as photographic **codes**. As we will see, many writers have argued that one may become a reader of one's own pictures, too; teasing out meanings that go beyond questions of factual memory and emotional response, giving a different sort of understanding to the history they represent.

Possibly the most frequent – and most important – image in anyone's snapshot collection is the simple shot of a subject presenting themselves to the camera, standing, perhaps in front of a famous monument or beside a car or house, but basically just *being there*. Yet this is the least readable of images, depending heavily on knowledge of the subject, on why the picture was taken and on its context. As Stuart Hall pointed out in relation to portraits of black Britons from the 1950s – dressed in their best and presenting themselves with great dignity – such innocence will always be deceptive, subject as it is to pressures from outside the frame (Hall 1991). The calmest portrait may offer evidence of recovery from illness or survival against the odds, and the most conventional of snaps may conceal dreadful abuse (Williams 1994: 31). Discrimination, persecution and social injustice are rarely explicit. 'How will you understand your past when all you have is photographs?' asks Ilan Ziv in his film about memories of the Holocaust.[10]

A rereading and re-viewing of family pictures came with the radical history movements of the 1970s, which brought different ways of understanding

10 *Tango of Slaves* written and directed by Ilan Ziv, TX 31 January 1994, Channel Four Television.

152

history, more sensitive to the type of information carried by everyday documents, including personal snaps. Not only academic historians, but also reminiscence groups, women's groups and local historians, set out to challenge the politics of traditional history writing by looking at the past from a different perspective. There was a desire to write history from below, to listen to ordinary people's accounts and to recapture the texture of ordinary lives. Those who had been hidden from history – women, black people, working-class people and many minorities – insisted on writing their own histories that ran counter to the dominant view of events, and they used personal photographs as part of the process. Arguing that women's stories have been concealed by the conventional ways of recording history, women writers drew on personal pictures to fill those absences. Projects included getting elderly women to recall their times at work, and tracing female ancestors (Grey 1991; Stanley 1991). Radical photographic movements – Camerawork, Hackney Flashers and others – joined in a campaigning attack which took on convention, capitalism and the ideology of the family.

To look back at personal pictures and tease out their meanings has meant that various different approaches to history have been brought into play. First, *community* histories have been recognised; histories of specific groups of many different kinds, say, the working class from the North-east of England or recent immigrants from Bangladesh. Personal photographs expect to be understood within an interpretive community, a group of users who share the same understandings of pictures which record and confirm valued rites of passage and culturally significant moments (Bhabha 1990: 17). Pictures of events such as anniversaries, religious holidays and weddings are symbols of social integration. They have different significations for different cultural groups, who bring an instant recognition to the details by which the meaning of the event 'subtly overwhelms the personal aspect of the picture and fills it with allusions to tribe and ritual' (**Hirsch 1981: 59**).

Even while acknowledging such visible community cues, *family* stories may cut across communal meanings. Julia Hirsch discusses wedding photographs of mixed marriages which must find a way of dealing with two sets of cultural conventions. Family histories often tell of conflict with a community or marginality to it, of migration and mobility across the generations, so that the photographs which accompany family members shift in and out of different contexts of understanding (Solanke 1991). On investigation, many people find that their stories tell of hybridity and cultural mixing. Ursula Kocharian put together an album to show the complex ancestry of her sons, born in Bradford, because 'so many families were uprooted from their countries of origin due to political events'.[11] By 'reading' the pictures, and referring to influences from popular culture, she produced a document in which cultural, political and family changes are displayed. Ursula's husband, Serge, comes from Iran, where his Armenian family fled from the Turkish massacres of 1915. Her own father came from Poland to fight alongside the

JULIA HIRSCH (1981) **Family Photography: Context, Meaning and Effect**, New York: Oxford University Press

11 Information from conversations with Ursula Kocharian.

The influence of Hollywood
even got to Iran in the 1950s
Serge's uncle, Haroot in striking
pose on the right!

Below, Serge's father Samuel
Approx. 1940.
"The adventurer" with rifle
and ammunition. Ready
to go Tiger hunting in
Northern Iran and gold
prospecting.
Didn't get a tiger – or any
gold!

Galipse was, single, educated
and a career woman (Matron
of a large hospital in the
capital Tehran)
How sad that 40 years
after the first picture was
taken she was forced to
wear the Muslim "chador".
after Khomeini's Islamic
revolution.
Even though, in fairness.
they are allowed to remain
Christians (Armenian Orthodox)
They must conform to the
Muslim dress code.

Above and right. Galipse.
Serge's aunt on his mothers
side.
The influence of Wallis Simpson
obviously reached Iran
in the 1940's!

3.17 From the album of Ursula Kocharian

My father (standing, left.) <u>1942</u>
Fighting with the BRITS after
fleeing Poland.

Photo above - one of the many
Army Photos taken by my
father during the war. This
one is the English Cromwell Tanks
1944/45
Afterwards he settled in England
with his Swiss bride and
had Barbara (my sister) in
1951.

And here they are, our children Alex & Joe (both named after
Great Grandfathers) with Serge. Both born in Bradford, W. Yorks
and only here as a result of so many of our family being
uprooted from their countries of origin because of political events.
World War II on my family's side and the 1914 Armenian Massacre
and 1979 Iranian revolution on Serge's

British during the Second World War; his album, which he had published at his own cost, was a record of the Polish regiment's campaigns across Germany. The long pressure of political history, invisible in the simplicity of the family photographs of the two boys, has shaped the family's movements, through wars, revolutions and enforced migration.

Just as family histories fit uneasily with histories of communities, *personal* histories remain part of, yet often at odds with, the histories of families. These three different modes rub up against each other, each one important in its own right, but questioned and often invalidated by the others in a recurring dissonance that frequently underlies discussions of personal photographs.

The more ceremonial the occasion, confirming familial and communal rituals, the more important it is that certain rules are followed in the production of the photographs that mark the event. Weddings must provide pictures of the bride and groom together, dressed in the clothes that make the occasion special. 'We do not care whether it was taken, like so many other ceremonial photographs, the day before the wedding or three hours later; we care only that the man and woman look like bride and groom and uphold the decorum of formal weddings' writes Julia Hirsch (1981: 62). This is one occasion for which a professional photographer (who knows the photographic rules and will abide by them) is usually engaged, for the power of such photographs is precisely in their embrace of convention.

Nevertheless, recognising their role in creating cohesion often goes along with resisting that cohesion at a personal level. Pictures which live up to expectations give enormous pleasure precisely *because* their familiar structure is able to contain the tension between an ideal image and the ambivalence of lived experience. They offer a framework within which understandings of the various realities we inhabit may come into play. While the historian is looking for the truths of the past, the user of a personal collection is engaging in acts of recognition, reconstructing their own past and setting a personal narrative against more public accounts (Walkerdine 1991; Watney 1991; Kuhn 1995).

The work of photographer and writer Jo Spence has shed new light on the construction of complex identities, drawing on personal photographs and family albums for her own, intensely personal work. While family pictures may, on the surface, act as social documents, a closer examination reveals the complex of interrelations and scandals that weave through the soap opera of personal life (Isherwood 1988; Martin 1991; Spence 1991). The placing of divorced spouses, children from a previous marriage, disgraced relatives, gay relationships, even awkward and sulky teenagers, poses problems for those who want their pictures to abide by the conventions. The very hints and puzzles they contain have enticed both detectives of family history and those who want to explore the ways in which their present identity carries the weight of the past. Personal pictures may act as an emotional centre for individual self-exploration. Autobiography, 'memory work' and forms of self-expression

3.18 Jo Spence/Dr Tim Sheard, *Greedy – I recreate my journey into emotional eating, a rebellion against parental disapproval*, 1989 (original in colour)

based on settling accounts with the past have become central to feminist approaches. The disjunction between image and remembered experience, the uncertain borderline between fantasy and memory, the tracing of identity and a sense of self back through one's parents and their sense of *themselves*, the opportunity to relive or re-enact the past – these have all been ways in which family photographs have been used to recapture personal history and make sense of individual lives (Spence 1987; Kuhn 1995).

Jo Spence began by using the snapshots of her childhood to draw attention to the codes of domestic photography. At the age of five, her mother photographed her with her bubble curls and coy smile to look just like Shirley Temple. When she became a teenager she herself took up the pose of the glamorous pin-ups of 1950s cinema. In her exhibition *Beyond the Family Album* at the Hayward Gallery in London in 1979, she offered her awareness of the sickness, shame and struggles of everyday life as a commentary on the conventional smiles of the snapshots themselves. Annette Kuhn has written that they seemed 'conspicuous by their ordinariness . . . but in aggregate the work felt utterly out of the ordinary' (Spence 1995: 20). It contributed to a revaluation of photographic genres, so that snapshots could no longer be ignored as trivial and irrelevant.

Jo Spence went on to explore her childhood experience in her own photographic work. In collaboration with Rosy Martin she staged possible family pictures in a dramatic performance of concealed relationships and submerged emotion. The work developed into a practice she described as a form of therapy, working through traumatic moments and reliving the intensities of childhood usually accessible only through **psychoanalysis** (Spence 1987). Her work was embattled and engaged, determined to explore the taboos and hidden truths which bedevil family histories. She dealt with class, as she reflected on her working-class upbringing and the half-articulated exclusions that implied; she dealt with gender, approaching the world from an uncompromising feminist perspective with a campaigning edge; and she dealt with subjectivity, always 'putting myself in the picture' in a form of 'politicised exhibitionism' (Spence 1987; Spence 1995: 94). Her most striking images represent her struggles with illness as she faced an operation for breast cancer in 1981. In a series of pictures that were also an ironic commentary on the process of photography itself, she asserted her right to define her own body. Ten years later she faced the ultimate taboo with her approaching death from leukaemia, but the project of photography remained with her until the last. In one of the few pictures which show her in the hospice where she died, she is lying to one side of the bed, almost pushed off its edge by the dozens of photographic prints spread across it. Her revelation of inner pain and her dialogue with her own body proved an inspiration for many and gave an impetus to a new generation of women photographers.

Other writers, including Annette Kuhn and Valerie Walkerdine, have also used the snapshots of their childhood to tease out the ways in which personal

3.19 Valerie Walkerdine as the Bluebell Fairy

memory and childhood fantasy overlap, and how both interleave with the social and with popular culture. Such memories are rarely comfortable. Looking at pictures of oneself as a child can be a disturbing experience, recognising in the calm exterior of an image the traces of a turbulent inner world. In a series of articles using the insights of psychoanalysis, Valerie Walkerdine writes of an obsession with sickness, death and incestuous sexuality as she repeatedly re-contextualises a snapshot of herself in carnival dress as the 'Bluebell Fairy': 'Even when the images of myself present me as the feminised object of the male gaze, as a pretty little girl who smiles for the camera, there is a terrible rage underneath' (Walkerdine 1991: 40). Critical work like that of Jo Spence and Valerie Walkerdine lays bare the trauma of an ordinary childhood. Revelations about child abuse and family discord indicate that worse horrors may underlie the aspirational surface of the innocent family snapshot. Family secrecy can give way to family horror story.

Yet late twentieth-century traumas have not only come from within. With the expansion of poverty and the decay of inner city neighbourhoods, the

159

happy memories promised by the Kodak snapshot are a remote possibility for the disaffected youngsters and struggling single parents living on desolate estates that have been abandoned by a shrinking welfare state. The privatised pleasure-loving family is looking increasingly defensive as the gap widens between the comfortably off and the dispossessed. Family images which came to epitomise 1990s Britain were the school photos of the 11-year-old boys who murdered toddler James Bulger, and the fuzzy image from a surveillance camera which failed to prevent that atrocity (Kember 1995).

Despite the privacy of family discourse, the public narratives of community, religion, ethnicity and nation cannot be put aside. As the twentieth century ended, the public media have themselves begun to look back on personal upheavals suffered during those years. Millions now watch television programmes that trace the secret histories of ordinary people, often using their personal snapshots. In the 1990s it became common for hitherto unspoken memories to be given public expression, be they of the repressed sexuality of the early years of the century or of global traumas, like those undergone by survivors of the Holocaust or Hiroshima. Often, such dreadful memories can only be given voice many years after the event, and the pictures treasured by those who tell their story have been used not to remember but to forget.

As Ursula Kocharian's snapshots show, for huge numbers of people migration and dispossession are part of recent history. Journeys always disrupt borders, and more journeys are made from economic pressure or are enforced by war or political rupture than are made purely for pleasure. Where do family albums record the memories of atrocities past? Only in sudden disappearances and truncated lives. Violence is only hinted at in the pictures of 'the old country' kept by immigrants and refugees. Whether from Czechoslovakia, Hungary and Poland, or from Somalia, Sri Lanka or Colombia, the previous generations who seem so composed in their portraits have so often perished in wars or concentration camps. And yet the second generation is often ashamed of its parents: they speak with an accent, their food is different, they cling to the past and their memories are a burden to their children. Their parents look like other people's postcards (Kalogeraki 1991: 40).

Yet, snapshots can be objects which enable the ego to 'bear the difference between now and then',[12] and more comfortable generations are able for the first time to look back at traumas suffered by their relatives. They include middle-aged people like the sole survivor from a cultured Jewish family in Slovakia, who set about making a 'family album' which attempted to piece together obliterated family histories.[13] Andrew Dewdney launched an investigation into hybridity and mixing with a group of teachers and students in Sydney. They were the children of immigrants to Australia from Greece (driven by economic necessity), and Vietnam (driven by war). He himself is from the English port of Bristol, made rich by the slave trade. In

12 Quoted from a lecture given by Mark Cousins at the Architectural Association, London 1994.

13 See also Serge Klarsfeld's meticulous collection of photographs of thousands of Jewish children deported from France, mostly to Auschwitz between 27 March 1942 and 22 August 1944, in *French Children of the Holocaust: A Memorial*, New York: New York University Press, 1997.

the resulting 'extended and shared family albums', the experiences of the native Australians proved as alienating as those first generation white Australians (Dewdney 1991).

Recently, a fascination with the personal has brought family photography into the galleries in new ways. Some photographers have taken the world of inner experience as their subject-matter, often incorporating snapshots or imitating their style (Williams 1994). Others have developed a sort of domestic hyper-realism, seeking out the squalor of everyday life. Notable are Richard Billingham's painful images which relentlessly record, in huge and garishly coloured panels, the apparent chaos of his parents' home. Several women photographers, including Sally Mann and Nancy Honey, have photographed their own children with an intimacy which has aroused criticism for its recognition of the warm sensuousness of childhood. Art historian Anne Higonnet comments that 'mothers know more than they used to' (Higonnet 1998: 197) and argues that a *maternal* view of children and domestic life is for the first time making its appearance (see also Hirsch 1997).

The possibility of a new way of looking opens up exciting possibilities for the re-evaluation of many genres of photography. The work of Sally Mann, in particular, has forced a questioning of easy judgements about the representation of childhood sensuality. However, this is the work of a photographic artist, produced and distributed within a context which is very different from that of the mundane family snapshot. Personal photography remains a minor discourse, a knowledge without authority. Even so we would do well to attend to what it has to tell us. Historians who take note of the details of everyday life and of ordinary people's accounts, feminist writers and photographers, artists of various kinds, are all now making use of personal pictures. The German artist Joachim Schmidt could, perhaps, have the last word. He collects snapshots, millions of them, sent to him from all over the world. His project is to display them in new contexts; sometimes as multiples of images that have an uncanny resemblance to each other, sometimes compared with the work of prestigious photographers. Here are picture faces of someone's old friends, slight but powerful images whose meanings are for ever lost, because their context has been lost. Personal pictures are also about forgetting.

ACKNOWLEDGEMENTS

I should like to thank Sue Isherwood; also Barry Lane, Pam Roberts, Kate Rousse and Debbie Ireland at the Royal Photographic Society; Guillermo Marin and Arthur Lockwood for bringing me albums and other material; and Arthur for his help in rephotographing the albums; Jenny Ransom for discussing her work at Kodak; Marian and Jeanette Covington, Paula Fascht and Ursula Kocharian for lending me their photographs and discussing their family histories with me, and many other people who showed and lent me personal pictures.

BIBLIOGRAPHY

KEY TEXTS

Barthes, R. (1982) *Camera Lucida*, London: Jonathan Cape

Coe, B. and Gates, P. (1977) *The Snapshot Photograph: The Rise of Popular Photography 1888–1939*, London: Ash and Grant

Ford, C. (1989) *The Story of Popular Photography*, Bradford: Century Hutchinson Ltd/National Museum of Photography, Film and Television

Hirsch, J. (1981) *Family Photography: Context, Meaning and Effect*, New York: Oxford University Press

Isherwood, S. (1988) *The Family Album*, London: Broadcasting Support Services

Kenyon, D. (1992) *Inside Amateur Photography*, London: Batsford

Linkman, A. (1993) *The Victorians: Photographic Portraits*, London: Tauris Parke Books

Linkman, A. and Warhurst, C. (1982) *Family Albums*, Manchester: Manchester Polytechnic. A fully illustrated exhibition catalogue with an introduction

Parr, M. and Stasiak, J. (1986) *'The Actual Boot': The Photographic Post-card Boom 1900–1920*, Bradford: A.H. Jolly (Editorial) Ltd/National Museum of Photography, Film and Television. Exhibition catalogue and introduction

Slater, D. (1983) 'Marketing Mass Photography' in H. Davis and P. Walton (eds) *Language, Image, Media*, Oxford: Blackwell

Spence, J. (1987) *Putting Myself in the Picture*, London: Camden Press

—— (1995) *Cultural Sniping*, London: Routledge

Spence, J. and Holland, P. (eds) (1991) *Family Snaps: The Meanings of Domestic Photography*, London: Virago

Tagg, J. (1988) *The Burden of Representation: Essays on Photographies and Histories*, London: Macmillan, especially chapter 1, 'A Democracy of the Image: Photographic Portraiture and Commodity Production'

Taylor, J. (1994) *A Dream of England: Landscape, Photography and the Tourist's Imagination*, Manchester: Manchester University Press

Thompson, F.M.L. (ed.) (1990) *The Cambridge Social History of Britain 1750–1850*, Vol. 2, *People and Their Environment*, Cambridge: Cambridge University Press

Williams, V. (1986) *Women Photographers. The Other Observers 1900 to the Present*, London: Virago (Revised edition 1991, *The Other Observers: Women Photographers from 1900 to the Present*.)

OTHER REFERENCES

Barrett, M. and McIntosh, M. (1982) *The Anti-Social Family*, London: Verso

Bede, C. (1855) *Photographic Pleasures*, London

Bernstein, B. (1971) *Class, Codes and Control*, Vol. 1, *Theoretical Studies Towards a Sociology of Language*, London: Routledge & Kegan Paul

Bhabha, H. (1990) 'Novel Metropolis', *New Statesman and Society*, 9 February

Bourdieu, P. (1965/1990) *Photography: A Middle Brow Art*, London: Polity Press

Burgin, V. (1982) *Thinking Photography*, London: Macmillan

Chanan, M. (1996) *The Dream That Kicks*, London: Routledge

Coe, B. (1989) 'Roll Film Revolution' in C. Ford (ed.) *The Story of Popular Photography*, Bradford: Century Hutchinson Ltd/National Museum of Photography, Film and Television

Crawley, G. (1989) 'Colour Comes to All' in C. Ford (ed.) *The Story of Popular Photography*, Bradford: Century Hutchinson Ltd/National Museum of Photography, Film and Television

Csikszentmihalyi, M. and Rochberg-Halton, E. (1992) *The Meaning of Things: Domestic Symbols and the Self*, Cambridge: Cambridge University Press

Davidoff, L. and Hall, C. (1976) 'The Charmed Circle of Home' in J. Mitchell and A. Oakley
  (eds) *The Rights and Wrongs of Women*, Harmondsworth: Penguin
Dewdney, A. (1991) 'More Than Black and White: The Extended and Shared Family Album' in
  J. Spence and P. Holland (eds) *Family Snaps: The Meanings of Domestic Photography*,
  London: Virago
Drake, M. and Finnegan, R. (eds) (1994) *Studying Family and Community History: 19th and
  20th Centuries*, Vol. 4, *Sources and Methods: A Handbook*, Cambridge: Cambridge
  University Press/Open University
Eco, U. (1979) *The Role of The Reader: Explorations in the Semiotics of Texts*, London:
  Hutchinson
Felman, S. and Laub, D. (1992) *Testimony: Crises of Witnessing in Literature, Psychoanalysis
  and History*, London: Routledge
Gabriel, T. (1995) *The Intolerable Gift*, unpublished conference paper, London: BFI
Geraghty, C. (1991) *Women and Soap Opera: A Study of Prime Time Soaps*, Cambridge:
  Polity Press
Grey, C. (1991) 'Theories of Relativity' in J. Spence and P. Holland (eds) *Family Snaps: The
  Meanings of Domestic Photography*, London: Virago
Gupta, S. (ed.) (1993) *Disrupted Borders: An Intervention in Definitions of Boundaries*,
  London: Rivers Oram Press
Hall, C. (1979) 'Early Formation of Victorian Domestic Ideology' in S. Burman (ed.) *Fit Work
  for Women*, London: Croom Helm
Hall, S. (1991) 'Reconstruction Work: Images of Post-War Black Settlement' in J. Spence and
  P. Holland (eds) *Family Snaps: The Meanings of Domestic Photography*, London: Virago
Hannavy, J. (1975) *Roger Fenton of Crimble Hall*, London: Gordon Frazer
Higonnet, A. (1998) *Pictures of Innocence: The History and Crisis of Ideal Childhood*,
  London: Thames and Hudson
Hiley, M. (1983) *Seeing Through Photographs*, London: Gordon Frazer
Hirsch, M. (1997) *Family Frames: Photography, Narrative and Postmemory*, Cambridge, MA:
  Harvard University Press
Holland, P. (1991) 'The Old Order of Things Changed' in J. Spence and P. Holland (eds) *Family
  Snaps: The Meanings of Domestic Photography*, London: Virago
—— (1992) *What is a Child?*, London: Virago
—— (1997) '"The direct appeal to the eye?" Photography and the Twentieth Century Press' in
  A. Briggs and P. Cobley (eds) *The Media: an Introduction*, Harlow: Longman
Holland, P. and Dewdney, A. (eds) (1992) *The Child, Seen but Not Heard?*, Bristol: Watershed
  Media Centre. Exhibition catalogue and introduction
Kalogeraki, K. (1991) 'My Father's Land' in J. Spence and P. Holland (eds) *Family Snaps: The
  Meanings of Domestic Photography*, London: Virago
Kember, S. (1995) 'Surveillance, Technology and Crime: The James Bulger Case' in M. Lister
  (ed.) *The Photographic Image in Digital Culture*, London: Routledge
Kuhn, A. (1991) 'Remembrance' in J. Spence and P. Holland (eds) *Family Snaps: The Meanings
  of Domestic Photography*, London: Virago
—— (1995) *Family Secrets: Acts of Memory and Imagination*, London: Verso
Lemagny, J-C. and Rouille, A. (1987) *A History of Photography*, Cambridge: Cambridge
  University Press
Lewis, B. and Harding, D. (eds) (1992) *Kept in a Shoebox: The Experience of Popular
  Photography*, Bradford: Yorkshire Art Circus/National Museum of Photography, Film and
  Television
Macdonald, G. (1979) *Camera: A Victorian Eyewitness*, London: Batsford; based on a Granada
  television series
Mann, S. (1992) *Immediate Family*, London: Phaidon
Martin, R. (1991) 'Unwind the Ties That Bind' in J. Spence and P. Holland (eds) *Family Snaps:
  The Meanings of Domestic Photography*, London: Virago

Mavor, C. (1996) *Pleasures Taken: Performances of Sexuality and Loss in Victorian Photographs*, London: I.B. Taurus

Musello, C. (1979) 'Family Photography' in J. Wagner (ed.) *Images of Information*, London: Sage

Penlake, R. (1899) *Home Portraits for Amateur Photographers*, London

Pryce, W.T.R. (1994) 'Photographs and Picture Postcards' in M. Drake and R. Finnegan (eds) *Studying Family and Community History: 19th and 20th Centuries*, Vol. 4, *Sources and Methods: A Handbook*, Cambridge: Cambridge University Press/Open University

Robertson, G., Mash, M., Tickner, L., Bird, J., Curtis, B. and Putnam, T. (eds) (1994) *Travellers' Tales: Narratives of Home and Displacement*, London: Routledge

Scharf, A. (1974) *Art and Photography*, Harmondsworth: Pelican

Slater, D. (1991) 'Consuming Kodak' in J. Spence and P. Holland (eds) *Family Snaps: The Meanings of Domestic Photography*, London: Virago

—— (1995a) 'Photography and Modern Vision: The Spectacle of "Natural Magic"' in C. Jenks (ed.) *Visual Culture*, London: Routledge

—— (1995b) 'Domestic Photography and Digital Culture' in M. Lister (ed.) *The Photographic Image in Digital Culture*, London: Routledge

Solanke, A. (1991) 'Complex Not Confused' in J. Spence and P. Holland (eds) *Family Snaps: The Meanings of Domestic Photography*, London: Virago

Soloman, J. (1995) 'Interrogating the Holiday Snap' in J. Spence and J. Soloman, *What Can a Woman do with a Camera?*, London: Scarlet Press

Sontag, S. (1978) *On Photography*, Harmondsworth: Penguin

Spence, J. (1991) 'Soap, Family Album Work . . . and Hope' in J. Spence and P. Holland (eds) *Family Snaps: The Meanings of Domestic Photography*, London: Virago

Spence, J. and Soloman, J. (eds) (1995) *What Can a Woman do with a Camera?*, London: Scarlet Press

Stanley, J. (1991) 'Well, Who'd Want an Old Picture of me at Work?' in J. Spence and P. Holland (eds) *Family Snaps: The Meanings of Domestic Photography*, London: Virago

Urry, J. (1990) *The Tourist Gaze: Leisure and Travel in Contemporary Societies*, London: Sage

Walkerdine, V. (1991) 'Behind the Painted Smile' in J. Spence and P. Holland (eds) *Family Snaps: The Meanings of Domestic Photography*, London: Virago

Warner, M. (1992) 'Women in the Victorian Family Album', *Creative Camera*, May

Watney, S. (1991) 'Ordinary Boys' in J. Spence and P. Holland (eds) *Family Snaps: The Meanings of Domestic Photography*, London: Virago

Werge, J. (1890) *The Evolution of Photography*, London

Williams, V. (1994) *Who's Looking at the Family?*, London: Barbican Art Gallery. Exhibition catalogue and introduction

CHAPTER 4

Constructions of illusion

Photography and commodity culture

ANANDI RAMAMURTHY

4.1 Victor Burgin, What does Possession mean to you?, 1974

Constructions of illusion

Photography and commodity culture

INTRODUCTION

The photograph as commodity

In the late twentieth century, commodity relations rule our lives to such an extent that we are often unaware of them as a specific set of historical, social and economic relations which human beings have constructed. Like any cultural and technical development, the development of photography has been influenced by its social and economic context. The photograph is both a cultural tool which has been commodified as well as a tool that has been used to express **commodity culture** through advertisements and other marketing material.

John Tagg has described the development of photography as 'a model of capitalist growth in the nineteenth century' (**Tagg 1988: 37**). The rise of commodity culture in the nineteenth century was a key influence on the way in which this technology was developed and used. The way in which photographic genres were affected by capitalism is illustrated in Tagg's essay on the demand for photographic portraits in the nineteenth century by the rising middle and lower-middle classes, keen for objects symbolic of high social status. The photographic portraits were affordable in price, yet were reminiscent of aristocratic social ascendancy signified by 'having one's portrait done'. Tagg describes how the **daguerreotype** and later the *carte-de-visite* established an industry that had a vast clientele and was ruled by this clientele's

JOHN TAGG (1988) 'A Democracy of the Image: Photographic Portraiture and Commodity Production' in **The Burden of Representation: Essays on Photographies and Histories**, Basingstoke: Macmillan

daguerreotype Photographic image made by the process launched by Louis-Jacques-Mandé Daguerre in France in 1839. It is a positive image on a metal plate with a mirror-like silvered surface, characterised by very fine detail. Each one is unique and fragile and needs to be protected by a padded case. It became the dominant portrait mode for the first decades of photography, especially in the United States.

carte-de-visite A small paper print (2½ × 4⅛") mounted on a card with the photographer's details on the reverse. This way of producing photographs for sale was developed by André-Adolphe Disdéri in France in 1854. Eight or more images were made on the same glass negative by a special camera with several lenses and a moving plate-holder. The prints were then cut up to size. Such prints could be produced in very large numbers.

ELIZABETH ANNE McCAULEY (1994) **Industrial Madness: Commercial Photography in Paris 1848–1871**, New Haven, CT, and London: Yale University Press

DON SLATER (1983) 'Marketing Mass Photography' in P. Davis and H. Walton (eds) **Language, Image, Media**, Oxford: Blackwell

'taste and acceptance of the conventional devices and genres of official art' (Tagg 1988: 50). The commodification of the photograph dulled the possible creativity of the new technology, by the desire to reproduce a set of conventions already established within painted portraiture. It was not, however, simply the perspectives and desires of the clients visiting photographic studios that encouraged the adherence to convention, but also the attempt, as McCauley has highlighted in her study of mid-nineteenth-century commercial photography in Paris, of the small business owners of these photographic studios both to establish themselves as part of a bourgeois class, as well as to assert the claim of photography as a highbrow art (**McCauley 1994**).

If we look at other photographic genres, we can also observe the way in which commodity culture has affected their development. Photojournalism for instance, like other journalism, is primarily concerned with the selling of newspapers, rather than the conveyance of 'news'. By the 1930s all commercial newspapers had begun to see the power of photography to captivate their readers' attention. The establishment of publications such as *Life* magazine in America and *Picture Post* in Britain saw the photographic image begin to command what was to be considered newsworthy and what was not. Newsworthiness usually meant the production of dramatic images which encouraged a kind of sensationalism that Susan Sontag has described as the production of 'spectacle' in photographic journalism – a spectacle that encouraged the sale of newspapers (Sontag 1979). Just as photographic genres have been affected by commerce, so has the development of photographic technology. The 'Instamatic' for instance was clearly developed in order to expand camera use and camera ownership. In turn, this technology limited the kind of photographs people could take (**Slater 1983**).

Were this chapter to discuss the commodification of photography in detail, it would be difficult to limit it, and it would most likely encroach on the subject area of every chapter in this book. Therefore this chapter will concentrate on the way photography has been used in representing commodity culture. In this sense, it will be as much about the decoding of visual commercial messages as about photography. Although the focus is on the specific qualities of photography in the production of commercial messages, photography forms part of a broader system of visual communication including painting, printing, as well as the broadcast media.

Photographs to represent commodity culture

One of the first instances suggesting the power of photography for advertisers dates back to the mid-nineteenth century, when the photographer Disdéri wrote an article offering 'indispensable advice' to exhibitors in the 1855 *Exposition Universelle* in Paris, emphasising the speed, exactitude and economy of photographic reproductions and suggesting 'wouldn't the propagation of a model of furniture appreciated by all the visitors to the exposition attract numerous orders to the manufacturer?' (McCauley 1994: 196). It is clear that as forms of mass production began to develop, the photograph, which constituted one of these forms, was also seen as a medium through which these commodities could be popularised and marketed. In this sense, from the very beginning, photographs were employed to induce desire and promote commodity culture.

The range of contexts within which photographs have been used to sell products or services is so enormous that we are almost unaware of the medium of photography and the language which has been created to convey commercial messages. Photographs for commerce appear on everything from the glossy, high-quality billboard and magazine advertisements to small, cheap flyers on estate agents' blurbs. Between these two areas there is a breadth of usage, including the mundane images in mail-order information and catalogues, the seemingly matter-of-fact but high-quality documentary-style images of company annual reports, the varied quality of commodity packaging, and of course the photography on marketing materials such as calendars, produced by companies to enhance their status. Within the traditional histories of photography, commercial photography has largely been ignored, despite the fact that photography produced for advertising and marketing constitutes the largest quantity of photographic production. While there are a number of critiques on advertising imagery, these tend not to be concerned with the photograph in particular. Other areas of commercial photographic production have received relatively no critical attention from scholars. Much of the history or literature that has been written has tended to be commissioned by the companies themselves or their associates, such as *Thirsty Work: Ten Years of Heineken Advertising* and *Some Examples of Benson Advertising*. These publications have also been unconcerned with the photographic aspect.

One possible reason for the lack of documentation and history-writing in this area is that commercial photography, for the most part, has not sought to stretch the medium of photography, since one of the key characteristics of photography within advertising and marketing is its parasitism. Advertising photography cannot be seen to constitute any kind of photographic genre; rather, it borrows and mimics from every existing genre of photographic and cultural practice to enhance and alter the meaning of lifeless objects – commodities. The way in which advertising photography borrows from other photographic genres in order to sell commodities can be seen from the beginning of the rise in advertising photography. It was during the inter-war years that photographs began to be generally employed within the advertising industry. This was partly due to the increased production of illustrated papers during the period, but also due to the development of a visually literate British public during the 1930s, the result of the dissemination of photography through the illustrated newspaper. As George Mewes of Photographic Advertising Limited (a studio which operated from 1926 to the late 1960s) wrote,

> now, the leading London dailies devote whole pages to photography, while the Sunday and Provincial press freely scatter photographs

throughout their editorial columns. Photographic news brought photographic advertising and a public that had been educated to visualise the world's events soon began to visualise its own needs.

(Quoted in Wilkinson 1997: 28)

Advertising photography, as photography curator Helen Wilkinson notes, began to appropriate first, journalistic methods of a seemingly 'realistic' style as well as the conveyance of narrative through a combination of image and text; and second, commercial cinematic conventions. For example, deep shadows to convey emotions were employed along with the close-up for a more naturalistic style of portraiture, which still retained an element of glamour. Some of the cinematic conventions of photography can be seen in stock photography sheets belonging to Photographic Advertising Ltd. One sheet represents head-and-shoulder portraits of women (figure 4.2). All the women have been shot in dramatic studio lighting and wear make-up, conventions which adhere to an image of cinematic glamour. All are photographed in a relatively relaxed manner and seem to reflect moments within a narrative. Some of the women are even involved in mundane activities like eating and drinking, actions which would not have been recorded in conventional portraiture. Thus they all appear to have a degree of naturalism which could be misconstrued as 'realism' despite their obvious glamour. The relationship between glamour and naturalism is a key aspect of 1930s advertising photography, as Wilkinson describes in relation to a 1930s Horlicks advertisement which depicts a close-up shot of a glamorous and attractive woman in a relaxed image of Horlicks-induced sleep. The degree of naturalism allowed the ordinary consumer to identify with the model and, combined with an image of glamour, provided a route to encourage desire that was transmuted to the product through the advertisement.

Glamorising mundane activities and commodities is part of the process through which photography has helped to imbue products with meanings and characteristics to which the commodity has no relationship. As Karl Marx noted, commodities are objects – usually inert – that have been imbued with all kinds of social characteristics in the marketplace. Marx called this process the fetishism of commodities, since in the marketplace (which means every place where things have been bought and sold) the social character of people's labour was no longer apparent, and it was the products of their labour instead that interacted and were prominent. Advertising images act to further fetishise commodities by investing products with what Marxists have described as false meanings. Whether we wish to describe these meanings as false or not, they are meanings that promote the culture of capitalism (see Williams 1980; Richards 1990). As Robert Goldman remarked in a study of 1980s advertising imagery: 'ads offer a unique window for observing how commodity interests conceptualise social relations' (**Goldman 1992: 2**). The representation of social relations in advertising has also been discussed

ROBERT GOLDMAN (1992)
Reading Ads Socially,
London: Routledge

4.2 Stock sheet W1910783 from the Photographic Advertising Ltd archive in other texts on the history and study of advertising (Leiss *et al.* 1986; Myers 1986).

ROLAND BARTHES (1977a) 'The Rhetoric of the Image' in **Image, Music, Text**, London: Fontana

JUDITH WILLIAMSON (1978) **Decoding Advertisements: Ideology and Meaning in Advertising**, London: Marion Boyars

The role of photographs in the production of signs that have fetishised commodities and represented commodity culture as natural and eternal became an increasing concern to scholars from the late 1950s onwards. Through a **semiological** analysis of commercial imagery, Barthes and others have suggested ways in which we can understand the role of photographs in the making and maintenance of **ideologies** and the hegemony of commodity culture (**Barthes 1973**; **Barthes 1977a**; **Williamson 1978**).

THE GRAMMAR OF THE AD

CASE STUDY: The commodification of human relations and experience – 'Omega and Cindy: time together'

The advertisement for Omega watches in the February 1999 issue of *Elle* magazine uses a traditional image of an attractive and glamorous woman – here Cindy Crawford – wearing an Omega watch.[1] Cindy is photographed in a surprisingly similar way to the women in the 1930s stock photography sheet discussed above, and indicates the endurance of this kind of glamour-girl image within commercial photography. Like many of the 1930s glamour girls, she is photographed isolated from any specific location, with heavy make-up, looking engagingly out at the viewer, with a half-open mouth suggesting sexual availability. She, like the 1930s girls, also appears in a relatively relaxed, candid pose. There are of course differences between the 1930s and late twentieth-century interpretations of the glamour girl. Cindy's loose hair and sporty tank top are used to suggest a late twentieth-century femininity which is supposedly more liberated. Although there are similarities between the stock photography sheets and the Omega image, we know that Cindy's photograph was taken specifically for this advertisement, not only because a supermodel has given her name to a product, but also because Cindy is depicted leaning her chin on her right arm on which she wears an Omega watch. The watch is given enormous focus in the image through its central position and its location next to Cindy's open mouth. The image of sensual desire which Cindy exudes is thereby transferred to desire for the watch. The notion of the watch carrying human characteristics is further encouraged through the text below, which reads 'Omega and Cindy: time together'. It is as though the watch is a human being with a personality with whom we can have a relationship. This feeling is further encouraged by the subsequent three pages of the ad, which present a diary of Cindy's day with Omega. Each page is captioned with a quotation from a classic text – Horace, K. Gibran, Keats – which suggests that the relationship and the watch are both as stimulating and enduring as the literature.

In advertising, photography and montage play a crucial role in the production of meaning and the commodification of human relations and experience.

1 Unfortunately it has not proved possible to get permission to reproduce this, or any other similar advertisement featuring a well-known actress or model.

Here, the juxtaposition of text and image, and the construction of the photograph, transmutes our desire for human relationships into a relationship between a person and a thing. This is represented as both attractive and satisfying. The commodification of human emotions and relation... ...most pervasive influences of modern advertising... ...our cultural associations with Cind... ...has proved herself to... ...and charity work are... ...has endured as a mod... ...tionship' it can pro... montage and the p... process, which when... these surface meaning... through manufacture... How much were the fa... paid? Were they allow... conditions like for the... these watches? Advertis... meanings of which are en... in which it appears natura... tion. These constructed m... accurately portray social rel... ...92: 35).

[handwritten note: when explaining the perfume adverts.]

The photographic message

In unravelling the meanings of images, Roland Barthes and others have tried to find systems which could be applied to help decode any photographic message. In his essay 'The Photographic Message', Barthes described photographs as containing both a denoted and a connoted message (**Barthes 1977b**). By the denoted message Barthes meant the literal reality which the photograph portrayed. In the case of the ad for Omega, this would be the image of Cindy Crawford wearing a watch (see case study). The second message, the connoted message, is one which he described as making use of social and cultural references. The connoted message is the inferred message. It is symbolic. It is a message with a code – i.e. Cindy Crawford signifies enduring beauty and glamour. When we look at documentary photography, the denoted image appears dominant. We believe the photograph to be 'fact', although, as Tagg has pointed out, it is impossible to have a simple 'denoted' message – all messages are 'constructed' (Tagg 1988: 1–5). The image for use in advertising, however, is different. We know from the start that it is highly structured. In the discussion on the Omega ad, I have already mentioned how the codes of glamour photography are employed in the image, as well as how the structuring of the watch in line with Cindy's mouth suggests a symbolic desire for Omega watches. The commercial

ROLAND BARTHES (1977b) 'The Photographic Image' in S. Heath (ed.) **Image, Music, Text**, London: Fontana photograph is therefore not perceived as primarily documenting real life. In this sense we are unconsciously aware when reading the image that the connoted message is the crucial one.

In trying to find systems for reading images, many scholars have adopted semiological methods first used in linguistics to decode visual signs:

> A sign is quite simply a thing -whether object, word or thing – which has a particular meaning to a person or group of people. It is neither the thing nor the meaning alone, but the two together. The sign consists of the signifier, the material object, and the signified, which is its meaning. These are only divided for analytical purposes; in practice a sign is always thing-plus-meaning.
>
> (Williamson 1978: 17)

If we use this system to analyse the Omega watch ad, we can read Cindy Crawford as a signifier of glamour and beauty which is the meaning signified. There are also many other signifiers in the image, for example, the black and white photograph, Cindy's half-open mouth, her loose hair and tank top, which all combine to signify a specific kind of femininity, glamour and beauty.

So what does the watch signify? To disentangle its meanings in the advertisement, it is useful to consider Roland Barthes' notion of a second-order semiological system, which he asserts exists in all ideological texts. In the second-order semiological system, the sign from the first level of signification becomes the signifier of the second level. In the ad for Omega, therefore, Cindy Crawford as a sign of enduring beauty and glamour acts as a signifier of Omega. The human characteristics of Cindy are interpreted as characteristics of an Omega watch. Second, the signifier of Cindy wearing an Omega watch in the context of the statement 'Cindy and Omega: time together' acts to signify an enduring and glamorous relationship. Barthes perceives this second level of signification as a form of myth, since in this second level of signification the production of ideology is paramount (Barthes 1973). In the case of advertisements such as this one it emphasises the ideological power of ads to commodify human relations.

In understanding the transfer of meaning between signs in an image, Judith Williamson and, later, Robert Goldman have suggested that the formal structure of an ad is significant (Williamson 1978: 24–26; Goldman 1992: 61–85). In one of the most widely adopted conventions of commodity advertising, an illustrative image of the product is montaged on to what could be described as the main mood image of the advertisement. Through this juxtaposition we are encouraged to transfer meaning. This convention is still applied in the Omega ad, although in a more sophisticated way. Cindy actually wears the watch, but the watch is photographed clearly and in hard focus – similar to most illustrative insets. The convention of montage is even more apparent on the subsequent diary pages of the advertisement, where the watch is highlighted from the rest of the black and white mood photograph by being in colour.

Apart from drawing our attention to the way in which formal structures create meaning, Judith Williamson also made an important point about the active involvement of the viewer in the production of meanings. She describes the viewer's role in producing meaning as 'advertising work' (Williamson 1978: 15–19). In describing this process, Williamson wished to emphasise our involvement in the maintenance and production of ideology. Later critics have also emphasised the way in which viewers interpret advertisements differently, depending on their experiences and cultural knowledge.

The transfer of meaning

In his essay 'Encoding/Decoding', Stuart Hall considered our involvement in the production of meaning (Hall 1993). He discusses how images are first 'encoded' by the producer, and then 'decoded' by the viewer. The transfer of meaning in this process only works if there are compatible systems of signs and symbols which the encoder and decoder use within their cultural life. Our background – i.e. our gender, class, ethnic origin, sexuality, religion, etc. – all affect our interpretation of signs and symbols. Our relationship and understanding of various forms of photography are part of those signs and symbols. Hall points to the fact that messages are not always read as they were intended, because our various cultural backgrounds lead to different interpretations. He suggests that there are three possible readings of an image: a dominant or preferred reading, a negotiated reading, and an oppositional reading. The dominant reading would comply with the meaning intended by the producer of the image. The importance of readers interpreting images as they were intended is obviously crucial for commercial messages, and is one of the reasons why advertisers use text and montage to restrict the ways in which we may interpret their images. Hall describes the negotiated reading as one which only partly conforms to the intended, dominant meaning. Finally the oppositional reading is one which is in total conflict with the meaning intended by the image-producer. Examples of ordinary people producing oppositional readings through graffiti have been collected by Jill Posner in *Spray it Loud* (Posner 1982). In *Reading Ads Socially*, Robert Goldman cites an example of a cigarette advertisement which was misinterpreted by many readers to create an oppositional meaning. In 1986, Kent cigarettes launched an ad campaign which depicted two people flying a kite on a page. In order to involve the viewer in the advertisement, the advertiser emptied the figures of content so that readers could literally place themselves in the ad. Viewers, however, interpreted the silhouetted figures as ghosts because of the health warnings about smoking to which we have become accustomed (Goldman 1992: 80–81). The question of reception brings into doubt the notion of global advertising which companies such as Coca-Cola and Benetton have tried to create. Can there really be worldwide advertising campaigns? People across the world will surely find different symbolic meanings in the same signifiers.

The creation of meaning through context and photographic styles

All photographs will be viewed by different people in different ways, whether in commercial contexts or not. The same photograph can also mean different things in different contexts. The commercial context, for example, can change the meaning of an image, just as different styles of photography will carry different messages. Let us look at an advertisement which does not use a style of photography normally associated with advertising. Because advertisers have traditionally been concerned with creating glamorous, fantasy worlds of desire for their products, they have tended to shy away from the stark, grainy, black and white type of imagery traditionally associated with documentary images and photojournalism and have gone instead for glossy, high-colour photography. Yet, at times of company crisis, or when companies have wanted to deliberately foster an image of no-nonsense frankness, they have used black and white imagery. In 1990, a short while after Nelson Mandela was released from gaol by the South African authorities, the Anglo-American Corporation of South Africa brought out an advertisement entitled 'Do we sometimes wish we had not fought to have Black trade unions recognised?' Underneath this title was a documentary photograph of a Black South African miner, in a show of victory (figure 4.3). At a moment when Anglo-American foresaw massive economic and political change, they attempted to distance themselves from the apartheid regime. Yet Anglo-American was by far the largest company in South Africa, 'with a near total grip over large sectors of the apartheid economy'.[2] While presenting this advertisement to the public, De Beers – Anglo's sister company, in which they had a 35 per cent stake – also cancelled their recognition agreement with the NUM at the Premier Diamond Mines, despite 90 per cent of workers belonging to the union. The frank and honest style of address which black and white provided hid the reality for black workers in South Africa. The miner depicted was in fact celebrating his victory against Anglo-American in 1987. Here, at another moment of crisis, Anglo-American have appropriated this image of resistance. The parasitism of advertising enables it to use and discard any style and content for its own ends. Anglo-American are no longer interested in fostering this image (they declined permission to have the advertisement reproduced here). There is an added irony in Anglo-American's use of this image, since it is not strictly speaking a documentary image at all, but a montage of two images used to capture the mood of the strike as the *Independent* saw it.

Black and white imagery has been used in other company contexts at moments of crisis. Carol Squiers has discussed the way in which they have been used in annual reports. Black and white, she notes, 'looks more modest

2 As stated in anti-Apartheid campaign literature of the time

4.3 South African miners demonstrating outside the offices of the organisation of South African mine owners. *Independent*, 26 August 1987

This photograph was used, torn from the newspaper page as it is here, by the Anglo-American Corporation of South Africa in their advertisement DO WE SOMETIMES WISH WE HAD NOT FOUGHT TO HAVE BLACK TRADE UNIONS RECOGNISED?, published in the *Guardian*, 2 April 1990

and costs less to print'. As Arnold Saks, a corporate designer, said: 'There's an honesty about black and white, a reality. . . . Black and white is the only reality' (**Squiers 1992: 208**).

Apart from specific ways in which certain forms of black and white photography have been used to signify specific characteristics of a company, advertisements that have tried to encourage the idea of rational consumer choice have adopted a kind of factual illustrative photography, which suggests an attention to scientific detail. An advertisement for Halfords children's bikes uses this kind of image to emphasise the inappropriateness of other manufacturers' children's handlebars. It is an interesting advertisement since the photograph does not actually represent their product, but a design fault in their rivals'. The advertisement also highlights the way in which the text of advertisements is crucial in anchoring their meaning (figure 4.4). Angela

CAROL SQUIERS 'The Corporate Year in Pictures' in R. Bolton (ed.) **The Contest of Meaning: Critical Histories of Photography**, Cambridge, MA: MIT Press

177

To appreciate Halfords adjustable brake levers, put your child's hand on this page.

This is the hand grip and brake lever of a child's bike, shown actual size.

According to the retailers, the bike is suitable for children as young as 4 years old.

The retailers, we hasten to add, are not Halfords.

Because all Halfords children's bikes are fitted with adjustable brake levers.

By turning a simple screw, you can adjust the reach of the brake levers to suit your child's hands.

As our picture demonstrates, not all children's bikes are made this way.

Which means not all children will be able to reach the brakes.

And if there's one thing more important than learning how to ride a bike, it's learning how to stop one.

HALFORDS WE GO THE EXTRA MILE.

4.4 Halfords children's bikes, *The Times Magazine*, 7 November 1998

Goddard discusses the way in which texts frame meanings in her recent book *The Language of Advertising* (Goddard 1998).

The symbolic value of using or not using a photograph has also been important for advertisers. Kathy Myers has explored the moments when advertisers have chosen to use and not use photographic images in an attempt to find symbols of ecological awareness (**Myers 1990**).

KATHY MYERS (1990) 'Selling Green' in C. Squiers (ed.) **The Critical Image: Essays on Contemporary Photography**, Seattle: Bay Press

178

HEGEMONY IN PHOTOGRAPHIC REPRESENTATION

Commercial photography constantly borrows ideas and images from the wider cultural domain. It is clear that when we point the camera we frame it in a thousand and one ways through our own cultural conditioning. Photographs, like other cultural products, have therefore tended to perpetuate ideas which are dominant in society. Commercial photographs, because of their profuse nature and because they have never sought to challenge the status quo within society (since they are only produced to sell products), have also aided in the construction and perpetuation of stereotypes, to the point at which they have appeared natural and eternal (see Barthes 1977a; Williamson 1978, part 2). Through commercial photography we can therefore explore hegemonic constructs of, for example, race, gender and class.

Photomontage – concealing social relations

One of the key ways in which commercial photography has sought to determine particular readings of images and products has been through **photomontage**. Advertisements are in fact simple photomontages produced for commercial purposes, although most books on the technique seem to ignore this expansive area. While socialist photographers like Heartfield use photomontage to make invisible social relations visible,[3] advertisers have used montage to conceal 'reality'. One of the peculiar advantages of photomontage, as John Berger wrote in his essay 'The Political Uses of Photomontage', is the fact that 'everything which has been cut out keeps its familiar photographic appearance. We are still looking first at things and only afterwards at symbols' (Berger 1972b: 185). This creates a sense of naturalness about an image or message which is in fact constructed. An early example of the photomontage naturalising social relations has been discussed by Sally Stein, who considers 'the reception of photography within the larger matrix of socially organised communication', and looks at the rise of Taylor's ideas of 'scientific management' in the factory, and the way these ideas were also applied to domestic work (**Stein 1981: 42–44**). She also notes how expensive it was to have photomechanical reproductions within a book in the early part of the century.

Yet in Mrs Christine Frederick's 1913 tract, *The New Housekeeping*, there were eight pages of glossy photographic images. This must have impressed the average reader. In her chapter on the new efficiency as applied to cooking, an image was provided which affirmed this ideology as the answer to women's work. The image consisted of a line drawing of an open card file, organised into types of dishes, and an example of a recipe card with a photograph of an elaborate lamb dish (figure 4.5). Despite Frederick's interest in precision, the card, which would logically be delineated by a black rectangular frame, does not match the dimensions of the file, nor does it contain practical information such as cost, number of servings, etc. which Frederick

3 John Heartfield was a German artist who used his talent to further both the anti-Nazi and socialist cause. His most celebrated work was produced for the Communist Party's illustrated newspaper *Arbeiter Illustrierte Zeitung* which included montages that exposed the rhetoric of Hitler's speeches, his sources of funding and the tragic impotence of organisations such as the League of Nations.

SALLY STEIN (1981) 'The Composite Photographic Image and the Composition of Consumer Ideology', **Art Journal**, Spring suggests in her text. As Stein points out, however, most readers must have overlooked this point when confronted with this luscious photographic image, which they would have accepted at face value.

> Because the page is not clearly divided between the file in one half and the recipe card in the other but instead flows uninterruptedly between drawing below, text of recipe, and photograph of the final dish, the meticulous organisation of the file alone seems responsible for the full flowering of the dish. As a symbolic representation of modern house work, what you have in short order is a strict hierarchy, with an emblem of the family feast at its pinnacle.
>
> (Stein 1981: 43)

The more down-to-earth questions of time and money are ignored and almost banished. In response to those who believed that her reading was too contrived, Stein wrote: 'If it seems that I am reading too much into this composite image, one need only note the title of Frederick's subsequent publication – *Meals that Cook Themselves*' (Stein 1992).

There are two key issues we can draw from Stein's analysis. First, the example highlights the power of the photographic image to foster desire. While a rather ordinary photograph of a cake may have impressed an early twentieth-century audience, in the twenty-first century we are also seduced by the use of the latest technology and luscious photography. The photography of food continues to produce tantalising images through the play of colour and texture. Dishes are often painted or glazed to highlight colours and textures to produce more and more mouth-watering images. Roland Barthes also discussed food advertising in his essay 'The Rhetoric of the Image' (Barthes 1977a). Using an advertisement for Panzani pasta he highlighted the sense of natural abundance that is often focused on in food advertising and photography, to encourage the notion of the naturalness of prepacked produce. The constant juxtaposition of uncooked fruit or vegetables with prepared food also conceals and thereby in effect dismisses the labour process. The total metamorphosis of a coconut into Carte D'Or's coconut ice cream (figure 4.6) is an extreme example of the ability of the latest technology – here digital photography– to deny the labour of cooking.

Concealing labour relations

This brings us to the second issue in Stein's analysis – the power of photomontage in the commercial context to conceal labour relations. Judith Williamson has also discussed this with regard to a Lancia car advertisement from around 1978. The image depicts the Lancia Beta in an Italian vineyard. It shows a man who appears to be the owner, standing on the far side of the car with his back towards us, looking over a vineyard in which a number of peasants are working happily. In the distance, on a hill, is an old castle (this image is illustrated in **Williamson 1979**).

4.5 Illustration from Mrs Christine Frederick's *The New Housekeeping*, 1913

4.6 Carte D'Or Coconut ice cream ad, *Good Housekeeping*, June 1998

Williamson asks a series of questions:

Who made this car? Has it just emerged new and gleaming from the soil, its finished form as much a product of nature as the grapes on the vine? . . . Who are these peasants? Have they made the car out in this most Italian field? . . . How can a car even exist in these feudal relations, how can such a contradiction be carried off? . . . What is this, if not a complete slipping over of the capitalist mode of

JUDITH WILLIAMSON (1979)
'Great History that Photographs Mislaid' in Photography Workshop (ed.)
Photography/Politics One, London: Comedia

production, as we survey a set of feudal class relations represented by the surveying gaze of possession, the look of the landlord with his back to us?

(Williamson 1979: 53)

Williamson also notes how the feudal Italian owner's gaze does not encompass both car (the product of industrial capitalism) and the owner's field of vision (the relations of Italian feudalism). She discusses the structure of the advertisement in order to understand why we don't question the contradictions of the image. The ad uses the traditional grammar of car advertisements with the showroom-effect camera angle, which intersects with the representation of 'Italianness'. The positioning of the car seems so casual that the man leaning against it could have just stopped to have a break and look at this Italian view. Maybe he is not Italian? Perhaps he will drive on and leave the 'most Italian' scene behind. The narrative of chance on the horizontal axis of the photograph naturalises the vertical axis of Italian castle, feudal relations and commodity ownership.

Contemporary advertisements also provide examples of the romanticised and non-industrial working environment. Hovis and other wholemeal bread producers have often used the image of the family bakery. Whiskey distillers have also used this image to represent their brand as one which has been produced with special attention and one that has the experience of time behind it. Jack Daniel's whiskey have used advertisements since 1995 which present a labour environment that could not possibly exist today (figure 4.7). The black and white photograph of a romanticised work environment seems to represent both the past and present. There is a reassuring sense of stability. The photograph also seems to illude us into believing that this is a 'real' world, especially since the whiskey bottle at the bottom of the ad, which we know to exist, is only engraved.

Gendered representations

While the concealing of class relations and the representation of commodity culture as natural and eternal is the most overwhelming construct of advertising, capitalism has also exploited racist and sexist ideologies. Much of the literature which considers racist and sexist imagery, however, while using commercial photography for examples, has tended to discuss broader cultural readings rather than the commercial or photographic context. (For the most recent and lucid example of these critiques see **Hall 1997**.) This section will discuss gendered representations. For explorations of 'race' and racism in commercial photography see case studies on pages 188–202 and 206–14.

The stereotypical and highly coded representations of women in popular culture have been given attention by many critics (**Berger 1972a**; **Winship 1987a**, 1987b; Williamson 1978). One of the key criticisms has been the way in which ads always represent women as objects to be surveyed. This has

STUART HALL (1997) **Cultural Representations and Signifying Practice**, London: Sage

JOHN BERGER (1972a) **Ways of Seeing**, London: BBC

JANICE WINSHIP (1987a) 'Handling Sex' in R. Betterton (ed.) **Looking On: Images of Femininity in the Visual Arts and Media**, London: Pandora

If you'd like to know more about our unique whiskey, write to us for a free booklet at the Jack Daniel Distillery, Lynchburg, Tennessee, USA.

TENNESSEE MEN and Tennessee maple account for the smoothness of Jack Daniel's Tennessee Whiskey.

We get these big chunks of hard maple from the hills around here. They're taken from high ground when the sap is low. Then, men like Billy Durm cut them in strips; stack them in ricks; and burn them to charcoal for smoothing our whiskey. Sometimes we joke about who's more important — the man or the maple? But after a sip of charcoal mellowed Jack Daniel's, you'll know that both are doing good jobs.

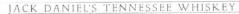

JACK DANIEL'S TENNESSEE WHISKEY

4.7 'Billy Durm', Jack Daniel's Tennessee Whiskey
A romanticised labour environment appears more real by its representation as a photograph

tended to increase the representation of women as both passive and objects of sexual desire. Erving Goffman has explored the body language used to represent men and women in his book *Gender Advertisements* to show how women in particular have been photographed for advertisements in ways that perpetuate gender roles (Goffman 1979). It is important to remember that the photographer always surveys his or her subject and personally selects what is believed to be worth photographing. The photographic process can also, therefore, exacerbate the voyeuristic gaze. Janice Winship has explored the contrasting ways in which men's and women's hands have been photographed in advertisements (see Winship 1987a). While male hands are usually photographed as active and controlling, female hands are invariably represented as decorative and caressing.

Winship's essay also draws attention to the increasing fragmentation of the body within recent commercial photography. It makes the body more easily commodified and packaged. In a content analysis of lipstick advertisements, Robert Goldman has pointed out that while most lipstick ads in 1946 depicted the whole body of a woman, by 1977 most ads only showed a part of the body. A Marks & Spencer make-up ad from *Marie Claire*, November 1998, highlights the continual fragmentation of women's bodies, with a series of women's lips montaged into the ad to express the range of lipsticks available. It is as though each part is like a commodity to be worn and discarded at will.[4] One of the most famous examples of the fragmentation of women's bodies was an advertisement for Pretty Polly tights, which depicted a woman's legs emerging from an egg. This objectification and fragmentation received criticism at the time. Oppositional graffiti included one that read 'born kicking'. As Pollock indicates, it was only 'after Picasso had visually hacked up the body, [that] we have been gradually accustomed to the cutting up of specifically feminine bodies: indeed, their cut-up-ness has come to be seen as a sign of that femininity'. Significantly, Pollock adds that this 'came to be naturalised by photographic representation in film, advertising, and pornography, all of which are discourses about desire that utilise the dialectic of fantasy and reality effects associated with the hegemonic modes of photographic representation' (Pollock 1990: 218)

Recent commercial photography has undoubtedly objectified both male and female bodies in the constant drive for commodification. It has also sometimes challenged traditional images of sexuality and gender in the increasing drive for niche marketing. Art photography has influenced commercial photography's representation of the body, and created a small space to challenge the traditional representations of men and women in advertising. A 1998 advertisement for Nokia uses a beautiful black and white photograph of a naked couple perfectly balanced on the man's arms with legs outstretched like those of dancers. The image represents both male and female bodies as strong and muscular and attempts to distinguish between the two as little as possible. Its style reflects a representation of desire that can be seen in the work of many gay photographers, who have been concerned with exploring images of masculinity and sexuality. While the image is photographically unusual for advertising, its content is interestingly slightly distanced from the Nokia company by the framing of the picture, like an art photograph at the top of the page. The use of a daring image is also legitimised by the caption – 'Simply poised for the future'. The image represents the future, not today.

4 It is worth noting, however, that despite the anonymity and objectification of the women's bodies in the image, the models used for the advertisement command much higher economic benefit from their work than the photographer. On asking Marks & Spencer for reproduction rights for this book, the company asked for £300 to be paid to each model and only £100 to be paid to the photographer.

Simply poised for the future.

It's hard to imagine improving on perfection. But that is exactly what has happened with the new Nokia 8110i. It has leapt ahead of its time and is now currently the only mobile phone poised to optimally deliver information on the Internet through Smart Messaging Services. The possibilities are endless; fax, e-mail, telebanking services could all be available to you at the touch of a button, virtually wherever you are. Yet the perfectly harmonised design of the 8110i still remains unique: curved, compact and beautifully distinctive. And there is a full range of Original Nokia accessories to choose from too. Find out why the Nokia 8110i is simply the shape of things to come. Call 0990 003110 today for a brochure.

www.nokia.com

4.8 Image Nokia ad, *Guardian Weekend*, Autumn 1998

FASHION PHOTOGRAPHY

So far I have concentrated on photographs within advertising, yet we cannot allow this area to subsume all discussion on photographs for commerce. Here, it is worth considering the genre of fashion photography, since this area of commercial photography has been particularly targeted with regard to discussions on the construction of femininity and gendered representations.

In *The Face of Fashion*, Jennifer Craik provides an historical account of the techniques of fashion photography from early photographic pictorialism of the nineteenth century, through the gendered constructions of the 1920s and 1930s which increasingly represented women as commodities, to the increasing dominance of the fashion photographer in the 1960s and the influence of filmatic techniques which led to clothes becoming more and more incidental within the fashion photograph. Craik also draws our attention to the increasing eroticism of 1970s and 1980s fashion photography. Most importantly she notes that the conventions of fashion photography are 'neither fixed nor purposeful' (**Craik 1994: 114**). It is perhaps for this reason that critical literature on the genre as a whole is sparse. Most of what has been written does not provide a critique of the genre as a whole, but tends to consider the constructions of gender and sexuality within these images. Femininity, as Craik notes, 'became co-extensive with the fashion photograph' by the 1930s. The heightened sexuality of the fashion image in the 1970s and 1980s, with the work of photographers such as Helmut Newton, has been discussed by Rosetta Brookes (**Brookes 1992: 17–24**).

The way in which women read fashion images of women has also been explored (see **Evans and Thornton 1989: ch. 5**). As Berger commented: 'Men look at women. Women watch themselves being looked at' (Berger 1972a: 47). As far as the photographic quality of the spreads is concerned, these have tended to be discussed in books, often commissioned by commercial enterprises such as *Vogue*, which eulogise these images and their relationship to '**Art**' photography. In this process the work of individual photographers has been discussed, rather than the genre itself. It is worth noting that even in their discussions of the fashion image and sexuality, Brookes, as well as Evans and Thornton, discussed the issue through key examples of work by particular photographers. Their essays provide critical case studies of fashion images from the 1960s, 1970s and 1980s by photographers such as Helmut Newton, Guy Bourdin and Deborah Turbeville. In marking out fashion photography as an area for discussion, it seems clear that the glossy images which are mostly discussed contrast to the fashion photographs of the average mail-order catalogue, which could be described as fashion illustration.

Several signs or features of the fashion image which have been pointed out by various writers are worth considering together in order to understand the genre. First, the transitory nature of fashion has impacted on the fashion image. Evans and Thornton have discussed this in terms of the ability of the fashion image to take 'extraordinary liberties' and get away with images which are unduly violent, pornographic or outrageous. Polly Devlin has pointed out the contradictory nature of the fashion image's transitoriness, since it aims to be both timely and timeless: 'Its subject is a product with built-in obsolescence, and the result may be an amusing, ephemeral picture or a monumental statement' (Devlin 1979: 113).

There are other contradictions apparent within the fashion image. Rosetta Brookes has suggested that in fashion photography 'we see the typical instead of the unique moment or event' (Brookes 1992: 17). Yet, at the same time as

JENNIFER CRAIK (1994) 'Soft Focus: Techniques of Fashion Photography', **The Face of Fashion**, London: Routledge, ch. 5

ROSETTA BROOKES (1992) 'Fashion Photography' in V. Ash and E. Wilson (eds) **Chic Thrills: A Fashion Reader**, London: Pandora

C. EVANS AND M. THORNTON (1989) **Women and Fashion: A New Look**, London: Quartet, especially ch. 5

producing the typical, fashion photographers have aimed to construct a sense of what is original and unique within a particular fashion. They have also tried to produce images which stand their ground beyond the transitory space of the magazine and the transitory nature of fashion, and for example enter the gallery or the coffee-table book. *The Vogue Book of Fashion Photography* and the major Victoria and Albert Museum exhibition and its accompanying catalogue *Appearances: Fashion Photography since 1945* are testament to this conflict (Devlin 1979; Harrison 1991). Both provide a good collection of images of the classical fashion photograph, although the historical essays tend to be uncritical of the genre. It is clear that there are tensions in the relationship between fashion photography and both advertising photography and 'Art' photography. The fashion image attempts to stand aloof from the undiluted commercial context of advertising, since most fashion spreads are commissioned by magazines which are not directly selling clothes. Yet the undeniable commercial angle has separated it from the 'Art' photograph, despite the inevitable commercial context of the latter.

The relationship of the fashion spread to magazines rather than the manufacturers also emphasises the importance of the images' ability to project 'a look, an image, a world' (Evans and Thornton 1989: 82). Val Williams' *Look at Me: Fashion and Photography in Britain* highlights the crucial role that particular magazines such as *Nova* in the 1960s and later *I-D* and *The Face* in the 1980s have played in developing conventions of challenge within certain areas of fashion photography, that encompassed discussions of race, sexuality and class within fashion and style. In constructing these multiple identities fashion photography enables us to view the social attitudes of a period.

Despite providing 'conventions of challenge', however, these magazines and the photographs within them are still subsumed within a culture of commodification in which identities, whether traditional or not, form part of a vast reservoir of appearances that can be packaged and sold. As Steve Edwards wrote, with regard to the *Next Directory*:

> As we flip the pages multiple identities whizz past our eyes. Distance and depth collapse into the intricate and exquisite surface of the image. What is there now to prevent us switching back and forth between these marvellous identities? She: now sipping tea on the lawn of the country seat, bathed in golden light, 'well-dressed, well-bred,' in that 'endless summer'. Now the belle of the southern states, young and raw, perhaps with an illicit negro lover. Now the cultured woman, on her travels through Europe in search of adventure. He: from the big city gentleman, to the rugged biker, to the fictions of Havana. These are the worlds that the photograph has to offer. . . . Our only choice is between its choices, we have no choice but to consume . . . or so the argument goes.
>
> (Edwards 1989: 5)

In creating worlds of illusion, fashion photography has been influenced by all other areas of photographic practice. Early portrait photography and the *carte-de-visite* had already established ways of photographing people in fashionable or dramatic clothing, which were adopted by early fashion photographers (Ewing 1991: 6–10). Fashion photographers such as André Barre, Irving Penn and Erwin Blumenfield have been influenced by art movements such as Surrealism. Bruce Weber's photographs for Calvin Klein have been influenced by the work of Leni Riefenstahl. The power of photojournalism and documentary photography in the 1930s also affected fashion images, especially as photographers moved between the genres. Yet, the concentration on what is contrived and stylised rather than the 'captured' moment, so revered in documentary, continues to set it apart. Films have also influenced fashion photography, both in terms of content and the creation of looks and styles and the way in which we are able to read what would otherwise appear as fragmentary and disjointed image sequences in the fashion spread. In creating images and 'looks', the fashion photograph – in its attempts to always find something new, different, glamorous and often 'exotic' – has also been influenced by the increasing experience of international travel. In the following case study we will therefore explore fashion and travel images together. This should indicate the impossibility of considering various commercial image-making forms in isolation. We live in a world dominated by lifestyle culture, whose conventions are 'neither fixed nor purposeful'.

CASE STUDY: Tourism, fashion and 'the Other'

In this case study we will consider a particular hegemonic construction from the nineteenth century – that of the exotic/primitive '**Other**' – and explore the way in which it has been exploited in the commercial world. Some of the most dominant ideological and photographic constructs were developed during the nineteenth century, a period of European imperial expansion. This history has affected the representation of black people in all forms of photographic practice (see Gupta 1986; Bailey 1988; *Ten/8* 16; *Ten/8* 2(3)). During the nineteenth century, the camera joined the gun in the process of colonisation. The camera was used to record and define those who were colonised according to the interests of the West. This unequal relationship of power between the white photographer and the colonised subject has been discussed by many (Freedman 1990; Prochaska 1991; Schildkrout 1991; Edwards 1992; Bate 1993). These early anthropological and geographical photographers were sometimes paid employees of companies who organised campaigns to explore new markets. Emile Torday, for example – an anthropologist who used photography as a research aid – was paid by the Belgian Kasai Company to explore the Congo.

This history of photography is integrally linked to colonial and economic exploitation. A sense of submission, exoticism and the 'primitive' were key feelings, which these photographers documented and catalogued. Through these images, the European photographer and viewer could perceive their own superiority. Europe was defined as 'the norm' upon which all other cultures should be judged. That which was different was disempowered by its very 'Otherness'.

During this period, the sense of 'Otherness' and exoticism was not only captured 'in the field' but was also exploited by photographers working in commercial enterprises. Malek Alloula has documented the genre of exotic/erotic colonial postcards which were sent back to France by French colonists. In his book *The Colonial Harem* he discusses images of Algerian women taken by French studio photographers in Algeria (**Alloula 1987**).

MALEK ALLOULA (1987) **The Colonial Harem**, Manchester: Manchester University Press

In the confines of the studio, French photographers constructed visions of exoticism which suited their own colonial fantasies and those of the European consumers of these images. The paid Algerian models could only remain silent to the colonisers' abuse of their bodies (figures 4.9 and 4.14). These images encapsulate Edward Said's description of Flaubert's Egyptian courtesan:

> She never spoke of herself, she never represented her emotions, her presence or history. He spoke for and represented her. He was foreign, comparatively wealthy, male, and these were historical facts of domination that allowed him not only to possess Kuchuk Hanem physically but to speak for her and tell his readers in what way she was typically oriental.

> (Said 1985: 6)

The dominance of photographs of women in these commercial images is not by chance. Colonial power could be more emphatically represented through gendered relations – the white, wealthy male photographer versus the non-white, poor female subject. These images, bought and sold in their thousands, reflect the commodification of women's bodies generally in society. They are also part of the development of postcard culture which enabled the consumption of photographs by millions. The production of exotic postcards also brought photographs of the 'Empire' and the non-European world into every European home. It was not only the photographs of non-European women which were sold: landscape photographs, which constructed Europe as developed and the non-European world as underdeveloped, were also popular (Prochaska 1991). These colonial visions continue to pervade contemporary travel photography, not only through postcards, but also in travel brochures and tourist ephemera.

Tourism

Today, many areas of commercial photography exploit exoticism and 'Otherness', along with the ingredient of glamour to invite and entice viewers and consumers. In this way, some of the ideological constructs of colonial domination have become so naturalised that we hardly notice them. In the tourist industry, images

Types Algériens. — Femme Mauresque. — ND Phot

4.9 French colonial postcard, c. 1910
White French photographers constructed their own colonial fantasies, which were sent by colonial officers in Algeria to relatives and friends in France

of exoticised women and children in traditional garb are used to encourage travel through tourist brochures, posters and TV campaigns. With submissive smiles and half-hidden faces these images, echoing those discussed by Alloula, continue to construct the East as the submissive female and the West as the authoritative male (figure 4.10). The non-European world is represented as a playground for the West. The bombardment of these images denies the reality of resourcefulness and intense physical work which actually constitutes most women's lives in the Third World. In the 1970s, Paul Wombell commented on this construct in a photomontage, which contrasted the fantasy tourist world

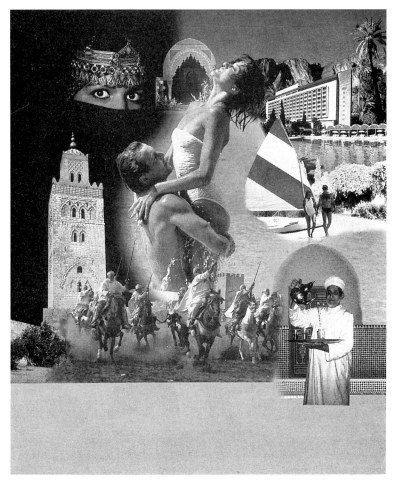

4.10 'Morocco', 1990
The 'East' is still represented as an exotic and erotic playground for the 'West'

with the reality for many Asian women workers in Britain (figures 4.11a and b). In many tourist advertisements, the image of work is so glamorised that we cannot perceive the reality.

The dominant photographic language of the tourist brochure has also affected how tourists construct their own photographs. These snapshots tend to reinforce the constructed and commodified experience of travel: what is photographed is that which is different and out of the ordinary. Most tourist snapshots also use a vocabulary of photographic practice which is embedded in power relations. Let us look at the photographs by Western tourists in the non-Western world. Tourism within Europe produces a slightly different set of

191

Rajput windows and the ethereal voice of the sitar.
Murals of the legends of Krishna and silks and brocades from Rajasthan.
A glimpse of India on your way to New York.

AIR-INDIA

4.11a

relations. In the non-Western world, the majority of tourists who travel abroad are Western. Automatically a relationship of economic power is established, both generally and in terms of camera ownership.

While Don Slater (1983) has discussed the contradictory way in which the expansion of camera ownership has not led to new or challenging photographic practices, in the non-Western world this contradiction between ownership and practice is less evident. Tourists, having already consumed an array of exotic and glamorised photographs of the place before arrival, search out these very images and sites to visit and photograph in order to feel that their trip is complete.

Ash trays and the extensive dirty floors of the airport.
The arrivals and departure board of Heathrow and the overalls from Acme.
A glimpse of exploitation on your way to New York.

IMMIGRANT-LABOUR

4.11b Montage, 1979

While many of the experiences revolve around architectural monuments, the desire to consume exotic/anthropological images of people has found a new trade, which has its parallel in the earlier studio-anthropological photography. In many tourist locations – in India, Morocco and Algeria, for example – men and women sit in elaborate garb which the tourist can recognise as traditional and, more importantly, exotic. These people wait for those willing to pay to have their photograph taken with them. Tourism creates its own culture for consumption. Just like the model in the studio, he or she is also paid by the photographer to conform to an image which has already been constructed.

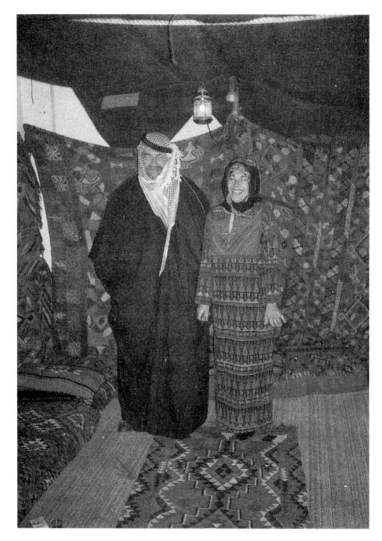

4.12 Tourist photograph
This photograph was taken in a carpet shop where tourists could dress up and role-play in a mock bedouin tent

Alternatively, at other sites, tourists can dress up as part of the exotic experience, and photograph themselves (figure 4.12). The trade in these new 'anthropological' images may have expanded to include the unknown snapshooter, but their purpose is not to encourage an understanding of a culture, but rather to commodify and consume yet another aspect of a place through the photographic image – the people.

194

Fashion

In fashion photography the consumption of 'Other' worlds is domesticated through the familiar context of the fashion magazine and the more-often-than-not white model. In some cases it is hard to know where one genre ends and the other begins. Within fashion, the ordinary is made to appear extraordinary, and vice versa. Fashion photography, as I have already mentioned, is blatantly concerned with the constructed photograph. It is also concerned with what is exotic, dramatic, glamorous and different. Therefore, it is easy to see how some photographers have moved between areas of anthropological and fashion photography. Irving Penn's *Worlds in a Small Room* is a series of constructed images of peoples from around the world, whom Penn photographed while on assignments for *Vogue* (Penn 1974). In these images the genres of fashion and visual anthropology seem to collapse. The images tell us little about the people, but say a lot about Penn's construction of these people as primitive and exotic. As with the fashion shoot, these images are contrived and stylised, and Penn is at pains to find what is extraordinary and to create the dramatic. The isolated space of the studio removes the subjects from their own time and space, in a similar way to the French colonial postcards discussed above (p. 189), and gives the photographer free rein to create every aspect of the image. Interestingly, Penn described this studio space as 'a sort of neutral area' (Penn 1974: 9). Yet, as we look through his book and peruse the photographs of Penn constructing his shots, the unequal relationship of power makes a mockery of the notion of neutrality.

The latent relationship between fashion and popular anthropological photography explains why the fashion magazine *Marie Claire* could include articles about ethnography without losing the tone of the fashion magazine. In their first issue, the article 'Arabia Behind the Veil' represented the jewellery and make-up of Arab women in a series of plates, like fashion ideas (figure 4.13). If we look closely at the images it is clear that the photographer has used just two or three models and dressed them differently to represent a series of styles, just like a fashion shoot.

In fashion photography we can see the continued use of the 'harem' image, for example, as the site of colonial fantasy and as being oppositional to the white 'norm'. In the November 1988 issue of *Company* magazine, a fashion spread titled 'Arabesque: Rock the Casbah – This is Evening Wear to Smoulder in' features non-white women in brocaded clothes, sitting and lying indoors on heavily ornamented fabrics, while pining over black and white photographs of men. The photographs of the women are bathed in an orangey, rich light. By contrasting colour and black and white photography, the men seem to appear more distant and further unobtainable. The representation of sexuality here is of an unhealthy obsession. In contrast, the fashion spread following it, 'Cold Comfort', features a white couple together, in a relationship of relative equality. Blue and brown predominate, in contrast to the previous spread, and the much more standard photographic lighting contrasts with the previous yellow haze,

Veils and face-painting techniques vary enormously between urban, rural and desert regions. Some girls start with make-up and 'graduate' to veils; women may combine the two, adding ornate jewellery or beadwork, head rings and, occasionally, hats
14

4.13 'Arabia Behind the Veil', *Marie Claire*, September 1988

to present images which seem much more matter-of-fact, like the denim clothing advertised. Here, however, matter-of-factness acts to represent Europe as rational in opposition to the irrational East.

In *Marie Claire*'s June 1994 issue, another pair of fashion spreads also provides an example of the oppositional way in which East and West are presented, not just through content, but also through photographic codes. In 'Indian Summer', the image of an exotic woman in physical and sexual abandon predominates women, then, adopted the veil with the same intention as the Arab women of today: as a shield against the visual aggression and intrusion of men. The most well-documented, archaic function of the veil, therefore, remains simply to protect and preserve.

Sustaining a certain ambiguity of identity is vital in the battle against destructive forces. Moslems often change their names when they enter a strange village or when they fall ill, to avoid tempting fate (understandably making the administration of health centres unduly complicated); and people here do not kiss due to the belief that an open mouth allows bad spirits to enter and the soul to escape. Veiling, make-up and name-changing are all different methods of separating the individual from the malevolent forces, whether human or spiritual, of the outside world.

There is a rigidly drawn division in Arabia between public life, at work, and private life, at home. This is hard for the outward-looking Westerner to grasp, but maintaining the extreme seclusion of the domestic sphere has, particularly in Saudi, developed over the centuries and become a kind of congenital male obsession. A woman who emerges from the confines of the home unveiled goes beyond inviting the advances of strangers; she is in fact, exposing the most vehemently guarded element, prize even, of private life.

Moslems are burdened with an inescapable pressure that comes from constant social surveillance. Each individual is considered responsible for the actions of his neighbours, so a form of sacred citizen's arrest exists whereby people can successfully become their brother's keeper. In Riyadh, even driving through an amber light might lead to the person being followed, detained and denounced by a complete stranger.

It may seem like a distorted view of independence, but the veil can actually serve to release women from the stress of such intense vigilance; behind the thick make-up or black curtain, many Arab women feel liberated by their anonymity.

And the veil does not in itself prevent women from educating themselves or working and can actually co-exist with a surprising amount of freedom. For instance, in a region to the east of Yemen, women – even though they accept the veil – still practise the custom of 'temporary marriage': a woman can, extremely easily, ▷

Maintaining the extreme seclusion of the domestic sphere has developed over the centuries to become a kind of congenital male obsession

15

the pages (figure 4.15), as in the previous spread and the colonial postcards already discussed (figures 4.9 and 4.14). The pages of this photo-story are almost like a film sequence with rapid cuts. As in the last 'Orientalist' sequence, this woman is alone, but the themes of physical and sexual desire are paramount. Many of the shots use wide angles to enhance their depth and, along with rich oranges and blues, it gives the sequence a heightened sense of physicality. The spread which follows this, entitled 'The Golden Age of Hollywood', contrasts

4.14 French colonial postcard, c. 1910
During the nineteenth century and today, the harem has remained a site for colonial fantasy, and a space which ensures the representation of the 'orient' as oppositional to the 'occident'

by representing white men and women together, in relative harmony (figure 4.16). This sequence is much more about glamour than 'Cold Comfort', yet here again the notion of rationality is also encouraged by the style of clothing as well as the standard photographic lens used. There is also an almost colonial feel to this fashion spread, through the sepia tones of the photographs and the 1930s styling. The other important difference between the two fashion spreads is that, while the latter concentrates on the clothing, the former concentrates on atmosphere. The context of these images within the fashion magazine leaves the predominantly white women as the surveyors of 'Other' women.

While I have discussed the use of colonial and exotic photographic messages in tourist and fashion photography separately, within the recent dominance of lifestyle culture there is little difference between these forms. Sisley's photo 'magazine' from Spring/Summer 1990 makes this clear. The subject of this fashion label's photo magazine was a Moroccan caravan tour. Along with the series of travel photographs of a European man and woman, presumably in Sisley clothes, is the male traveller's diary. There is no written information on

4.15 'Afternoon Dream' from 'Indian Summer', *Marie Claire*, June 1994
Rich reds and oranges dominate this scene in which the mood of sexual abandon that is created is more important than the display of clothes

4.16 From 'The Golden Age of Hollywood', *Marie Claire*, June 1994
In contrast to the 'East', Europe is represented as more rational and restrained

Salsa style. Ha
Tweed coat wit
Lurex collar
(£285) by
Vivienne West
Burgundy silk s
(from £170) fro
a selection by
Callaghan and
shirt (£129) by
cut to Rospuro.
Burgundy woolt
tights (£6.80)
by Fogal. Two b
Balmoral boots
(£200) by Paul
Harnden. Drop
earrings (from £
and gold and
ebony necklace
(from £180), bo
from a selection
by Dinny Hall.

4.17 Tourism and fashion marketing collide in this feature
Source: British *Elle*, November 1987

the clothes, and they are clearly not the main subject of the photographs, which concentrate on building up an atmosphere of unhindered travel. It is not just the fashion advertiser that has manipulated 'the exotic' into a lifestyle and a fashion statement. Fashion magazines such as *Elle* and *Vogue* have done the

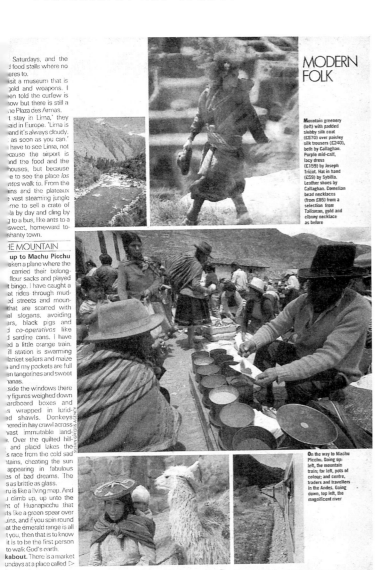

Saturdays, and the
d food stalls where no
ares to.
isit a museum that is
gold and weapons. I
en told the curfew is
now but there is still a
ne Plaza des Armas.
t stay in Lima,' they
said in Europe. 'Lima is
and it's always cloudy.
, as soon as you can.'
i have to see Lima, not
ecause the airport is
and the food and the
houses, but because
e to see the place *los
ntes* walk to. From the
ains and the plateaux
e vast steaming jungle
me to sell a crate of
la by day and cling by
g to a bus, like ants to a
sweet, homeward to-
shanty town.

HE MOUNTAIN

up to Machu Picchu
aken a plane where the
carried their belong-
flour sacks and played
t bingo. I have caught a
at rides through mud-
ed streets and moun-
that are scarred with
al slogans, avoiding
ers, black pigs and
d *co-operativos* like
d sardine cans. I have
ed a little orange train.
ill station is swarming
lanket sellers and maize
s and my pockets are full
en tangerines and sweet
nanas.
side the windows there
y figures weighed down
ardboard boxes and
s wrapped in lurid-
ed shawls. Donkeys
nered in hay crawl across
vast immutable land-
. Over the quilted hill-
and placid lakes the
s race from the cold sad
itains, cheating the sun
appearing in fabulous
es of bad dreams. The
s as brittle as glass.
ru is like a living map. And
u climb up, up unto the
nt of Huanapicchu that
ts like a green spear over
uins, and if you spin round
at the emerald range is all
t you, then that is to know
it is to be the first person
to walk God's earth.
kabout. There is a market
undays at a place called ▷

MODERN FOLK

Mountain greenery
(left) with padded
slubby silk coat
(£570) over paisley
silk trousers (£240),
both by Callaghan.
Purple mid-calf,
lacy dress
(£159) by Joseph
Tricot. Hat in hand
(£59) by Sybilla.
Leather shoes by
Callaghan. Cornelian
bead necklaces
(from £85) from a
selection from
Talisman, gold and
ebony necklace
as before

On the way to Machu
Picchu. Going up:
left, the mountain
train; far left, pots of
colour; and centre,
traders and travellers
in the Andes. Going
down, top left, the
magnificent river

137

same. *Elle*'s fashion spread from November 1987 entitled 'Weave a Winter's Tale of Fashion's Bright New Folklore' was shot in Peru, and combines photographs of the season's clothes with tourist brochure images (figure 4.17). The main text is of a travel diary, with a subtext of photo titles which combine tourist descriptions and clothing details that include prices. Here, Peru is turned into

201

the flavour of the month for fashion influence and tourism, which are not distinguished between in layout and photographic format. In a similar vein, *Vogue* focused on Egypt in their May 1989 issue.

Images and photographs for both these magazines are the key to their commercial success. Here, there is also no distinct line between the advertisement and editorial photograph. What is clear, however, is the dominance of commercial interest in all these photographic images, which are contrived and stylised and are 'positioned on a threshold between two worlds: the consumer public and a mythic elite created in the utopia of the photograph as well as in the reality of a social group maintained by the fashion industry' (Brooks 1992: 18–19).

THE CONTEXT OF THE IMAGE

Don Slater has criticised the semiotic critique of advertisements (characterised by writers such as Roland Barthes and Judith Williamson) for taking as assumed precisely what needs to be explained – 'the relations and practices within which discourses are formed and operated' (Slater 1983: 258). Barthes' and Williamson's readings of advertisements have provided a very limited social and historical context. Often even simple pieces of information, such as the magazine from which the images have been extracted and the date of advertisements, have not been mentioned. Liz Wells has commented on some of the limitations of *Decoding Advertisements*, especially Williamson's lack of consideration of multiple readings (Wells 1992).

While scholars have devoted some space to the understanding of a broad cultural context, the exploration of political and economic contexts is more rare. The vast array of commercial messages has also made their contextualisation increasingly difficult. It would be impossible to contextualise them all. Information about processes of production is not always easily available, and this increases the reality of consumption over that of production:

> What commodities fail to communicate to consumers is information about the process of production. Unlike goods in earlier societies, they do not bear the signature of their makers, whose motives and actions we might access because we knew who they were. . . . The real and full meaning of production is hidden beneath the empty appearance in exchange. Only once the real meaning has been systematically emptied out of commodities does advertising then refill this void with its own symbols. Production empties. Advertising fills. The real is hidden by the imaginary.
>
> (Jhally 1990: 50)

To decode photographs and advertising images more effectively, it is essential for us to understand their context. Let us take, for example, Williamson's reading of the Lancia car advertisement (1979). Would a discussion of Lancia manufacturing and car production in the late 1970s reveal more about the image?

Since the founding of the Lancia firm in 1907, Lancia had been known for their production of quality cars for gentlemen, as one writer described it. With increasing conglomeration in all industries throughout the twentieth century, Lancia, as a family firm, ran into trouble and was eventually taken over by Fiat in 1969 (Weernink 1979). The Beta saloon was the first car to be produced by Lancia after the merger. Fiat, which was known for producing smaller, cheaper cars, needed to distinguish the Beta from its own cars. Style and quality needed to be suggested, and 'Lancia – the Most Italian Car' was the slogan used to enhance the sense of stylishness of the Lancia range generally. It is this slogan which has been visualised in the 1979 advertisement discussed by Williamson.

Apart from asserting a sense of style and quality, why has Lancia chosen to represent any form of labour relations in the advertisement? Most car advertisements of this period tended to talk about the car itself and its features – for example, its economical use of petrol or the size of its boot. This advertisement does not discuss the car's actual features at all. In the late 1970s strikes took place in many major industries in Britain and Europe. In September 1978, for example, the Ford car workers at Dagenham went on strike for nine weeks. Car manufacturers generally must have wanted to maintain an image of good industrial relations. The illusion of the contented happy peasant worker in the vineyards depicted by the ad discussed earlier (see page 180–2) glosses over the general unrest that was present during this period. Finally, the image of the peasant worker could carry another function. During the mid-1970s, the car industry began to introduce microprocessors into production for increased automation. The peasant workers depicted in the ad, outside of industrial production, also acted to represent Lancia as a quality hand-crafted, gentleman's car.

Image worlds

Let us look at an example of marketing photography, where an understanding of the context within which images are produced helps us to perceive the extent to which commercial interests affect photographic practice. David Nye, in *Image Worlds*, gives us a detailed exploration of the context of production, dissemination and historical setting of General Electric's photographs between 1900 and 1930 (**Nye 1985**). As Nye notes, commercial photographers do not strive for uniqueness (as does the artist photographer), but rather for a solidity of a predictable character. In spite of their documentary appearance, Nye notes the contrast between the images produced by a socially concerned documentary photographer and a commercial photographer, even when the subject is the same. He compares two photographs of Southern textile mills, one by Lewis Hine, the other by a photographer working for General Electric. While Hine emphasises the people and children in the mills who work in

DAVID NYE (1985) **Image Worlds: Corporate Identities at General Electric 1890–1930**, Cambridge, MA: MIT Press potentially dangerous environments, the commercial photographer's image stresses machinery, electrification and technical progress (Nye 1985: 55–56).

Nye also notes how, by the beginning of the twentieth century, the management of General Electric discovered the need to address four distinct groups – engineers, blue collar workers, managers and consumers. Their desire to say different things to different groups affected the production of images for the company's various publications. While the *General Electric Review* (a company-sponsored scientific journal) used photographs which emphasised the machines, the publications for workers employed images which concentrated on the idea of the corporation as community.

Nye not only notes the varying sorts of photographs for different publications, but also the changing production of images over time. While images from 1880 to 1910 expressed a sense of relationship between workers and managers (they were often photographed together), images after this date present a picture of a workforce which was much more highly controlled by management. Nye details how by the 1920s General Electric had 82,000 workers in their employment, in contrast to 6,000 in 1885. The burgeoning workforce made management's role more important, and the artisanal skills of the previous era had also all but disappeared. Labour unrest began to increase during the 1910s. In 1917, partly in response to these conflicts, General Electric began to publish a magazine called *Works News* which was distributed to all blue collar workers twice a month. The paper did not address the general workforce, but was tailored to each site. The covers of the magazine produced a new kind of photographic image not previously used by the company. They featured individual skilled workers photographed from head to toe and engrossed in a piece of interesting work. This kind of image was repeated on the cover of nearly every issue of *Works News* (figure 4.18), and did not represent the reality for most of General Electric's employees; but, since these workers were individualised and isolated, the generalisation was only implicit. These kinds of images hardly existed inside the magazine, which concentrated instead on the workers – as a community which went on holiday, played in sports teams and participated in other forms of recreation. The style of the cover photographs had a history in Lewis Hine's work a decade earlier. He had aimed to represent and give dignity to 'real men' in difficult work. In adopting this style, the General Electric photographers were simply using it as a representational strategy to define the image world of the General Electric plant. It is only through an appreciation of the context of the image that we can understand the intent in the production of images by Hine and the General Electric photographer as different, and can therefore appreciate the different meanings of the image. The production of meaning is a process. As Marx noted in *Grundrisse*:

> It is not only the object that production creates for consumption . . .
> [It] also gives consumption its precise nature, its character, its finish.

4.18 Schenectady *Works News* General Electric, 2 November 1923
Images which represented individual workers engrossed in a piece of interesting work dominated the cover of
Works News during the 1920s. It did not represent the reality for most workers, but presented images which
gave a certain dignity and harmony during a period fraught with conflicts

. . . Hunger is hunger, but the hunger that is satisfied by cooked
meat eaten with a knife and fork is a different hunger from that
which bolts down raw meat with the aid of hand, nail and tooth.
Production thus produces not only the object but also the manner of
consumption, not only objectively but also subjectively.

(Marx quoted in Slater 1983: 247)

CASE STUDY: Benetton

This final case study will be used to draw together a number of strategies for considering commercial photography which have been suggested above. While giving due importance to economic and social contexts, it will also explore the language of particular ads, as well as their reception. Benetton's advertising photography challenges traditional boundaries and is also a rare example of an advertising photographer being constantly named, as one would be in the Art world. It is through his Benetton imagery that Toscani's work has entered the Art gallery and his name has become widely known.[5]

In 1984, when Toscani joined Benetton, the United Colors campaign began. Benetton suggests that the genesis of their multicultural image was by chance and that they were originally only concerned with the colour of Benetton jumpers, until somebody pointed out that 'it wasn't just the sweaters that came in different shades' (*The Face* 83, November 1987). Yet what were the economic reasons for using this kind of image? In 1978, Benetton's export market was 26 per cent of its total sales, but by 1981 its export share had increased to 40 per cent of its total output. By 1983, export sales exceeded domestic sales. In 1986 the Benetton Group was finally launched on the stock exchange. During the mid-1980s, therefore, the company changed from being an Italian (and family) company, to becoming an international player for world markets (Belussi 1987: 12–22). The company obviously needed a new image to express their growing importance internationally.

4.19 Benetton advertisement, 1987
Most of the early Benetton advertisements encouraged the notion of racial exclusivity. Europeans were invariably blond-haired and blue-eyed, and Africans were always very dark-skinned

5 Benetton imagery was shown in *The Globe* exhibition which toured the UK in 1989. The image of the new-born baby was also shown in an exhibition of images of motherhood at Boymans-van-Beunigen Museum, Rotterdam, Holland.

4.20 USSR, Benetton, 1987

Multicultural multinationalism

Just as Coke had exploited the image of world harmony in the 1970s, so Benetton too decided to foster a 'global' image. David A. Bailey has discussed these early images as a process of 'objectification and fragmentation' (Bailey 1989). By objectification he referred to the usual process of commodification – here of ethnicity – which takes place in advertising. The 'fragmentation' he referred to was the process whereby national cultures were reduced to caricatures in the Benetton ads, ignoring the flux within identities. Benetton's notion of international unity was constructed within a 'grammar of race' (**Back and Quaade 1993: 65**).

It is not the suggestion of unity in difference which was established, but rather the notion of difference as hegemonic. The African children selected as models are all black – in contrast to the white, blue-eyed Europeans (figure 4.19).

Benetton's multiculturalism was bound to be hegemonic. Operating through the confines of a multinational, the most superficial reading of Benetton's images between 1984 and 1989 suggest that global harmony can be achieved by wearing Benetton clothes. These images, however, are not ideologically innocent. All these images were taken in the confines of the studio, where make-up, lighting, poses, etc. were completely controlled by Toscani. Let us look at an advertisement made up of two double-page spreads which depict a young Russian boy, dressed in red Benetton clothing and sporting Soviet regalia (figure 4.20),

L. BACK AND V. QUAADE (1993) 'Dream Utopias, Nightmare Realities: Imagining Race and Culture within the World of Benetton', **Third Text** 22

4.21 USA, Benetton, 1987

and a young American girl called Stacey Reynolds in denim clothing (figure 4.21) (*The Face*, March 1987). 'Stacey' is obviously a mythic character since two different American girls are given this name in Benetton advertisements.

Toscani says different things about America and the USSR through the models' poses and regalia. The Soviet boy stands straight, and salutes us with a stern expression on his face. In his left hand, he carries a paper rocket in army camouflage colours – perhaps a reference to the arms race. In contrast, the American girl smiles at us gently and carries a model of the Statue of Liberty. Symbolically, we have the gentle America presented as the upholder of liberty, contrasted with the stern and uncompromising USSR that is presented as responsible for the buildup of arms. In many Benetton photographs there is clear support for capitalist ideology. In another image, a Chinese boy, dressed in blue, carries a copy of Chairman Mao's 'Little Red Book'. The book is upside down.

The Benetton manufacturing model

The stinging contradiction in Benetton's image of global harmony can be seen by exploring their context of production. Benetton's business success rests on their 'flexibility in manufacturing', which allows the company to respond quickly to changes in fashion trends. Through a computerised network that links retailers with the Benetton headquarters, Benetton is immediately made aware of fast-selling items, which can then be reproduced according to demand. This entails a large amount of subcontracting, a system that encourages small work-shops with non-unionised labour, and homeworking which is notorious for being badly paid (Mitter 1986: 112–115; Phizacklea 1990: 14–16). As far as the relationship of this Western company to Third World workers is concerned, this too is not a picture of world harmony. Much of Benetton's success in world markets is linked to the establishment of the multifibre agreement, which limits clothing imports from the Third World for the benefit of European manufac-turers. Second, the system of subcontracting has been used by many companies in the West to franchise out unskilled 'shell making' to factories in the Third World, where labour is cheap. It is clear that in 1988, Benetton were looking to exploit the labour of the Third World. As Luciano Benetton said in the Channel 4 programme, *How to Survive Lifestyles*, in 1988,

> We want also to analyse the opportunity of manufacturing in Far East
> Asia, because we have solved for the next future (sic) the problem of the
> competition coming from those countries and the best way to face the
> competition is to combine our technology with very low . . . labour cost.

Shock advertising – ahistoricism and ambiguity

Already aware that their advertising campaigns were being read ambiguously, Toscani discarded the slightly sugary image of children smiling sweetly for a series of bold images which played on contrasts, particularly that of skin colour. Before 1989, Benetton's images still seemed to relate to the genre of studio fashion photography. Benetton clothes and other accoutrements of fashion were worn by the models, who were positioned in a shallow space. After 1989, this relationship collapsed and the clothes ceased to be represented at all. Back and Quaade (1993) have described the 1989 to 1991 phase as that of 'Racialisation and Ambiguity'. The notion of racial essences continued; but beyond this, racist imagery and history were evoked. This series included the image of a black woman nursing a white child, as well as an image of a black and white man handcuffed together. Both images created an uproar in America, as well as discontent in Britain. The former image clearly echoed slave rela-tions, where black slave mothers nursed white children (figure 4.22). The image also dehumanised the black woman through the way it was cropped – she is a headless unidentifiable 'Other'. This image was not born in isolation. We can even find fashion quotations for it. The torso of a Dahomey woman was photographed by Penn in a similar way. Her headless body is totally objecti-fied and dehumanised, and is presented for consumption to the predominantly white viewer – she cannot even look back (see Penn 1974: 39). Benetton, however, suggested that their advertisement represented 'racial' harmony, with the portrayal of black and white together.

Images do change meaning according to their context; yet images, like every-thing else, are historically based and cannot avoid the meanings and symbolisms

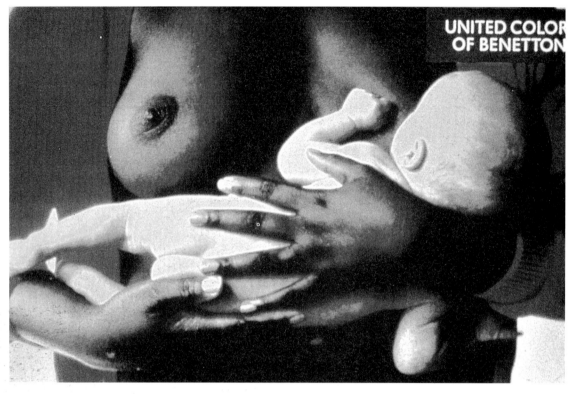

4.22 'Black Mama', Benetton, 1989
Slave relations of black women nursing white children were clearly echoed in this image. The black woman is also dehumanised here into an unidentifiable 'Other'

which the past puts upon them. Benetton, however, with dollars in their pockets, chose to suggest that they could ignore history and empty these images of meaning. They insisted that they could not be responsible for how they were decoded by individuals. Historical interpretation was dismissed as individual interpretation. Yet, as Vittoria Rava, Benetton's advertising manager, commented: 'we believe our advertising needs to shock – otherwise people will not remember it' (Graham 1989). Historical referencing was essential for the campaign's effectiveness. Following the storm over these advertisements in the United States, Benetton's sales figures fell in America. In sneering response, Toscani and Benetton released a series of fluffy animal pictures – a black sheep kissing a white wolf; a black dog and white cat – as though to absolve the previous images of any racist context, and to present Benetton as primarily interested in bold photographs which depicted contrast. The Benetton experience of 'global advertising' clearly indicates the impossibility of globalism. Photographs are read differently in different cultures and countries.

210

Pseudo-documentary and the courting of controversy

The controversy of Benetton images increased as Benetton discarded the constructed fantasy image of advertising for the seeming realism of photo-documentary. This third phase of advertising has been described as an experimentation with 'pseudo-documentary' whose overriding theme is 'a fetishisation of images of abject catastrophe' (Back and Quaade 1993: 74). The new campaign included the photographs of David Kirby dying from AIDS (figure 4.23), an African soldier holding a human femur behind his back, a burning car in an Italian street, an albino Zulu girl being shunned by others and an image of poor black people scrambling into a waste lorry. In using these images, Toscani defied the boundaries of photographic genres, in which the 'reality' of the documentary image stands in stark contrast to the fantasy world of advertising. Luciano Benetton argued that in using these images they were not attempting to be 'eccentric or provocative' but that it was 'an attempt to get away from traditional advertising in the belief that it has no power and no value any more' (Baker 1991: 29). The collapsing of these genres, however,

4.23 David Kirby, Benetton, 1992
Documentary images such as this one raised questions about what was morally acceptable within an advertisement. The contrast between the 'realism' of documentary and the fantasy world of advertising also collapsed

caused outrage. The photograph of the man dying from AIDS, the Zulu girl and the fire-bombed car had all been published earlier in documentary contexts, but the context of commodity sales inflamed people's passions and opinions. As has been noted above, the production of meaning is a process, and that process is affected by the photograph's context. The promotion of Benetton has been carried out primarily through the instigation of controversy. It must surely be for this reason that the company has at times refused to recognise or perhaps has exploited the quandaries which editors of magazines have faced. Ambiguity after all has increased the controversiality of images and courted free publicity. *Elle* magazine, for example, accused Benetton of deliberately sending advertisements to magazines just before printing deadlines to make it difficult for magazines to avoid using particular advertisements. On another occasion, Benetton refused to substitute the advertisement representing an albino Zulu girl being shunned by other girls for the *New Yorker*. The paper was running a piece about Malcolm X and racial tension in the same issue, and they did not want viewers to think that they were mixing advertising and editorial. Benetton argued, 'To ask us to pull this ad because they thought their readers would misconstrue it in the context of the story sets up a dangerous precedent' (Savan 1990: 47).

Yet during the LA riots of 1992, Benetton, of their own accord, withdrew their billboards of a burning fire-bombed car from the streets of LA. Suddenly Benetton seemed to care about the new meanings which their images could create. They replaced this image with one of people of various ethnic backgrounds smiling broadly. Of course, on this occasion, Benetton again exploited the free publicity of the news cameras. CNN sent a camera crew to document the event. Fred Bacher commented on Benetton's approach: 'What I find offensive about the ads is not their extreme violence; it's their trendy ambiguity. Benetton's ads are not constructed to help their consumers form ideas about social issues' (Bacher 1992: 45–46).

In reading these 'pseudo-documentary' images, we must remember that Benetton has not just added their green logo. These photos have been cropped and touched up, in a similar way to which a commercial photographer might enhance the image of a cake to give it greater visual appeal. The original black and white photo of Kirby was hand-coloured by Benetton (figure 4.23). One interesting fact about Benetton's use of documentary images is that until 1995 they have always been in fantastic colours, despite the rich black and white documentary tradition. This must be a deliberate decision on the part of Benetton, in order to complement their slogan. The enhanced colouring on some of the images seems to give these photographs a surreality which is disturbing and has added to the distaste which has been felt for their use.

By 1994, Benetton had moved beyond the pseudo-documentary, but continued to refer to conflict situations. Still playing with photographic genres, Toscani photographed the bloodstained clothes of a soldier from former Yugoslavia in catalogue-style photography. The distaste of and for this image and others has led Benetton retailers in Germany, USA and France to take out lawsuits against the company, in the belief that Benetton's ad campaigns have added to their losses.

Colors and the politics of location

In 1992 Benetton launched *Colors*. The magazine has provided Benetton with an avenue to highlight issues, which their advertisements have touched on. Subtitled 'a magazine about the *rest* of the world' (my emphasis), the centrality of Europe is undeniable. Each issue deals with a subject such as 'race', ecology, immigration, food, etc. The presentation of information is fragmented. What is bizarre and quirky is given importance. 'The rest of the world' remains a space for exoticism and fantasy. In the magazine, form also appears to be as, or more, important than content. Whether dealing with shopping, rubbish or cosmetic surgery, Toscani isolates products or fragments of the human body, photographing them frontally, in a shallow space, in a similar way to the image of a perfume bottle inset in an advertisement. Isolated and often distorted in size, objects are fetishised and appear surreal. Through *Colors* Toscani high-lights issues without projecting any particular opinion – 'trendy ambiguity' pervades. From a photographic and image point of view *Colors 13* is particu-larly interesting, because unlike previous issues there are no words, and many of the photographs are framed in their traditional rectangular shape. It is only at the end of the magazine that we find the written word. The editorial gives us a simple outline about how we read images that could be found in any photography textbook. Here Benetton, targeted for their use of imagery, turn into an educator of visual literacy. They consider the ambiguity of photographs as well as the way in which editors and photographers crop and retouch images in order to create a 'picture of reality that corresponds with their style or poli-tics'. They make no qualms about adding – 'we do that at *Colors* too', but there is no explanation of what their politics or attitudes to anything may be, and the fragmentation and bizarre juxtaposition of images only mystify further.

While the earlier issues of *Colors* appear to have been used to legitimise the content of their previous advertising campaigns, more recently Benetton has used *Colors* to shock and push the boundaries of what it is acceptable to discuss within the marketing arena. At the beginning of 1998 Benetton produced an issue of *Colors* devoted to death, which could be seen as the ultimate taboo issue. Toscani could not get advertisers to buy space in this issue, which contained such things as a guide to suicide (O'Reilly 1998). It is worth noting that following this issue, a number of fashion advertisers such as Pepe also used the death theme in their advertisements, to produce shocking images which glamorised death rather than enabling greater understanding. Benetton's shock tactics have also been explored recently by Pasi Falk who describes them as the Benetton–Toscani effect (**Falk 1997**).

Benetton's advertising and photography is integrally linked to their corpo-rate image making. It was even their advertisements which furnished the

PASI FALK (1997) 'The Benetton–Toscani Effect – Testing the Limits of Conventional Advertising' in Mica Nava *et al.* (eds) **Buy This Book**, Seattle: Bay Press company with a new logo. And Benetton's advertisements have become so divorced from the sales of any particular product, that they function much more clearly in the enhancement and creation of their image worldwide. The advertising campaigns and Toscani's photography have not only furnished the magazine *Colors* with visual material, but have also been converted into art postcards that are sold everywhere from Helsinki to Manchester. As Luciano Benetton writes in *Global Vision*, a Benetton publication which documents the company's development and marketing and provides a visual catalogue of their advertising:

> Our international image and the substance of our company are the same – a global group open to the world's influences and engaged in a continuing quest for new frontiers.

> (Benetton 1993)

The 'United Colors' campaigns have certainly visualised this imperialist philosophy.

BIBLIOGRAPHY

KEY TEXTS

Alloula, Malek (1987) *The Colonial Harem*, Manchester: Manchester University Press
Back, L. and Quaade, V. (1993) 'Dream Utopias, Nightmare Realities: Imagining Race and Culture within the World of Benetton', *Third Text* 22
Barthes, Roland (1973) *Mythologies*, Granada (first published 1957)
—— (1977a) 'The Rhetoric of the Image' in S. Heath (ed.) *Image, Music, Text*, London: Fontana
—— (1977b) 'The Photographic Message' in S. Heath (ed.) *Image, Music, Text*, London: Fontana
Berger, John (1972a) *Ways of Seeing*, Harmondsworth: Penguin
Brookes, Rosetta (1992) 'Fashion Photography' in J. Ash and E. Wilson (eds) *Chic Thrills: A Fashion Reader*, London: Pandora
Craik, Jennifer (1994) 'Soft Focus: Techniques of Fashion Photography' in *The Face of Fashion*, London: Routledge
Evans, C. and Thornton, M. (1989) *Women and Fashion: A New Look*, London: Quartet
Falk, Pasi (1997) 'The Benetton–Toscani Effect – Testing the Limits of Conventional Advertising' in Mica Nava, Andrew Blake, Iain MacRury and Barry Richards (eds) *Buy this Book*, London: Routledge
Goldman, Robert (1992) *Reading Ads Socially*, London: Routledge
Hall, Stuart (ed.) (1997) *Representation, Cultural Representations and Signifying Practices*, London: Sage
McCauley, Elizabeth Anne (1994) *Industrial Madness: Commercial Photography in Paris 1848–1871*, New Haven, CT, and London: Yale University Press
Myers, Kathy (1990) 'Selling Green' in C. Squiers (ed.) *The Critical Image: Essays on Contemporary Photography*, Seattle: Bay Press
Nye, David (1985) *Image Worlds: Corporate Identities at General Electric 1890–1930*, Cambridge, MA: The MIT Press
Slater, Don (1983) 'Marketing Mass Photography' in H. Davis and P. Walton (eds) *Language, Image, Media*, Oxford: Blackwell

Squiers, Carol (1992) 'The Corporate Year in Pictures' in R. Bolton (ed.) *The Contest of Meaning: Critical Histories of Photography*, Cambridge, MA: The MIT Press

Stein, Sally (1981) 'The Composite Photographic Image and the Composition of Consumer Ideology', *Art Journal*, Spring

Tagg, John (1988) 'A Democracy of the Image: Photographic Portraiture and Commodity Production' in *The Burden of Representation: Essays on Photographies and Histories*, London: Macmillan

Williams, Val (ed.) (1998) *Look at Me: Fashion and Photography in Britain, 1960 to the Present*, London: British Council

Williamson, Judith (1978) *Decoding Advertisements: Ideology and Meaning in Advertising*, London: Marion Boyars

—— (1979) 'Great History that Photographs Mislaid' in Photography Workshop (ed.) *Photography/Politics One*, London: Comedia

Winship, Janice (1987a) 'Handling Sex' in R. Betterton (ed.) *Looking On: Images of Femininity in the Visual Arts and Media*, London: Pandora

OTHER REFERENCES

Bacher, Fred (1992) 'The Popular Condition: Fear and Clothing in LA', *The Humanist*, September/October

Bailey, David (1988) 'Re-thinking Black Representations', *Ten/8* 31

—— (1989) 'People of the World' in P. Wombell (ed.) *The Globe: Representing the World*, York: Impressions Gallery

Bailey, David and Hall, Stuart (eds) (1992) *Critical Decade Ten/8* 2(3)

Baker, Lindsay (1991) 'Taking Advertising to its Limit', *The Times*, 22 July, p. 29

Bate, David (1993) 'Photography and the Colonial Vision', *Third Text* 22

Belussi, Fiorenza (1987) *Benetton: Information Technology in Production and Distribution: A Case Study of the Innovative Potential of Traditional Sectors*, SPRU, University of Sussex

Benetton (1993) *Global Vision: United Colors of Benetton*, Tokyo: Robundo

Benson, S. H. (n.d.) *Some Examples of Benson Advertising*, S. H. Benson Firm

Berger, John (1972b) 'The Political Uses of Photomontage' in *Selected Essays and Articles, The Look of Things*, Harmondsworth: Penguin

Bishton, Derek and Rearden, John (eds) (1984) *Black Image-Staying On Ten/8* 16

Devlin, Polly (1979) *Vogue Book of Fashion Photography*, London: Condé Nast

Edwards, Elizabeth (ed.) (1992) *Photography and Anthropology 1860–1920*, New Haven: Yale University Press

Edwards, Steve (1989) 'The Snapshooters of History', *Ten/8* 32

Ewing, William (1991) 'Perfect Surface' in *The Idealising Vision: The Art of Fashion Photography*, New York: Aperture

Freedman, Jim (1990) 'Bringing it all Back Home: A Commentary on *Into the Heart of Africa*', *Museum Quarterly*, February

Goddard, Angela (1998) *The Language of Advertising: Written Texts*, London: Routledge

Goffman, Erving (1979) *Gender Advertisements*, London: Macmillan

Graham, Judith (1989) 'Benetton "Colors" the Race Issue', *Advertising Age*

Gupta, Sunil (1986) 'Northern Media, Southern Lives' in Photography Workshop (ed.) *Photography/Politics: Two*, London: Comedia

Hall, Stuart (1993) 'Encoding/Decoding' in S. Durring (ed.) *The Cultural Studies Reader*, London: Routledge (first published 1980)

Harrison, Martin (1991) *Appearances: Fashion Photography Since 1945*, London: V&A

Jhally, Sut (1990) *Codes of Advertising*, London: Routledge

Leiss, W., Kline, S. and Jhally, S. (1986) *Social Communication in Advertising*, Toronto: Methuen

Mayle, Peter (1983) *Thirsty Work: Ten Years of Heineken Advertising*, London: Macmillan

Mitter, Swasti (1986) 'Flexibility and Control: The Case of Benetton' in *Common Fate Common Bond; Women in the Global Economy*, London: Pluto

Morris, Roderick C. (1992) 'The Best Possible Taste', *Spectator*, 15 February

Myers, Kathy (1986) *Understains: Sense and Seduction in Advertising*, London: Comedia

O'Reilly, John (1998) 'Death is Probably the Last Pornographic Issue Left', *Guardian*, 2 February

Penn, Irving (1974) *Worlds in a Small Room*, London: Studio Vista

Phizacklea, Annie (1990) 'The Benetton Model' in *Unpackaging the Fashion Industry: Gender, Racism and Class in Production*, London: Routledge

Pollock, Griselda (1990) 'Missing Women – Re-Thinking Early Thoughts on Images of Women' in C. Squiers (ed.) *The Critical Image: Essays on Contemporary Photography*, Seattle: Bay Press

Posner, Jill (1982) *Spray it Loud*, London: Routledge

Prochaska, David (1991) 'Fantasia of the Phototheque: French Postcard Views of Senegal', *African Arts*, October

Richards, Thomas (1990) *Commodity Culture in Victorian Britain*, London: Verso

Said, Edward (1985) *Orientalism*, London: Penguin (first published 1978)

Savan, Leslie (1990) 'Logo-rrhea', *Voice*, 24 November, New York

Schildkrout, Enid (1991) 'The Spectacle of Africa Through the Lens of Herbert Lang', *African Arts*, October

Sontag, Susan (1979) *On Photography*, Harmondsworth: Penguin

Stein, Sally (1992) 'The Graphic Ordering of Desire: Modernisation of a Middle-Class Women's Magazine 1919–1939' in R. Bolton (ed.) *The Contest of Meaning: Critical Histories of Photography*, Cambridge, MA: The MIT Press

Weernink, Wim (1979) *La Lancia: 70 Years of Excellence*, London: Motor Racing Publications

Wells, Liz (1992) 'Judith Williamson, Decoding Advertisements' in *Reading into Cultural Studies*, London: Routledge

Wilkinson, Helen (1997) '"The New Heraldry": Stock Photography, Visual Literacy and Advertising in 1930s Britain', *Journal of Design History*, 10(1)

Williams, Raymond (1980) 'Advertising the Magic System' in *Problems in Materialism and Culture*, London: Verso

Winship, Janice (1987b) *Inside Women's Magazines*, London: Pandora

CHAPTER 5

The subject as object

Photography and the human body

MICHELLE HENNING

5.1 Physique image from *Physique Pictorial*, 4(3), Fall 1954

The subject as object
Photography and the human body

INTRODUCTION

The photographic body in crisis

Since the late 1980s an extraordinary number of photographic practices and critical texts have taken the human body as their central subject. The photography historian **John Pultz** suggested that this is to do with the emergence of new forms of critical theory and 'body politics' (Pultz 1995: 7–10). Artists as diverse as Jo Spence, Cindy Sherman and Annette Messager have used photography in ways which challenge the idealisation of the female body in traditional nudes. And photography is used by, for example, the installation artists Mona Hatoum and Adrian Piper to critique ideas of racial difference.[1]

Some writers have argued that social crises, notably the AIDS epidemic, have politicised the photographic representation of the body and sexuality (Foster 1996: 122–123). Official representations of the AIDS crisis were opposed by agitational graphics groups such as Gran Fury, and artists such as Nan Goldin documented the impact of the epidemic on actual communities and individuals (Dubin 1992: 197–225; Crimp and Rolston 1990; Kotz 1998). The fascination with the body has also been linked to the advent of new technologies and forms of technical knowledge, including new means of rapidly reproducing and distributing photographic images, and developments in genetics and medicine which appear to offer the possibility of radically transformed bodies (Ewing 1994: 9). The writer Chris Townsend

JOHN PULTZ (1995)
Photography and the Body,
London: Weidenfeld & Nicolson

1 The work of these artists, and others named in this chapter is reproduced in widely available monographs and exhibition catalogues. It has not been possible to include full publication references for all of them.

argued that there have been two separate crises: first, a crisis of 'the body and social despair' and second, a crisis relating to looking, 'to the cultural uses of photography, and to disintegrating myths about the medium' which leads to conflicting views over how photography should be used to represent the human body (Townsend 1998: 8).

However, the anthropologist **Carole S. Vance**'s writing on photography and censorship in the US shows how ideas about bodies and bodily practices, and about the meanings and uses of photographs, are deeply interconnected (Vance 1990). Unlike Townsend she sees the 'crisis of looking' and the 'crisis of the body' as closely related. Instances of censorship bring to light the way that conflict between different interest groups relates to conflicting ways of understanding and interpreting photography.[2] Photographs of human bodies are caught up in social struggles over the legitimacy of different sexual practices and identities, and different views about the meanings and uses of photographs have political implications.

These struggles are as old as photography, but they became particularly vivid in the late twentieth century with the rise of both sexual politics and religious fundamentalism. At the same time the globalisation and diversification of media and the targeting of specialised interest groups made the range of photographic representations of the body more visible than ever. In this chapter we consider not just this recent history but also older examples which show the social significance of photographs of and about bodies.

The chapter is organised thematically rather than chronologically, to allow discussion of a number of current and historical photographic practices and debates. There are, inevitably, some important issues not discussed here, such as the representation of disability or the controversies over the photographing of children. However, the ideas and theories introduced in this chapter may be applied to a wider range of examples than those specifically considered here.

In the first section we look at how photography has been used historically as part of a broader attempt to 'read' people's bodies: especially in relation to racial and ethnic classifications and the description and analysis of social deviancy. The next section considers how gender and sexuality are visually coded in certain kinds of photographs, focusing particularly on erotic or 'soft porn' photographs. The third section attends to the ways in which the camera as a technology intervenes in the body, and also how it represents the body's relationship with technology, through a consideration of medical imaging, early avant-garde photography and contemporary advertising images. The final section explores the photographic representation of death and corpses, and the view that photography is a practice deeply associated with death.

EMBODYING SOCIAL DIFFERENCE

By the end of the nineteenth century photography was being used to classify people into 'types', illustrating and extending the Victorian sciences of

CAROLE S. VANCE (1990) 'The Pleasures of Looking: The Attorney General's Commission on Pornography versus Visual Images' in Carol Squiers (ed.) **The Critical Image: Essays on Contemporary Photography**, Seattle: Bay Press

2 This was vividly demonstrated in the reactions to Robert Mapplethorpe's touring photographic exhibition *The Perfect Moment* (1989) and to Andres Serrano's 1987 photograph *Piss Christ*. See Dubin 1992.

phrenology and **physiognomy**. The success of these popular sciences in the late nineteenth century has been described as part of a 'vast attempt at deciphering the body' in which the desire to classify bodies according to visual appearance is justified by the belief that the surface reveals hidden depths; in other words, that the outer surfaces of the body could be read as a series of signs or codes revealing or expressing inner character (Magli 1989: 124). Both phrenology and physiognomy appealed to a popular enthusiasm for classification according to 'type', and both became popular in the 1840s and 1850s at the same time as photography. 'Typological' classification was reassuring to the urban middle classes because its convenient generalisations helped make the mass of strangers in the city seem more familiar. As the sociologist Simmel noted, visual appearances were particularly important in a period when new means of public transport meant that many social encounters were primarily visual encounters: 'Before the development of buses, railroads and trams in the nineteenth century, people had never been in a position of having to look at one another for long minutes or even hours without speaking to one another' (Simmel quoted in Benjamin 1938: 38).

Simplified, popularised versions of physiognomy and phrenology could be used to counteract the anonymity of urban life, and provided 'a method of quickly assessing the characters of strangers in the dangerous and congested spaces of the nineteenth century city' (Sekula 1989: 348). These 'sciences' are not, however, as harmless as they first appear. Whilst they may have reassured the dominant class, physiognomy and phrenology were also deployed as a means of social control via photography. Because it shows us only surfaces, photography is ideally suited to physiognomic and phrenological interpretation, and it became part of an increasingly professionalised and systematic police force.

The photographer and theorist **Allan Sekula** argues that the photographs taken for police and prison records should be seen alongside the portrait photographs which flourished at the same time. People were encouraged to read portraits using physiognomy, so the portrait of the respectable citizen emphasised facial characteristics associated in physiognomy with moral character and citizenship. The photographic police archives also relied on a physiognomic norm: the 'average man' was the physical and social ideal against which the criminal body was measured (Sekula 1989: 347, 354–356).

Photography historian **John Tagg** has also discussed photographs of criminals, using the work of the French social historian **Michel Foucault** (see also margin note p. 56) to understand how photography is used to 'discipline' people. Discipline in Foucault's sense refers to processes of surveillance, identification, classification, labelling, analysis and correction – as opposed to older regimes of punishment which did not seek to understand the deviant/deviation but rather to eliminate it. According to Foucault, in modern society, power is dispersed through social institutions (such as schools, asylums, prisons) and exists in insidious ways in everyday practices. The construction of archives is

phrenology was developed at the end of the eighteenth century by Franz Josef Gall. It was based on the idea that the contours of the skull could give clues to the mental functioning of the brain.

physiognomy was an ancient science, systematised in the 1770s by Johann Caspar Lavater, which claimed to read the character of a person through the classification of the features of head and face. Lavater saw a 'correspondence between the external and the internal man, the visible superficies and invisible contents' (Lavater 1789 quoted in Lalvani 1996: 48)

ALLAN SEKULA (1989) 'The Body and the Archive' in Richard Bolton (ed.) **The Contest of Meaning: Critical Histories of Photography**, Cambridge, MA: MIT Press

JOHN TAGG (1988) **The Burden of Representation: Essays on Photographies and Histories**, London: Macmillan

5.2 Filing card using Bertillon's 'anthropometric' system, 1898
The standardised police records initiated by Bertillon produce 'a portrait of the product of the disciplinary method: the body made object' (Tagg 1988: 76)

crucial to the everyday ways in which disciplinary power is exercised. Tagg quotes texts from the 1850s through to the 1970s which lay down strictures for photographing social deviants for the purpose of police, prison, asylum and legal archives. At first the photographic archive was a vast accumulation of unclassified and often unrecognisable photographic portraits, but in the 1880s a French bureaucrat, Alphonse Bertillon, developed techniques to standardise police records and enable identification of repeat offenders. His filing card system involved detailed measurements of the criminal, description of identifying marks, and use of two photos – front view and profile – which were taken using standardised focal length and lighting (Lalvani 1996: 109; Sekula 1989: 357–363).

To study the disciplinary uses of photography means considering the ways in which people are represented, arranged for the camera, made available to be gazed at, and placed in a system of signification which codes and classifies them. As Tagg notes, we can see

> a repetitive pattern, the body isolated; the narrow space; the subjection to an unreturnable gaze; the scrutiny of gestures, faces and features; the clarity of illumination and sharpness of focus; the names and number boards. These are the traces of power, repeated countless times, whenever the photographer prepared an exposure, in police cell, prison, consultation room, home or school.
>
> (Tagg 1988: 85)

Perhaps one of the most striking photographic techniques derived from physiognomy and phrenology is composite portraiture. This was introduced by Francis Galton in the 1880s. Galton developed a technique for superimposing a number of photographed faces of people with shared characteristics or circumstances. The composite image produced in this way supposedly revealed hereditary physical characteristics, the surface 'symptoms' of innate biology. At first he presented his technique as useful in the diagnosis of disease, but he also attempted to use composite portraiture to reveal the

5.3 Francis Galton, *The Jewish Type*, composite photographs, 1883
Joseph Jacobs, the Jewish man who commissioned these images, saw them as validating Jewish identity, but they also reinforced Galton's own anti-Semitic views

5.4 Nancy Burson, *Warhead I*, composite image, 1982
Using computer imaging to superimpose faces, Nancy Burson updates the composite imaging technique invented
in the nineteenth century

characteristic physiognomy of different 'types': the faces superimposed may
all have committed the same crimes, or belong to the same ethnic groups.
Galton's method is centred around a concept of race: using phrenology and
physiognomy, he naturalised social differences by describing social 'types' in
terms of biology, that is, along the lines of race. In his work, different cultural
groups or social classes appear as separate races with definite and visible physical characteristics.

So the popular sciences of phrenology and physiognomy, combined with
new photographic techniques, produced a new and fundamentally racist vision
of society. It is perhaps not surprising to learn that the racial classificatory system
which Galton developed was later embraced by Nazism. It was Galton, the
pioneer of composite photography, who introduced the 'science' of eugenics.
Eugenics proposed that intellectual and moral qualities were hereditary and that
some races were therefore superior to others. As well as conveniently providing
a justification for European colonialism, eugenics represented class differences as
biological, viewing the inclination of the lower social classes towards deviance
as the result of a lack of hereditary good qualities.

These photographic practices are not confined to the nineteenth century. For instance, Sekula compares Galton's work to the recent use of composite (digital) photography by the American artist Nancy Burson, questioning the social and political implications of Burson's practice (Sekula 1989: 377). Burson's work questions nuclear weapons policies, advocates social welfare and tackles the conventions of feminine beauty, but like phrenology it emphasises surface appearances. It has also been argued that the fact that Burson has used her methods to help find missing children 'returns the art of composite portraiture to the purposes for which Galton originally designed it', for police detective work (Taylor 1997: 57).[3]

Computer-generated composites have also become a form of entertainment: 'Foto Morphosis' photo-booths combine the faces of two individuals to produce their 'virtual reality' child.[4] Composite imaging of a different sort, the 'photo fit', is regularly used by the police to attempt to identify criminals, and is based on classifying facial features according to type (this kind of mouth . . . or this kind?). Aspects of physiognomy and phrenology also exist today in market research attempts to identify and classify the consumer, just as the nineteenth century attempted to characterise strangers in the urban crowd. Most advertising today is too sophisticated to simply provide visual representation of the 'ideal consumer', but it still frequently deploys images of individuals as 'types'.

OBJECTS OF DESIRE

Objectification and images of women

Even erotic imagery depended on the classification of social types, though not primarily through physiognomy. Clothing and props act as signifiers of class and occupation in Victorian pornography. These images represented social types considered to be sexually available: for example, the laundress. The art historian Eunice Lipton has shown how, in Paris, the laundresses' low pay, visibility (the laundries were open on to the street) and tendency to drink wine to counteract the heat of the laundry led to their reputation as sexually 'loose' women (Lipton 1980). Other Victorian pornographic images showed women and couples in clearly middle-class domestic surroundings.[5]

Today, erotica also works through classifying its subjects into recognisable types – in this way it makes different women appear sexually available to a presumed heterosexual male viewer. And, just as the criminal photograph reduces the depicted person to a series of signifiers, so pornographic images offer women as available objects of fantasy by attaching certain meanings to a narrow set of signifiers.

In the 1970s and 1980s such representations of women became a focus of feminist criticism. Feminists questioned the existing distinctions between legitimate and illegitimate images (such as 'hardcore' pornography) which

3 However, it could be argued that finding missing children is a different kind of activity from establishing the criminal 'type'.

4 'I had Bill Clinton's Baby', **Marie Claire** 104, April 1997, p. 92. Even this mechanised composite uses racial typology – as well as programming in the preferred sex of your child you can choose your child's racial characteristics from 'Asian, Afro-Caribbean, Hispanic or Caucasian'.

Chapter 4 gives a contemporary example of the way this works: some of Benetton's ads, while ostensibly about global harmony, use visual signifiers of racial and ethnic identity which reproduce ideas of absolute racial difference.

See figure 3.4 in chapter 3 which hints at this reputation, though more explicitly sexualised images of laundresses were also common.

5 Detailed discussion of Victorian erotic and pornographic photography can be found in Solomon-Godeau (1991); Kendrick (1987), and Williams (1995).

5.5 Anonymous stereoscope photograph from around 1895
The plants, fabrics and lamp in this image are used to suggest a bourgeois interior

6 The argument against the traditional 'hard'/'soft' distinction is put by Brown (1981).

7 Solomon-Godeau concludes that 'it may well be that the most insidious and instrumental forms of domination, subjugation and objectification are produced by mainstream images of women rather than by juridically criminal or obscene ones' (Solomon-Godeau 1991: 237).

were based on degrees of explicitness of nudity and/or sexual activity.[6] Advertising and publicity images as well as erotica were criticised for eroticising the female body in a way which turned women into mere objects for a male gaze, a process usually termed **objectification**.[7]

The concept of objectification has special relevance to photography. In one sense photography inadvertently objectifies people by turning them into things to be looked at (Solomon-Godeau 1991: 221–222). But it has also been suggested that in everyday life women are already constituted as objects to be looked at and men as 'possessing the **gaze**'. According to this argument, women internalise the male gaze to the point that they survey themselves. This relationship has been expressed by the critic John Berger:

> Men look at women. Women watch themselves being looked at.
> This determines not only most relations between men and women
> but also the relation of women to themselves. The surveyor of
> woman in herself is male: the surveyed female. Thus she turns herself
> into an object – and most particularly an object of vision: a sight.
>
> (Berger 1972: 47)

If women are already objectified by the male gaze, and if objectification is in any case what photography does, then photographic images of women are doubly 'objectifying' (see Solomon-Godeau 1991: 221–222). We need to consider not only how photographs present women's bodies for a male viewer but also how this process spills over into everyday life and into how men view actual women, and how women view themselves. In relation to this 'spilling over', the everyday cultural objects, domestic settings and familiar poses used in soft porn and advertising are significant, because, as feminist theorist Beverley Brown has argued, this limited visual vocabulary operates as a 'short-cut' to sexual fantasy and in turn, leaves everyday life with a 'certain afterglow' (Brown 1981: 138–140). In advertising, this process is part of the attempt to eroticise commodities (see chapter 4).

Fetishism, voyeurism and pleasure

Photography theorists have made use of psychoanalytic theory to analyse how photographic images construct women as objects for a male gaze, and how the visual pleasures of looking at such images are implicated in the exercise of power. In particular the concepts of **voyeurism** and **fetishism** have been influential. These concepts were most famously formulated by Sigmund Freud, and have been developed by more recent psychoanalysts, notably Jacques Lacan, Melanie Klein and Luce Irigaray (see Gamman and Makinen 1994: ch. 3). However, we will focus here on the terms as they were initially developed by Sigmund Freud (Freud 1905, 1927). (See also note p. 31).

A Freudian approach considers the spectator's experience of visual pleasure in terms of his or her subjectivity which is shaped from early childhood. This visual pleasure or **'scopophilia'** is usually understood as an erotic pleasure gained in looking at another person or at images of other bodies. This pleasure is voyeuristic when it is dependent on the object of this gaze being unaware, not looking back. Voyeurism is a form of objectification which Freud saw as originating in childhood curiosity. At its extreme, it becomes an obsessive sexual practice. Voyeurism describes a mode of looking related to the exercise of power in which a body becomes a spectacle for someone else's pleasure, a world divided into the active 'lookers' and the passive 'looked at'. To some extent photography, by the very nature of the medium, invites voyeuristic looking, although some photographs, such as those which depict a normally private or taboo activity and a subject apparently unaware that they are being photographed, are more explicitly voyeuristic (Sontag 1977: 11–14). The concept of voyeurism is applicable not only to sexualised or erotic images, but also in relation to the depiction of colonised peoples and of disability as spectacle.

Another concept which has been central to Freudian analyses of photography is fetishism (see Burgin 1983). In Freudian psychoanalytic theory an important moment in the shaping of the self is the point at which the child becomes aware of sexual difference and moves away from its early close relationship with its mother: this process of entry into sexuality is what produces, in some people, sexual fetishism. Freud's definition of fetishism is derived from older definitions, in which an inanimate object takes on special powers such as warding off danger and misfortune and is the centre

8 In particular, it is a useful corrective to the tendency towards a literal interpretation in which a pornographic image which does not include a woman's head has 'decapitated her', or flattening lighting made for a 'one-dimensional' representation. Instead, a reading based in the concept of fetishism suggests flattening and fragmentation are part of the process by which the pleasures of looking at the image, or handling the object (a magazine page, a photograph), are translated into the pleasure of looking at (or imagining touching) the depicted body.

CHRISTIAN METZ (1985) 'Photography and Fetish', **October** 34, Autumn

LAURA MULVEY (1975) 'Visual Pleasure and Narrative Cinema' Reprinted 1989 in **Visual and Other Pleasures**, London: Macmillan

9 In 1957 Roland Barthes observed similar qualities in the cinematic representation of the face of Greta Garbo (Barthes 1986: 56–57).

10 However, an advertisement such as this is clearly intended for a female readership. Even taking into account Berger's argument that women internalise the male gaze, the Freudian theory of fetishism is inadequate in explaining the fetishistic qualities of these advertisements, for in Freud's explanation, the fetishist is male (Gamman and Makinen 1994: 37–44, 95–105).

of religious rituals. In Freud's interpretation, an object becomes a fetish when it becomes the focus of (usually male) sexual desire. The male child develops an unconscious fear of castration at the sight of a woman's body, and fetishism is one means of allaying this anxiety: in a process termed 'disavowal' the fetishist knows but suppresses his knowledge of her 'lack' (of a penis) and idealises objects associated with the woman (for example, shoes).

The use of Freud's concept of fetishism to explain visual pleasure is controversial because it relies on the theory of male castration anxiety (Gamman and Makinen 1994: chs 3 and 6). Nevertheless, it is useful for thinking about the ways in which certain photographic styles and techniques are linked to objectification.[8] For instance, the film theorist **Christian Metz** argued that a photograph works like a fetish because it freezes a fragment of reality, 'cutting off a piece of space and time . . . keeping it unchanged while the world around continues to change' (Metz 1985: 85).

In the same way, fetishism, in Freud's interpretation, involves freezing a moment (the moment before the trauma of recognition) and fixating on a fragment, an object associated with the woman. Most of all, the photograph can be a fetish because of its physicality – we can touch and hold a photograph: 'The familiar photographs that many people carry with them always obviously belong to the order of fetishes in the ordinary sense of the word' (Metz 1985: 87).

But perhaps the reason why the theory of fetishism has been so important in analysing film and photography is that it helps to account for the ways in which visual images seem so often to objectify and fragment women's bodies in a way that is not common in representations of the male body. In a well-known essay, the film theorist and film-maker **Laura Mulvey** used the theory of fetishism to explain ways in which certain films objectify the female star. She suggested that the female figure on screen is potentially troubling to male spectators: 'the woman as icon, displayed for the gaze and enjoyment of men, the active controllers of the look, always threatens to evoke the anxiety it originally signified' (Mulvey 1989: 21).

Mulvey contended that the male spectator is unconsciously reminded of the traumatic moment when he recognised sexual difference. One way he can deal with this is by disavowing it through fetishism. Mulvey suggests that certain films turn the represented figure of a female star (such as Marlene Dietrich) into a fetish by bringing together the beauty of the film as spectacle, the play of light and shadows, with the beauty of the woman as object. Close-ups, lighting and make-up fragment, flatten and render the female face one-dimensional (Mulvey 1989: 21–23).[9] The formal qualities of the projected image are the reassuring substitute object which distracts the male spectator from the threat which the woman poses.[10]

Although Mulvey is discussing motion film, we can see similar qualities in the representation of the female face in current cosmetic advertisements in women's magazines. Here, a blank space in the image stands in for flesh:

the faces are flattened with no shadows visible, reduced to a set of facial features arranged on a smooth and atonal expanse of skin. In this way the medium and image are conflated, the glossy, smooth feel of the magazine page stands in for the woman's skin (see Burgin 1986: 19).

Class and representations of the body

One useful question raised by the debates around photographic images of women is how we distinguish a feminist political opposition to these images from a more conservative disgust at the portrayal of aspects of the body that are normally kept hidden from public view (Rodgerson and Wilson 1991: 28). The cultural theorist **Laura Kipnis** uses the example of the porno-graphic magazine *Hustler*.[11] Kipnis argues that *Hustler* needs to be understood in terms of class as well as gender, since it sets out primarily to provoke and disgust the 'establishment' (Kipnis 1992: 373–391).

To understand what disgust has to do with class, we need to look briefly at the history of attitudes towards the body. The historian Norbert Elias has described the change in attitudes that occurred as part of a shift from feudal society to a capitalist system in Europe. He suggested that, as a new class becomes dominant, it transforms the dominant ideas about the body and bodily decorum which had prevailed in the old social order (Elias 1994).

Medieval, feudal society was rigidly hierarchical, and control of bodies was a central part of social control of the population. But, as the Russian literary theorist **Mikhail Bakhtin** pointed out, in the medieval carnival these hierarchies were disrupted, and ideas of bodily decorum ridiculed or ignored. Carnival was the legitimate space where bodily excess was celebrated, where the lower body, orifices, reproduction, eating, defecation and copulation, pregnancy, birth and death were openly represented (Stallybrass and White 1986: 13; Dentith 1995: ch. 3).[12]

Bakhtin referred to this carnivalesque body as the 'grotesque' body. In the grotesque conception of the world, birth and death are cyclically related, and bodies are understood in collective terms, linked to one another and the world and continually growing and changing. Gradually, the grotesque body of the carnival was displaced by the dominant representation of the body, epitomised by the classical nude. The classical body is a smooth, orifice-less and self-sufficient body. While the grotesque tradition represents the body as ever-changing, from birth to death, and connected to the earth and to other bodies, 'classical' representations of the body omit these aspects: 'The ever unfinished nature of the body was hidden, kept secret; conception, pregnancy, childbirth, death throes, were almost never shown' (Bakhtin 1984: 29).

One way the merchant classes in the sixteenth century and the industrial bourgeoisie in the eighteenth century maintained their political **hegemony** was through strictures about bodily control and decorum. Capitalist society places enormous emphasis on individualism, constructing a strict separa-tion between the 'private' and the 'public'. Increasingly, the classical body

LAURA KIPNIS (1992) '(Male) Desire and (Female) Disgust: Reading Hustler' in Lawrence Grossberg *et al.* (eds) **Cultural Studies**, London and New York: Routledge

11 *Hustler* had been used by Andrea Dworkin to demonstrate the misogyny she believes to be central to pornography (Dworkin 1981: 29–30). Kipnis' argument is a critique of approaches such as Dworkin's, which focus exclusively on gender in their discussions of pornography.

12 Other writers argue that it was legitimate precisely because it made it easier for those hierarchies to remain in place the rest of the time See Stallybrass and White 1986: 13; Dentith 1995: 73–74.

Mikhail Mikhailovich Bakhtin (1895–1975) Bakhtin was one of a group of Soviet philosophers and theorists. In 1929 many of the group were arrested by Stalin's regime. From 1929 until his death in 1975, Bakhtin worked in internal exile in the Soviet Union.

His work focused on culture as a reciprocal process, and especially on the relationship between representation and social conflict, in which subordinate groups modify and reinterpret the representations produced by the dominant social class. His work was controversial and subject to censorship, since it defended the idea of multiple and conflicting perspectives ('heteroglossia') at a time when the Stalinist government was attempting to impose one ideological worldview. Bakhtin's most famous writings include the essays written in the 1930s and early 1940s, published in *The Dialogic Imagination* (trans. Caryl Emerson and Michael Holquist, University of Texas, 1981).
In these essays Bakhtin sees the novel as distinct from the official artforms of the epic and poetry, in that it engages with everyday spoken language. For Bakhtin, the novel is on the side of popular culture, against authoritative culture. Bakhtin also wrote about the writers Rabelais and Dostoevsky in books eventually published in the mid-1960s: *Rabelais and his World* (trans. Hèïène Iswolsky, Indiana University Press, 1984) and *Problems of Dostoevsky's Poetics* (trans. Caryl Emerson, University of Manchester Press, 1984). Central to these writings is the concept of carnival.

LINDA WILLIAMS (1995) 'Corporealized Observers: Visual Pornographies and the Carnal Density of Vision' in Patrice Petro **Fugitive Images**, Bloomington: Indiana University Press

became the publicly acceptable representation of the body in modern society, while those aspects associated with the lower body and the body's connection with the world were banished to the realm of the private, seen as disgusting and shameful, displaced into illicit and secret representations which were unmentionable and invisible in 'polite society' (Stallybrass and White 1986: 188). However, the advent of photography as mass reproduction made this division increasingly hard to control and the representation of the disgusting, the base, the distasteful became a means of challenging social hierarchies.

Kipnis sees *Hustler* in this light. She contrasts *Hustler's* use of photography with the more 'tasteful' images of *Playboy* and *Penthouse*:

> The Hustler body is an unromanticized body – no vaselined lens or soft focus: this is neither the airbrushed top-heavy fantasy body of Playboy, nor the ersatz opulence, the lingeried and sensitive crotch shots of Penthouse, transforming female genitals into *objets d'art*. It's a body, not a surface or a suntan: insistently material, defiantly vulgar, corporeal.

> (Kipnis 1992: 375)

But being insistently 'grotesque' does not necessarily make an image politically radical. The targets of carnivalesque ridicule and attack were just as often social outsiders or those considered inferior, such as women. To understand a reaction of shock or disgust at a photograph may mean paying attention to complicated intersections of categories such as class and gender. Middle-class women's disgust at the explicit representation of women's bodies for a male audience is inseparable from their own relationship to images of women's bodies and to their own bodies. Attempts to legally restrict the distribution of explicit photographs of women's bodies or of sexual activity were carried out to protect 'ladies' against seeing such representations, though the film historian **Linda Williams** suggests that they saw them nevertheless (Williams 1995: 25). This attitude to middle-class women as (potential) viewers of sexually explicit imagery is part of a wider ideology which incited in middle-class women a disgust at their own bodies. 'Ladies' were encouraged to develop a delicate 'feminine' sensibility premised on the repression and unmentionability of bodily experiences such as menstruation, excretion, and even childbirth: 'Since "respectable women" were defined precisely by their self-distancing from such indecent domains they were the social group most remote from any access to available symbolic articulations of the lower body' (Stallybrass and White 1986: 188–189).

By the late nineteenth century these 'symbolic articulations' included photographs. Even today, a middle-class woman's first encounter with a pornographic magazine may be an encounter with carnivalesque pleasures from which she knows she is excluded; she is not the intended viewer of these images, though she may be the object of the fantasies. Her disgust at these images may be a combination of her learned disgust at the lower body, her horror at the knowledge of her own exclusion (a body like hers is offered up for the pleasure of the readers, while she has had so little access to such representation) as well as feminist outrage at the ways in which the conventions of pornographic imagery construct the woman as an object of male sexual fantasy.[13]

The anti-pornography campaigns

Although, as Kipnis argues, feminist analyses of pornography have tended to underestimate the significance of class, they have effectively drawn attention to its often extreme misogyny and its role in women's subordination. In the 1980s a number of feminist campaigns against pornographic imagery gained momentum, such as the 'Off the Shelf' campaign organised by the Campaign Against Pornography in the UK.[14] These campaigns were influenced by the American Radical Feminists, such as Robin Morgan, who argued that 'Pornography is the theory – rape is the practice' and Andrea Dworkin, who famously stated: 'Pornography *is* violence against women' (Rodgerson and Wilson 1991: 26; Dworkin 1981). Dworkin's critique of pornography is passionate and almost evangelical in style, and has been very influential. It differs from previous forms of feminism in seeing texts (both visual and written) rather than social discrimination, as central to male dominance. However, it depends on a very narrow interpretive approach to photographs, and offers little evidence for the view that a photograph can be a *cause* of violence against women (Kendrick 1996: 231).

Other feminists, such as the group Feminists Against Censorship, argued that the anti-pornography campaigns risked undermining women's right to enjoy sexual and erotic imagery (Chester and Dickey 1988; Rodgerson and Wilson 1991; Segal and Macintosh 1992). A number of writers have pointed out how the category 'pornography' is a misleading one, and that we should pay attention to the range of images and audiences for whom 'pornography' has widely differing meanings and uses. As the critic Katherine Enos puts it:

> For conservative feminists and the religious right, pornography is the theory, the rape and murder of women the practice. For queer culture, the production of their own pornographies can be a self-affirming form of representation in a straight culture where a 'lesbian kiss' on TV is so unheard of as to be a matter of public debate.
>
> (Enos 1997/1998)

As the above quote implies, anti-pornography feminism found allies in political groups which were usually opposed to feminism. Whilst left-wing political parties were happier to support feminists on this issue than on many other feminist arguments, the religious Right also found it acceptable, even

13 Disgust and desire are not necessarily mutually exclusive: 'disgust always bears the imprint of desire. These low domains, apparently expelled as "Other", return as the object of nostalgia, longing and fascination' (Stallybrass and White 1986: 191).

14 Previously, attention had focused on writing rather than images. One explanation for feminism's new focus on the visual image is that most visual erotica seemed to be *of* women and *for* men, while written erotica more frequently addressed a female audience. The Kinsey report research of the 1940s suggested that women are less sexually aroused by images than by literature, and this view is still commonly held. Walter Kendrick points out that attitudes to pornography in America (and Britain) have now shifted so much that '"Pornography" now means pictures, preferably, moving pictures' (Kendrick 1996: 243).

15 The feminist lawyer Catherine MacKinnon drafted anti-pornography legislation in Minneapolis which was then adopted by right-wing legislators in Indianapolis and New York (legislation subsequently declared unconstitutional).

DEBORAH BRIGHT (1998) **The Passionate Camera: Photography and Bodies of Desire**, London and New York: Routledge

taking on board aspects of feminist arguments, such as the objectification argument.[15] However, as the artist and writer **Deborah Bright** argues, the right wing, particularly in the United States, was primarily interested in responding to the new-found visibility of many minority communities and tackling what they saw as 'enemies within', such as 'immigrants, those on public assistance, young unemployed black men, unwed mothers, and gay men and lesbians' (Bright 1998: 1). State-funded arts agencies in the United States were relatively supportive of community-based art in the 1970s and 1980s. Right-wing groups responded by attacking state funding of photographic images which dealt with issues related to minorities, and especially to homosexuality. In particular they questioned the funding by the National Endowment for the Arts (NEA) of exhibitions of photographs which they saw as undermining norms of decency. They considered images which could be read as pornographic, sacrilegious or blasphemous as unsuitable for state funding; this usually meant photographic representations of bodies, body parts, bodily fluids or sexual practices. Most notorious were the 1989 attacks on exhibitions of the photographs of Robert Mapplethorpe and Andres Serrano, both funded by the NEA, leading to (self-) censorship of this work by museums and galleries, and to legislation restricting the NEA's grant-giving powers (Bright 1998: 6–7).

Photography and homoerotic desire

Whereas feminist writers have pointed to photography's role in naturalising or reinforcing gender hierarchy, Christian fundamentalists see certain kinds of photographs (or photographs of certain subjects) as naturalising and endorsing improper or illegitimate activities and identities. They attribute particular power to photographs because of their immediacy, tending to treat the photograph as directly reflecting reality, and somehow capable of causing deviant behaviour. Carole S. Vance has argued that, because it is very easy to change a photograph's meaning through recontextualising it, campaigners could elicit support through exposing unfamiliar audiences to, for instance, decontextualised images of naked children or sadomasochistic sex (Vance 1990).

It was the visibility of forms of sexual 'deviance' – in particular, homosexuality – to which the new Right objected and their aim was to suppress this visibility through legislative measures. The conservative tendency to idealise an earlier America, of the 1950s, is partly based in a belief that images appealing to such deviant desires were a more recent phenomenon.

While it is true that in the 1950s gay men and lesbians had little access to images or media representations which represented homosexuality at all, and those which were available usually portrayed it in a negative light, some writers have argued that the homoerotic desire was addressed by certain images and texts, but that this was done in highly coded ways to avoid censorship. The art historian **Emmanuel Cooper** explains how the American 'physique' magazines of the 1950s, which were primarily photo-

EMMANUEL COOPER (1990) **Fully Exposed: The Male Nude in Photography**, London: Unwin Hyman graphic magazines depicting toned and muscular male bodies for a male readership, legitimated their male readership's interest through the use of visual references to classical antiquity (Cooper 1990: 100–101). These classical references work in a dual way: legitimating the images by emphasising their aesthetic (rather than erotic) nature; and simultaneously working as coded references for the readership, drawing on the homoerotic associations of ancient Greek art and culture.

However, the art historian Gavin Butt argues that the repressive culture of 1950s America meant that readings were fragile, based in connotations and associations dependent on the viewer's own homoerotic desire. The heavily coded nature of the image is evidence of the illegitimate and unspoken nature of such desire at the time, rather than of a thriving 'gay' identity (Butt 1998: 280). As well as references to classical art, the physique photos included certain 'campy' references. For instance, in figure 5.1, (p. 218) the use of studio props emphasises the contrived nature of the image, avoiding any attempt to make the image appear naturalistic. In addition, the poses struck by the models are not so much accurate copies of classical poses but a 'kitsch approximation' which emphasises the image's own artifice (Butt 1998: 279; Cooper 1990: 102) (for a discussion of kitsch and camp, see p. 237). Even the models' carefully developed bodies had homoerotic associations, displaying developed torsos yet 'slim-hipped, with the legs of ballet dancers' (Michael Bronski, quoted in Butt 1998: 280). These images predate the 1970s, when male homosexual identity became more visible and distinct, and specifically gay cultural forms were constructed.

In the 1980s, a new sexual politics, partly developed in response to government policies regarding HIV and AIDS, rejected older gay and lesbian attempts to be accepted within the status quo and instead challenged the dominant construction of 'normal' versus 'deviant' through a revival and re-inflection of the category 'queer'. Queer activists demanded public visibility for people and practices deemed 'abnormal' or 'unnatural' in the face of a history of social invisibility and repression.

Part of this new sexual politics was a re-evaluation of the cross-dressing which was an important part of working-class 'butch/femme' lesbian culture in the early twentieth century. Previously, this had been dismissed by feminist lesbians as a sign of repression, and as reinforcing old 'inversion' theories of homosexuality (in which lesbians are 'mannish' women). Queer politics shed a different light on this history, celebrating cross-dressing as undermining fixed gender roles. Whilst lesbian photographers challenged anti-pornography feminism by producing lesbian erotica, including SM images, queer photographers emphasise role-playing and cross-dressing, questioning the stability and naturalness of gender.

5.6 Del LaGrace Volcano, from the _Hermaphrodyke: Self-Portraits of Desire_ series, 1995 (original in colour)

The British photographer Del LaGrace explores and undermines the signifiers of gender in erotic imagery. While these images differ from the physique magazine images in explicitly challenging normative sexuality, they too emphasise their own constructedness through the inclusion of the shutter release cable, which also blurs the line between photographer and photographed

CASE STUDY: _LA CICCIOLINA_ (figure 5.7)

This chapter has outlined a number of different arguments and theories related to the photographic representation of the human body. Using a case study we can explore how these general arguments might be applied to a specific image: a photograph of the Hungarian-Italian 'porn star' Ilona Staller, known as _La Cicciolina_.

5.7 *La Cicciolina* (original in colour)
In Italy, Ilona Staller is a well-known porn star who performs in hardcore stage shows and films, as well as
modelling for softcore magazines. In June 1987 she was elected to the Italian Parliament as an MP for the
Italian Radical Party. This photograph is taken by Riccardo Schicchi, with whom she usually works

Earlier in the chapter, I looked at how erotic imagery uses props and settings
to classify bodies as social types. This tendency impinges on people's everyday
lives, insofar as this typology is then applied to actual people: affecting, for
instance, how men view women, and how women view themselves. Yet
Schicchi's photographs of *La Cicciolina* suggest that photographs do not have
to use this vocabulary to 'count' within the porn/erotica industry. The props in
the photograph shown here – (painted) bubbles, a gold waistcoat, a goose,
and broken classical columns – do not add up to any recognisable everyday

235

situation, nor are they readable signifiers of class or social position. The only obvious connotations are of fairy-tales, signified by the goose (and its fairy-tale connection with gold). *La Cicciolina* herself is clearly situated as a figure of fantasy, not a real social type or 'girl next door'.

The lack of realism in pornographic colour photography was noted in the 1950s by one of the founders of Cultural Studies in Britain, Richard Hoggart. He commented on the new 'technicolour cheesecake' magazines which he saw as part of the Americanisation and de-politicisation of British working-class culture.

> Everything has been stripped to a limited range of visual suggestions – can one imagine a musky body-smell, un-artificially disordered hair, an uneven texture to the skin, hair on the arms and legs, beads of perspiration on the upper-lip, on one of these neatly-packaged creatures?

> (Hoggart 1957: 191)

Hoggart then goes on to imply that this lack of realism might encourage 'sexual immorality'.[16] His view contrasts interestingly with the way the right-wing anti-pornography campaigners of the 1980s read photographs as direct, scarcely mediated, reflections of real situations (Vance 1990).

In fact Hoggart's description could apply to the *Cicciolina* image, with its absence of shadows and three-dimensional space. As noted above, this flattening is particularly common in photographs of women, making the pleasure of looking at the person depicted inseparable from the visual and tactile pleasure provided by the picture. It turns the photograph into a fetishistic substitute, defusing the threat suggested by the female body. The same visual qualities produce what Bakhtin characterises as the classical body. The classical body represses or conceals aspects of real existence in favour of an idealised norm. As Kipnis argued, more 'respectable' softcore magazines such as *Playboy* and *Penthouse* tend towards smooth, unblemished classical bodies. Schicchi and Staller take this to an extreme, so that even in the more explicit images *La Cicciolina*'s body is decidedly un-corporeal, with atonal expanses of skin and often lacking any body hair.

However, the more typical photographic spreads of *Penthouse* and *Playboy* are naturalistic; that is, they attempt to pass as reality through invoking 'everyday' situations and settings. In contrast, the images of *La Cicciolina* have become increasingly anti-naturalistic over the course of her career. Whilst early images present her in conventional erotic poses with honey-blonde hair and little make-up, by the mid-1980s she sports white-blonde hair, startling ginger eyebrows, scarlet lips and bright blue eyelashes, and poses with increasingly bizarre props in front of painted backdrops. Staller and Schicchi's approach can be compared to the tactics of the Radical Party, for whom Staller stood as candidate. This minority party achieves its political ends by disrupting Parliament from within, its playful humour standing in contrast to the seriousness of the main political

16 'Are such things likely to increase sexual immorality among young people? I find it hard to imagine much connexion between them and heterosexual activity. They may encourage masturbation: in their symbolic way they may promote that kind of sealed-off sexual response' (Hoggart 1957: 191–192).

parties. Similarly, these photographs could be seen as disrupting the naturalism of softcore pornography, taking up and exaggerating existing tendencies such as the lack of perspectival depth and the use of props.

It is interesting to compare this explicitly 'staged' quality with the emphasis on artifice which characterised the 1950s physique photographs discussed above, and also with the use of studio photography and role-playing in recent 'queer' photography. Although the *Cicciolina* pictures have very little in common with the work of Del LaGrace Volcano, the use of colour, painted surfaces and playful quotation of styles and settings resemble the work of the French photographers Pierre et Gilles. These qualities could be understood in terms of 'camp' which is characterised by humorous artifice and flamboyance. Yet 'camp' has been defined as a 'queer aesthetic', which loses its political significance if applied to 'straight' culture (Meyer 1994: Introduction). Thus the visual style of Schicchi's photographs of *La Cicciolina* could be read as a heterosexual appropriation of the camp aesthetic. However those very same qualities could be understood in terms of 'kitsch'. This was originally a derogatory term applied to forms of popular culture considered as cheap, garish, sentimental or vulgar (Greenberg 1939). More recently the term has taken on other associations, so that 'kitsch' taste also refers to the knowing, ironic preference of an educated middle class for objects and images usually dismissed as 'low' culture.[17] The wide availability of the *Cicciolina* photographs, as postcards and poster-books, could be seen as evidence that even softcore porn, seen as one of the lowest and most irredeemable forms of popular culture in the late 1970s and early 1980s, became by the 1990s capable of being rehabilitated through irony.

TECHNOLOGICAL BODIES

The camera as mechanical eye

Recent writers have considered photography in terms both of the bodies depicted and of its relationship to the bodies of the viewer and of the photographer (Crary 1990; Jay 1993). They suggest that photographs should not be thought of in terms of a single, centred and disembodied 'gaze' but as part of a new visual practice which presumes an embodied observer. **Jonathan Crary** places photography in the context of a range of popular nineteenth-century toys and devices which produce illusions of movement or depth. Devices such as **mutoscopes** and **stereoscopes** were enjoyed precisely because they 'tricked the eye' and, as Linda Williams has suggested, because of the tactile bodily sensations they provided since the observer engaged with them by holding the eyepiece of the machine or cranking a handle (Williams 1995: 14).[18]

Early scientific uses of photography give us an idea of its significance for understanding the human body. In the 1880s the French scientist Etienne-Jules Marey used photography to explore human and animal physiology. As

17 'Neo-kitsch is intentional, and it capitalises on an acquired taste for tackiness. It is a popularisation of the camp sensibility, a perspective wherein appreciation of the "ugly" conveys to the spectator an aura of refined decadence, an ironic enjoyment from a position of enlightened superiority' (Olalquiaga 1992: 45).

18 Williams argues that understanding photography in relation to the body is particularly crucial for erotic images since the observer engages with them by touching their own body as well as the machine through which they are viewing or the paper of the image (Williams 1995: 14).

JONATHAN CRARY (1990) **Techniques of the Observer: On Vision and Modernity in the Nineteenth Century**, Cambridge, MA: The MIT Press

The **mutoscope** was one of many entertainment devices developed as a result of the Victorian fascination with the phenomenon of persistence of vision, in which the human brain retains an image for a fraction of a second longer than the eye actually sees it. The mutoscope was an arcade machine invented in 1895 by Thomas Edison. It was basically a mechanised version of a flipbook, in which a person looked through a viewer and cranked a handle to flip the photographs inside, which gave the images the illusion of continuous movement. The **stereoscope** was a form of entertainment popular from the 1850s. It consisted of either a hand-held or a cabinet-style viewer and pairs of photographs on cards. The pictures were taken from different viewpoints corresponding to the spacing of the eyes. The stereoscope was constructed so that each eye only sees one photograph, giving the impression of a three-dimensional image. Sometimes tinted tissue paper was used as a backing, adding colour to the image when seen through a backlit viewer; or pinpricks included to simulate sparkling jewels or streetlamps; or objects painted on the tissues so that they would suddenly appear when held to the light.

5.8 Women using stereoscopes in late nineteenth-century France
This photograph is a reminder that women, as well as men, enjoyed optical toys and the pleasures of spectatorship

MARTA BRAUN (1992)
Picturing Time: The Work of Etienne-Jules Marey (1830–1904), Chicago: University of Chicago Press

See chapter 3, pp. 128–9 for more discussion of stereoscopes.

the photography theorist **Marta Braun** explains, Marey developed special cameras and photographic techniques to study human and animal locomotion (Braun 1992: ch. 3). His contemporary, the American artist Eadweard Muybridge, performed similar experiments. His images of a horse in motion, published in 1878, were sensational because they showed for the first time that horses ran in a different way than was usually pictured.

Through their photography Marey and Muybridge opened up to vision things that the human eye could not perceive. This ability of photographic technology to expand the capabilities of the human eye was noted by writers, photographers and film-makers in the early part of the twentieth century. In the 1920s and 1930s the camera (both the still and the motion camera)

5.9 Etienne-Jules Marey
Marey's 'chronophotographic' studies can be understood as part of the drive to increase the efficiency of human motion in the military, in industry and in sport

was understood as a kind of mechanical eye. As the Soviet film-maker, Dziga Vertov, expressed it:

> I'm an eye. A mechanical eye. I, the machine, show you a world the way only I can see it. I free myself for today and forever from human immobility. . . . My way leads towards the creation of a fresh perception of the world. Thus I explain in a new way the world unknown to you.
>
> (Vertov 1923 quoted in Berger 1972: 7)

The literary critic and philosopher Walter Benjamin also commented on the ability of photography and film to expand what could be perceived by the human eye. For Benjamin, this was part of their utopian, liberatory potential: in enabling people to see the world in new ways, it offered them the possibility of questioning and ultimately changing their everyday lives (Benjamin 1936: 229–230).

The idea that the camera transforms the way we see the world is even more pertinent today with the advent of new non-photographic imaging media such as X-rays (radiography), ultrasound and magnetic resonance imaging, and new techniques such as tomography that allows cross-sections or slices through the body to be imaged. Together with microscopic photography (micrography), these technologies enable us to see aspects of the body not visible to the naked eye (Ewing 1996).

Thus the camera is an extension of the photographer's body, a kind of prosthesis, but it also threatens to take over and displace the eye: it gets between the viewer and the viewed and 'shapes reality according to *its* terms' (Krauss 1986: 116). The experience of looking through the camera, and the conventions surrounding photographic practice, affect the way we see. Thus the camera can be understood as one of a number of 'prosthetic' machines (including telephones and computers) which we may treat as extensions of our own bodies but which change the ways we physically engage with the world. Seeing through the camera is different from seeing without it and, since photography, seeing is a changed practice.

LISA CARTWRIGHT (1995)
Screening the Body: Tracing Medicine's Visual Culture,
Minneapolis and London: University of Minnesota Press

The camera also affects the way we value our own sense of sight: the cultural theorist **Lisa Cartwright** has argued that in medicine, photography and cinematography 'supplanted or replaced sensory perception', since the data produced via these techniques came to be seen as having more authority than the doctor's or technician's own observations (Cartwright 1995: 34).

The very presence of the camera transforms the scene, it *intervenes* in reality. Medical uses of photography and other imaging technologies show how it intervenes in the body of the photographed subject: nineteenth-century surgical experiments combined photography and cinematography with vivisection, as in the 1898 film of a dog's beating heart (Cartwright 1995: 20). Other medical imaging techniques had inadvertent and unexpected effects on bodies, producing tumour and cancers (notably radiography; see Cartwright 1995: chs 5 and 6).

Although intervention is seldom this extreme, photographic and non-photographic imaging techniques actively transform the body in the process of representing it. Even Marey's studies of bodies in motion intervened in the body they represented. Marey attempted to remove from the picture all features of the body not connected to its motion, all the 'readable' signs which the physiognomist is anxious to record. Through his photographic technique, 'Marey effectively reorganised the body to make it embody its own status as an object subject to laws of temporality and duration' (Cartwright 1995: 36).

Marey was involved in the 'science of work', the European equivalent of the 'scientific management' techniques of the American Frederick Winslow Taylor. From 1911, Frank Gilbreth, a follower of Taylor, used Marey's chronophotographic techniques to break down, analyse and reorganise the movements of a person at work (Braun 1994: 340–348; Lalvani 1996: 139–168). The shift from the analysis and classification of bodies, as in physiognomy, towards their corrective transformation is described by Michel Foucault, as part of a general shift in the exercise of power in the modern period.

The body as machine

5.10 Hannah Höch, *Das schone Madchen* (The Beautiful Girl), photomontage (original in colour)
The photomontages of the Dada artist Hannah Höch celebrate the 'New Woman', playfully juxtaposing magazine images of women with photographs of machine parts, but also seem critical of the uniform, idealised and machine-like mannequins depicted in the same magazines

The photographs and films of Marey and Gilbreth are among a large number (including industrial, commercial, medical and art photographs) which contributed to a perception of the human body as a machine. This perception depended on a highly idealised and utopian concept of the efficient, smooth-running machine, which ignored the ways in which certain kinds of machines mutilate bodies (for example, in factories and war).

In popular culture, an uneasy mixture of traditional ideas of femininity and the new image of the disciplined, machine-like body informed the repre-

5.11 *Hans Bellmer with first Doll*, 1934

sentation of women. In 1920s Germany, women's magazines enthusiastically showed female aviators and female celebrities beside their cars, while advertising photographs depicted women as automaton-like mannequins (Lavin 1993: 3, 59 and 132).

Avant-garde artists used new photographic techniques both to celebrate technology and to critique it.[19] The political stakes of this became clear in the late 1930s, as Nazi ideology embraced a version of the machine body. This combined ideas of classical perfection from ancient Greek art with the racial classifications of nineteenth-century physiognomy, and Fordist/Taylorist ideas of the ideally machine-like, efficient and uniform worker. The ideal male body was a self-contained, muscular, armoured machine.

Some avant-garde photography challenged the image of the body as machine favoured by Taylorism and the Nazi emphasis on the male body as a disciplined fighting machine. The art historian **Hal Foster** shows how Hans Bellmer's Surrealist photographs of dismembered and mutilated dolls, which can be read as deeply misogynistic and paedophiliac, have different connotations in this historical context. Bellmer's photographs of distorted bodies, complete with prosthetic limbs, are simultaneously a rebuke to the militaristic ambitions of Fascism and Fascist ideas of bodily (and racial) purity, and a reminder of the real mutilations produced by technological warfare (Foster 1993: 114–120).

The relationship between technology and the body continues to be ambivalently and uneasily represented. In a 1998 advertisement for the Saab 9–3 car (see figure 5.12), the photographic/digital montage blending car seat and human torso recalls the avant-garde use of **photomontage**. However, avantgarde montage depended on the incongruous and violent juxtaposition of bodies and machine parts. Here, the seamless blend of chair and torso suggests a painless transition from human to technological. The seat seems more human than the torso, its head-rest becomes a kind of head, and it has wrinkles, while the torso is asexual, with no hairs or irregularities, its flesh a polite shade of beige, smooth as a mannequin. The head is missing but not severed; instead the neck discreetly fades into shadow. Thus the advertisement humanises technology, presenting the merging of technology and the body as desirable but also as inherently safe. The text confirms this: 'you actually feel like part of the car itself. Joined at the hip, as it were.'

The ad has the task of picturing the intermingling of body and machine without reminding us of the violent collision of flesh and metal which happens in a car crash. To tread over this line would undermine the ideology of the harmlessness of technology which it is promoting, and make the image disturbingly suggestive of death.

19 Maud Lavin notes that 'the Berlin Dadaists prided themselves on both affirming and negating their principal themes. While they were applauding the newly rationalized man – associated in their minds with the machine, the engineer, and the Soviet artist Vladimir Tatlin – they were also satirizing man-as-machine idealism, particularly as it had been played out in the carnage of World War I' (Lavin 1993: 16).

HAL FOSTER (1993) **Compulsive Beauty**, Cambridge, MA, and London: The MIT Press, chs 4 and 5

photomontage The use of two or more originals, perhaps also including written text, to make a combined image. A montaged image may be imaginative, artistic, comic or deliberately satirical.

5.12 Advertisement for Saab, 1998
One of the themes central to current representations of the body is the merging of the corporeal and the technological, and the potential displacement of the body by the machine. By presenting a seamless merging of human and machine, this advertisement reassures us of the harmlessness of the car, and conceals the fact that technology can pierce and shatter bodies

PHOTOGRAPHY AND DEATH

The representation of death was common in painting prior to the invention of photography, and then in early photography, but it is usually assumed that the practice of photographing dead relatives or friends stopped, particularly in English-speaking countries. Anthropologist Jay Ruby has challenged this perception, showing that the practice continues in present-day America, but has come to be seen as shameful, or highly private, and is seldom discussed, and the photographs are seldom displayed publicly (Ruby 1995: 161). Death is among those aspects openly represented in medieval carnival but is increasingly relegated to the private realm in the modern era.

Ruby's study also shows that the fact that nineteenth-century photographers were frequently commissioned to produce post-mortem photographs does not necessarily mean that theirs was a culture much more comfortable with death than our own. Great effort was made in early post-mortem photography to present the corpse as merely asleep, in keeping with funerary practices and cultural representations which represent death as a deep sleep (a notion still present in the modern 'chapel of rest') (Ruby 1995: 63–72).

Even so, until about 1880, post-mortem photography was a publicly acceptable practice, with photographs of corpses displayed openly in American homes, and professional photography studios advertising the service. Its gradual concealment indicates a change in attitudes towards photography, as well as in ideas and practices related to death. Originally, the significance of corpse photography was to preserve a likeness. For many bereaved people, photographs still privately serve this function, but a new public unease has grown around photographing the dead.

Photography has associations with death because of its ability to objectify – this is expressed by **Susan Sontag**: 'All photographs are *memento mori*. To take a photograph is to participate in another person's (or thing's) mortality, vulnerability, mutability. Precisely by slicing out this moment and freezing it, all photographs testify to time's relentless melt' (Sontag 1977: 15).

SUSAN SONTAG (1977) **On Photography**, Harmondsworth: Penguin

The qualities which make a photograph work as a fetish – its immobility and silence, its ability to freeze a past moment – are the same qualities which associate it with death (Metz 1985: 83–84). Current attitudes to post-mortem photography may also result from the twentieth-century tendency to accept photographs as reflections of the real (Rosler 1991). **Roland Barthes** has argued that our horror at photographs of corpses is related to our faith in photographic realism. Since, according to Barthes, we tend to conflate the real and the live, a photograph of a corpse seems to attest 'that the corpse is alive, as *corpse*: it is the living image of a dead thing'; in other words, the corpse appears to have been live at the moment of its encounter with the camera (Barthes 1981/1984: 78). Photography renders the living immobile, frozen: the living person photographed may subsequently die, but remains preserved in the photograph, while the dead body photographed is 'horrible' since it is given the same 'immortality'. According to Barthes, photography 'produces Death while trying to preserve life' (Barthes 1981/1984: 92; Jay 1993: 450–456).

ROLAND BARTHES (1981) **Camera Lucida**, New York: Hill and Wang, republished in London by Fontana, 1984

Though nowadays commercial photography studios do not photograph corpses, a number of art photographers have done so – notably Andres Serrano and Sue Fox. Sue Fox's mortuary photographs perhaps seem more 'horrific'

5.13 Post-mortem daguerreotype of child, Boston, c. 1850s
An example of the mid-nineteenth-century tendency to photograph the dead as if they were asleep

20 For reproductions and
discussion of Sue Fox's
photographs see Townsend
1998.

than Serrano's because their documentary-style composition has the effect
which Barthes noted: of making the dead seem alive.[20] Whilst Fox depicts
the corpse dissected, as meat, stripped of personality, Serrano's photographs
continue the Victorian tradition of making the dead appear asleep, and include
poignant details, such as the mark left on a child's flesh by the elastic of its
sock. Although this is a kind of realism, these photos are also highly staged
and decontextualised: only the titles suggest that they are taken in a morgue.
Serrano's morgue series is similar to his series depicting body fluids, including the (in)famous *Piss Christ*, in that the attraction of the refined classical
composition and sumptuous colour of the photograph conflicts with the
horror or disgust associated with the 'grotesque' aspects of the body depicted.

SUMMARY

In his classic study of the nude, the art historian Kenneth Clark claimed
that the photograph's relationship to reality meant that the idealisation
fundamental to the classical nude could never be achieved: the body in a
photograph is always a particular body, a real, naked, human being, however
idealised (Clark 1956: 4).

As the examples in this chapter demonstrate, campaigns and conflicts over
photographs of the body hinge on this relationship between photography and

5.14 Andres Serrano, *The Morgue* (Fatal Meningitis II), 1992 (original in colour)
Serrano's morgue photographs draw on the nineteenth-century tradition, blurring the line between sleep and death

reality and the extent to which the photograph is understood as a reflection of reality. Yet it is also clear that photography is one of the means by which individuals are constructed as social subjects: the use of photographs in medicine, policing and in scientific studies of work shows how photography participates in the disciplining of the body. A photograph constructs different meanings for human bodies through the way it represents them, and some photographs may conform to and reproduce dominant ideas about sex, about race, about what it is to be human, male or female, whilst other photographs challenge these ideas. However, these meanings are not firmly attached to particular methods, techniques or styles; instead the significance of particular ways of photographing bodies changes with its context. For instance, the composite photos of Francis Galton, Nancy Burson, and those produced by a photo-booth all depend on viewing people as 'types', but all serve different social purposes. Similarly, the muscled male body and the classical aesthetic could be associated with either a coded homoeroticism (in American physique magazines of the 1950s) or the deeply homophobic culture of Fascism. In all instances, photographs do not simply speak of 'the body' but of particular bodies, of social groups and the relationships of power between them.

BIBLIOGRAPHY

KEY TEXTS

Barthes, Roland (1981) *Camera Lucida*, New York: Hill and Wang, republished in London by
  Fontana, 1984
Braun, Marta (1992) *Picturing Time: The Work of Etienne-Jules Marey (1830–1904)*,
  Chicago, IL: University of Chicago Press
Bright, Deborah (ed.) (1998) *The Passionate Camera: Photography and Bodies of Desire*,
  London and New York: Routledge
Cartwright, Lisa (1995) *Screening the Body: Tracing Medicine's Visual Culture*, Minneapolis
  and London: University of Minnesota Press
Cooper, Emmanuel (1990) *Fully Exposed: The Male Nude in Photography*, London: Unwin
  Hyman
Crary, Jonathan (1990) *Techniques of the Observer: On Vision and Modernity in the
  Nineteenth Century*, Cambridge, MA: The MIT Press
Foster, Hal (1993) *Compulsive Beauty*, Cambridge, MA, and London: The MIT Press, chs 4 and 5
Kipnis, Laura (1992) '(Male) Desire and (Female) Disgust: Reading Hustler' in Lawrence
  Grossberg, Cary Nelson and Paula A. Treichler (eds) *Cultural Studies*, London and New York:
  Routledge
Metz, Christian (1985) 'Photography and Fetish', *October* 34, Autumn
Mulvey, Laura (1989) 'Visual Pleasure and Narrative Cinema' in *Visual and Other Pleasures*,
  London: Macmillan
Pultz, John (1995) *Photography and the Body*, London: Weidenfeld & Nicolson
Sekula, Allan (1989) 'The Archive and the Body' in Richard Bolton (ed.) *The Contest of
  Meaning: Critical Histories of Photography*, Cambridge, MA: The MIT Press
Sontag, Susan (1977) *On Photography*, Harmondsworth: Penguin
Tagg, John (1988) *The Burden of Representation: Essays on Photographies and Histories*,
  London: Macmillan
Vance, Carole S. (1990) 'The Meese Commission' in Carol Squiers (ed.) *The Critical Image:
  Essays on Contemporary Photography*, Seattle: Bay Press
Williams, Linda (1995) 'Corporealized Observers: Visual Pornographies and the Carnal Density
  of Vision' in Patrice Petro *Fugitive Images*, Bloomington: Indiana University Press

OTHER REFERENCES

Bakhtin, Mikhail (1984) *Rabelais and His World*, Bloomington: Indiana University Press.
  Originally completed in 1946, first published in 1965
Barthes, Roland (1986) 'The Face of Garbo' in *Mythologies,* London: Grafton Books, essays
  originally published in 1957
Benjamin, Walter (1936) 'The Work of Art in the Age of Mechanical Reproduction' in
  Illuminations, London: Fontana, 1973/1992
—— (1938) 'The Paris of the Second Empire in Baudelaire' in *Charles Baudelaire: A Lyric
  Poet in the Era of High Capitalism*, London: Verso, 1985
Berger, John (1972) *Ways of Seeing*, Harmondsworth: Penguin
Brown, Beverley (1981)'A Feminist Interest in Pornography: Some Modest Proposals' in Parveen
  Adams and Elizabeth Cowie (eds) (1990) *The Woman in Question*, London and New York:
  Verso
Burgin, Victor (1983) 'Photography, Phantasy, Function' in *Thinking Photography*, London:
  Macmillan
—— (1986) *The End of Art Theory: Criticism and Postmodernity*, London: Macmillan
Butt, Gavin (1998) *Men on the Threshold: The Making and Unmaking of the Sexual
  Subject in American Art 1948–1965*, Unpublished Ph.D., University of Leeds

Chester, Gail and Dickey, Julienne (eds) (1988) *Feminism and Censorship: The Current Debate*, Bridport, Dorset: Prism Press

Clark, Kenneth (1956) *The Nude*, Harmondsworth: Penguin, 1960

Crimp, Douglas and Rolston, Adam (1990) *AIDS Demo/Graphics*, Seattle: Bay Press

Dentith, Simon (1995) *Bakhtinian Thought: An Introductory Reader*, London: Routledge

Dubin, Steven C. (1992) *Arresting Images: Impolitic Art and Uncivil Actions*, London and New York: Routledge

Dworkin, Andrea (1981) *Pornography: Men Possessing Women*, London: The Women's Press

Elias, Norbert (1994) *The Civilising Process: Vol. 1, History of Manners,* Oxford: Blackwell

Enos, Katherine (1997/1998) 'Crash & Pornography Culture', www.pomegranates.com

Ewing, William (1994) *The Body*, London: Thames and Hudson

—— (1996) *Inside Information: Imaging the Human Body*, London: Thames and Hudson

Foster, Hal (1996) 'Obscene, Abject, Traumatic', *October* 78, Autumn

Freud, Sigmund (1905) 'Three Essays on Sexuality', in Vol. 7 of Sigmund Freud (1953–1964) *Standard Edition of the Complete Works*, trans. James Strachey, London: Hogarth Press

—— (1927) 'Fetishism', in Vol. 7. of Sigmund Freud (1953–1964) *Standard Edition of the Complete Works*, trans. James Strachey, London: Hogarth Press

Gamman, Lorraine and Makinen, Merja (1994) *Female Fetishism: A New Look*, London: Lawrence and Wishart

Greenberg, Clement (1939) 'Avant-Garde and Kitsch', in *Art and Culture*, Boston, MA: Beacon Press, 1961

Hoggart, Richard (1957) *The Uses of Literacy*, Harmondsworth: Penguin, 1959

Jay, Martin (1993) *Downcast Eyes: The Denigration of Vision in Twentieth Century French Thought*, San Francisco: University of California Press

Kendrick, Walter (1987) *The Secret Museum: Pornography in Modern Culture*, New York: Viking, republished in 1996 by the University of California Press

Kern, Stephen (1983) *The Culture of Time and Space 1800–1918*, Cambridge, MA: The MIT Press

Kotz, Liz (1998) 'Aesthetics of Intimacy', in Deborah Bright (ed.) *The Passionate Camera: Photography and Bodies of Desire*, London and New York: Routledge

Krauss, Rosalind (1986) *The Originality of the Avant-Garde and Other Modernist Myths*, Cambridge, MA: The MIT Press

Lalvani, Suren (1996) *Photography, Vision, and the Production of Modern Bodies*, Albany: State University of New York

Lavin, Maud (1993) *Cut with the Kitchen Knife: The Weimar Photomontages of Hannah Höch*, New Haven, CT: Yale University Press

Lipton, Eunice (1980) 'The Laundress in Nineteenth Century French Culture', *Art History*, Vol. 3, No. 3, abridged version in Francis Frascina and Charles Harrison (1983) *Modern Art and Modernism: A Critical Anthology*, HarperCollins

Magli, Patrizia (1989) 'The Face and the Soul', in M. Feher with Ramona Naddaff and Nadia Tazi (eds) *Zone 4: Fragments for a History of the Human Body, Part Two*, Cambridge, MA: Zone/MIT Press

Mellencamp, Patricia (1992) *High Anxiety: Catastrophe, Scandal, Age and Comedy,* Bloomington: Indiana University Press

Meyer, Moe (ed.) (1994) *The Politics and Poetics of Camp*, London: Routledge

Olalquiaga, Celeste (1992) *Megalopolis: Contemporary Cultural Sensibilities*, Minneapolis: University of Minnesota Press

Rodgerson, Gillian and Wilson, Elizabeth (eds) (1991) *Pornography and Feminism: The Case Against Censorship*, London: Lawrence and Wishart

Rosler, Martha (1991) 'Image Simulations, Computer Manipulations, Some Considerations' *Ten-8* 2(2) *Digital Dialogues*

Ruby, Jay (1995) *Secure the Shadow: Photography and Death in America*, Cambridge, MA, and London: The MIT Press

Segal, Lynne and Macintosh, Mary (eds) (1992) *Sex Exposed: Sexuality and the Pornography Debate*, London: Virago

Solomon-Godeau, Abigail (1991) 'Reconsidering Erotic Photography: Notes for a Project of Historical Salvage', in *Photography in the Dock*, Minneapolis: University of Minnesota Press

Stallybrass, Peter and White, Allon (1986) *The Politics and Poetics of Transgression*, Ithaca and New York: Cornell University Press

Taylor, Mark C. (1997) *Hiding*, Chicago, IL, and London: University of Chicago Press

Townsend, Chris (1998) *Vile Bodies: Photography and the Crisis of Looking*, Munich and New York: Prestel-Verlag and Channel Four Television Corporation

CHAPTER 6

On and beyond the white walls

Photography as Art

LIZ WELLS

6.1 Karen Knorr, *Analytical Inquiry into the Principles of Taste*, from *Country Life*

On and beyond the white walls

Photography as Art

INTRODUCTION

> The history of art photography *is* an extraordinary picture story.
> Individual images, extracted from the larger histories of technology,
> economics, politics, and popular culture, are stripped of their context
> and meaning and then placed in a time line of formal invention.
> And photographs consciously created as art fit right into that
> aesthetic context, all on their own. Photographic images are
> intentionally made into, or are made as, beautiful, prized objects.
>
> (Heiferman 1989: 20)

Photography is significant as a means of visual communication. But the
history of photography as **Art** focuses not so much upon photographic
communication as upon photographs as objects, reified for their **aesthetic**
qualities. It follows that, typically, such histories focus upon pictures, and
the works of specific practitioners. Thus, the story of photography as art
tends to be presented as a history of 'great', or 'master' (*sic*), photographers.
Such accounts not only divorce photography as fine art from the larger
history of photography with its ubiquity of practices, but also rarely engage
with broader political issues and social contexts.

   This chapter considers debates relating to the status of photography as
fine art. In particular, it discusses photography and the art gallery. The first

section focuses on nineteenth-century debates and practices, noting that from its very inception photography was conceptualised in terms of both its apparent ability to accurately transcribe from reality and in terms of its expressive potential. The principal focus of the chapter is twentieth-century photography considered in the context of Western modern, and postmodern art movements. In modernism, the emphasis was upon the photograph as a specific medium with particular qualities or attributes. Subsequently, postmodern theory loosened the focus on the formal, viewing the photographic as a particular language or sign system. Finally, the chapter discusses funding structures, the gallery system, publishing, and the international context. The chapter is written from a British perspective: obviously Britain cannot be considered in isolation from broader debates and developments, but attention is given to particular British manifestations. For instance, Britain is not unique in providing state finance for the Arts, but, as is indicated in the brief discussion of the Arts Council funding system in the final section of the chapter, particular **ideological** assumptions characterise British provisions.

As with any overview, a word of caution is appropriate: this discussion should be taken as a starting point for fuller exploration of sets of debates, not as a comprehensive compendium. For instance, choice of photographs for illustration has been restricted to landscape. In the third case study, focus on one genre allows more immediate comparison of form, content and subject-matter than would be the case with a random compilation of images. Landscape also contrasts with the emphasis on people (in personal albums, in the streets, or as 'body') in previous chapters.

The status of the photograph as Art

In 1989, 150 years after Fox Talbot's announcement, the Royal Academy, London, mounted its first ever photography exhibition, *The Art of Photography*. Arguably this represented the acknowledgement by the Arts establishment that has been sought, variously, throughout photography's history.

Photographs have been exhibited right from the inception of photography. They were included in the Great Exhibition of 1851, and the Royal Society of Arts organised its first show of photography in 1852.[1] In the nineteenth century, there were no mass media of the sort taken for granted now, so exhibition was one of the prime ways of communicating information about new technological developments. But, from very early days, critics and practitioners disagreed as to the status of photography as Art.

This debate begs the question as to what is meant by 'Art'. In this chapter we use 'Art' to refer to fine art practices relating to the gallery and the Arts establishment, by contrast with more general understandings of photography as an 'art' or expressive skill.[2] Many claims have been made for photography as Art. Art tends to be acclaimed for perceptions on the condition of humankind. The artist is characterised as a special sort of 'seer', or visionary

MIKE WEAVER (1989a) **The Art of Photography**, London: Royal Academy of Arts

1 The 1851 exhibition, a celebration of British achievements, was held at the purpose-built Crystal Palace, London. The Royal Society of Arts is also London-based.

2 The term 'Art' is used to indicate focus upon Arts institutions and gallery exhibition. This follows Raymond Williams' distinction between 'art' as creative skill and 'Art', used in Britain since the early nineteenth century to refer to the Art establishment, a network of galleries,

of 'truth', poetically expressed. In the case of photography, the artist is viewed as transcending 'mere recording' of events, offering a unique perspective on or insight into people, places, objects, relationships, circumstances.

Photography impacted on the role and status of painting. Writing in the 1930s, Walter Benjamin argued that the 'aura' associated with the uniqueness of the work of fine art such as a painting would wither in favour of the photograph, which he welcomed as a more democratic – or less exclusive – medium because of its potential for mass reproduction (Benjamin 1992b). Here it is the anti-elitist potential of photography which is being stressed. Noting a number of moments of transition in the late nineteenth and early twentieth centuries in which photography was central to art movements, **Peter Wollen** argues that

> For photography to be an art involves reformulating notions of art, rejecting both material and formal purism and also the separation of art from commerce as distinct semiotic practices that never interlock.
>
> (Wollen 1982: 188)

Other critics, including curator and historian Beaumont Newhall, have based claims for photography on its formal and expressive qualities which accord with the Western, post-Renaissance tradition. Such claims stem from connoisseurship; that is, valuation of the sensitive and the precious within photography. They are not necessarily intended to assert parity of status with older Art forms.

In considering the status of nineteenth-century photography it is important to remember that art and technology, the expressive and the mechanical, were viewed as distinct. This distinction characterised the reception of photography and attitudes towards it. Photography of record aimed for maximum precision and detail, whereas pictorial photography was expected to conform to aesthetic conventions in terms of composition and subject-matter, highlighting particular features in order to stress their significance. For many photographers, it was creative potential along with its apparent accuracy of transcription that was the source of fascination with the medium.

However, they did not necessarily see themselves as fine artists. For instance, British photographers such as Julia Margaret Cameron or Lady Clementina Hawarden, whose work might now be viewed as Art, did not themselves make this claim. Likewise, as historian Margaret Harker notes, combination printing, using two or more 'negatives' (glass plates) in order to achieve particular pre-visualised results, was common from the 1850s. This could be viewed as an artist's approach to using the medium. Yet she affirms that the first attempt to promote photography as *fine art* was not made until a Camera Club exhibition in Vienna in 1981 (Harker 1979). By contrast, Aaron Scharf, in relation to the Paris photography exhibition of 1855, describes photographers including Durieu, Nadar and Bayard as '"immigrants" to the Fine Arts' (Scharf 1974: 140). As we see, there is also some

museums, funding organisations, publishing and festivals (Williams 1976). The notion of Art as a specialised field of practice has been criticised variously, for instance, in Soviet Constructivism, or, more recently, in postmodern practices such as publishing imagery on the internet, exhibiting on (advertising) hoardings, or organising community-based arts projects.

PETER WOLLEN (1978) 'Photography and Aesthetics', **Screen 19(4)**, Winter, reprinted in *Reading and Writings*, London: Verso and New Left Books, 1982

See also chapter 1, pp. 46–9, discussion of Newhall, and of his *The History of Photography*.

disagreement between historians as to when photography was first viewed as Art.

Thus, we should distinguish between claims made by photographers for themselves, or for particular movements, and claims made at a later stage by historians, critics and curators. For instance, Soviet revolutionary artists aimed to take work out from the gallery into everyday social life, viewing art as both an essential tool in the re-education of the mass of the Russian people and as 'art for the people'. Nowadays, retrospectives of this work are curated for Art galleries, spaces which the Soviet artists would surely have viewed as bourgeois and elitist! Likewise, early twentieth-century documentary, originally destined for publications in social surveys, magazines or books, now takes pride of place within the gallery and the archive. Peter Galassi, as curator of an exhibition of highlights from the photography archive at the Museum of Modern Art in New York, distinguishes between photography intended as Art and 'vernacular' photography, noting the differing lineages of work now included within the same collection (Galassi 1995). This distinction over-simplifies a complex history. It may be useful as a means of classification for museums and archives which, in the late twentieth century, have become increasingly prominent – with curators increasingly influential – in both the conservation of history and its interpretation. However, precisely because of the influence of the museum in constructing what are inevitably selective histories of the medium, over-simplified categorisation has become a source of concern for academics.

EARLY DEBATES AND PRACTICES

The complex relations between photography and Art

Understanding the relationship between photography and painting in the nineteenth century involves a number of interconnected considerations. Photography in Britain and France was initially heralded for its technical recording abilities. With few exceptions, the emphasis was upon *picture-taking* rather than *picture-making* – to echo a distinction made by Margaret Harker (Harker 1979). She suggests that the development of the art of photography in the late 1850s can partly be accounted for through the increasing involvement of people trained as artists. They brought with them a concern for form and composition and, in particular, the use of light. She notes that the use of photographs as illustrations for poetry or literature, or as picture narrative and allegory, also dates from the late 1850s. **Mary Warner Marien** argues that what she terms High Art Photography:

MARY WARNER MARIEN (1997) 'Art, Photography and Society', Chapter 3 of **Photography and Its Critics, A Cultural History, 1839–1900**, Cambridge/New York: Cambridge University Press

> orchestrated separate media. High Art photographs blended theater, printmaking, and painting with photography. Actors or other players were posed singly or in a *tableau vivant*. Interestingly, specific paintings were only occasionally replicated in High Art Photography.

For the most part, these images rendered original conceptions, illustrating religious or moral precepts often in the manner of maudlin genre painting and popular Victorian prints. By partaking in the established didactic function of the fine arts, High Art photographers attempted to skirt objections to the medium's inartistic verisimilitude.

(Warner Marien 1997: 87)

In this section we consider first the influence of the transcriptive qualities of photography within changing nineteenth-century fine art practices; second, photography democratising Art; and third, photography, aesthetics and Western Art. In the following section we discuss pictorialism, and claims for the photograph as fine art made by photographers at the turn of the century. Writing on *Art and Photography* **Aaron Scharf** (1974) emphasises uses of photographs by artists; for example, as reference notes. Only in the later chapters on twentieth-century Art movements does he acknowledge the photograph as art in its own right. As both **Van Deren Coke** and Aaron Scharf have indicated, a number of artists used photographs as study devices, eliminating the need to pay for models or to spend long periods of time sketching. For some, these photographic 'sketches' ultimately took over as works in their own right. For example, the French caricaturist, Nadar, first used photography as the basis for satirical portraiture, later acknowledging the photographs themselves.[3] But the use of photography also allowed artists to extend their range of references, returning from both urban 'public' spaces and rural 'open' spaces with photographic notes to support paintings made in the studio. Photographs could be used as research notes, or as models for painting. For instance, Aaron Scharf notes that Manet used photographs of the Mexican emperor, and of soldiers, when working on his paintings of the emperor's execution. Scharf also includes two examples, a riverscape and a seascape, by the French realist painter, Gustave Courbet, which seem to be based directly upon contemporary photographs (Scharf 1974: 127).

Realism and systems of representation

Courbet and Manet were prominent among artists associated with nineteenth-century Realism within which photography was implicated as an aid to painting. Discussing the implications of Realism as an historical movement in painting and in literature, in France and elsewhere, Linda Nochlin has suggested that the degree of social change experienced during the Industrial Revolution in Britain from the late eighteenth century, and the political revolutions in France, induced artists to explore everyday social experience (Nochlin 1978). Noting the dominance of Realism as a radical movement from about 1840 until 1870 to 1880, she suggests that there are a number of associated ambiguities including, crucially, the issue of the relation between **representation** and 'reality', itself a problematic concept. She argues that:

AARON SCHARF (1974) **Art and Photography**, London: Allen Lane, Pelican Books, revised edition

VAN DEREN COKE (1972) **The Painter and the Photograph**, New Mexico: University of New Mexico Press

3 This was clearly indicated in sketches, photographs and tear sheets from the collection at the Paris Bibliothèque Nationale exhibited at the Maison de Balzac as part of *Mois de la Photo*, 1990.

Key archive in Britain: The National Gallery, London for a collection of nineteenth-century French paintings (including one version of Manet's *The Execution of the Emperor Maximilian*)

The commonplace notion that Realism is a 'styleless' or transparent style, a mere simulacrum or mirror image of visual reality, is another barrier to its understanding as an historical and stylistic phenomenon. . . . Realism was no more a mere mirror of reality than any other style and its relation *qua* style to phenomenal data . . . is as complex and difficult as that of Romanticism, the Baroque or Mannerism. So far as Realism is concerned, however, the issue is greatly confused by the assertions of both its supporters and opponents, that Realists were doing no more than mirroring everyday reality. . . . These statements derived from the belief that perception could be 'pure' and unconditioned by time or place.

(Nochlin 1978: 14)

Central to her approach is the contention that perception is culturally conditioned.

Paris underwent massive architectural and cultural change in the first half of the nineteenth century, becoming, in effect, the first modern city. Modes of vision, and subject-matter appropriate for Art, were up for debate. Writing at that time, French poet and philosopher, Baudelaire, argued that the painter of 'modern life' should focus on the contemporary, upon the movement and change which had revolutionised everyday experience. He was among the first critics to support Realism's challenge to previous aesthetic convention through the introduction of everyday subjects and ordinary people into pictures, and through the use of less 'finished' styles of painting than those expected or in keeping with the conventions of the French Academy of Art. Yet he made no particular connection between Realism and photography, dismissing the latter as an inferior form of artistic expression due to its mechanical nature. Thus his view of the potential and limitations of the camera seems in line with that, for instance, of critics who dismissed Courbet's series of large-scale pictures of the rural community in Ornans on a number of grounds, including not only the everyday content of the image but also, as one critic put it, its appearance as 'a faulty **daguerreotype**'. Yet, photography, in a whole range of practices, was central to changing ways of seeing.

Aesthetic conventions reflect broader sets of ideas. For instance, since the Renaissance, Western Art has used perspective as the principal system of visual organisation. Perspective involves a single, central viewing point. It has been argued by some critics that this system, in prioritising one central viewing position, reaffirms individualism (that is, the emphasis on the individual which emerged within entrepreneurial capitalism). In other words, a particular political philosophy is reflected and reaffirmed through image-making conventions. In photography, focus, which refers to the use of the camera lens to give a 'sharp' image of objects which may be in differing parts of the picture, interacts with perspective to support ways of seeing

daguerreotype Photographic image made by the process launched by Louis-Jacques-Mandé Daguerre in France in 1839. It is a positive image on a metal plate with a mirror-like silvered surface, characterised by very fine detail. Each one is unique and fragile and needs to be protected by a padded case. It became the dominant portrait mode for the first decades of photography, especially in the United States.

based upon geometric mapping of space. That camera optics conform to the rules of perspective meant that photographic notes could support composition in painting. As film theorist, Bill Nichols, has suggested, 'Renaissance painters fabricated textual systems approximating the cues relating to normal perception better than any other strategy until the emergence of photography' (Nichols 1981: 52). Indeed, as has been noted, one of the claims made was that the photograph had the technical ability to reproduce from actuality with more accuracy than any other form of representation. As such, photography, itself a part of scientific and technological development, seemed to fit within the spirit of modernity, as well as offering realist possibilities for representing aspects of modern life.

Photography extending Art

Photography supported painting. It also encroached very directly upon genres of painting such as portraiture, not only taking over some of the work of painters, but also extending the compass of the work. For instance, while few could afford the time and cost of sitting for a painted portrait, the studio photographer could offer a similar service much more cheaply. As such, portraiture became more democratically available. Both high street studios and the touring 'jobbing' photographer became common from the mid-nineteenth century (see chapter 3). This did not prevent a continuing hierarchy; the painted portrait was still commissioned by the wealthy and the aristocracy. But it did allow a greater number of people the status of seeing themselves pictured.

Furthermore, photography provoked artists to re-examine the nature and potential of paint as a particular medium. Photography appeared to be more successful than painting in capturing likenesses. It also had a sense of instantaneity which painting lacked. It has been suggested that photography encouraged the Impressionist painters to experiment with manners of painting which could also capture a sense of the moment, and the passage of light. It is a truism that photography 'released' painting from its responsibility for literal depiction, allowing it to become more experimental. The developing relationship between the two media was considerably more symbiotic.

Another respect in which photography may be said to have extended Art was in its role as the re-presenter of art objects. It was no longer necessary to travel to Florence to see paintings commissioned by the Medicis, or to Egypt to contemplate classical architecture and artefacts; you could attend slide talks, or visit an exhibition, and view reproductions. Virtual reality, with its possibilities of seemingly travelling around a painting or sculpture, viewing it from every possible angle, now makes the 2D black and white photograph appear highly limited as a means of showing an art object. But, at the time, the possibility of seeing photographs of art objects was highly radical. Among the first illustrated art histories was an 1847 limited edition book of Spanish Art which included sixty-six **calotypes** by Fox Talbot (Scharf 1974: 160).

Key galleries in Britain: National Portrait Gallery, London Scottish National Portrait Gallery, Edinburgh (See Photography archives, pp. 354–7, for museums, galleries and archives outside Britain)

calotype Photographic print made by the process launched by William Henry Fox Talbot in England in 1840. It involved the exposure of sensitised paper in the camera from which, after processing, positive paper prints could be made. Not much used in England in the early days, because it was protected by Fox Talbot's own patents, but its use was developed in Scotland, especially by David Octavius Hill and Robert Adamson.

PETER GALASSI (1981) **Before Photography**, New York: MOMA

MARK HAWORTH-BOOTH (1992) **River Scene, France**, Los Angeles, CA: J. Paul Getty Museum

MIKE WEAVER (ed.) (1989b) **British Photography in the Nineteenth Century: The Fine Art Tradition**, Cambridge: Cambridge University Press. A collection of essays on major photographers of the Victorian era

Photographs not only reproduced Art, they also mirrored Art in making pictures in accordance with established fine art conventions. *Before Photography*, **Peter Galassi**'s comparative study of photographs and paintings within the same genres, draws our attention to continuities in aesthetic convention including compositional similarities. Likewise, in a more detailed manner, **Mark Haworth–Booth** has examined the construction of *River Scene, France* by Camille Silvy, which was a combination print involving staging people within the rural setting (figure 6.2). Not only does its composition echo traditional aesthetics, but the image romanticises the pastoral (in line with many examples of landscape paintings).

Indeed, staged photographs depicting idealised or mythical scenes became common from the 1850s onwards. Among earlier examples is the work of Julia Margaret Cameron. She invited friends, family and servants to pose for her, either for portraits or as actors within her dramatic scenarios. Since she moved in Victorian middle-class circles, this legacy includes portraits of well-known artists, writers and intellectuals, including Alfred Lord Tennyson and

6.2 Camille Silvy, *River Scene, France*, 1858
Two exposures combined to create the idealised rural scenario

260

Charles Darwin. But it is her tableaux which have significance in relation to Art. Cameron's photography coincided with Pre-Raphaelite Art in Britain.[4] Through mythologising the past, the Pre-Raphaelites arguably represented a conservative response to modernity. Cameron likewise staged mythical scenes, using costumes and titles to indicate the poetic.

Julia Margaret Cameron was one of a number of serious 'amateurs' who figure prominently in the history of photography in Britain. Others were more professional, in the sense that photography was their source of income. For instance, Swedish painter-photographer, Oscar Rejlander, set up a commercial studio in Victoria, London. But he became known for his allegorical compositions, in some cases of a scale equivalent to paintings. For example, 'The Two Ways of Life', involving a number of models playing roles ranging from the religious (charity) to the debauched (gambling), was nearly three feet (one metre) long. It was made from thirty separate photographs, entailing pre-visualisation on a grand scale. Such work reflected Victorian preoccupations, including religion, class and morality. This particular picture must have accorded with social concerns acceptable to the Establishment – it was purchased by Queen Victoria in 1857.

Thus pictures made by Victorian photographers reflected conventions and tensions in other areas of Victorian Art. Indeed, photography itself impacted on such tensions and aesthetic developments, with emphasis upon interpretation rather than upon accuracy of recording. In line with other areas of the Arts there was an emerging schism between those preoccupied with the realist concerns of nineteenth-century industrialisation and those with more expressive aspirations.

Photography claiming a place in the gallery

In 1892 a number of photographers seceded from the Photographic Society of Great Britain – which in the 1870s and 1880s had emphasised the science and technology of photography, and offered no support for the progress of photography as Art. Led by Henry Peach Robinson, they formed the Linked Ring Brotherhood (which did include a few women). Robinson suggested:

> It must be admitted by the most determined opponent of photography as a fine art that the same object represented by different photographers will produce different pictorial results and this invariably not only because the one man uses different lenses and chemicals than the other but because there is something different in each man's mind which somehow gets communicated to his fingers' ends and thence to his pictures.

(**Harker** 1988: 46)

Retrospectively labelled 'pictorialist', typically their imagery was soft focus, with metaphoric connotations, often drawing upon traditional fable and

4 The Pre-Raphaelites were a group of British artists of whom Dante Gabriel Rossetti (the son of an Italian refugee), William Holman Hunt and John Everett Millais were the most famous. Taking nature as their primary subject, they sought to retrieve what they viewed as a simplicity and sincerity in art which had been lost in the Renaissance. Examples of their work may be found in many English municipal galleries (the most extensive collection is in Birmingham City Art Gallery).

MARGARET HARKER (1979) **The Linked Ring: The Secession Movement in Photography in Britain, 1892–1910**, London: Heinemann

NAOMI ROSENBLUM (1997) **A World History of Photography**, London and New York: Abbeville Press, ch 7 on Pictorialism

6.3 Henry Peach Robinson, *The Lady of Shalott*, 1860–1861
A medieval tale interpreted allegorically

allegory (figure 6.3). Again, the Pre-Raphaelites may have been one source of influence. Defining pictorial photography, Mike Weaver notes the aim:

> to make a picture in which the sensuous beauty of the fine print is consonant with the moral beauty of the fine image, without particular reference to documentary or design values, and without specific regard to personal or topographical identity.
>
> (Weaver 1986: Preface)

Membership of the Linked Ring was international, with photographers in other secessionist movements in Europe and the USA joining by invitation. In France the first exhibition of the newly formed Photo-Club of Paris was held in 1894; in Germany Hamburg became the centre for art photography. The Photo-Secession in New York, which was founded by Alfred Stieglitz (a member of the Linked Ring) was not established until 1902. Its objectives echoed the emphasis on the expressive potential of the medium which characterised the European movements. However, membership was restricted to Americans. Margaret Harker suggests that this was to facilitate the raising of standards within American photography to exceed those in Europe. Stieglitz had previously organised a number of exhibitions of work by European painters, introducing the Impressionists to New York and bringing what he considered to be the best in Art to America.[5] He also founded and edited *Camerawork*, published from 1903 to 1917, described by Aaron Scharf as 'undoubtedly one of the most influential journals ever published to be concerned equally with art and photography' (Scharf 1974: 240).

Given the complexity of the relation between photography and painting, and the extent to which photographers since the mid-century had sought 'artistic results', why was there such emphasis on photography as Art at the end of the century? One factor is that secessionism coincided with the development of technologies such as roll film and the box camera, which allowed the casual amateur to take photographs. Serious amateurs, in claiming artistic status, were also marking a distinction between themselves and the newly emerging mass market in photography.

Furthermore, dissent within photography, represented by the various secessionist groups, echoed dissent more generally within the Arts. The end of the nineteenth century witnessed the challenge posed by the Impressionists in painting, Naturalism in theatre[6] and, indeed, the birth of cinema. It also witnessed the development of lithographic techniques necessary for the mass reproduction of photographs in print. It was an era of considerable change. The pictorialists claimed the photograph as Art, but this claim was made at a time of challenge to dominant aesthetics. Pictorialism not only seems conservative now, to many people it probably seemed overly traditional then. Indeed, tension, debate and dissent characterised the era. Peter Henry Emerson is known for his picturesque renderings of life in East Anglia. Defining 'picturesque', Harker notes 'emphasis on acute observation and appreciation of scenery; an understanding of proportion and perspective in landscape; and the conception of architecture at one with its natural environment (not to be considered in isolation)' (Harker 1979: 27). Emerson's emphasis was upon what he termed 'Naturalistic Photography', which was the title of his book published in 1889. He advocated realism and 'truth-to-nature' as opposed to the impressionist or the idealistic. For this reason he has been viewed by some critics as a forerunner of modern photography. But his concern with composition and differential focusing, including soft focus where appropriate, would have allowed him a place within Pictorialist circles had he so desired. Well-documented disputes with H.P. Robinson were probably the main cause of his exclusion. He remained in the Photographic Society and is credited with responsibility for Royal acclaim, hence the change of title to the Royal Photographic Society (RPS).[7]

Aside from illustrated talks, the exhibition was the principal space for public display of photographs.[8] Claiming photography as Art did not mean seeking different forms of display so much as claiming different cultural significance. Relevant historical research to date is limited, but it should not be assumed that the Victorian gallery operated like the contemporary gallery.

5 The Impressionists, mid-to late nineteenth century, include Monet, Cezanne, Pisarro, Bonnard, Morisot, Renoir, Van Gogh and Sisley. Relatively informal technique seemed to offer a vision of the world which was both instantaneous and subjective. Their concern to find ways of painting which reflected light, movement and speed echoed an emphasis on modernity and immediacy by critics such as Baudelaire, although the subject-matter treated by many of the artists was rural or natural rather than urban. The most extensive collection is in the Musée D'Orsay, Paris, but most major art collections (including the Metropolitan Museum of Art, New York and the National Gallery, London) offer examples.

6 Naturalism in painting now refers to close observation and detailed study of external appearances. Naturalism in late nineteenth-century theatre referred to drama in which social environment was depicted as the primary influence on characters, actions and events. Key dramatists include the Scandinavians Henry Ibsen and August Strindberg.

7 The RPS remains a major photographic institution to this day. Paradoxically, perhaps, it is now the major archive for nineteenth-century British Pictorialism, holding work by many of those who led the secessionist challenge to the Photographic Society.

8 Books of photographs date from the very early days with Henry Fox Talbot's *The Pencil of Nature* or Anna Atkins' use of

photographic illustrations in her studies of flora. But each image had to be hand printed. Therefore books could only be produced in limited editions.

For instance, gallery display conventions emphasised quantity of work, rather than the singularity of the specific image. Paintings, prints and photographs were hung floor to ceiling, with little regard to size or frames (figure 6.4). Since it would be almost impossible to view those hung at floor or ceiling level, certain parts of the wall were, in effect, pride of place. An example of this may be found in the Round Room at Birmingham Museum and Art Gallery, England, which has been hung to demonstrate the style of the gallery in 1885 (although with only about fifty paintings rather than nearly ninety, as originally). The legacy – and difficulties – of this style of hanging may also be seen annually, particularly in the print sections, at the Royal Academy Summer Show. Galleries were not painted white, and lighting was limited, in contrast to the visibility standards of the late twentieth century. Just seeing monochrome images must have been difficult, let alone discerning the detail of resolution and tonal contrast for which the Pictorialists strived.

Indeed, the Linked Ring were instrumental in introducing changes to the gallery, emphasising the presentation of the picture. Photographer Frederick Evans is credited with the introduction of mounts in more muted colours in

6.4 Thurston Thompson, *Exhibition Installation*, 1858
Installation shot of the fifth exhibition of the Photographic Society of London, 1858. Photographs were framed and matted but crowded in blocks, some so high or low as to render them difficult to see

order not to distract from the delicacy of detail and imagery achieved through the various photographic printing and toning processes. Photographs were framed more uniformly and less heavily than previously; more wall space was allocated to each picture, and the hanging space restricted to the central area of the wall, not too high or too low. Although the concentration of photographs would surprise viewers accustomed to late twentieth-century gallery conventions, the Pictorialists did set new standards of display at the time.

THE MODERN ERA

Modernism and Modern Art

> The Modern Movement in the twentieth century has often involved painters and sculptors in an exploration of the idea that art has a purely formal language in which meaning is conveyed by shape, texture, colour and size. This exploration has been in a shifting dialogue with the traditional subjects of art, such as landscape, the figure and still life.
>
> (Tate Gallery, St Ives, Cornwall, 1995)

Key galleries in Britain: The Tate, Liverpool and London. The Tate, St Ives, is largely devoted to English Modernism

In his essay 'When Was Modernism', cultural critic Raymond Williams notes that the idea of the Modern began to take on what he terms 'a favourable and progressive ring' in the mid-nineteenth century (Williams 1989). He adds that, in its more specific use, 'Modern' soon developed into a categorisation of a number of art movements broadly located between the 1890s and the 1940s, so that by 1950 it was possible to contrast 'Modern Art' with 'contemporary Art'. 'Modernism' increasingly came to refer to avant-garde art movements within which the emphasis was on the specific medium and experiments in forms of expression, rather than on subject-matter. Williams notes a number of social factors which contributed to making the early twentieth century the key era of artistic change. These included the dislocation of artists caused by war and revolution, which contributed a sense both of art movements as international and of the artist as somehow outside of modern society and therefore in a position to offer a particular perspective on it. He also cites the growth of publishing, noting that the Futurists, Surrealists, Cubists, Constructivists and others announced the birth of their new Art movement through manifestos published in magazines or journals.

American critic Clement Greenberg wrote extensively on the subject of Modernism, taking the position that Art is autonomous from its social context of production. He emphasised the *medium*, and method of expression, arguing that 'the essence of Modernism lies . . . in the use of the characteristic methods of a discipline to criticise the discipline itself, not in order to subvert it but in order to entrench it more firmly in its area of competence' (Greenberg 1961: 308). His influence as a critic, and his unequivocal support for abstract Art, contributed to the international respect

6.5 Bill Brandt, *Prior Park, near Bath*, 1936
Straight photography used with great compositional effect to describe the contours of the park, and of the sculptural urn in the foreground

accorded to American Abstract Expressionism (including painters such as Mark Rothko and Jackson Pollock).

Earlier, in 1939, Greenberg had distinguished between avant-garde art, and 'kitsch', by which he meant the popular and the commercial 'product of the industrial revolution which urbanised the masses of Western Europe and America and established what is called universal literacy' (Greenberg 1939: 533). For him the avant-garde was the historical agency which functioned to keep culture alive in the face of capitalism. At this point in his development as a critic, Greenberg acknowledged the social and historical contexts in which the experience of Art occurs, asserting that the avant-garde was a type of political engagement.

Modern Art came to occupy a relatively autonomous, arguably elitist position which remained unchallenged until the 1960s. The internationalism of Modern Art rests on this notion of autonomy. If art is viewed as *not* context-specific it can be assumed that it communicates regardless of national and cultural differences. Artist-critic Victor Burgin has commented sardonically on such assumptions:

> *Art* is an activity characteristic of humanity since the dawn of civilisation. In any epoch the *Artist*, by virtue of special gifts, expresses that which is finest in humanity. . . . The visual artist achieves this through modes of understanding and expression which are 'purely visual' – radically distinct from, for example, verbalisation. This special characteristic of art necessarily makes it an autonomous sphere of activity, completely separate from the everyday world of social and political life. The autonomous nature of visual art means that questions asked of it may only be properly put, and answered, in its own terms – all other forms of interrogation are irrelevant. In the modern world the function of art is to preserve and enhance its own special sphere of civilising human values in an increasingly dehumanising technological environment.
>
> If these beliefs sound familiar – perhaps even self-evident – it is because they long-ago became part of the received common-sense we in the West learn at our mother's knee.
>
> (Burgin 1986: 30)

Modern photography

Greenberg condemned the literal in painting. By contrast, he welcomed it in photography:

> The art in photography is literary art before it is anything else: its triumphs and monuments are historical, anecdotal, reportorial, observational before they are purely pictorial. . . . The photograph has to tell a story if it is to work as art.
>
> (Greenberg 1991: 131)

In his view the photograph was transparent, documentary, and marked by speed and ease (relative to painting): 'All visible reality, unposed, unaltered, unrehearsed, is open to instantaneous photography' (Greenberg 1991). This view clearly prioritised **straight photography**, by then well established in American documentary, over American photographic **Formalism** which, in its mid-century heyday, was experimental and more gallery oriented.

Broadly speaking, Modern photography sought to offer new perceptions, literally and metaphorically, using light, form, composition and tonal contrast

H.H. ARNASON (1988) **A History of Modern Art**, London: Thames and Hudson. This revised and updated third edition includes photography as the central vocabulary of the image. As contemporary critic, Peter Wollen, has noted:

> During the 1910s the pictorialist paradigm began to crack. It moved, however, not towards greater intervention, but towards less. The straight print triumphed, shedding at the same time its *fin-de-siècle* aesthetic pretensions and overcoming its resistance to photography of record. Not only was the gum process rejected but also softness, darkness, blurriness and *flou* altogether. Following the crucial innovations of Strand and Sheeler, ambitious photography accepted illumination and sharpness. The way was cleared by the new machine aesthetic of modernism, which gave fresh confidence to the photographer and validated clarity and precision . . . pictorialism transmuted into a new modernist photography of geometrical compositions, machine forms, hard-edge design and clear delineation of detail.
>
> (Wollen 1982: 180–181)

As Wollen goes on to note, this is the era when the pictorial and the documentary came together under the influence of new principles of composition. Photographers such as Florence Henri (France) or Paul Strand (USA) seem to have echoed the Cubists in their concern with form. In the case of many of Strand's more famous photographs people are depersonalised to the extent that they become anonymous figures in the cityscape (see, for instance, Wall Street, or Central Park, both 1915 to 1916). Wollen engages with the aesthetic implications of this new photography, arguing that the camera as machine does not in itself make the photograph more objective (and therefore less amenable to the expression of particular perceptions), 'it simply substitutes discovery for invention in the traditional categories of classical aesthetics' (Wollen 1982: 182). Here it is the process of realisation of the image which is at stake. Put more bluntly: creativity resides in the artist, not in the technology.

Concern with form and precision can be seen at its extreme in what we now term American Formalism, for example, in the work of Edward Weston and Tina Modotti, whose abstract visual poetics concentrated on tone and shape rather than on the subject of the image. Edward Weston defined his approach as both abstract and realist, emphasising the observational basis of the photograph. Beaumont Newhall has stressed the interdependence of the technological and the aesthetic in Weston's work, noting his insistence upon pre-visualisation of the image. Weston sought clarity of form and extolled the camera for its depth of focus and its ability to see more than the human eye. The f/64 Group, founded in 1932 by a number of American photographers, including Weston, Imogen Cunningham and Ansel Adams, was so-called precisely to reflect the emphasis upon sharpness of image. Their approach emphasised photography as a specific type of medium with its own optical, chemical and consequent aesthetic properties. Unlike other photographic movements of the time, Formalism sought gallery exhibition. Indeed, work by these photographers is now highly prized (and priced) and is included in all major photography archives as examples of one of the most significant photography movements of the twentieth century.[9]

Photographers move geographically and aesthetically over a lifetime, changing their style and subject-matter, their work reflecting differing political contexts. Photography figured extensively within European avant-garde movements of the 1910s to 1930s, but in ways which did not necessarily pose images as Art or lead to gallery exhibition. Here emphasis on reconstruction in Europe subsequent to both the First World War and to the Russian Revolution offered obvious social and political context and a sense of immediacy. Discussing photography and architecture in Europe between

9 Curiously, Stieglitz never showed Edward Weston's work in New York in his Madison Avenue gallery, named An American Place, which he ran from 1929 to 1946. However, in the second half of the twentieth century almost all major historical surveys or gallery overview exhibitions give prominence to the work of the American Formalists. The individual photographers are featured in a number of monographs so their work is easily found in bookshops and libraries.

6.6 Edward Weston, *Dunes, Oceano*
Photographic seeing with emphasis on the rhythm of form

the wars, Ian Jeffrey describes 1920s photographic modernism in Europe as engaged with social totalities and worthy of respect, 'premised on selflessness, transcending local and even national affiliations' (Jeffrey 1991: 60). By contrast, he notes more archaic subject-matter in the 1930s, with its more romantic focus on secret worlds and marginalised people within the city. The imagery of Krull, Atget, Brassai can be viewed as more conversational, in a classic documentary manner, less experimental and less inclined to celebrate the promise of a new social order so eagerly supported in the first half of the 1920s. In effect, reminding us of the changing European political circumstances, Jeffrey proposes that optimism in the 1920s was superseded by a retreat into romanticism in the 1930s and, crucially, that this can be discerned in the shifting subject-matter and style of the image.

In order to examine developments in slightly more detail, we offer two case studies. First, we focus on ways in which art and design were implicated politically in social reconstruction both in Soviet Constructivism and in the German Bauhaus. These movements show artists reaching out beyond the gallery system. Second, we consider photography in relation to a specific art movement – namely Surrealism – noting, in particular, the intellectual currencies which informed Surrealism, its multidisciplinary nature, and subsequent comments and reappraisals. Each case study is intended to offer an example of ways in which photography, caught within specific broader movements, might be analysed and contextualised. Each also draws attention to the emphasis upon aesthetic radicalism which typified Modern movements. That the studies focus on more-or-less simultaneous moments in history is also important as it indicates something of the diversity of projects, ideas, influences and debates which may obtain at any one time.

CASE STUDY 1: Art, design, politics – Soviet Constructivism and the Bauhaus

A brief background

Discussing experimentation in Russian art from the 1860s to the early 1920s, Camilla Gray traces a number of strands within Russian Modern Art, ranging from spiritual interest in medieval icon painting to a realism which mirrored developments in other parts of Europe (Gray 1962). In the mid-nineteenth century, 'The Wanderers' – a group of Russian painters who, like their contemporaries in France, had broken from the Russian Art Academy – committed themselves to developing art which was about the everyday. Links with Paris, Munich and Vienna, especially immediately after the failure of the 1905 Revolution, led to a number of major exhibitions in Moscow and St Petersburg wherein Russian artists showed alongside their Western European contemporaries. By the time of the 1917 Revolution there was an identifiable avant-garde which, in the paintings of

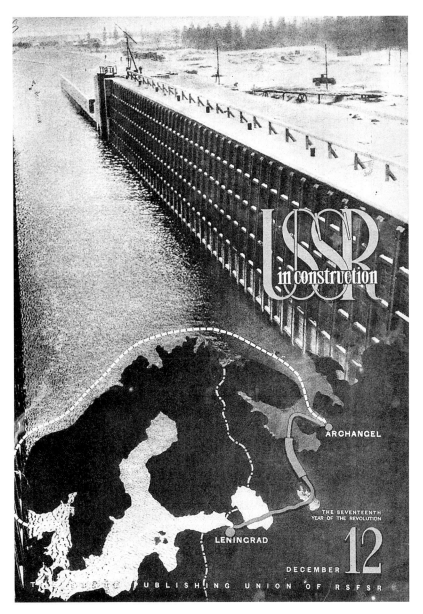

6.7 Alexander Rodchenko, *White Sea Canal*, from *USSR in Construction* 12, 1933

One example of the geometric style and the commitment to a new angle of vision, literally and metaphorically, which characterised both the Bauhaus and Constructivism

Malevich, Popova, El Lissitzky, paralleled Cubism in France in exploring the surface of the canvas and the nature of artistic language.

Experiments in the social role of art

The success of the 1917 Revolution led to a new political context, one in which the nature and social role of art was hotly debated. A number of artists, led by Malevich, stressed the formal and spiritual supremacy of art in itself. A Russian form of Modernism. Others emphasised proletarian culture advocating a social role for artist-workers in the vanguard of Revolutionary change. The new situation encouraged a radical aesthetics. Painter-photographer Alexander Rodchenko asserted that:

> Art has no place in modern life. It will continue to exist as long as there is a mania for the romantic and so long as there are people who love beautiful lies and deception. . . . Every modern cultured man must wage war against art, as against opium. . . . Photograph and be photographed.
>
> (Rodchenko 1928)

For Rodchenko and the other Constructivists, new art involved, first, the depersonalisation of practice, that is, taking art out of the realm of individual artistic expression; second, logical laboratory study of form and composition; third, analysis of rules governing the nature of artistic communication. That photography was technological made it particularly appropriate. Art set out to renegotiate itself as a type of practice which was utilitarian in foregrounding design and function, and selfless from the point of view of the artist. As such it represented the socialist ideals of the Revolution. Soviet Constructivism flourished for about a decade, before being superseded by Socialist Realism with its focus on glorification of the worker, the peasant and 'heroes' of the Revolution.

Constructivist photography

For the Constructivists, photography was a popular form which, through its usage in posters, magazines and publishing, could be at the forefront of taking new ideas to the people. Emphasising art's post-Revolutionary responsibilities, Rodchenko stated that he was fed up with 'belly button' shots, by which he meant photographs composed conventionally shot from waist level through cameras with their viewfinder on top. He argued for full exploration of the geometry of the image which would, literally and metaphorically, engineer a new angle of vision. Indeed, for Rodchenko photography was the true modern art. He argued that, unlike painting and sculpture which he viewed as outdated, photography could express the reality of post-Revolutionary society. Thus, in the case of Soviet Constructivism, the issue was not one of photography attempting to claim status as Art, but rather a democratisation of artistic practices in the service of social and cultural revolution within which photography, by its enquiring nature and its ubiquity, could play a leading role.

The integration of art and design

Shifting political circumstances are also reflected in the fortunes of the German Bauhaus (1919–1933), which was founded in Weimar under the leadership of Walter Gropius. It moved to Dessau in 1925, by which time Herbert Bayer, photographer and typographer, was a key influence; and to Berlin in 1932, before disbanding in consequence of the election of Hitler's National Socialists. (Many Bauhaus theorists were exiled to the United States where they formed The Chicago Art Institute.) The Bauhaus was a clear response to the destruction and dereliction witnessed during the First World War. 'Bauhaus' literally means 'house for building'. Like Soviet Constructivism, the Bauhaus was multi-disciplinary, although architecture came to be the central concern. Taking the notion of reconstruction as the central tenet, Bauhaus theorists emphasised the relation between form and function, and stressed what they saw as a potential unity of art, design and the everyday (see Rowland 1990). Their radical approach was not uncontroversial. For instance, Frankfurt School theorist, Walter Benjamin, expressed impatience with such experimentation, accusing the 'new objectivity' photographers of the Bauhaus of making the world artistic rather than making Art mundane. For Benjamin, emphasis on form detracted from the democratic characteristics of photography which, in his view, should be a comprehensible means of communication for everyone. He opposed formalism and abstraction because, he argued, experimentation in visual languages tends to be exclusive, and therefore elitist.

A new instrument of vision

The Bauhaus viewed radicalism in photography in different terms. László and Lucia Moholy-Nagy were perhaps the best-known photographers associated with the Bauhaus. They stressed ways in which use of light, mechanical reproduction and the possibility of sensitive printing expressed the machine aesthetic of the Modern Age. In parallel with the Soviet emphasis upon photo-eye as the modern method of communication, Moholy-Nagy emphasised the relation between the mechanical nature of the camera, form, the use of light and visual perception, arguing that photography enhances sight in relation to time and space (Moholy-Nagy 1932). Like Benjamin, their writings opposed the reification of the individual artist. Unlike Benjamin, they stressed the compositional qualities of the image, viewing this as central to the means of expression.

CASE STUDY 2: Art movements and intellectual currencies – Surrealism

What was Surrealism?

It is always relevant and, in academic terms, interesting, to trace links between the general intellectual climate of any era and aesthetic developments.

CHRISTOPHER PHILLIPS (ed.) (1989) **Photography in the Modern Era: European Documents and Critical Writings 1913–1940**, New York: MOMA

ABIGAIL SOLOMON-GODEAU (1991) 'The Armed Vision Disarmed: Radical Formalism from Weapon to Style' in **Photography at the Dock: Essays on Photographic History, Institutions and Practices**, Minneapolis: University of Minnesota Press

JOHN WILLETT (1978) **The New Sobriety, Art and Politics in the Weimar Period**, London: Thames and Hudson

Surrealism took the idea of the individual psyche as its theoretical starting point, thus particularly reflecting the **psychoanalytic** work of Sigmund Freud. Surrealism emphasised artistic processes whereby the imaginary can be recorded through automatic writing or drawing which would thus offer insights into the world of thought and therefore disrupt taken-for-granted perceptions and frames of reference. For the Surrealists, the artist was the starting point or material source of what was to be expressed. Freud distinguished between the Id, the **unconscious** instinctual self, and the Ego, the largely conscious socialised self. Likewise, Surrealists distinguished between 'thought' and 'reason', and aimed to bypass what they saw as the **repressive** nature of reason in order to express what they viewed as natural desires.

Surrealism has been regarded as attempting to replicate the world of dreams. This is premised directly on Freud's dream theory wherein he argued that analysis of the manifest content of dreams offers perception on subjective responses to experience. However, this is to oversimplify, as the aims of Surrealism were complex and, to some extent, changed over time. They included a direct attack on the nature of Art; many of the early Surrealists were also involved in the First World War anti-Art movement, Dada (Ades 1974). Both Dada and Surrealism were interventionist in challenging what was happening in the gallery. For instance, Marcel Duchamp placed a urinal in the gallery claiming that the location made it 'Art'.

French poet André Breton described 'A desire to deepen the foundations of the real; to bring about an ever clearer and at the same time ever more passionate consciousness of the world perceived by the senses' (Breton 1978: 115). In the late 1920s, Surrealists, led by Breton, called for adherence to Marxist dialectical materialism and to the ideal of revolution. This caused splits in the Paris-based group (including the expulsion of Salvador Dali because of his support for Fascism in Spain). Fundamentally, Surrealism was premised on challenging philosophical distinctions between interior experience and exterior realities. The radicalism of Surrealism lay in its aims: to disorient the spectator; to push towards the destruction of conventional ways of seeing; and to challenge rationalist frameworks.

Fine art movements transcend national boundaries, albeit reflecting particular national features. In exploring photography as Art, it is necessary to take account of the interplay between that which characterises specific social and political circumstances, and more general international contexts. For instance, the first Surrealist Manifesto was published in Paris in 1924, but the first International Surrealist Exhibition in Britain did not take place until 1936, by which time, arguably, the movement had lost its more experimental edge.[10] Furthermore, a number of the original Paris-based group became members of the Communist Party. In Britain, with Roland Penrose as the key Surrealist artist and exponent, the emphasis lay more on visual form and psychoanalytic references than on political revolution.

10 Held in London at the New Burlington Galleries in Burlington Gardens; that is, in a modern gallery.

6.8 Lee Miller, *Portrait of Space*, near Siwa, Egypt, 1937
An example of a Surreal juxtaposition of interior/exterior to achieve a dreamlike effect. Mirrors frequently feature, referencing reflection. Possibly the inspiration for Magritte's *Le Baiser*

Surrealist photography

How does lens-based imagery, including photography, fit within Surrealism? For Dali, the mechanical nature of the camera was liberating: 'photography sets imagination free', he claimed. Breton stated:

> The invention of photography has dealt a mortal blow to the old modes of expression, in painting as well as in poetry, where automatic writing, which appeared at the end of the nineteenth century, is a true photography of thought.
>
> (Breton 1978: 7)

He also noted approvingly that 'belief in an absolute time and space seems to be vanishing', a reference to the photograph's ability to picture the past, or the geographically distant, and welcomed the fact that 'today, thanks to the cinema, we know how to make a locomotive *arrive* in a picture' (1978: 7). Despite the involvement of artists such as Herbert Bayer, previously associated with the Bauhaus, Surrealist photography clearly differed both in principle and in vision from the Formalist 'new objectivity' of the Bauhaus. Stressing the imagination as the source of insight on experience, the Surrealists used **photomontage**, double exposure, **rayographs**, or **solarisation**, in order to produce disorienting imagery.

Critical reappraisals

Feminism has provoked reappraisal of Surrealism in recent years, both through debates about patriarchal attitudes in psychoanalysis and, more specifically, through new art history. Women figured in Surrealism as artists but, until recently, their position and contribution has been largely ignored (see Chadwick 1985, 1998). Reinstatement has focused attention on the work of many women Surrealists, including photographers Lee Miller and Claude Cahun. Indeed, allegedly Lee Miller 'discovered' solarisation by opening a darkroom door, not realising that Man Ray was printing.

The feminist critique has also drawn attention to the role of woman as muse. Considered from a feminist perspective, the expression of unconscious desires, central to Surrealist imagery, seems merely an excuse for male heterosexual fantasy. 'Woman' is objectified. The distorted or fragmented female figure is a common motif. Hans Bellmer's female dolls most obviously degrade and violate woman through her disfiguration or dismembering. Surrealists viewed such imagery as an expression of innate but repressed desire, and no doubt welcomed the challenge to bourgeois boundaries of permissibility. With hindsight, and in the light of feminism, the misogyny is clear.

Reappraisal has also focused upon the relation between photographic representation of the real, and the surreal effect, for instance, of doubling a particular motif within the image or of distortion. The taken-for-granted realism of the photographic became the source of the *coup d'oeuil* effect which often operated to disorient the spectator. Rosalind Krauss notes metaphoric effects: 'we see with a shock of recognition the simultaneous effect of displacement and condensation, the very operations of symbol formation, hard at work on the flesh of the real' (**Krauss and Livingston 1986: 19**). The shock emanates from the refusal of the transcriptive realism expected of photography.

Modern photography, the gallery and the archive

Nowadays Modern photography is central to the archive. Historical connoisseurship has created a canon of photographers whose imagery is now highly regarded. This was not always the case. In Britain, the main impetus in photography for most of this century was in documentary and photojournalism, studio portraiture and commercial art. From about 1905 (towards the

---

photomontage The use of two or more originals, perhaps also including written text, to make a combined image. A montaged image may be imaginative, artistic, comic or deliberately satirical.

rayographs, solarisation Aesthetic techniques associated in particular with the work of Man Ray and Lee Miller. Solarisation involves brief exposure to light during printing thereby altering tonal contrast. Likewise rayographs or photograms, cameraless photographs, made by placing objects on photographic paper then exposing to light, were discovered by accident. (The technique had been known about in the nineteenth century but not exploited. See Krauss and Livingston 1986: 229.)

ROSALIND KRAUSS AND JANE LIVINGSTON (1986) **L'Amour Fou**, London: Arts Council of Great Britain

RUDOLF E. KUENZLI (1991) 'Surrealism and Misogyny' in Mary Ann Caws, Rudolf Kuenzli and Owen Raaberg **Surrealism and Women**, Cambridge, MA: The MIT Press end of Pictorialism) photography had little visibility in the art gallery. The work of British photographers – such as Bill Brandt and George Rodgers, whom we now celebrate – was not made initially for gallery exhibition, nor was it necessarily widely known. Bill Brandt's now famous collection *Perspective of Nudes* was not published until 1961.

Developments can be mapped through a number of exhibitions. A major retrospective of photographs by Bill Brandt, curated in 1969 for MOMA, New York, arrived at the Hayward Gallery on London's South Bank in 1970. *The Land: 20th Century Landscape Photographs*, also by Bill Brandt, was exhibited at the Victoria and Albert Museum in 1975. A now forgotten show, *Spectrum*, at the Institute of Contemporary Arts (ICA), London, in 1969, included four British-based photographers – Tony Ray Jones, Enzo Ragazzini, Dorothy Bohm, Don McCullin – and encompassed straight photography, optical experiments, photojournalism and portraiture. In 1975 the Arts Council organised a touring exhibition, *The Real Thing, An Anthology of British Photographs 1840–1950*. Thus a diversity of work was brought into focus.

Key collection: The Print Room, Victoria and Albert Museum, London

LATE TWENTIETH-CENTURY PERSPECTIVES

The American and European Avant-garde art movements of the 1960s emphasised idea and process over the conventions of painting and sculpture. The war in Vietnam, the civil rights movement in America, the development of feminist politics and theory, and the student protests of 1968, were reflected in works that were challenging to the status quo, to ideas about the artist as apolitical and working alone, and to art institutions.

(*Comment and Commitment: Art and Society 1975–1990*, Tate Gallery, London 1995)

Conceptual art and the photographic

Photography in the 1960s was centrally implicated in the expansion of the mass media, including fashion shots, album covers for long-playing (33⅓) records, photojournalism (the *Sunday Times* colour supplement was launched in 1962). In the Art gallery, two parallel developments in the 1960s and 1970s contributed to shifting the position of photography. First, pop artists such as Andy Warhol (USA), Roy Lichtenstein (USA), David Hockney and Richard Hamilton (both British) started to use the photographic in order to reference and comment on lifestyles and consumerism.[11] To echo Roland Barthes, many elements within their pictures were *déjà-lu* ('already read'). This was the whole point. Raymond Williams has suggested that in the 1960s the two dimensions of the modern, radical aesthetics and technological change, came together in the pictures of artists whose work engaged with the revolution in mass culture consequent upon developments in technology and communications such as television (Williams

11 Pop Art in the 1960s essentially commented upon evidence of transformation into a consumerist society. Artist Richard Hamilton described Pop Art as popular, transient, expendable, low cost, mass produced, young, witty, sexy, gimmicky, glamorous and big business.

1989). Indeed, photography arguably contributed to creating a more visually sophisticated audience than had previously obtained: 'that painters have used photographs does not legitimise photography; on the contrary, such cross-pollination has primarily helped *painting* remain a vital and effective medium' (Coleman 1979: 121). Through Pop Art the photographic gained a presence in the gallery (see Alloway (1966) for an account of British Pop Art). Second, in Conceptual Art the photographic became accepted as a valid medium of artistic expression. It was in the 1970s that American Art magazines, including *Artforum* and *Art in America*, took photography into their remit. As photo-theorist, John Roberts, has argued:

> Photography was the means by which conceptual art's exit from Modernist closure was made realisable as *practice*. Yet photography itself was of little interest to most conceptual artists, producing a situation in which critical agency is given to the photographic image without photography becoming theoretically self-conscious as a medium. Photography, then, had an indirect function: it allowed conceptual art to reconnect itself to the world of social appearances without endorsing a *pre*-Modernist defence of the pictorial.
>
> (Roberts 1997: 9)

Modernist theory had focused on the medium. By contrast, Conceptual Art stressed ideas. Artists were concerned to draw attention to the manner or vocabulary of expression; also, to contexts of interpretation, that is, the influence of the situation within which the spectator responds to the image or art object. Indeed, in a number of instances artists placed a statement about an art object in the gallery, thereby focusing attention on the idea, rather than the object (which might never have been actually made). From the postmodern theoretical perspectives of the 1990s/2000s the notion of explicitly requiring spectator interpretation comes as no surprise. But, at the time, Conceptual Art, especially in its more critical or political forms, consti-tuted a challenge to the Art establishment (see Harrison and Wood 1993). In conceptual photography the characteristics of the medium could be used as a part of the means of expression of an idea. Thus, for instance, Keith Arnatt's sequence of digging himself into a hole in the ground (figure 6.9) is obviously, at one level, a metaphoric reference to the well-known phrase. But the documentary idiom secures a sense that this event literally did take place through demonstrating the sequence of moments in time.

Conceptualism challenged the dominance of abstract Formalism. It was not that it denied the significance of form. Rather, form was brought into play differently with a view to social, political, metaphysical, or simply humorous, comment. However, as photography became accepted within Conceptual Art, so attention came to be paid to photographs (pictorialist, formalist and documentary) and to photography history. In effect, Conceptual Art offered photography a bridge into the gallery.

JONATHAN GREEN (1984) 'The Painter as Photographer' in **American Photography**, ch 9, New York: Harry N. Abrams

6.9 Keith Arnatt, *Self Burial*, TV Interference Project, 1969
Photograph on paper, 467 × 467 cm. The humour of the piece of work emanates from the realism attributed to photography. One way of testing the implication of choice of specific medium, and therefore the implied comment on the nature of the medium, is to imagine what interpretational shift might occur if the sequence had been, say, painted

This era featured other challenges which, although incorporating some of the aesthetic characteristics of formalism, took for their starting point ideas which were anchored socially (rather than aesthetically). For instance, the 'new topographics' photographers, including Lewis Baltz (USA) and Bernd and Hilla Becher (Germany), explored the act of looking through the detailed mapping of industrial edifices or locations.[12] Similar images are blocked next to one another, thereby bringing into question the degree of detailed discrimination involved in day-to-day perceptions. Clearly this work drew on the emphasis upon detailed seeing typical of, for instance, the f/64 group. But the new topographics, in charting the industrial landscape, implied a social and environmental questioning which did not figure in American Formalism. Land Art also dates from this period. Here, the photograph is

12 The term 'new topographics', used in the 1970s, refers back to nineteenth-century topographical work, especially the photographic charting of the American West.

the record, and the final product, of an intervention within the rural. Work by British artists, including Richard Long and Andy Goldsworthy, has become well known not through direct experience of the results of their investigations and interventions, but through their photographs. The sculptural intervention ameliorates, deteriorates, and becomes reabsorbed within the environment. Ultimately only the picture remains.

Photography and the postmodern

Since the 1970s there have been significant developments in Art practices founded in the new centrality of critical ideas to the visual arts, and in what was often referred to as the 'return to the figurative'. Of course the figurative had never entirely disappeared. The 'return' was more a question of a regeneration of interest in the representational on the part of curators and critics, now moving beyond Modernist preoccupations with the specificity of each medium. For example, as noted, Conceptual artists referenced the media and used 'found' images and materials not previously associated with fine art. New Art also posited questions of representation. By the 1980s Art had ceased to be self-obsessed, was looking outward beyond the boundaries of the gallery, taking on contemporary issues and making a range of references that ruptured Modernist assertions of the autonomy of Art.

Critical theorist, Douglas Crimp, suggested that photography contributed centrally within this challenge to the museum and gallery:

> From the parochial perspective of the late-1970s art world, photography appeared as a watershed. Radically reevaluated, photography took up residence in the museum on a par with the visual arts' traditional mediums and according to the very same art-historical tenets. New principles of photographic connoisseurship were devised; the canon of master photographers was vastly expanded; prices on the photography market skyrocketed. Counterposed against this reevaluation were two coincident developments: a materialist history of photography and dissident photographic practices . . . taken together and brought into relation, they could tell us something about Postmodernism, a term coming into wide use at just that time.
>
> (Crimp 1995: 2)

Thus, from the 1970s on, emphasis upon conceptual ideas and critical practices contributed to creating a place for the photographic within the Art gallery. Furthermore, photography contributed to the regeneration of art practices. The sources of this shift are complex. First, the radicalism of 1968 in Europe heralded a Left cultural agenda in the 1970s. This underpinned critical interrogation of dominant cultural practices. Examples may be found in the work of then British-based artists Victor Burgin and Mary Kelly, both of whom, notably, wrote about photographic practices as well as making photographic work. Second, and as a part of this, Modern theory had begun to be questioned across many realms of academic enterprise, from the scientific to the aesthetic. In the fine arts this questioning took off earlier in North America than it did in Europe. Thus, in Britain, the third influence was new American Art, including photographically based work by artists such as Cindy Sherman and Barbara Kruger. (See Nairne 1987, ch 4; Kruger 1983, 1990; Sherman 1997.)

Barry Lane, photography officer at the Arts Council from 1973 to 1995, attributes the burgeoning of interest in photography in the 1970s to three key factors.[13] First, developments including community arts, performance art and 'happenings' signified a broadening of definitions of 'Art'. As already noted, photography breached the gallery around this time. Second, developments in America lent impetus and contacts for fostering photography in Britain. Third, there were energetic claims from within the British documentary movement for the artistic integrity of the medium, and such claims were further fuelled by the commercial success of leading British 1960s photographers.

Art education reflected the changes. In England in the 1970s there was a move to consolidate art schools within the newly established polytechnics and to upgrade courses from diploma to degree status. This involved changing the erstwhile 'liberal studies' agenda to a more purposeful critical appraisal of art history. Art school graduates, who subsequently formed the new generation of gallery curators, were increasingly well informed and interested in exhibiting a greater range of ideas-based work. Not only had photography moved into the art gallery but, more broadly, critical ideas moved on to the agenda in photography education; an agenda that was increasingly influenced by feminist perspectives and critiques. A number of new degrees in photography became established wherein 'theory' meant thinking about photography **semiotically**, and in relation to questions of identity, gender and representation.[14] By the 1990s, digital imaging was adding its voice to the claims (see chapter 7).

Developments do not proceed in an orderly and coherent fashion. Whilst digitally produced work takes its place alongside the straight photograph and constructed imagery, the relative lack of photographs in a number of major museum collections indicates that photography is still seen by some as a lesser Art. The corollary of the new emphasis upon ideas and critiques was that, from the mid-1980s, straight photography found itself positioned ambiguously. On the one hand, museums established photography sections[15] but on the other hand it became more difficult to retain the space within the contemporary gallery. The foothold established in the 1970s came to seem precarious. This was expressed partly in the practical issue of scale. Photography galleries had been designed to accommodate the standard-format image. A number of the newer photo-media galleries, which were larger scale (often converted

13 Interviewed by Liz Wells, April 1995.

14 The most prominent example was at the Polytechnic of Central London in the 1980s. Tutors then included Victor Burgin and Simon Watney, both of whom have published extensively on art and culture.

15 For instance, the Museum of Modern Art, New York has a number of galleries permanently dedicated to photography, as does the National Museum of Photography, Film and Television in Bradford, Yorkshire, England; the V&A, London, opened a permanent space for photography exhibition in 1998.

from disused industrial buildings), became key institutions within the new debates. The standard photograph became harder to show, smaller pictures being dwarfed within cavernous warehouse – now, gallery – spaces.

More particularly, the position of photography changed partly as a consequence of fashion and the focus on the postmodern. Since the 1970s lens-based media, including photography, video, slide projection and installation have been absorbed within broader fine art practices. Furthermore, by the 1990s irony, parody and pastiche increasingly featured within the armoury of the artist. It is no accident that a key exhibition of contemporary British photography at the Victoria and Albert Museum in 1988 was titled *Towards a Bigger Picture*. The *double entendre* of the title referred in particular to the extension of photography within Art practices and to diversity of subject-matter. But it also referenced conceptual understanding of ways in which scale contributes to the claim for place within the Art gallery. For example, very small-scale work, carefully mounted and framed, inherits the sense of the precious associated with miniature painting. It demands close-up and detailed looking. Preciousness is emphasised if individual works are hung with space between them. By contrast, large-scale photographic works claim the status traditionally accorded to academic painting and other Art made for public spaces. They also assert their presence and, therefore, the significance of their theme or subject-matter. Such pictures engage with contemporary myth in ways which echo the ideological and political involvements typical of classical painting.

New constructions

Discussing pluralism in American Art in the 1970s, critic Corinne Robins comments on the increasing eclecticism of photography, noting:

> Photographers concentrated on making up or creating scenes for the camera in terms of their own inner vision. To them, reportage as such had become the job of the video artist, who had the heritage of *cinéma vérité* behind him [*sic*]. To the 1970s camera people, realism belonged to the earlier history of photography and, as seventies artists, they were embarked on a different kind of aesthetic quest. It was not, however, the romantic symbolism of photography of the 1920s and 1930s, with its emphasis on the abstract beauty of the object, that had caught their attention, but rather a new kind of concentration on narrative drama, on the depiction of time changes in the camera's fictional moment. The photograph, instead of being presented as a depiction of reality, was now something created to show us things that were felt rather than necessarily seen.
>
> (Robins 1984: 213)

fabrication The crafting of images which have been **staged** or appropriated and adjusted for the camera. The term is more common within American photography than European, referencing the craft base of the medium. It stands by contrast with 'constructed' imagery, which inflects the directorial approach in more political terms through referencing both Soviet Constructivism and theories of deconstruction.

Central to the postmodern is an emphasis on **construction**, the forging, **staging** or **fabrication** of images. Pictures are preconceived by the artist.

282

Constructed photography includes photomontage, **staged imagery, image-text** works, slide-tape installations, photographs derived from Land Art; indeed, any photographic imagery wherein the conceptual engineering of the artist is clearly evident. Contemporary photographers as divergent in concerns as Bernard Faucon, Mary Kelly, Peter Kennard, Barbara Kruger, Richard Long, Mari Mahr, Cindy Sherman, Susan Trangmar and Joel-Peter Witkin all fall within this broad category. The notion of construction derives from two sources: first, the idea that art can intervene politically, as in the example of the Soviet Constructivists or of the German *monteurs*. Second, in postmodern terms, 'construction' directly relates to **deconstruction** theory and practices. Both approaches refuse to take the world at face value. Constructed imagery in effect *critiques* what Grundberg has defined as 'concentration on the literal surfaces of things and on subject matter that seems to speak for itself' (Grundberg 1990: 82).

For instance, in the example of Karen Knorr's series *Country Life*, country-side becomes a setting for reflections upon bourgeois taste and lifestyle (figure 6.1, page 252). Likewise, Patricia Townsend uses double exposure techniques to provoke a sense of dislocation which reminds us that we are objects of the look, as well as lookers, and that walls conceal metaphorically as well as literally (see frontispiece, p. xxii). In each case, the images use the **indexical** qualities of the photographic – that is, the way in which the photograph draws upon actuality – as part of their vocabulary of expression, but only a part of it. Each invites the spectator to actively *read* the image, and all, variously, implicate questions of subjectivity and **identity**.

There are a number of methods whereby the interpretive latitude of an image may be contained. These include photomontage, sequencing and image-text techniques. We also have to take account of factors beyond the image itself. The mounting and framing of pictures – whether single images, or series, or sequences – is not neutral. Framing contributes to the rhetoric of the image through delineating the edge of the picture, that which is put into the frame. It also acts as a margin between the work and the wall on which it hangs. The established convention in post-Renaissance Art of framing paintings means that the frame also signifies the special status of a picture. However, the meaning of the frame is ambiguous: from the point of view of the gallery wall it is a part of the picture, but from the point of view of the picture it dissolves into the wall. In relation to the single image, this ambiguity is relatively clearly comprehended. Within sequences, or blocks of images, the play of the frame is more complex: the frame not only plays between the setting and the image, but also interacts with other frames within the grouping of pictures.

Written text commonly accompanies both single pictures, and series, groups or sequences. Written text includes titles, captions, artists' statements, poetry, or forewords which accompany an exhibition or book publication. Titling, and the signature of the artist, contribute to the claim for the status of the image as Art. Titles may be cryptic, or metaphoric, operating to

staged images Described by American critic A.D. Coleman as 'falsified documents', this refers to the creating of a scene for the camera (as in staging within theatre).

image-text Pictures within which visual imagery and written text are integrated in order to effect a play of meaning between them.

extend resonances, or they may be primarily descriptive. For instance, a title such as *Rome, 1975* or *Waiting Room* specifies place or type of location. However, the caption does not simply anchor; writing constitutes a further signifier within the complex interaction of discourses with which the spectator engages. For instance, the title *Rome* at the very minimum means something different to an Italian than to someone of another nationality. Titles, or captions, simultaneously anchor, and become implicated in, play of meaning. The refusal of a title, as in *Untitled*, is likewise not neutral. This implies that the image is to 'speak for itself'.

Writing operates complexly. This is often particularly so in constructed imagery within which text is montaged as an integral element. Here the verbal is articulated not only as a poetic reference but also as a visual element. Colour, handwritten or typographic style, placing, scale, prominence – all contribute to how we read the overall piece. Likewise, artists' statements do not simply contextualise, or determine a position from which the work is to be read, although, of course, they do offer this. If an artist is viewed as a special sort of seer, offering particular insights into the world of experience, then his or her statement contributes to this claim for authority.

Towards the postmodern in Britain

Any attempt to overview recent thematic developments is fraught with difficulty, not only because of diversity but also because of the lack of the benefit of hindsight. Nonetheless, concentrating on developments in Britain, we have selected some examples of group exhibitions from the late 1970s through to the early 1990s as a focus for discussion.[16]

A note of caution: gallery administrators and curators are caught up in the fashionable. An overview of exhibitions does not necessarily tell everything about contemporary developments – although it might say quite a lot about the politics of the gallery. For instance, as **Brett Rogers** suggests in her introduction to *Documentary Dilemmas*,

> Ignored by the art world which favours big pictures and high prices, and outstripped by technology that gives the edge to television and digital developments, documentary photography has also come under harsh scrutiny from post-modern critics, who question its tendency to separate and exploit certain groups of people, serving up the poor as exotic fare for voyeuristic consumers.
>
> (Rogers 1994: 5)

She goes on to suggest that this has led to the ignoring of new rhetorical strategies in use within documentary, including fill-in flash, colour, scale, captioning, sequencing, and the use of text within the image. Trends within curatorship, criticism and, indeed, the international Art market, marginalise some areas of practice. Any attempt to define trends and developments should acknowledge this.

16 Space does not allow discussion of all group shows, let alone the many single-person shows which have attracted attention during this period, but they are traceable through *Creative Camera* and *Portfolio*.

BRETT ROGERS (ed.) (1994) **Documentary Dilemmas: Aspects of British Documentary Photography 1983–1993**, London: British Council. This exhibition was curated for an international tour, and included work by John Davies, Anna Fox, Julian Germain, Paul Graham, Anthony Haughey, Chris Killip, John Kippin, Karen Knorr, Martin Parr, Ingrid Pollard, Paul Reas, Paul Seawright and Jem Southam

Furthermore, as Mary Kelly has noted, there is a sense in which the gallery itself, although of central symbolic significance, is less important in the history of artistic production than catalogues, books, reviews, and other accompanying, more permanent, forms of reproduction of work (Kelly 1981). Exhibitions are ephemeral. It is published reviews, catalogues or books, rather than the shows themselves, which reach the wider audience. In this section, discussion is based upon catalogues and reviews, so no account is taken of how each show was hung within the particular gallery space.[17]

In 1979 The Arts Council mounted *Three Perspectives on Photography*, a show of recent British photography, at the Hayward Gallery, on London's South Bank. This exhibition makes an interesting contrast to the 1991 Arts Council show, *Shocks to the System*.

Three Perspectives on Photography was organised as three different groups of work, each separately curated, thus acknowledging diversity of approaches. In so doing it appeared radical at the time. Section One, on 'Photographic Truth, Metaphor, and Individual Expression' included series of photographs – each captioned – by six (male) photographers. Stylistically the images reflected a modernist emphasis on photographic seeing. But Paul Hill, in his introduction to the section, stressed the expressive and metaphoric dimensions of the photograph, opposing any simple equation of believability with truth. Indeed, suggesting that the photograph should be understood as a *symbol* for that which is depicted, he drew attention to what would now be termed the semiotics of the image.

Of even more significance retrospectively are the two following sections: 'Feminism and Photography' and 'A Socialist Perspective on Photographic Practice'. Neither of these topics would figure in so blunt a way by the 1990s. Feminist perspectives, on the whole, have been taken on board, some might say diluted through incorporation. By contrast, socialism had been marginalised, and would be a distinctly unfashionable exhibition title! By 1991, a decade later, nothing so succinct as three perspectives could be claimed. The imagery included in *Shocks to the System* was largely made during, and influenced by, the Thatcher decade. Here it is not Left art which is emphasised so much as a range of different visual methods of drawing attention to subjective and political issues and complexities, often employing humour or parody. The show was multicultural, and reflected the diversity which now obtains in gallery photographic practices.

Women's photography

The mere mention of the phrase 'women's art' sends shivers down the art establishment spine – more radical feminists on the war-path! Feminism, advocacy of women's rights on the ground of equality, is usually misinterpreted to mean exclusively female, probably radical and, more than likely, shaven-headedly lesbian. It's curious how this misconception perpetuates!

(Libby Anson, *Untitled #7*, Winter 1994/1995)

17 In viewing exhibitions, you should take into account particular relations set up between the work of different photographers and consider how this contributes to interpretation. One obvious question: What work is hung at the entrance point? Does this indicate a central theme or preoccupation?

Three Perspectives on Photography, London: Arts Council, 1979; *Shocks to the System*, London: The South Bank Centre, 1991. The latter catalogue includes thirty-seven photographers represented by one photograph, and a mini-biography. Two further shows – *About 70 Photographs*, ed. CHRIS STEELE-PERKINS, curated from the Arts Council collection in 1980, and GERRY BADGER and JOHN BENTON-HARRIS, *Through the Looking Glass*, London: Barbican Art Gallery, 1989 – also demonstrate something of the diversity of practices within mainstream gallery photography in the 1980s. Both include straight photography alongside more conceptual works

Key resources in Britain: Women's Art Library and Magazine, London. Established 1982 as a slide library, publication archive and national/international membership network. (Magazine retitled *Make* in 1996.) IRIS Women's Photography Archive, Staffordshire University, a slide library of contemporary work

The resurgence of feminism in the 1970s challenged the patriarchal establishment. This challenge included a set of questions about women, representation and Art, which led to critical work on three key fronts. First, examination of ways in which women have been represented in Western Art. Within patriarchy, active looking has been accorded to the male spectator. 'Woman' becomes the object of his **gaze**. Although this does not only concern 'the nude', the representation of naked women for visual consumption formed one obvious focus for accusations of sexism in visual culture. Fundamentally it was argued that the term 'nude', central to the visual arts tradition, lent a guise of respectability to the practice of naked women being objectified for **fantasy** libidinous gratification. Second, feminist art historians pursued the archaeological project of rediscovering and drawing attention to the work of women artists, previously ignored or marginalised. Third, women in art schools, galleries and publishing asserted a right for space devoted to contemporary women artists. The revolution took several forms. In art education the art history curriculum was brought under scrutiny, and various guises whereby sexism figured in the studio were challenged. Alongside this, the demand was made that galleries and publishers should examine their record in exposing the work of women artists – and set out to rectify it. Protests were mounted against exhibitions showing work deemed offensive to women.

Question: Do women have to be naked to get into the Metropolitan Museum of Art?
Answer: Less than 5% of the artists in the Modern Art sections are women, but
85% of the nudes are female – Guerilla Girls

VAL WILLIAMS (1986) **Women Photographers: The Other Observers 1900 to the Present**, London: Virago (second edition published as *The Other Observers: Women Photographers 1900 to the Present*). This was researched and curated for the National Museum of Photography, Film and Television in Bradford, Yorkshire as a touring show with accompanying book, although it is the text which has become the classic introduction to the recuperation of a range of types of work by women

CONSTANCE SULLIVAN (ed.) (1990) **Women Photographers**, London: Virago. This book concentrates on high-quality reproduction of photographs by women historically, with a view to reclaiming their work for the canon

This revolution obviously influenced photography, itself forging space in the Art gallery. Three projects stand as key examples. They relate, respectively, to the diverse history of photography, modern aesthetics and postmodern gallery-based practices. First, in *Women Photographers: The Other Observers 1900 to the Present*, writer-curator **Val Williams** traced and surveyed a range of work, from high street studio portraiture to fashion photography, from the documentary and photojournalistic to the snapshot, and to contemporary feminist practices. The purpose was to expose the names and work of women photographers, previously hidden from history, and to demonstrate the diversity of practices within which they had been active. This exhibition, with its broad remit, opened at the National Museum of Photography, Film and Television; significantly, a photography organisation (as opposed to an Art gallery). It contrasts with the second example, **Constance Sullivan**'s selection, also entitled *Women Photographers*, which more specifically recuperates women as artists in terms of the precepts and principles of modern photography. From the point of view of considering photography and the Art gallery in the context of contemporary, postmodern practices, the third example, *Shifting Focus*, curated by **Susan Butler**, was of central import for both its focus upon contemporary work made for the gallery and its internationalism. Most significantly, *Shifting Focus* posited the question: What happens when women look? If, traditionally, women have been the object of the gaze, the viewed rather than the viewer, the represented rather than the author of representation, what happens when she takes a more active role? Butler was concerned to explore ways in which, in exercising the right to look, women alter the terms of visual culture which, as feminist art historians have argued, was premised upon unequal viewing relations.

The 1994 (British) Signals Festival of Women's Photography continued the overall aim to draw attention to, encourage and celebrate work by women, both within and without the gallery. Indeed, now it is common-place for exhibitions to include work by women artists. But perhaps the strength and confidence of women's work is best testified by the shift to more specifically themed exhibitions, for example, self-portraiture, war, the family, lesbian identity. The presence of women photographers in the gallery is now taken for granted. Furthermore, the shift in focus has influenced new themes within the work of male photographers.[18]

The influence of women's photography within the gallery thus goes beyond simply securing a rightful place for work by women. Feminist theory posed a more fundamental critique of aesthetic conventions and practices. This has led to determined retrieval of the terms of visualisation. As American artist, Barbara Kruger, asserted in one of her renowned photomontages, 'we will not play nature to your culture'. Women's photography has now moved beyond critiques of representation to exploration of relations of looking. The terms posed are increasingly diverse: for example, in relation to the body. Katrina Lithgow depicts naked pregnant women in a matter-of-fact manner which both asserts woman's right to represent herself and refuses romanticisation. More experimentally, in both aesthetic and technological terms, Mona Hatoum revealed internal organs of the body normally only subjected to the medical gaze. Each, variously, poses questions of identity using the body as a focus. This has been critiqued or dismissed as a retreat into the personal. (It may, indeed, reflect a sense of the limited influence of the artist within contemporary global politics.) However, it also reflects the influence of the central tenet of psychoanalysis, namely, that the individual subject is formed through cultural experience. As subject-matter within photography, 'the body' implicates broader cultural concerns (see chapter 5).

Questions of identity

> Post structuralist thinking opposes the notion that a person is born
> with a fixed identity. . . . It suggests instead that identities are
> floating, that meaning is not fixed and universally true at all times for
> all people, and that the subject is constructed through the
> unconscious in desire, fantasy and memory.
>
> **(Bailey and Hall 1992: 20)**

SUSAN BUTLER (1989) **Shifting Focus**, Bristol/London: Arnolfini/Serpentine. The catalogue comments internationally on contemporary work by women. Also DIANE NEUMAIER (ed.) (1996) **Reframings, New American Feminist Photographies**, Philadelphia: Temple University Press

18 Examples include John Coplan's imaging of the male body (Tate collection), Paul Rhys' exploration of his relationship with his father (included in *Who's Looking at the Family*, Barbican Gallery, London, 1994) and David Lewis' appraisal of the black body within anthropology (*The Impossible Science of Being*, The Photographers' Gallery, 1995).

DAVID A. BAILEY and STUART HALL (eds) (1992) **Ten/8** 2(3), **Critical Decade**

From the perspective of the present, contemporary art practices appear to be marked by diversity, if not incoherence. Arguably this diversity variously reflects issues of identity. Psychoanalytic theory suggests that images, through offering points of identification, offer fantasy resolutions for subjective angst. Identification, in this context, refers to processes whereby the individual subject assimilates an aspect, property or attribute of that which is seen, and is transformed, wholly or partially, after the model which the other – in this instance the image – provides. Personality is constituted through such imaginary identifications. Thus Art may be seen as feeding our need for a clear sense of identity and of cultural belonging. This is a continuous process of apprehension and reassurance, since identity is neither uniform nor fixed, and is constantly subject to challenge and shift. In other words, any sense of self-location through the contemplation of the photographic image is temporary. Indeed, desire for reassurance may be one of the factors propelling us to keep on looking at images.

Black and British

Curator Sunil Gupta has noted that the history of black photography in Britain is brief. As a movement, he ascribes its early development to funding initiatives taken by Labour-controlled local city councils in the early 1980s context of Thatcherism, and of inner-city racial tension (Gupta 1990). Key exhibitions and initiatives included *Reflections of the Black Experience* (curator, Monika Baker, Brixton Art Gallery, 1986), which, as a primarily documentary show, offered evidence not only of the diversity of black experience in Britain but also of the presence of good black photographers. The Association of Black Photographers, later Autograph, was formed soon after this to promote the work of black photographers across a range of fields. Meanwhile, *D-Max* (curator, **Eddie Chambers**) toured work for the gallery by British Afro-Caribbean photographers.

EDDIE CHAMBERS (1999) 'D-Max: An Introduction' in **Run Through the Jungle**, Annotations 5, London: INIVA

Racism, the post-colonial context and the desire to explore ethnic difference, mean that questions of identity figure centrally in black Art. Obvious avenues of exploration include the dislocated family, diaspora, internationalism, and media representation of '**the Other**' of British culture. Exhibitions which have explored these themes include *Disrupted Borders*, which connected work from widespread parts of the world – including Finland, India, North America – all of which in some way treated questions of cultural integration or marginality (**Gupta 1993**), and *Mirage*, which included work, in a range of media, by black artists from Europe and North America (Bailey, ICA, 1995). A number of British-based photographers are prominent within new black Art practices. These include Ingrid Pollard (figure 6.10), whose work regularly poses questions of history and heritage, and David A. Bailey, whose 1987 series on the family album was the subject of the following evocative description:

SUNIL GUPTA (ed.) (1993) **Disrupted Borders**, London: Rivers Oram Press

Key resources in Britain: Institute of International Visual Arts (INIVA), London, an umbrella organisation coordinating multicultural initiatives; African and Asian Artists Slide Library, University of East London

"pastoral interlude"
... it's as if the Black experience is only lived within an urban environment.
I thought I liked the Lake District; where I wandered lonely as a Black face in
a sea of white. A visit to the countryside is always accompanied by a feeling
of unease; dread ...

6.10 Ingrid Pollard, from *Pastoral Interludes*, 1987 (original in colour)

Against the background of a 'Made in England' clock and a
montage of snapshots, a family album is displaced by a Black
magazine which in turn is displaced by the screaming headlines
of a tabloid newspaper. As the clock ticks on, marking the shifting
historical context, the changing assemblages of images address
the contradictions between private and public representations
of race.

(Gilane Tawadros in Haworth-Booth 1988: 41)

Explorations of post-colonial identity typically interlink the political
and personal. Two themes predominate: first the legacy of colonialism; and
second what it is to be British, regardless of ethnic identity, given 'New
Europe'. Post-colonial preoccupations are clearly marked in Black Art, but
likewise figure within Scottish and Irish Art. To take an example: black artist
David Lewis has pictured the map of Africa as a chessboard for a game

played by European players (*D-Max*). Scottish artist Ron O'Donnell depicted a map of Scotland with a noose round the Highlands (*I-D Nationale*, Portfolio Gallery, Edinburgh, 1993). The point is similar. Questions of lineage and heritage within European Britain are central to the contemporary cultural agenda.

Likewise, in North America, the end of the twentieth century witnessed developing interest in Latin American photography. This partially reflects increasing Hispanic population and influences, especially in the southern states of the USA. But the interest in what the *New York Times*, in reviewing *Image and Memory* by **Watriss and Zamora**, described as 'vast national subconscious made visible and waiting to be fathomed', begs more complex explanation. Arguably it also reflects what might be defined as neo-colonial concerns with identity; Latin America geographically is both the closest threat to USA political supremacy and also offers the nearest exotic from the point of view of commerce, travel and fascination with other cultures. Research, exhibition and publishing of historical and contemporary photography from Central and South America feeds this fascination.

PHOTOGRAPHY WITHIN THE INSTITUTION

Questions of national identity are not only reflected in art practices but also in the centrality of the gallery and museum. This is particularly marked in the burgeoning British heritage industry. In 1939, the Victoria and Albert Museum, London (V&A), home of the National Collection of the Art of Photography, mounted a small centenary exhibition. In 1972, the museum hosted a major exhibition of nineteenth-century photography including over 800 pictures, entitled '*From Today Painting is Dead*': *The Beginnings of Photography* (a quote from artist Paul Delaroche in the 1840s) organised by the Arts Council in conjunction with the National Portrait Gallery and the Science Museum. This coincided with other developments in Britain, including the opening of the Photographers' Gallery in London, 1971, and of Impressions Gallery, York, in 1972. Stills Gallery, Edinburgh, was set up in 1977, and the Association of Welsh Photographers, later Ffotogallery, Cardiff, in 1978. Plans to establish the National Museum of Photography, Film and Television (NMPFT) in Bradford, as a branch of the Science Museum, were announced in 1980. Also in 1980 the Royal Photographic Society (RPS) moved its library and archive from London to Bath. The Scottish Photography Archive, part of the National Galleries of Scotland, was established in 1984 and, by 1995, included over 20,000 photographs. Thus, the 1970s and 1980s were characterised not only by the extension of provision for photography collections and exhibitions, but also by an increase in major institutions located away from London. In 1998 the V&A opened the Canon Photography Gallery dedicated to exhibitions of photographic art.

WENDY WATRISS and LOIS ZAMORA (eds) (1998) **Image and Memory: Photographs from Latin America 1866–1994**, Austin: University of Texas Press. Drawing from the more than 1000 images exhibited at Houston's FotoFest in 1992, this book documents the work of fifty photographers from ten countries. The photographs range from the opening of the Brazilian frontier in the 1880s to documentary images from El Salvador's recent civil war to works of specifically aesthetic and experimental nature.

This echoes a general expansion whereby by the mid-1980s there were over 2000 museums and galleries in the United Kingdom, with new ones opening at the rate of one a fortnight. Discussing *The Heritage Industry*, Robert Hewison argues that 'in the twentieth century museums have taken over the function once exercised by church and ruler, they provide the symbols through which a nation and a culture understands itself' (Hewison 1987: 84). Museums have become key patrons of Art, influencing priorities and pricing within the Art market. Given the monumental dimensions of some new centres (for instance, the Pompidou Centre, Paris, or the planned Bankside extension to the Tate in London), galleries also influence the conceptual scale of imagery. The photograph has been used extensively within the expanding museum to both document and celebrate the history. It has also been implicated in critiquing this 'heritage industry' (Taylor 1994: 240ff.).

Funding for the Arts in Britain involves private, commercial and public sources; it is essentially a mixed economy. Typically, exhibition organisers seek private or commercial sponsorship as well as revenue from admission tickets and sales such as postcards and catalogues. Many public galleries are partly funded by local authorities, regional arts boards or the Arts Council of England. (Wales, Scotland and Northern Ireland each have their own provisions.) Alongside this is the network of national, regional and local museums and art galleries, often Victorian in origin, which, again, are funded by both the national government and local authorities.

The subsidy system in England

Central to the subsidy system is the Arts Council of England (ACE) which is appointed by government as an independent or 'arms'-length' organisation, financed and monitored through the Department of Culture, Media and Sport. ACE works in liaison with a network of regional arts boards in England and Wales.[19] The Arts Council has included architects, critics, academics, business people, as well as established artists and writers. In effect, the government trusts appointees to take decisions which do not contravene government interests. The set-up both perpetuates the notion that the arts are outside politics and leaves the arts in a marginal position in terms of financial and cultural policy debates in Parliament. Of course, this is not the same thing as saying that the arts are apolitical.

The establishment has been criticised as attempting to use the Arts to assert **hegemonic** influence. This is not just a question of social class, nor of history and heritage. The Arts Council, and interrelated systems of influence such as arts criticism, have been accused of metropolitan myopia; that is, failing to acknowledge that which occurs outside of major cities, particularly London. Furthermore, past policy priorities often failed to take account of ethnic diversity. The Greater London Council (dissolved by the Conservative Government in 1985) took a lead in supporting multicultural initiatives.[20]

19 Photography became an identifiable concern in 1967, when a committee was set up to advise the Council's visual arts panel on photography exhibitions. A full-time officer responsible for photography was appointed in 1973.

20 Furthermore, the community arts movement of the late 1960s and 1970s posed a challenge to static notions of what constitutes Art and demanded democratisation not only in terms of education and access to the Arts but in the definition of Arts activities acknowledged (Braden 1978).

The range and diversity of photography organisations and practices poses a problem for the Arts Council, more accustomed to developing artistic and financial policies for established arts organisations and practices:

> With its base in modern technology and its place in the contemporary communications media, photography is an art form that goes beyond the traditional arts. While one small sector may be found within fine art institutions, most independent photography belongs in a far broader range of cultural, community and educational institutions.
>
> (Arts Council 1987)

There is a key distinction to be made between photography galleries, and Art galleries such as the Tate, which include photographically produced work within their collection as Modern Art, but have no particular policy towards photography. Photography galleries have a narrower remit in terms of focus upon the particular medium (whether chemically or digitally based), but a much broader cultural remit in, potentially, displaying and interrogating all aspects of photography as visual communication, historically and now. Photography is situated both within the fine art gallery system and beyond it. This inevitably poses problems when it comes to determining the scope of public subsidy within a system which, in the case of the Arts Council, has its origins in fine art practices.

In practice, in the 1980s/90s, the Arts Council and the regional arts boards financed publishing and marketing of photography books and magazines, commissions for photographers, major exhibitions including touring exhibitions, initiatives in training and education, provision of research, information and advice services, and a network of regional centres for photography which typically include a gallery, digital workshop and darkrooms, and provide a local or regional focus for education and training. In 1998 Yorkshire hosted a year of focus on photography and digital imaging, initiated by ACE and funded both publicly and commercially.[21] Thus, in the 1980s and early 1990s two subsidy systems operated in parallel: direct finance for museums and major galleries, and indirect finance through the Arts Council system for living artists (Hewison 1987). But this is to oversimplify: for instance, museums, including the V&A and NMPFT, not only maintain archives but also collect contemporary work, thereby, in effect, supporting photographers. Furthermore, since the late 1990s, the national lottery in Britain has offered a further source of funding for galleries involved in larger-scale initiatives such as building works.

21 Paradoxically, this same year witnessed the demise of a number of galleries devoted primarily to the photographic, including Camerawork in East London and Zone Gallery in Newcastle.

Curators and exhibition contexts

Photography exhibitions tour nationally and internationally – and, increasingly, feature as websites as well as physical entities. Museums and galleries commission exhibitions which are 'hired' by other galleries; it is not uncommon for exhibitions to be 'on the road' for two years. They are curated by one or more people, whose role includes researching the exhibition concept, the selection (or commissioning) of work, planning how the work will be hung within the exhibition space, and writing a significant part of any accompanying book or catalogue. The power of the curator, operating regionally, nationally or, increasingly, internationally, has come into question in recent years. Of course curators take initiatives which contribute to the exposure of work. But they may also regularly favour certain artists, or types of work, at the expense of others. Furthermore, it has been suggested that curators often act more as 'creators', putting together theme exhibitions which, however relevant and interesting, serve as much to advance themselves as to showcase the work of artists.

The archive, the critic and the curator interact with the international market for both contemporary and historic photographic work. International auction houses, such as Christie's or Sotheby's, note the influence of exhibitions (and events, such as the death of an artist) on auction prices.[22] Considering places in which the validation and valuation of art occurs, **Sandy Nairne** notes the key influence of the private gallery, the private collector, the public museum and the art magazine (Nairne 1987).

Commercial art dealers scrutinise trends in order to maintain their position in a competitive market. In Britain, the market for both old and contemporary photography is a relatively new phenomenon; a response, perhaps, to both the renewal of interest in the photograph in the 1970s and 1980s and the increasing emphasis upon private commercial practices which characterised 1980s Thatcherism. But 'collection' as a commitment on the part of particular individuals or businesses is not new. Indeed, royal patronage for artists, since the Renaissance, has taken precisely this form. The key purchasers may now be entrepreneurs rather than the Royal Family, but patronage through payment for ownership of the art object persists. As Walter Benjamin suggested in 1931, 'The most profound enchantment for the collector is the locking of individual items within a magic circle in which they are fixed as the final thrill, the thrill of acquisition, passes over them' (Benjamin 1992a: 62).

Outside the mainstream

Photography has also challenged dominant aesthetics in a range of contexts, usually with some commitment to political empowerment. Central to the politics of representation is the question of whose experience is validated. This motivated the work of many contemporary women and black artists in the 1980s and early 1990s. In this respect the gallery is sometimes overtly a site of political engagement. In community arts, the emphasis is not so much on exhibition or publication as on the darkroom as workshop and on ways in which photographic seeing can contribute to self-esteem and the fostering of social and political perceptions. Community workshops and schools-based initiatives have offered a number of opportunities for photographers to run a

22 For example, in 1995, prior to auction, a collection of paintings and photographs by Man Ray was exhibited at the Serpentine, one of London's higher profile public galleries for contemporary art.

SANDY NAIRNE (1987) 'Value, Commodity and Criticism' in **State of the Art, Ideas and Images in the 1980s,** London: Chatto & Windus range of projects. Among the best known was the Cockpit in London in the 1980s. Projects often take the form of workshops for teachers or community workers, who then take back ideas to their schools or local areas. Some of these projects owe their roots to high profile initiatives such as international festivals whose organisers are concerned not to overlook the locality in which they are based.

Internationalism: festivals and publishing

The 1980s also saw a burgeoning of international photography festivals. The first such international festival was established as an annual meeting place and showcase for photography at Arles, France, in 1970. Others, such as Houston (biennial since 1986) and Rotterdam (more or less biennial since 1988), have been loosely based upon the same model involving some thematic focus, a number of lectures and events, opportunities for less-experienced or less-established photographers to show their portfolio to known photographers, critics and curators and, in certain instances, some form of schools- and community-based spin-off. Another major European festival is the biennial Paris *Mois de la Photo* which, since 1980, has taken place throughout the city. *Fotofeis*, the biennial Scottish International Festival of Photography, ran from 1993 to 1997. England has no regular, large-scale international festival, although there have been a number of one-off themed festivals; for instance, the 1994 Signals Festival of Women's Photography and the Photo '98 Year of Photography and the Digital Image. Contemporary Photography Fairs, commercial enterprises, increasingly feature as do photography auctions.

The purpose of festivals is to offer a focus, meeting place and showcase for photography. As such they contribute to raising the profile of photography nationally and internationally. Along with gallery exhibitions, photography magazines and books, they profile trends in photography and the work of particular photographers. But festivals require attendance and participation. This contrasts with photography publishing which, in principle, can attain widespread distribution through bookshops (although few bookshops stock much other than a few more popular titles by 'household name' photographers). Furthermore, as has been noted, publications outlive festivals and exhibitions. It is photography magazines such as the two-monthly *Creative Camera*, based in London, or the biannual *Portfolio*, based in Edinburgh, which trace debates and developments, and shape history, through featuring the work of particular photographers, discussing contemporary issues, and reviewing shows and books. Likewise in the United States, *Aperture* and *Afterimage* offer regular coverage of new work and current debates.

The gallery as context

Galleries are particular sorts of meeting places, often including coffee bars and/or bookshops. Arguably, the gallery network not only offers visual pleasures but also operates to reassure a certain sense of intellectual and cultural elitism. Part of the pleasure of looking at pictures lies in discussing images, in sharing responses. This assumes and reaffirms biographical and cultural similarities in terms of class, gender, ethnicity, education and interest or involvement in the Arts. Sociologist Terry Lovell has suggested that 'the discerning of aesthetic form itself must be seen as a major source of pleasure in the text – the identification of the "rules of the game", and pleasure in seeing them obeyed, varied and even flouted' (Lovell 1980: 95). Galleries have specific profiles in relation to this. For instance, organisations such as Camerawork in East London and Side Gallery, Newcastle, both of which were prominent in the 1980s, were founded in socialist commitment.

The political significance of the contemporary gallery is complex. There is a sense in which curator, critic, audience and artist are all complicit in perpetuating an exclusive system which functions hegemonically in ways which seem relatively detached from economic imperatives. On the other hand, the private collector, and the public museum and Art gallery, along with the public subsidy system, exercise a significant degree of economic influence on developments within the Arts.[23]

23 See for instance Stuart Alexander, 'Photographic Institutions and Practices' in Michel Frizot (1998) *A New History of Photography*, Cologne: Konemann.

CASE STUDY: Landscape as genre

Having raised some issues pertaining to the institution, it seems appropriate to end this chapter on photography as Art through a brief historical overview of one genre of photographic practice.

Genre

Developed within film studies to reference clusters of movies of a similar sort (such as the Western, melodrama, film noir), the term 'genre' refers to types of cultural product. But genre is not simply a classification. Genres carry with them specific sets of histories, practices, ideological assumptions and expectations, which shift over time to take account of changing cultural formations. We have chosen the example of landscape, but the principal point about change and continuity can be examined in relation to any chosen genre.

Landscape as genre

There is a key distinction between 'land' and 'landscape'. In principle, land is a natural phenomenon, although most land, especially in Britain, has been subjected to extensive human intervention (creating fields, planting crops, shoring up the coastline, and so on). 'Landscape' is a cultural construct. It dates from seventeenth-century Dutch painterly practices, but became central to English painting. The eighteenth-century English landscape painting did not simply echo the Dutch, but re-articulated the genre to incorporate the increasing emphasis on technological achievement (Bright 1990) – a clear example of accommodation to particular cultural circumstances!

Landscape can be defined as vistas which encompass both nature and the changes which humans have effected in the natural. Broadly interpreted, this includes sea, fields, rivers, gardens, buildings, canals, and so on. It thus encompasses emblems of property ownership (such as fences), or of industrialisation (such as mines or factories). Typically, English landscape pictures rarely depict work or, if they do, romanticise the rural labourer. For the aristocracy, landed gentry and nineteenth-century industrialist, land ownership symbolised hereditary status or entrepreneurial success. As John Berger has argued, landscape paintings operated to reassure this status (Berger 1972).

Landscape photography

In considering landscape as an example of a genre within photography, we are concerned first to identify typical aesthetic and socio-political characteristics of landscape imagery; and second to explore ways in which the genre has accommodated change, reinvented and reinvigorated itself over time. Landscape photography has largely inherited the compositional conventions of landscape painting. Typically landscape photographs are a lateral rectangle – it is no accident that 'landscape format' has come to describe photographs where the width is greater than the height. Compositionally, the 'golden rule' of one-third/two-third horizontal proportions is usually obeyed, as are the rules of perspective.[24]

24 As with all genres, there are exceptions. Aside from constructivist experiments, exceptions might include more metaphoric imagery, dealing, for instance, in landscape and memory, or pictures shot close-up which draw upon the conventions of still life as well as landscape.

British landscape photography is founded as much in the documentary endeavours of travelling photographers, at home and abroad, as in the gallery. Thus there are two key lines of inheritance within landscape photography: on the one hand, straight photographs, topographical in intent, on the whole echoing the composition of the classic landscape painting, and, on the other hand, more pictorial images constructed in accordance with a preconceived idea, be it poetic, mythological or critical import. As with all genres, landscape also reflects new aesthetic ideas; for instance, Surrealist dreamlike states (figure 6.8, page 275) or the Constructivist compositional radicalism based on the ideal of a new angle of vision (figure 6.7, page 271).

Historical development and change

By the nineteenth century, 'landscape' also stood as an antidote for the visual and social consequences of industrialisation, offering a view of nature as therapeutic, a pastoral release from commerce and industry. Art movements such as Romanticism and Pictorialism reflected such changing attitudes: ignoring ways in which the industrial actually impacted on the visual environment, Romanticism in painting reified the rural idyll. This reification is reflected in photographs of the time. For instance, Camille Silvy's *River Scene, France* (figure 6.2, page 260) is a carefully staged myth about the calm, leisure and pleasure of the countryside. There are several examples of seascapes, for instance, by Gustave le Grey (also French) wherein combination printing has, similarly, been used to effect pleasing scenes; for instance, clouds above the serene waters.

As we have seen, such stagings are taken further in Pictorialism, within which people were frequently depicted in close relation to what was perceived as 'natural' environment, with no stated documentary or topographical location. Thus, for instance, *The Lady of Shalott* is re-presented by Henry Peach Robinson as a picturesque tale (figure 6.3, page 262). Here landscape becomes the background against which a story is staged.

Unlike Britain, and, indeed, most of Europe, the American West is characterised by vast open spaces. Nineteenth-century pioneers, such as Carleton Watkins, whose work is now central to the photography archive, were employed to chart land prior to its opening up by, in his case, the laying of the Pacific Railroad. Mary Warner Marien notes the differing cultural contexts within which European and American landscape photography developed:

> Where English and European amateurs might craft an antimodern,
> picturesque photograph that lamented the decline of an agriculturally
> based society, Watkins synthesized a soaring sublime based on wilderness.
> . . . The viewer of his photographs is often flung out over and above
> dizzying, deep chasms. The immediate sensation is one of transcendence
> and invincibility, a feeling profoundly different from the quiet reflection
> and nostalgic passivity evoked by much European amateur landscape
> photography. Indeed, a sense of the sublime, vested in natural wonders
> like Niagara Falls and Yosemite but transferable to human works like the
> railroad, is characteristic of nineteenth-century American cultural life.
>
> (Warner Marien 1997: 95–96)

New aesthetics

Modern landscape photography has been particularly associated with American photographers, including Ansel Adams, Imogen Cunningham, Minor White and Edward Weston, who subscribed to the notion of pure photographic seeing. Modern photographers stressed the aesthetic and spiritual dimensions of landscape, producing elegant and elegiac abstract imagery. Edward Weston's images, in which the sharpness of the realisation of the photograph is tempered with the rhythm of form, offer prototypical examples (figure 6.6, p. 269).

Genres typically are characterised by continuity through change, by an ability to re-form in order to incorporate new aesthetics and circumstances. Landscape is no exception. Now fences, the railway, brick walls, motorways, pylons, signs and hoardings have all, variously, become rendered as a part of traditional imagery and myth. Of course, 'translations' are involved: landscape photographs are often monochrome, the countryside represented in terms of shape and tonal gradings. The fundamental point is that the photograph re-inflects subject-matter in terms which reflect current cultural currencies. In this sense, the Modernist landscape, with its emphasis on aesthetics, was one moment in the regeneration of the genre. The focus upon more obviously intrusive cultural elements, or industrial legacies, in the work of Ray Moore or John Davies, for instance, offers another.[25]

25 Work by most of the photographers mentioned in this section can be found in monographs published under their name, or in exhibition catalogues published variously.

The modern and the postmodern

Analysis of aesthetic and ideological change involves engagement with broad socio-economic and political circumstances as well as with aesthetics. But genre analysis is always best pursued through comparison of specific examples. For instance, in this chapter there are two compositionally somewhat similar square-format photographs, by Bill Brandt (figure 6.5, p. 266) and Karen Knorr (figure 6.1, p. 252). Both use photographic techniques and conventions to effect a sense of harmony. Yet they are different in import. Brandt's image is a documentary statement, the location is given. Knorr's, through the presence of the man and the book, and the caption, offers a conceptual comment upon English culture, one which provokes critical interpretation. The difference between the Modern aesthetic, and the postmodern critique, is marked.

The politics of landscape

A number of contemporary British photographers, including Keith Arnatt, John Davies, John Kippin, Ingrid Pollard and Jem Southam, engage in critical terms with notions of landscape, commenting, for example, on the legacy of indus-trialisation whether it be rural industry such as tin-mining (Southam) or the Northern industrial landscape (Davies), or on the implicit racialisation of pastoral imagery (Pollard). Fay Godwin's work on land, access and property rights offers a further significant example. Landscape imagery reflects and reinforces partic-ular ideas about class, gender, race and heritage in relation to property rights, accumulation and control (see Taylor 1994; Wells 1994). A number of contem-

6.11 John Kippin, *Pilgrims*, 1994 (original in colour)

porary photographers have made it their business to question this. John Kippin's work on the commodification of heritage (figure 6.11) is one such example. The contrast between this type of contemporary emphasis and the nineteenth-century idyllic image is obvious from a comparison of the work of Kippin, or Pollard, with Silvy or Peach Robinson.

Others are less overtly concerned with the socio-political, working in terms which echo earlier formalist preoccupations but which also reflect current ecological concerns or, indeed, explore issues of perception, subjectivity and the gaze. Here work by British-based artists as diverse in their concerns as Bill Hirst, Susan Trangmar and Lynn Silverman stand as prominent examples.[26] Yet all these pictures 'fit' within landscape as a genre, and contribute to its regeneration, typifying the attitudes and discourses characteristic of particular eras. As can be seen through considering the various examples of landscape included in this chapter, there are a whole range of questions to be brought into play when discussing specific fields of practice and, indeed, it is productive to analyse genres in terms both of specific historical traditions within visual culture and of contemporary issues and aesthetics.[27]

26 See Bill Hirst (1994) *Fractal Landscapes*, Manchester: Cornerhouse; Meaghan Morris (1988) 'Two Types of Photography Criticism Located in Relation to Lynn Silverman's Series' in *The Pirate's Fiancee*, London: Verso; John Stathatos on Susan Trangmar's installation 'Amidst', *Portfolio* 19, 1994, Edinburgh: Portfolio. Each of these artists is asking formal questions about imagery and perception as well as metaphysical questions about the experience of being in open space.

27 It has not been possible to include full publication references for all the artists named in this chapter. Most university library catalogues offer search facilities by keyword, in this instance, the name of the artist. Many dealers, galleries and museums have websites offering information on artists and their work, sometimes including book and magazine references.

BIBLIOGRAPHY

KEY TEXTS

Arnason, H.H. (1988) *A History of Modern Art*, London: Thames and Hudson, third edition (updated and revised to include photography)

Arts Council (1979) *Three Perspectives on Photography*, London: Arts Council

—— (1991) *Shocks to the System*, London: The South Bank Centre

Badger, Gerry and Benton-Harris, John (eds) (1989) *Through the Looking Glass*, London: Barbican Art Gallery

Bailey, David A. and Hall, Stuart (eds) (1992) *Ten/8* 2(3), *Critical Decade*

Bright, Deborah (1990) 'Of Mother Nature and Marlboro Men: An Inquiry into the Cultural Meanings of Landscape Photography' in Richard Boston (ed.) *The Contest of Meaning*, Cambridge, MA: The MIT Press

Butler, Susan (1989) *Shifting Focus*, Bristol/London: Arnolfini/Serpentine

Chambers, Eddie (1999) 'D-Max: An Introduction' in *Run Through the Jungle*, Annotations 5, London: INIVA

Coke, Van Deren (1972) *The Painter and the Photograph*, New Mexico: University of New Mexico Press

Galassi, Peter (1981) *Before Photography*, New York: MOMA

Green, Jonathan (1984) 'The Painter as Photographer', *American Photography*, New York: Harry N. Abrams

Gupta, Sunil (ed.) (1993) *Disrupted Borders*, London: Rivers Oram Press

Harker, Margaret (1979) *The Linked Ring: The Secession Movement in Photography in Britain 1892–1910*, London: Heinemann

Haworth-Booth, Mark (1992) *River Scene, France*, Los Angeles, CA: J. Paul Getty Museum

Krauss, Rosalind and Livingston, Jane (1986) *L'Amour Fou*, London: Arts Council of Great Britain

Kuenzli, Rudolf E. (1991) 'Surrealism and Misogyny' in Mary Ann Caws, Rudolf Kuenzli and Owen Raaberg *Surrealism and Women*, Cambridge, MA: The MIT Press

Nairne, Sandy (1987) *State of the Art, Ideas and Images in the 1980s*, London: Chatto & Windus

Phillips, Christopher (ed.) (1989) *Photography in the Modern Era: European Documents and Critical Writings 1913–1940*, New York: MOMA

Rogers, Brett (ed.) (1994) *Documentary Dilemmas: Aspects of British Documentary Photography 1983–1993*, London: British Council

Rosenblum, Naomi (1997) *A World History of Photography*, London, Paris, and New York: Abbeville Press

Scharf, Aaron (1974) *Art and Photography*, Harmondsworth: Pelican, revised edition

Steele-Perkins, Chris (ed.) (1980) *About 70 Photographs*, London: Arts Council of Great Britain

Sullivan, Constance (ed.) (1990) *Women Photographers*, London: Virago

Watriss, Wendy and Zamora, Lois (eds) (1998) *Image and Memory: Photographs from Latin America 1866–1994*, Austin: University of Texas Press

Warner Marien, Mary (1997) *Photography and Its Critics, A Cultural History, 1839–1900*, Cambridge and New York: Cambridge University Press

Weaver, Mike (1989a) *The Art of Photography*, London: Royal Academy of Arts

—— (ed.) (1989b) *British Photography in the Nineteenth Century: The Fine Art Tradition*, Cambridge: Cambridge University Press

Willett, John (1978) *The New Sobriety, Art and Politics in the Weimar Period*, London: Thames and Hudson

Williams, Val (1986) *Women Photographers: The Other Observers, 1900 to the Present*, London: Virago (revised edition 1991 *The Other Observers: Women Photographers from 1900 to the Present*)

Wollen, Peter (1978) 'Photography and Aesthetics', *Screen* 19(4), Winter, reprinted in *Readings and Writings*, London: Verso and New Left Books, 1982

OTHER REFERENCES

Ades, Dawn (1974) *Dada and Surrealism*, London: Thames and Hudson

Alexander, S. (1998) 'Photographic Institutions and Practices' in Michel Frizot *A New History of Photography*, Cologne: Konemann

Alloway, Lawrence (1966) 'The Development of British Pop' in Lucy R. Lippard (ed.) *Pop Art*, London: Thames and Hudson

Arts Council (1972) *From Today Painting is Dead*, London: Arts Council

—— (1975) *The Real Thing, An Anthology of British Photographs 1840–1950*, London: Arts Council

—— (1987) *Independent Photography and Photography in Education*, London: Arts Council

Benjamin, Walter (1992a) 'Unpacking My Library' in *Illuminations*, London: Jonathan Cape, 1970; Fontana, 1973/1992. Originally published in *Literarische Welt*, 1931

—— (1992b) 'The Work of Art in the Age of Mechanical Reproduction' in *Illuminations*, London: Jonathan Cape, 1970; Fontana, 1973/1992. Originally published in *Zeitschrift fur Sozialforchung* 5(1), 1936

Berger, John (1972) *Ways of Seeing*, Harmondsworth Penguin

Braden, Su (1978) *Artists and People*, London: Routledge & Kegan Paul

Brandt, Bill (1961) *Perspective of Nudes*, London: The Bodley Head

Breton, André (1978) *What is Surrealism?* Selected Writings in F. Rosement (ed. and introduction), London: Pluto Press

Bright, Deborah (1990) 'Of Mother Nature and Marlboro Men: An Inquiry into the Cultural Meanings of Landscape Photography' in Richard Boston (ed.) *The Contest of Meaning*, Cambridge, MA: The MIT Press

Burgin, Victor (1986) *The End of Art Theory: Criticism and Postmodernity*, London: Macmillan

Chadwick, Whitney (1985) *Women Artists and the Surrealist Movement*, London: Thames and Hudson

—— (1998) *Mirror Images: Women, Surrealism and Self-Representation* Cambridge, MA:
The MIT Press

Coleman, A.D. (1979) *Light Readings*, New York: Oxford University Press

Crimp, Douglas (1995) *On the Museum's Ruins*, Cambridge, MA: The MIT Press

Galassi, Peter (1995) *American Photography 1890–1965*, New York: MOMA

Godfrey, Tony (1998) *Conceptual Art*, London: Phaidon

Gray, Camilla (1962) *The Russian Experiment in Art*, London: Thames and Hudson

Greenberg, Clement (1939) 'Avant-Garde and Kitsch' reprinted in C. Harrison and P. Wood (eds)
(1992) *Art in Theory 1900–1990*, Oxford: Blackwell

—— (1961) 'Modernist Painting' reprinted in F. Frascina and J. Harris (eds) (1992) *Art in
Modern Culture*, London: Phaidon

—— (1991) 'Four Photographers', first published 1964, reprinted in *History of Photography*
15(2), Summer

Grundberg, Andy (1990) 'On the Dissecting Table' in Carol Squiers *The Critical Image*, London:
Lawrence and Wishart

Gupta, Sunil (1990) 'Photography, Sexuality and Cultural Difference', *Camerawork Quarterly*
17(3)

Harker, Margaret F. (1988) *Henry Peach Robinson*, Oxford and New York: Blackwell

Harrison, Charles and Wood, Paul (1993) 'Modernity and Modernism Reconsidered', chapter 3
of Paul Wood, Francis Frascina, Jonathan Harris and Charles Harrison *Modernism in
Dispute*, London: Yale University Press/Open University Press

Haworth-Booth, Mark (ed.) (1975) *The Land: Twentieth Century Landscape Photographs*,
selected by Bill Brandt, London: Gordon Fraser Gallery

—— (ed.) (1988) *British Photography: Towards a Bigger Picture*, New York: Aperture

Heiferman, Marvin (1989) 'Everywhere, All the Time, for Everybody' in Marvin Heiferman and
Lisa Phillips (eds) *Image World*, New York: Whitney Museum of Art

Hewison, Robert (1987) *The Heritage Industry*, London: Methuen

Hutchison, Robert (1982) *The Politics of the Arts Council*, London: Sinclair Browne

Jeffrey, Ian (1991) 'Morality, Darkness and Light: The Metropolis in Pictures' in Martin Caiger-
Smith *Site Work*, London: The Photographers' Gallery

Kelly, Mary (1981) 'Reviewing Modernist Criticism', *Screen* 22(3): 41–62

Kruger, Barbara (1983) *We Won't Play Nature to your Culture*, London: Institute of
Contemporary Arts

—— (1990) *Love For Sale: The Words and Pictures of Barbara Kruger*, New York: Harry N.
Abrams, Inc

Lovell, Terry (1980) *Pictures of Reality*, ch 5.3, London: BFI

Moholy-Nagy, László (1932) 'A New Instrument of Vision', reprinted variously, including in Mike
Weaver (ed.) (1989) *The Art of Photography*, London and New Haven, CT: Yale University
Press

Neumaier, Diane (ed.) (1996) *Reframings, New American Feminist Photographies*,
Philadelphia: Temple University Press

Nichols, Bill (1981) *Image and Ideology*, Bloomington: University of Indiana Press

Nochlin, Linda (1978) *Realism*, Harmondsworth: Penguin

Pollock, Griselda (1977) 'What's Wrong with "Images of Women"?', reprinted in R. Parker and
G. Pollock (eds) (1987) *Framing Feminism*, London: Pandora Press

Roberts, John (ed.) (1997) *The Impossible Document: Photography and Conceptual Art in
Britain 1966–1976*, London: Camerawords

Robins, Corinne (1984) *The Pluralist Era: American Art 1968–1981*, New York: Harper & Row

Rodchenko, Alexander (1928) 'Against the Synthetic Portrait, for the Snapshot', published in the
Moscow journal *Novy LEF: New Left Front of the Arts* in C. Phillips (ed.) (1989) *Photography
in the Modern Era: European Documents and Critical Writings 1913–1940*, New York: MOMA

Rowland, Anna (1990) *The Bauhaus Source Book*, ch 6, Oxford: Phaidon

Sherman, Cindy (1997) *Retrospective*, London: Thames and Hudson

Solomon-Godeau, Abigail (1991) 'The Armed Vision Disarmed: Radical Formalism from Weapon to Style' in *Photography at the Dock: Essays on Photographic History, Institutions and Practices*, Minneapolis: University of Minnesota Press

Taylor, John (1994) *A Dream of England: Landscape, Photography and the Tourist's Imagination*, Manchester: Manchester University Press

Weaver, Mike (1982) *Photography as Fine Art*, London: Thames and Hudson

—— (1986) *The Photographic Art*, London: Herbert

Wells, Liz (ed.) (1994) *Viewfindings, Women Photographers: 'Landscape' and Environment*, Tiverton, Devon: Available Light

Williams, Raymond (1976) *Keywords*, London: Fontana

—— (1979) 'The Arts Council', *Political Quarterly*, Spring

—— (1989) 'When Was Modernism' in *The Politics of Modernism*, London: Verso

Wollen, Peter (1982) 'Photography and Aesthetics' in *Readings and Writings*, London: Verso and New Left Books

CHAPTER 7

Photography in the age of electronic imaging

MARTIN LISTER

7.1 David Bate, Baroque Sheep, 1999, from the series *Animal Thoughts*

Photography in the age of electronic imaging

INTRODUCTION

During the past ten years, the traditional mechanical and chemical processes of photography have been augmented by the use of digital cameras and scanners, specialist image-processing software, and new ways of digitally storing, transmitting and exhibiting images on-line. With the initial impact of new image technologies, at the end of the 1980s, there were frequent pronouncements about the impending death of photography. This was a premature and ill-founded claim. It was typical of the fears which radical technological change tends to generate amongst the practitioners of a traditional medium, and it neatly echoed the very fears that photography once held for artists in the nineteenth century. The actual effects of the new technologies upon the various practices of photography are both more subtle and complex, as was photography's impact upon the **autographic** arts, and they do not include its 'death'.

For many photographers, the new digital technologies and processes are now an essential part of their post-production practices, and have blurred the edges between older specialisms, especially between photography, typographic and graphic design, editorial work, and still and moving image production. For others, digital technologies have indeed all but replaced **analogue** technologies: optical lenses are replaced by digital and virtual cameras, films by discs, physical darkrooms and optical enlargers by computers and software. However, images that have their source in a camera lens pointed at the world and a destination in the ink on a printed page are clearly as numerous and culturally important as ever. It is the processes that intervene between these two points that are digital, electronic and interactive, and frequently involve telecommunications systems for exchanging work in progress and as a means of distributing and exhibiting images.

However dramatic they are, these technological transformations are only the latest in a number of such transformations that are part of photography's history, and alongside them the practice of traditional chemical photography continues. But it does so in the context of newly expanded possibilities, and in the process takes on a new kind of identity as a historical form. Like lithography and painting before (as they themselves were displaced by photography), 'pure' photography has become more of a specialist activity with a distinctive aesthetic and a set of connotations rather than what it was for much of the twentieth century: the ubiquitous, taken-for-granted and culturally dominant means of image-making. As with painting in the age of photography, film and cinema in the age of television and video, or the telephone in the age of the internet, the older forms continue but are repositioned in relation to the new. It is along these lines that we need to think about photography in the age of electronic imaging.

In the past decade, this process of relocation and negotiation between photography and the new digital image technologies has been intense, and new ideas and theories have proliferated in the effort to grasp and understand the nature of the process and its cultural significance. This chapter outlines and discusses the critical issues raised by the impact of new technologies upon the practices of photography and ensuing debates.

It starts by looking at the terms in which the practical impact of digital technology on photography was initially conceived in the early 1990s. It then proceeds to explore the ensuing debates about the cultural significance of these practical and technological changes. First, it considers the various claims that the advent of new image technologies are bringing about a new era in visual culture. Second, it considers some challenges to this view. These come from critics who stress elements of cultural continuity which run across technological change; continuities of social and cultural use which are common to photographic and digital technologies. Third, it outlines the debate about the perceived threat that digital technology poses for the faith we have had in the special truth value of photographs, especially those of documentary photography and photojournalism. Finally, it places some of the ideas discussed earlier in the chapter in a larger historical context. This is the transition of capitalist societies in the late twentieth century from modernity to postmodernity, especially as expressed in the aesthetic and cultural forms of modernism and postmodernism.

PhotoVideo

In 1991 an exhibition called *PhotoVideo: Photography in the Age of the Computer* was held at the Photographer's Gallery, London. In the catalogue of the show the curators stated:

Until recently, at least, it was possible to define photography as a process involving optics, light-sensitive material and the chemical processing of this material to produce prints or slides. Today, though, that definition is subject to change. Technological innovations . . . are shifting photography from its original chemical basis towards electronics. . . . It is not overstating it to say that the advent of this new technology is changing the very nature of photography as we have known it.

(Bode and Wombell 1991)

PAUL WOMBELL (ed.) (1991) **PhotoVideo: Photography in the Age of the Computer**, London: Rivers Oram Press

The authors pointed directly to the process which was at the centre of the technical developments in question: the use of computers to digitise photographs (and video). In their catalogue essay they began to think through some of the practical implications of encoding photographs as 'units of electronic information' (see box E, p. 334). However, they stressed that probably more significant than the capacities of the new technologies to change *how* images are produced, distributed and used, are the *ideas* to which the changes are giving rise: 'Perhaps the most profound effect of these new technologies is their capacity to challenge categories and assumptions that have been at the heart of traditional ways of seeing and thinking' (Wombell 1991: 5). The main challenges they saw were as follows. First, that 'With the arrival of new and increasingly seamless ways of editing and changing images, our traditional belief that the "camera never lies" is brought into question. Who, they ask, stands to lose when the 'truth' of the photographic image stops being accepted?[1] On the other hand, they saw a very different kind of creative challenge appearing as 'these new forms of electronic image-making are providing artists and photographers with new ways of representing this changing visual and cultural landscape'. Other contributors to the catalogue raised political issues about the use of the new image and information networks for the surveillance of Europe's black population (Piper 1991) and the question of exactly what motivations and sets of ideas were driving investment in the new image technologies (**Robins 1991**).

In *PhotoVideo* we saw the beginnings of the complex, and even contradictory, critical responses to technological change which have been followed through in subsequent debate and thought. At their heart, there is a warning that some important traditional values and uses of photographs are likely to be undermined, while on the other hand there is a sense of new horizons opening up for image-making in a fast changing world. There is also a sense that the new technologies raise questions about power and politics, and that we should be interested in finding out why, and how, we came to develop these technologies.

1 The authors' use of scare quotes in relation to the 'camera (that) never lies' and the concept of photographic 'truth' already signal the direction in which qualifications to these fears was to go.

K. ROBINS (1991) 'Into the Image: Visual Technologies and Vision Cultures, in P. Wombell (ed.) **Photovideo: Photography in the Age of the Computer**, London: Rivers Oram Press

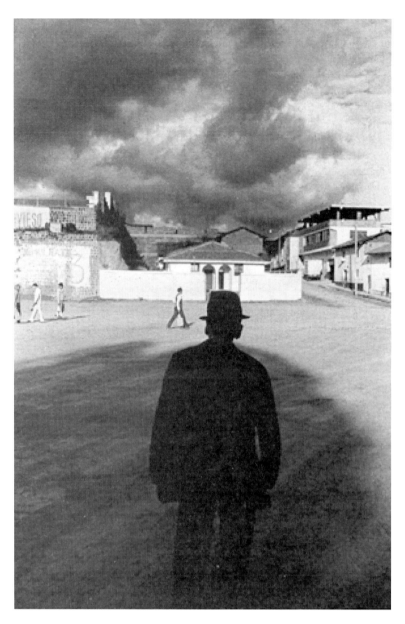

7.2 Pedro Meyer's image El Asombrado. The title of this photograph, shown at the Photovideo Exhibition in 1991, contains a play on words. Sombrero – hat, asombro – astonishment, sombra – shadow. This was an image that the photographer valued but the exposure was the last on a roll of film and was badly damaged. Each chemical print that he made from the negative took 'countless hours' and the traces of the manual restoration were always visible. This image has been electronically restored. The image now exists as a file of digital information, a perfect original from which thousands of perfect prints can be made. It was transmitted for publication in this book in digital form. Some might mourn the loss of the traces of the 'artist's hand' in the process (the preservation of the paradoxical idea of a photographic original). A more progressive view would see that the new technology facilitates the reproduction and circulation of the photographer's vision.

BOX A Digitising photographs – the initial implications

- A shift in the location of photographic production: from the chemical darkroom to the 'electronic darkroom' of the computer.
- The outputting of single photographic originals in an expanded range of ways, from 'hardcopy' through transparencies and varying forms of print, to the computer and TV screen.
- An unprecedented ease, sophistication and invisibility of enhancing and manipulating photographic images.
- The entry of photographic images into a global information and communications system as they become instantaneously transmissible in the form of electronic pulses passing along telephone lines and via satellite links.
- The high speed transmission of news images which are no longer containable within territorial and political boundaries.
- The conversion of existing photographs and historical archives into digital storage banks which can be accessed at the screens of remote computer terminals.
- The potential of the new information and image networks for greatly extending the practices of military and civil surveillance.
- The unprecedented convergence of the still photographic image with previously distinct media: digital audio, video, graphics, animation and other kinds of data in new forms of interactive multi media.

See also boxes B to F.

Thinking about digital images: some initial points

What are we looking at?

There are images which are visibly marked by the electronic means of their transmission, such as the break down of a 'photographic' image into horizontal lines (a 'video effect'). Such features have now come to connote immediacy or authenticity in much the same way as the grainy black and white news photograph did in contrast to high resolution, full-colour feature or advertising photographs (Becker 1991). In much the same way, the electronically produced 'transitions' between still images, which are a feature of multimedia authoring software such as Macromedia Director, have rapidly become conventions. As the image on a computer monitor breaks up and fades through a veil of simulated grain, 'the photographic' is signified.

For the most part, however, the significant differences between the purely photographic and the digitally registered photograph lie in the way it was 'taken' or transmitted, not simply the way it looks. Hence, in thinking about 'pre' and 'post' electronic 'photography' we are not always faced with evident and visible differences in the images themselves. This is because it is precisely the capacity of the new image technologies to register (in the case of digital cameras), carry, mimic or simulate photographic images in increasingly undetectable ways. It is this factor that has given rise to ethical debates in many areas of photographic practice, especially in the case of documentary photography and photojournalism.

Similarly, in the case of the impact of digitisation on archive images, picture libraries and image banks, the issues are ones of access, transmission and the use of images which *continue to look like photographs* but which have been stored in an immaterial and malleable digital form.

'Photographs' and 'photographic images'

In the growing critical literature about photography and new image technologies, two related sets of questions have been asked. Which set is asked depends on the nature of the critic's interest in photography. One set of questions tends to be of a broadly philosophical kind. They are about the **epistemological** and **ontological** status of visual images. The epistemological questions ask what kind of *knowledge* a digital rather than a photographic image provides us with and *how* it does it. The ontological questions are asked about what kind of thing an image is (or is now coming to be) as it becomes encoded as electronic data, *in what form or material and where does it now exist*?

At other times the questions are framed differently. Traditionally, a main way of understanding images has been to think of them as referring to, or depending upon, objects in the real world. They represent, and in the case of photography are caused by, these objects. With the application of electronic and digital technologies to image production, can we still understand the 'image world' in which we live as continuing to refer beyond itself to a prior reality? Has it become autonomous; a 'virtual' realm of illusion and spectacle, effectively challenging older ideas about photographic representation? What kind of power are images coming to have; is their power magnified by the new means of production and transmission, or is it being devalued? With what effects and under whose control? (For further discussion of these points see the later section in this chapter 'Walter Benjamin and the precedent of the age of mechanical reproduction'.)

These latter sorts of question lead us more directly to a major issue which requires a more historical and sociological approach. How do current developments relate to an earlier 'age of mechanical reproduction' in which the photographic image has been so important? Is the use of digital image and other new communications technologies bringing about a further expansion and intensification of the age of mass reproduction? If so, are we looking at more of the same; at differences and transformations within larger processes of continuity? Or is the new digital and electronic culture qualitively different from the photographic one; is a new language and a new way of seeing

BOX B Analogue and digital

Traditionally, images have been analogue in nature. That is, they consist of physical marks and signs of some kind (whether brush marks, ink rubbed into scored lines, or the silver salts of the photographic print) carried by material surfaces. The marks and signs are virtually inseparable from these surfaces. They are also continuously related to some perceivable features of the object which they represent. The light, for instance, cast across a rough wooden table top, becomes an analogous set of tonal differences in the emulsion of the photograph. A digital medium, on the other hand, is not a transcription but a conversion of information. In short, information is lodged as numbers in electronic circuits. It is this feature of digitisation which has meant that images can now exist as electronic data and not as tangible, physical stuff. Some of the key differences can be set out as follows:

Analogue

transcription: the transfer of one set of physical properties into another, analogous, set

continuous: representation occurs through variations in a continuous field of tone, sound, etc.

material inscription: signs inseparable from the surface that carries them

medium specific: each analogue medium bounded by its materials and its specific techniques

Digital

conversion: physical properties symbolised by an arbitrary numerical code

unitised: qualities divided into discrete, measurable and exactly reproducible elements

abstract signals: numbers or electronic pulses detachable from material source

generic: one binary code for all media, enabling convergence and conversion between them

Digitisation is also the effective precondition for the entry of photographic images into the flow of information which circulates within the contemporary global communications network. It is their translation into a numerical code that now enables them to be electronically transmitted. For the above reasons, questions have arisen about the place of images in time and space, where they can be said to actually exist, about how and where they are stored when in electronic form, how and by whom they can be accessed, used, owned and controlled.

For a full discussion of the analogue/digital distinction see: TIMOTHY BINKLEY (1993) 'Refiguring Culture' in P. Hayward and T. Wollen (eds) **Future Visions: New Technologies of the Screen**, London: BFI being born? Will the established institutions of media and art continue to be involved or are new networks and opportunities for communication and creativity being opened up?

These two sets of questions – the philosophical and the socio-historical – can also be thought of as arising from different ways of thinking about photography. On the one hand, there is a primary interest in understanding the impact of digital technology on the *specific properties of original chemical photographs* (fine, framed prints or the individual snaps collected from Quick Print); on the other hand, there is an emphasis on the wider implications of new technology for the more generic 'photographic image' of *mass reproduction and 'mass' culture.*

This latter image culture is based upon photographic originals, but ones which are processed by other graphic and reprographic technologies, and are a key element in a range of other media forms: newspapers, magazines, books, supersite posters, educational and publicity material. The term 'the photographic image' is often used to denote this broader range, and also the constituent images of film and cinema (while we have to be careful to remember other factors such as time, narrative, and the different kinds of exhibition and institution that are involved). Finally, by one more extension, the term can include the images of video, which share some of the lens-based and analogue features of the chemical photographic process, although these images are registered electromagnetically.

A 'POST-PHOTOGRAPHIC' ERA?

With the adoption of the term 'post-photographic era', a more decisively historical and epochal dimension was given to the thinking about new image technologies. The term was probably given its currency in the title of a book by **William Mitchell**, although the term was earlier used in *Photo Video* (Wombell 1991: 150).

Mitchell saw the emergence of digital image technology as one of a number of historical moments in which we can identify 'the sudden crystallisation of a new technology [which] provides the nucleus for new forms of social and cultural practice and marks the beginning of a new era of artistic exploration' (1992: 20). For Mitchell, the 1990s, which finally saw the effective and widespread application of computers to image-making, was just such an historical moment; one which was comparable to the 1830s and the revolutionary birth of photography itself.

In an equally dramatic tone, the art historian Jonathan Crary spoke of 'the rapid development in little more than a decade of a vast array of computer graphics techniques' as bringing about 'a transformation in the nature of visuality probably more profound than the break that separates mediaeval imagery from Renaissance perspective' (Crary 1993: 1). While Crary himself asked questions about the completeness of this 'break', this was a bold claim

A-M. WILLIS (1990) 'Digitisation and The Living Death of Photography' in P. Hayward (ed.) **Culture, Technology and Creativity in the Late Twentieth Century**, London: John Libbey and Co Ltd

WILLIAM J. MITCHELL (1992) **The Reconfigured Eye: Visual Truth in the Post-photographic Era**, Cambridge, MA: The MIT Press and one which, in other contexts, has been contested (Virilio *et al.* 1988; **Robins 1995**).

Such claims have done more than encourage a wave of speculation about what such digital futures may hold. They also led to a renewed interest in the emergence of earlier image and communication technologies and the claims that accompanied them (Marvin 1988; Boddy 1994). They continue to bring about a new kind of interest in the early histories of photography, film, radio and television as a way of researching the historical grounds for speculating about the direction of current change (Punt 1995; Slater 1995).[2]

In a parallel development there is now much interest in the history of the computer, especially the manner in which it came to be applied to image-making, as the machine which is credited with this epochal transformation (**Darley 1990, 1991**).

The end of the 'Cartesian dream' and new ways of seeing?

For William J. Mitchell the application of the computer and digitisation to image-making has brought an age of ('false') innocence to an end. This was the 150-year period during which chemical photographs provided us with images that we could comfortably regard as 'causally generated truthful reports about things in the real world', which could be confidently distinguished from 'more traditionally crafted images, which seemed notoriously ambiguous and uncertain human constructions' (Mitchell 1992: 225).

Mitchell argues that the once fixed and stable images of photography 'served the purposes of an era dominated by science, exploration, and industrialisation'. He sees this historical period coming to an end 'as we enter the post-photographic era' and have to face again 'the ineradicable fragility of our ontological distinctions between the imaginary and the real, and the tragic elusiveness of the Cartesian dream' (Mitchell 1992: 225). In his view, the new image technologies have unsettled older, established attitudes and beliefs in the status of images. He sees digital technology as taking us beyond the historically specific and temporary limits of photographic 'seeing' in a progressive movement which is in tune with a postmodern age (see 'The postmodern connection' later in this chapter).

In calling up the name of the seventeenth-century philosopher René Descartes, Mitchell is pointing to the 'Cartesian' tradition in Western philosophy which bears his name. In broad and simplified terms, this has generally come to stand for a search for certain and objective knowledge through the exercise of scientific reason; for a disinterested and rational method of enquiry untainted by the feelings and subjectivity of the observer. The attainment of such certain knowledge by an abstract reason exercised by a 'disembodied' mind is the 'Cartesian dream' to which Mitchell refers.

By the early nineteenth century such a search for scientific knowledge had taken a fiercely empirical turn and had been extended to the study of

K. ROBINS (1995) 'Will Images Move Us Still?' in M. Lister (ed.) **The Photographic Image in Digital Culture**, London and New York: Routledge

2 A recent example of this renewed interest in the history of photography understood as a technology in general and an image technology in particular is Patrick Maynard's book *The Engine of Visualisation* (1997).

A. DARLEY (1991) 'Big Screen, Little Screen: The Archaeology of Technology', **Ten-8 2(2) Digital Dialogues**
A. DARLEY (1990) 'From Abstraction to Simulation: Notes on the History of Computer Imaging' in P. Hayward (ed.) **Culture, Technology, and Creativity in the Late Twentieth Century**, London: John Libbey and Co Ltd

the social as well as the natural world within the social philosophical framework known as **positivism**. This was characterised by an exclusive concern
for empirically verifiable and measurable facts. A connection between this
'positivist' method and the birth of photography has been frequently noted.
As John Berger (1982) has put it,

> The camera was invented in 1839. Auguste Comte was just
> finishing his Cours de Philosophie Positive. Positivism and the
> camera and sociology grew up together. What sustained them all
> as practices was the belief that quantifiable facts, recorded by
> scientists and experts, would one day offer man such total
> knowledge about nature and society that he would be able to
> order them both.
>
> (Berger and Mohr 1982: 99)

As real as this historical link with positivist social science may have been,
photography has never been exclusively contained within positivism's
framework or limited to such uses. It is, however, an aspect of photography's
history which is being thrown into sharp relief by theorists of post-
photography like Mitchell, who stress the mechanical process and optical
realism of analogue photography as a radical contrast to a new digital 'age
of electro**bricolage**'.

For Jonathan Crary, the constructed or 'virtual' visual 'spaces' of computer-
generated imagery are radically different from the 'mimetic capacities of film,
photography, and television'. The latter depended upon 'a point of view
static, or mobile, located in real space' while the techniques of computer
imaging 'are relocating vision to a plane severed from a human observer'.
As the new image technologies become 'the dominant models of visualisation', Crary believes that 'Most of the historically important functions of the
human eye are being supplanted by practices in which visual images no
longer have any reference to the position of an observer in a "real" opti-
cally perceived world' (Crary 1993: 2).
Both Mitchell and Crary sketch out a scenario in which seeing and representing the world through a camera lens, from a definite position in space,
are giving way to new forms of vision and image.

This is a vision in which older lens-based images are either converted into
electronic data or new images are constructed directly from data which simulate the appearance of a photograph. These images can be infinitely change-
able, as they continually circulate within global telecommunication networks,
available for convergence with one another and other 'abstract visual and linguistic elements' (Crary 1993). Further, these images do not necessarily refer
to anything that is empirically verifiable as 'real' but to ensembles of concepts,
other images and data.

It is not difficult to see how, on this way of thinking, the traditional hand-
me-down, Cartesian framework for thinking about how we observe the

bricolage A process of
improvisation in which various
elements and 'bits and pieces'
are joined together to make
something. In French a
bricoleur is a handyman, and
bricolage refers to DIY. The
term has been adapted for use
within digital imaging by
adding the prefix 'electro'.

7.3 Albrecht Dürer, 'Draughtsman drawing a nude', 1538
Dürer depicts one of many apparatuses in the history of art through which the appearance of the world was organised in relation to the position of the observer. It is an apparatus and a way of seeing which is later embodied in the camera. It also, as Lynda Nead observes, already positions the female as the object of the male gaze (Nead 1992: 11)

external world is deemed to have become hopelessly inadequate. Faced with Crary's vision of the new image technologies, the question no longer seems to be 'can an observer see clearly from their position?', but whether we, as observers, have any fixed or secure position from which to see anything that is material and stable! New possibilities for vision and visualisation are opening up, as the computer extends the realm of what the visual sense encompasses. On the one hand, we (or perhaps, given the globally and locally uneven distribution of technologies and information circuits, 'some of us', would be more accurate) can 'see' distant planets, the inside of a beating heart, a molecule that is a concept, we can move through buildings which have not been built, we can window-shop in cyberspace. On the other hand, the qualities and formal means of images are undergoing certain kinds of change; this is probably most remarkable in terms of the spectacular extremes of scale and detail, of focus and viewpoint, of subtle and dramatic kinds of juxtaposition, in the degree of fragmentation and fusion, and in the trans-formation and mutation of images that we are coming to regularly see in the advertisements on our television screens. There is a scrambling, to an unprecedented degree, of the real and the imagined.

We will not, however, as Crary argues, get far in understanding our newly 'precarious' position within this shifting scenario of images and imaging tech-nologies if we fail to see it in a historical context (for there are precedents of sorts) and take account of the forms of social and cultural power which drive and shape such developments (Crary 1993: 2).

BOX C: Digital simulation

The simulation of photographs: the production of images which have the appearance of a chemical photograph but which are constructed from information which is processed within the computer.

This use of computers represents a dramatic assault on the notion of photographic causality: the sense that photographs are caused by the objects and the lights that make those objects visible. This is the manner in which digital technology is being used to generate images, which have a photographic appearance, from pure data. The images which are constructed in this way have no traditional photographic referent. Such a 'photograph' may be based on knowledge of, but not caused by, the action of light reflected by a particular object. But what it does refer to is *other photographs*. In fact the whole motivation in the generation of many such images is that they carry the authority and information of a photographic image (and in the way that a photograph carries such information). Given this aim, the continuity of photographic codes between chemical and digital photographic production is strong.

Such 'object-based' systems work by using the computer to define the geometry of an object and then to render its surfaces by the application of algorithms which simulate the object's constructed surface according to information about viewpoint, location, illumination, reflection, etc. This

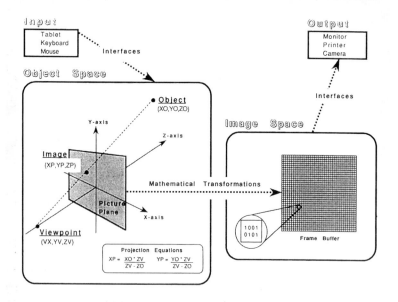

7.4 Diagrammatic representation of the concept of a 'virtual camera'

7. 5 Computer-generated image of billiard balls
This image of impacting billiard balls is a computer simulation of 'photographic seeing'. These particular balls do not exist and neither does the room which is reflected on their surfaces. They are constructed mathematically and their surfaces are rendered according to the computer's 'knowledge' of the action of light upon specified kinds of surface, over a given distance and from a certain position and source, etc. The balls are represented in movement as if photographed with a shutter speed of 1/250 of a second. The realism to which this computer-generated image aspires is the 'look' of a photograph; realism equals the signifying means of the photographic image

ability of the computer to construct objects in space is in direct line with the perspectival geometry of the Western pictorial tradition. This has its roots in the work of fifteenth-century painter mathematicians and art theorists of the early Italian Renaissance, such as Leon Battista Alberti, Piero della Francesca and Paolo Ucello.

In this sense, the computer's simulation of photographic images shares much with the constructed perspectival views of early Renaissance painters. They both construct views of the physical world which are centred on the eye of a spectator in a given position, and they do so by organising information about objects, spaces, and the behaviour of light which is the result of observation, data and its rigorous conceptual systematisation. The greatest challenge to both is the representation of the human figure and, to date, it seems reasonable to judge that the computer-generated image has some way to go to match the achievements of the painter. But, in other ways, the computer has been used to produce images which precisely mimic the look of the world as seen by a camera.

WALTER BENJAMIN AND THE PRECEDENT OF THE AGE OF MECHANICAL REPRODUCTION

WALTER BENJAMIN (1970a)
'The Work of Art in the Age of
Mechanical Reproduction' in H.
Arendt (ed.) **Illuminations**,
Glasgow: Fontana/Collins

As many art and photographic historians have been quick to see, current developments echo **Walter Benjamin**'s classic account of the impact of photography upon the handmade image in his 1936 essay 'The Work of Art in the Age of Mechanical Reproduction'. (See also note p. 17.)

The parallel has been so compelling that a good deal of the writing which deals with current developments explicitly plays with Benjamin's original title (including the title of this chapter itself). Articles and scholarly papers with titles which echo Benjamin's abound; transposing the 'Mechanical Age' to the Electronic, the Cybernetic, the Digital, the Post-Photographic Age, Era, or Culture. The newspaper pastiche 'Mute', which reports on new media and related techno-cultural issues, once sported the banner, 'The Work of Art in the Age of Post-Mechanical Reconstruction!' (Nichols 1988; Virilio *et al.* 1988; Grundberg 1990; Malina 1990; Jukes 1992).

Why is this so? Benjamin, writing over sixty years ago, offered two basic sets of propositions about the epochal significance of film and photography as means of mechanically reproducing images.

The first concerned the power of a new image technology, photography, to **reproduce autographic** images. A second set concerned the particular ways that the camera – still and moving – represented the contemporary world itself. These two sets of propositions are now being transposed in efforts to think about the impact of digital technology upon photography.

Benjamin pointed out that mechanical reproduction substituted 'a plurality of copies for a unique existence' (Benjamin 1970: 223). These were not copies in the sense of fakes (they could not be passed off for the original) or imperfect handmade copies, but were the outcome of an independent technical process. Through this process, images which had previously existed in one place at one time could now be seen simultaneously by a variety of new audiences in a diverse range of situations. Knowledge of the work was no longer restricted to being in the presence of the original. The images were no longer dependent upon their original contexts for their meaning and became open to multiple interpretations and readings. They could also be put to new uses. For instance, it became possible to compare and connect images that were previously separated in space and time. Reproduction created a new kind of portable cultural object (Lury 1992: 396) which was free from the controlled environments and rituals of the church, the civic state, and the aristocratic cultures in which the unique handpainted image had been predominantly produced and used.

Now, it is the photographic image itself which is subject to a similar process as it is converted, reproduced or simulated in digital form, stored electronically, and transmitted by telecommunications networks. Hence, the question arises as to whether there is a second 'electronic' or 'digital' revolution in visual culture which is usurping the role of photography in the 'age of mechanical reproduction' which Benjamin first described.

Benjamin's second set of propositions concerned the camera itself. He recognised that photography developed as a part of the scientific and technological endeavours of nineteenth- and early twentieth-century industrial capitalism. The physical context of this development was the nineteenth-century city. He stressed the way that urban experience was newly characterised by speed, rapid change and a fragmentation of everyday experience. This was brought about by new transport and communications systems, by the industrial division of labour on the production line, and by the separation of leisure and work in a wage labour economy. Benjamin argued that a rapid succession and juxtaposition of shifting viewpoints and experiences confronted the city dweller in their everyday lives. The new industrial and urban environment bombarded him or her with an unprecedented level of physical and psychological shocks (Benjamin 1970b).

Benjamin sees the camera and its images as making this bewildering environment possible to contemplate. He points to the way that still photography renders faithfully the plethora of everyday detail that would normally be overlooked. He points to factors such as the way in which the photographic camera can put the 'eye' in places that it could not otherwise be, or the way in which the shutter freezes action not perceivable by the eye alone. With movie film the speed of human and mechanised action was slowed down. Through editing, a range of shots, frames and actions, matching the bewildering viewpoints of the city dweller, could be put together in a coherent narrative. Benjamin suggests that, in this period, a kind of 'optical unconscious' was revealed by the camera, just as, through psychoanalysis, 'the instinctual unconscious' was discovered.

So, in Benjamin's view, photography, and then cinematography, were particularly suited to depict the changed environment of industrial societies and, moreover, they could reach mass urban audiences rather than small elites. They represented a new way of organising perceptions within the dramatically changed environments of early twentieth-century cities. In his 1988 essay, 'Postmodernism and Consumer Society', Fredric Jameson proposed that our perceptual skills and habits are again lagging behind our apprehension of a new kind of urban environment, represented most clearly in the new forms and spaces of postmodern hotels and shopping centres.

> My implication is that we ourselves, the human subjects who happen into this new space, have not kept pace with that evolution . . . [of postmodern architectural space] . . . we do not yet possess the perceptual equipment to match this new hyperspace . . . in part because our perceptual habits were formed in that older kind of space I have called the space of high modernism.
>
> (Jameson 1993: 198)

Jameson makes it clear that he sees himself as following in Benjamin's footsteps when making this point (Jameson 1993: 202). Similarly, albeit in the sphere of visual representation rather than architectural space, it is now being argued, by theorists like Mitchell and Crary, that we are moving rapidly into a time where the new means of digital and electronic imaging are coming to supersede those of the age of mechanical reproduction. As they do, they suggest that new kinds of perception are being born, which are adjusted to a world in which significant global economic, technological and cultural change is again taking place on a scale that is likened to that of industrialisation itself.

Although he is interested in film rather than still photography, **Bill Nichols** investigated the idea of such a parallel in his 1988 essay, 'The Work of Culture in the Age of Cybernetic Systems' (1988: 27). Here, following Jameson (1984), he drew up three parallel lists of the technological, legal and cultural features of three stages of capitalism – the entrepreneurial, monopoly and multinational. With more emphasis on social and economic processes, David Harvey (1989: 174–179) has also reproduced a number of charts which represent the changes that have been seen to take place in the transition from industrial capitalism to present conditions, variously described as 'late capitalist', 'disorganised capitalist', 'postmodern', 'post-industrial' and' post-Fordist'. In a much reduced form the kinds of change which are pointed to in this way of thinking are as follows:

BILL NICHOLS (1988) 'The Work of Culture in the Age of Cybernetic Systems', **Screen** 29(1), Winter

the mechanical camera	the electronic computer
the photograph	the digital image
industrialism	a 'post industrial age'
the modern era	postmodernity
modernism	'postmodernism'
rationalism/positivism	structuralism/post-structuralism

For a fuller discussion of the different kinds of virtual reality technology and the experiences they provide see: Michael Heim (1995) 'The Design of Virtual Reality', in Mike Featherstone and Roger Burrows (eds) **Cyberspace, Cyberbodies, Cyberpunk: Cultures of Technological Embodiment**, London, California and New Delhi: Sage

BOX D Virtual reality and the dematerialisation of the image

Systems of sensors which respond to the body's actions and shifting positions in physical space can be related to simulated visual projections of other bodies, objects and spaces. Frequently the resulting images are relayed to binocular screens mounted close to the eye and are seen to become both physically and conceptually interactive with the viewer, now rethought as 'user' or even 'author' of the 'virtual' environments which they perceive visually and sense kinaesthetically.

It is with such developments that ideas about a post-photographic era meet the scenarios of 'virtual reality' (VR). This is where the techno-dreaming starts. It is important to stress that, beyond research laboratories and 'shoot-em-up' arcades, 'virtual realities' are not socially available in any way that matches the concept. At this time, the apparatus is presently more of a 'discursive' than a material object; that is, it is something that is reported rather than seen. It is something that is talked and speculated about, and represented in other media: cinema, TV, novels, comics, rather than used (Hayward 1993). In this way contemporary VR technology has much in common with the status of the camera obscura throughout the eighteenth century. Then, according to the research of Crary, the main use of the apparatus was not to produce images but as an object which stimulated philosophical reflection and speculation on the nature of perception and knowledge (Crary 1993: 29). It was a model for thinking about the nature of knowledge and reality.

Virtual reality technologies have given rise to a speculative, quasi-philosophical set of ideas; a cluster of speculative propositions about the future and the nature of change in visual culture. It is being argued that virtual reality technologies will usher in a culture beyond representation, a culture in which images do not in some way refer to, and mediate a socially given reality, but are, virtually (that is, 'for all intents and purposes'), reality itself. Or, in a somewhat more measured formulation, the promise is that the whole human sensorium will be engaged in an electronic environment that will become 'virtually' indistinguishable from the social and material realities which people inhabit or may wish to inhabit. It will make the Renaissance use of pictorial perspective to render the imaged world continuous with the spectator's physical space seem like a primitive form of hieroglyphics. Here, the speculation is that the very sense of the viewer being before a material image, of reading a text, will cease. The notion of a viewer will become redundant as we actually inhabit constructed sensory worlds.

Virtual reality stands ultimately for the aspiration to dissolve material images altogether; the removal of any material interface between vision and image. Whilst being quite remote from the practical production of photographic images, a relationship is frequently proposed by seeing VR as a new stage in a **teleology** of the cinema. It is seen as a progressive technological fulfilment of the cinema's illusionistic power, which, on this view, was itself an heir to still photography, the camera obscura, and the centred eye of the perspectival tradition of image-making.

TECHNOLOGICAL CHANGE AND CULTURAL CONTINUITY

We have seen that much thought about the place of photography in an age of electronic imaging has been based upon ideas of ruptures, breaks and radical change, not only in the means of producing images, but also in culture at large. However, alongside these propositions, other media theorists and historians have argued that such a view fails to take enough account of photography's history in particular, and the kind of relationship that new technologies have to cultural change in general. They argue that such claims place too much emphasis on the evident technological difference between photographic and digital processes. A preoccupation and fascination with technological difference obscures important elements of continuity in the cultural meaning and uses of technologies.

Rather than simply see a break between the 'old' chemical technology and the 'new' electronic and digital one, these critics argue that we also have to see how both are shaped and developed by powerful social and cultural forces which run through nineteenth- and twentieth-century Western culture. The *difference* between analogue and digital image technologies is only one factor within a much larger context of *continuities and transformations*. In short, in order to assess the significance of new image technologies we also have to look at how images are *used*, by whom, and for what purposes.

For instance, a major use of new image technologies is to be found within medicine, where they are being used to make the interior of the living body visible. Some writers have stressed the way in which such new, non-invasive, medical imaging techniques can be seen as liberatory and wholly benign (Stafford 1991). However, in her study of the way in which these technologies are being used to produce and construct images of the body within medical science, Sarah Kember argues that the highly mediated images of CAT scans and Magnetic Resonance Imaging have their antecedents in nineteenth-century medical photography. For Kember, 'there is in fact no clear separation between photo-mechanical and electronic imaging in the context of the surveillance and classification of the body' (Kember 1995: 95–6). Both, she argues, participate in the gendered power relations of an increasingly technologised, masculine medical science which seeks to dominate the female body with its connotations of the 'natural' and 'maternal'.

In order to see the kinds of cultural continuity which run through technological change, we have to pay attention to the institutions and social sites in which new image technologies are being applied, and to the established cultural forms and practices which are being extended and transformed through such use. These sites are predominantly ones in which the photographic image has long been put to work: in the production of news, in the making of art, in advertising, in military and civil surveillance, in the production of spectacle and entertainment, education and pornography, to name only the more obvious ones.

Before looking more closely at two examples of such sites and uses, we will note a number of more general ways in which the use of digital technology can be seen as an acceleration or intensification of photographic processes that have a lengthy history. To see, in fact, that digital technologies are used to continue and build upon photographic forms.

Photography's promiscuity: its historical interface with other technologies, sign systems and images

> Throughout its history, photography has always enjoyed a complex relationship with other text-based or visual information media.
>
> (Bode and Wombell 1991: 4–5)

The new digital media, in their interactive, multimedia forms, are being celebrated for their capacity to generate **polysemic** meanings which involve the viewer's active participation. The two main bases for this are the capacity of digitisation to bring about, first, a convergence of previously separate media and, second, an 'interactive' relationship between the viewer and the text (see Box F, pp. 338–9).

The first wave of critical responses to digital image technology have overwhelmingly valued this capacity to produce layered and open-ended images which are always in creative process. By being included within digital multimedia programmes, it can seem that photographic images are newly exposed to multiple contexts of sound, other images, speech and text, etc. Multiple, alternative, radical and unexpected meanings are then seen to be the result of this new kind of complex of messages. Moreover, such meanings can now be discovered or created by the viewer (or 'user') of multimedia, as they interact with material which is structured with their participation in mind.

In this celebration of 'new' media, an opposition is often made, or implied, with an idea of an older 'pure' photography which was an 'automatic' source of fixed, singular and stable meaning (Robins 1991: 56–60; Lister 1995: 8–11). The evident technological difference between photographic, camera-based processes on the one hand, and digital, computer-based processes on the other, also becomes the basis for constructing different intellectual and creative conceptions of practice, production and, in particular, of what is involved in viewing or using images. There are, indeed, differences to be thought about, as there were between the traditional practices of working with still or moving images, or there was between making 'silent' and 'talking' movies. However, it is an altogether different matter to jump to the conclusion that the convergence of older media brings about a completely novel and unprecedented situation. There is also a danger here that 'convergence' is assumed to be an inevitable achievement of the technology, rather than a matter of how it is used, what it is used for, and whether, in any particular case, it is of value to use it.

The degree to which these factors of convergence and interactivity can be seen as entirely new features of 'digital' art, media and communications is dependent on failing to take into account a number of factors. When such factors are included in our thinking, the frequently made opposition between the photographic and the digital turns instead into a picture of the latter extending and building upon some key aspects of the former. This is important to remember; otherwise, two difficulties arise.

See chapter 4 for a fuller discussion of codes, pp. 172–84

First, the degree to which digital image production draws upon the received conventions and codes of older media is lost to sight. 'Codes' are not just a matter of routine practice or 'know-how', but have ideological weight. This means that there is a danger that a rich resource can, in fact, be drawn upon, but without an informed, critical awareness of the politics of representation which have been developed around these practices. Second, the euphoric over-evaluation of digital 'culture' which is achieved by means of simple and ahistorical oppositions casts photographic culture in a poor light and obscures its continuing power and complexity (Robins 1991: 56–57).

Three features of photographic culture will indicate how the meanings and uses of photographs, in a pre-digital period, have involved issues of convergence and relationships with other media. (For a discussion of the limits of the current opposition between ideas of the 'passive' viewer of photographs and the 'interactive' user of digital multimedia, see Lister 1995b.)

- Mass-produced, mediated and hybrid 'photographic images' have circulated throughout the twentieth century. This has depended upon a convergence of photography with print, graphic, electronic and telegraphic technologies. As John Tagg put it, 'the era of throwaway images' began in the 1880s with the introduction of the half-tone plate. It was this interface of the chemical photograph with print technology which 'enabled the economical and limitless reproduction of photographs in books, magazines and advertise-ments, and especially newspapers' (Tagg 1988: 56). In 1903 the telegraphic transmission of half-tone images became possible and the *Daily Mirror* launched a photo-telegraphy service as early as 1907 (Harvie *et al.* 1970).
- Photographic images have seldom been met in isolation. They are embed-ded and contexted in other signifying systems, primarily, those of the written or spoken word, graphic design and the institutional connotations of power, authority, neutrality or glamour. As Barthes (1977a: 15) puts it, the photograph is at the centre of 'a complex of concurrent messages'. In a newspaper these are the text, the title, the caption, the layout, and even the title of the newspaper or publication itself: a photograph can change its meaning as it passes from the page of the conservative to the radical press. Photography as an element in a complex of 'concurrent messages' pre-dates the technological convergence of the new hybrid media.

The Daily Mirror

THE MORNING JOURNAL WITH THE SECOND LARGEST NET SALE.

No. 2,649.   Registered at the G.P.O. as a Newspaper.   SATURDAY, APRIL 20, 1912   One Halfpenny.

ONE OF THE THOUSANDS OF TRAGEDIES WHICH MADE THE TITANIC WRECK THE MOST HORRIBLE IN THE WORLD'S HISTORY.

Of the 903 members of the crew of the Titanic, only 210 have been saved. This means tragedy upon tragedy for Southampton, where the majority of the men lived, for by this appalling disaster mothers have been robbed of sons, wives of husbands and young girls of sweethearts. Yesterday was a terrible day in the history of the town, though it put an end to all suspense. A list of the saved was posted outside the White Star offices, and mothers and wives who had been hoping against hope eagerly read the names, only to find that their worst fears were realised. For some, of course, the list contained glorious news, but they hushed their joy in the presence of the terrible grief of their friends and neighbours. The photograph illustrates one of the many tragedies, and shows two women anxiously awaiting the posting of the list, and what happened in Southampton yesterday has been happening in New York and London for five days. *Daily Mirror* photograph.

7.6 Front page of the *Daily Mirror*, 22 April 1912
An early use of a screened photograph printed with text

- The sheer number of photographs circulating in the world, and the frequency with which we meet them, is also a basis of their *intertextuality*. None is free-standing. Each one is a small element in a history of image production and a contemporary 'image world'. Within this environment, the photographic image gains its meaning by a continual borrowing and cross-referencing of meanings between images. The still photograph quotes a movie, the cinematographer adopts the style of an advertising photographer, the music video mimics an early silent movie.

We can now consider this argument for continuities of use and cultural meaning between pre- and post-digital photography by looking at two brief case studies. They are chosen from many possible ones. Whilst not discussed here, equally strong examples can be found in the production of erotica and pornography (Graham 1995), and the relationship of digital image culture to domestic snapshots (Slater 1995).

CASE STUDY: War and surveillance

From the original watchtower through the anchored balloon to the reconnaissance aircraft and remote sensing-satellites, one and the same function has been indefinitely repeated, the eye's function being the function of a weapon.

(Virilio 1989: 3)

The remote digital video cameras, sensors and image processors used in modern warfare have taken over and extended an historic role of photography. Paul Virilio clearly has in mind that an early use of photography was the mounting of a camera in a balloon for the purpose of aerial reconnaissance. In this way vision and its record were placed in the service of military intelligence; it was given a new vantage point and power. This has been built upon ever since, as a sequence of new image technologies has been harnessed to, and often developed for, military surveillance purposes. With the contemporary use of satellites, remote sensing technology, digital enhancement of images, and the establishment of global information networks, this early means of lifting a mechanical eye above the enemy has continued to develop. A point has been reached where the entire planet is 'becoming encapsulated by whole networks of orbital devices whose eyes, ears, and silicon brains gather information in endless streams' which produce a kind of 'portrait of what is happening on planet earth painted electronically in real time' (Robins 1991: 72).

In the nineteenth century portable, if cumbersome, darkrooms were trundled out to war. As early as the 1850s Fenton was commissioned by the British government to photograph the Crimean War, and Brady worked the battlefields of the American Civil War. By the First World War, photography played a key part in reporting war and and providing propaganda for the public at home. In 1991 the Gulf War revealed the scale and depth to which technologies of surveillance and so-called 'information' technologies had reached. The domestic television set became the mesmerising end point of an electronic image chain which started with a digital camera travelling on the nose of a

7.7 The Arc de Triomphe and the Grand Boulevards, Paris, from a Balloon, 1868, by Nadar (Gaspard Felix Tournachon)
A (civil) example of how, within twenty years of its invention, the camera was airborne and pointing to its usefulness as a tool of intelligence gathering and surveillance

7.8 NASA, Johnson Space Center, Houston, Texas. STS-52
'Earth View (Sinai Peninsula)'

smart bomb (Druckery 1991). Immersed in real-time simulations, pilots attacked by computer and video, functioning 'as components in the virtual domain of the military technological system' disembodied and dislocated from material reality. Visual surveillance systems have become simulation systems. The gathering of data and intelligence was converted into a real-time digital image of war which paralleled an awful reality that few of us in the West could know or, mercifully, experience.

A highly selective and orchestrated spectacle of this war, at least partly derived from the same material, was relayed to the domestic television set. When Paul Virilio called this war 'the first totally electronic war', we can, as Ian Walker (1995) has pointed out, take this phrase 'in two ways, to describe how the war was fought *and* how it was represented'. At many points these two aspects came together, as 'the most potent images were those taken by the military themselves' which were then relayed on through the world's media. The journalists and war correspondents, like the rest of us, saw the war mainly on television. Photographers were reduced to taking pictures of military personnel pointing to video monitors at prearranged press briefings. However, the 'invisibility' of the Gulf War and the highly mediated nature of the images received is squarely in the tradition of 'self censor-ship [imposed] in the name

328

7.9 Press photographer photographing the Gulf War in progress. Access to the war action is confined to a video screen at a military briefing

7.10 Sophie Ristelhuber, Fait, 1992

Photograph from the exhibition and book *Aftermath*. Still photography was practically and officially made almost impossible during the 1991 Gulf War, but Sophie Ristelhuber's camera offers an alternative and critical view of the aftermath of the events 'in considered retrospect' (Walker 1995) of social cohesion' which has been part of war reporting and photojournalism from the Great War to the Falklands (Taylor quoted in Walker 1995).

Ian Walker has also argued that in this new context, where the photographer is removed from the scene of cybernetic warfare and its electronic reporting, photography continues to play a role in offering us a view of events 'in considered retrospect' (Walker 1995). Considering Sophie Ristelhuber's photographs of the aftermath of the Gulf War, Walker agrees with Taylor that it is ill-informed simply to oppose photography's old role as reportage to its recent displacement and deconstruction by digital image technology. He points instead to the range of political and aesthetic strategies which an artist like Ristelhuber brings to their use of photography. He then suggests that the future of the medium may lie in such critical-artistic interventions and not in the traditional genre of documentary photography and photo-reportage.

CASE STUDY: Popular entertainment

Photography was . . . only one of many instruments, institutions, and practices designed to engage, astonish and entertain the eye; only one of a vast array of machines for the production of spectacle.

(Neale 1985: 23–24)

While we may not associate the still photograph with spectacular effect, Steve Neale reminds us that the stereoscope was one of the most popular ways of viewing photographs in the nineteenth century. Projected images for entertainment (both painted and photographic) as in the Phantasmagoria, and other environments in which transparent and backlit images were presented to audiences (the Diorama, the Eidophusikon) were very much part of the culture in which photography emerged.

All of these machines were united by their '"astonishing" capacity for realism and painstakingly detailed representation'. With their use of light and movement, they lured and manipulated the spectator's gaze. With the coming of electricity and mechanical music towards the end of the nineteenth century these luminous photographic entertainments became the technical and cultural antecedents of cinema, which, in one of its earliest forms – Edison's Kinetoscope – was an arcade machine designed to be used by individual viewers (Neale 1985).

Currently, two major popular forms which digital image technology has taken are those of the console-based interactive computer game for domestic use, and the 'coin-op' arcade game (Haddon 1993). The magazine *CD Rom Today* reports that the gross US turnover for computer games now equals that of the Hollywood movie industry (Dewdney and Boyd 1995). The interactivity which is central to the design and use of personal computers has major roots in the arcade game, the 'earliest form of interactive software to find a mass market' (Haddon 1993). The imagery of interactive CD-Rom also strives for the high

7.11 Viewers at a Panorama
Source: Buck Morss (1991) *The Dialectics of Seeing: Walter Benjamin and the Arcades Project*, Cambridge, MA: The MIT Press, p. 82

7.12 Photograph of a contemporary games arcade

resolution of the photographic image in combination with full motion video and stereo sound. These are held in audio-visual structures, exhibited on luminous screens, which invite the individual viewer to navigate in and out of parallel or forking narrative paths which frequently draw upon a range of traditional narrative genres borrowed from cinema or television.

In these ways digital CD-Rom can be understood as a developed electronic version of many preceding forms of visual entertainment which has, as one of its roots, these nineteenth-century forms of photographic entertainment and spectacle (Dewdney and Boyd 1995).

DIGITISATION AND THE QUESTION OF PHOTOGRAPHIC TRUTH: THE ISSUES FOR PHOTOJOURNALISM

As was noted at the beginning of this chapter, a fear for the demise of photographic truth was one of the initial responses to digital image technology. We have also seen how the fervour raised by the prospect of a new 'techno-culture' has led to this issue being frequently raised in over-simple terms: terms which suffer from an ignorance of theories of photographic representation.

Theories of photographic realism

Traditional claims about photography's truth value have rested upon the causal relationship between the photographic image and the real world. In realist theories, photography was primarily defined by its technical basis: the way in which light reflected by an object or event in the real world is registered on the film emulsion (or, in the case of video, on electromagnetic tape). The photograph was understood as an index or trace of what had caused it. But it has long been clear that this aspect of the photo-mechanical process has only a small part to play in the meanings that a photograph has. (For discussions of realist theories of photography and their fallacies see Snyder and Allen 1975; Snyder 1980.) Subsequently, the ambiguously complex meanings of photographs have been understood to be the result of complex technological, cultural, ideological and psychological processes in which indexicality is but one element.

Despite this recognition, it is currently this **indexical** quality which is stressed above all others in the polarised debates of the 'photography equals old, bad and limited' versus 'the digital equals new, good and open-ended' kind. Such positions and debates short-circuit much of what has been understood about photographic representation. They divert attention from the whole range of decisions, conventions, codes, operations and contexts which constitute photographic meaning. However, even where ill-informed oppositions are avoided, there is still a sense in which many practitioners feel that the ethics and politics of photographic representation are under threat.

This is the position taken by Fred Ritchin, a photographer and teacher of photojournalism, who has claimed that 'the new malleability of the image may eventually lead to a profound undermining of photography's status as an *inherently truthful* pictorial form' (**Ritchin 1990b: 28**; my emphasis). This, however, is not the only way in which the issues are being conceived. **Martha Rosler**, an artist and critical theorist, argues that they cannot be posed in terms of photography's essential or inherent truth value. Her thinking on the matter proceeds by stressing that 'Any familiarity with photographic history shows that *manipulation is integral* to photography' (1991: 53; my emphasis). In the face of what she sees as 'slightly hysterical' pronouncements that 'photography as evidence of anything is dead', Rosler wants to remember a more complex history of photography in which contradictions abound and its objective realism is not an essential quality of the medium. Instead, as we shall see, she argues that photographic truth is based upon a set of historically and culturally specific beliefs about photographs as documents.

We will first attend to Ritchin's thoughts on the issue which express some widespread concerns that are close to the professions of documentary and photojournalistic practice. Rosler's different perspective on the issues will be more fully outlined in the following section, as they properly belong within the wider debates about the status and meaning of images in a 'postmodern' world.

Ritchin and 'the end of photography as we know it'

For Ritchin, the choices the photographer makes at the point of exposure (which can now be digitally altered in retrospect), together with subsequent editorial and post-production manipulations, have been so greatly extended by the use of computers that ethical problems now arise 'with the greatest urgency' (1990a: 29). He believes that traditional manipulations of photographs were somehow held in ethical check and were usually undertaken without 'damaging the image's integrity'. New digital image technologies, however, mean that an 'editor has the ability to reach into the guts of a photograph and manipulate any aspect of it', much in the way that texts can be edited and the writer's meanings subtly but effectively altered.

Ritchin, whose thinking is haunted by an Orwellian nightmare of a future digital dystopia (1990a: 3), searches for strategies which will enable photojournalists to ward off the digital undermining of their vocation. He is too keenly aware of the **semiotic** complexities and the politics of photojournalism to be able to seek reassurance in any simple idea of photographic realism. He recognises that the genre of documentary photography has long been the subject of critical debate, and that naive reflection theories have for some time ceased to inform most documentary photographic education and practice (1990b: 28). And, given this history of critical debate, Ritchin then sees 'the application of computer technology to photography' as a second challenge to what he calls 'photography's putative capacity for reliable transcription'.

F. RITCHIN (1990a) **In Our Own Image: The Coming Revolution in Photography**, New York, Aperture; (1990b) 'Photojournalism in the Age of Computers' in C. Squiers (ed.) **The Critical Image** Seattle: Bay Press, pp. 28–37

M. ROSLER (1991) 'Image Simulations, Computer Manipulations, some Considerations', **Ten-8 2(2), Digital Dialogues**

BOX E Digital encoding

The encoding of the 'message without a code' (Barthes 1977b: 36) – the conversion of original analogue photographs to digital images.

Digital technology facilitates the introduction of a matrix of tiny manipulable elements at the physical base of the photographic image. This amounts to an 'infection' of the stable analogue photographic image by an intrinsically fluid and malleable digital code.

The material basis of the chemical photograph, the photographic emulsion, is a granular structure of silver halides dissolved in gelatin and spread onto a plastic or acetate base. This emulsion holds the nearest thing there is to a photographic 'mark': the tiny light-sensitive grains of silver, the constituent bits out of which an image is configured. This material basis of the photograph has long been industrially produced. It is put in place by workers in the factories of Kodak, Ilford, Fuji or Agfa. The individual photographer has never had access to this level of signification, except to

control the degrees of contrast which various intensities of light reflected from an object in the real world bring about within this granular field. It is this sense, that something pre-exists the photographer's intervention in the forming of an image, that underpins our belief in the chemical photograph's special claim to veracity.

The computer with its immaterial field of binary switches has unlocked this inaccessible level of signification. Chemical grain can be scanned by a set of linked Charge Coupled Devices to become digital pixel. Digital pixel can also be made to mimic chemical grain. In short, a code has been imported into, has translated and reconfigured, the granular field of the chemical photograph. With this code in place the photographic image (now strictly speaking the 'photographic' image) becomes manipulable to a fine degree.

7.13 A three-stage illustration of the principle of digitising a photograph

The tones or colours of the chemical photograph which are represented by a seamless and random grain are divided into a grid of small picture elements (pixels). Each area of the grid is then assigned a number which corresponds to the brightness of a grey scale or to the three primary colours. Changes in resolution, definition and contrast can be achieved by changing the value of these pixels, and even the configuration of the image can be invisibly altered by removing or adding pixels

Ritchin entertains two responses to this second challenge. First, he plays with the idea of securing a protected category of stable, verifiable images, whose epistemological and ethical status would, in some way, be officially accredited. One can imagine some kind of 'kite mark' or official caption stating that this is a 'certificated' chemical photograph or an 'ethically manipulated' digital photograph (1990b: 28–37). With this suggestion Ritchin comes close to occupying a defensive, rearguard position that William Mitchell foresees for photojournalists:

> Protagonists of the institutions of journalism, with their interest in being trusted, of the legal system, with their need for provably reliable evidence, and of science, with their foundational faith in the recording instrument, may well fight hard to maintain the hegemony of the standard photographic image.
>
> (Mitchell 1993: 7)

Second, Ritchin (1990b) avoids basing his defence of photojournalism on any form of technological veracity and shifts it to the ground of authorship. In fact, Ritchin's best argument is based upon a claim for some parity between the photojournalist and the journalist who writes, where the authority of the writer's report is based upon the reputation of the author and the institutions for which they work. Finally then, Ritchin seems to accept that the value of the photographic image in a digital age will not be secured by tracing its truthfulness to its origins in a photo-chemical process. Rather, it must rest on the conscience and reputation of the photographer who made the image. In this one respect, he comes close, as we shall see, to Martha Rosler's argument.

Overall, Ritchin casts the difficulty for photojournalism in a digital age as a largely personal and ethical problem – a problem for individual photographers and picture editors as they are pitched into a situation where truth and integrity are ever harder to defend against what he sees as an inherently unscrupulous and deceitful digital technology.

THE POSTMODERN CONNECTION

In this section we will revisit a number of ideas that we have met so far. This is in order to see how accounts of post-photography form part of a larger analysis or story about the distinctive features of the culture of late capitalist societies; what has come to be described as the condition of post-modernity (Harvey 1989). Three sets of ideas are particularly relevant in this respect.

- First, Rosler's views on photography's inherent manipulability and her argument that we have to see present developments as part of a longer history of nineteenth- and twentieth-century mass media: a history of the mass production and consumption of images as commodities.

- Second, the kind of view that Mitchell advances about the emergence of a new 'post-photographic era', together with a current interest in reapplying Benjamin's ideas to current developments in visual culture, which proposes that digital image technology represents a new way of seeing within changed cultural and economic conditions.

- Third, a popular and widespread excitement about the birth of a new 'techno-culture' based upon digital technology, virtual realities, interactive media and the internet, in which the production and transmission of visual images plays a central part. This has led to a devaluation and a rapid **historicisation** of photographic culture. It is seen, suddenly, as an outmoded culture which is finally limited to a recording function and a naive desire to gain an objective view of the world, while digital image technology restores and extends the creative and imaginative possibilities of the image.

Rosler and the commodification of images

In the previous section, we saw how Fred Ritchin argued that a kind of photographic integrity was at stake as digital image technology dramatically increased the possibilities of image manipulation. We can now return to this issue by looking more closely at the arguments of Martha Rosler. By reminding us of the part that photography itself has played in creating a market in images, appearances and illusions throughout the twentieth century, she offers us a view of the fragility and partialness of the 'modern' idea of photographic truth. In doing so, she sketches a tradition of critical thought which long precedes the advent of digital images and which points to a longer historical process, in which the photographic image has served to bring about a condition where we 'prefer the sign to the thing signified, the copy to the original, fancy to reality, the appearance to the essence' (Rosler 1991: 61).

In her essay 'Image Simulations, Computer Manipulations: Some Considerations', Rosler has no time for the opposition between photographic truth and digital manipulation which has become central to much discussion about 'post-photography'. She warns that 'critical considerations of the possibilities of photographic manipulation tend to end with the tolling of the death knell of *truth*. This discussion will not end that way'. The manipulation which Rosler sees as integral to photography itself is shown by any familiarity with photographic history from the very earliest uses of multiple negatives by photographers like Oscar Rejlander.

In Rosler's thinking, any sense of there being a crisis of photography's truth value is to fundamentally mistake what is going on. She agrees that we may no longer look at photographs 'as ways of communicating *facticity*, but that doesn't amount to asserting that "truth is dead" or that "photography is used up"'. Rosler argues that we are mistaken if we think that the changes which are taking place are simply or primarily caused by the new technologies, or that some kind of essential 'nature of photography' is now undergoing change. Rather, we need to look at wider cultural factors and recognise that our ideas and beliefs about photographs, as well as many other things, are changing.

Rosler stresses the importance of understanding that the **straight photography** of documentary and journalism is a genre. It has its own history, a politics, and institutional frameworks (of the press and broadcasting) which lend it its special, if contestable, authority. The term 'straight photography' points us to a way of making photographs in which evident artifice, construction and manipulation are avoided as a matter of principle. It does not, and cannot, mean an unmediated, uncrafted photograph or an image which is not the result of intention and shaping by the photographer. The very choice to work in this way, to avoid dramatic and rhetorical artificial lighting, for example, to resist any setting up and orchestration of the subject, or the many manipulations and devices of the darkroom, is itself the outcome of working with ideas and making choices within a wider set of possibilities.

For Rosler, the question is not how accurately or objectively photographs represent the appearance of reality but whether they, or any other kinds of image, can be used to 'tell the truth' about a reality whose appearance can itself be an illusion. In seeing the issue this way, Rosler points to the openly manipulative, alternative traditions of photography, represented by the **photomontages** of the Dadaists and John Heartfield. This was a way of using photography that sought to prise open and dismantle appearances in order to point to the social realities that their surfaces do not reveal. Rosler sees these political photomontages as sharing with the early practitioners of photography, those who used multiple negatives to overcome the limitations of orthochromatic film, a search for a '*truer truth,* one closer to conceptual adequacy'. If, then, manipulation is recognised as integral to photography, it is best embraced and consciously directed.

> If we want to call up more hopeful or positive uses of manipulated images, we must choose images in which manipulation is itself apparent, not just as a form of artistic reflexivity but to make a larger point about the truth value of photographs and the illusionistic elements in the surface of (and even definition of) *reality*. . . .
>
> Here we must make the requisite bow to Brecht's remark about the photo of the exterior of the Krupp works not attesting to the conditions of slavery within.
>
> (Rosler 1991: 58)

Rosler argues that the 'identification of photographs with objectivity is a modern idea' and it is one that may be passing together with many other certainties of the modern age, such as a belief in progress. The meanings that images carry, whether photographic or digital, are not 'fully determined by the technologies used in their production', but they are shaped by the ideas and beliefs that are invested in and brought to them.

Rosler sees 'the questioning of photographic truth' as part of a 'more general cultural delegitimisation [that] is at work in industrial societies'. Rosler has in mind Guy Debord's theory of a 'society of the spectacle' in which the cultural industries of capitalist societies, which centrally included photography, have turned the very look of the world, its appearance, into a type of marketable commodity (Debord 1970). This, Rosler argues, was the material basis for a far-reaching change in the status of images, and it is one that substantially took place across the late nineteenth and the first half of the twentieth century, prior to the emergence of digital image technologies.

Images, then, had already been severed from any simple equation with 'truth' in the earlier history of the mass production of images, advertising, cinema, propaganda, popular visual culture and spectacular entertainment. The question of the truth value of images or the reliability of the evidence which they provide does not simply rest on the kind of technology which was used to produce them, whether mechanical, electronic or digital. The use of photographs for propaganda purposes, argues Rosler, 'neither began nor will end with the electronic manipulation of photographic imagery'.

BOX F Convergence, multimedia and interactivity

[Y]ou can take a video-tape or a laser disc of a film, and you can send the signal to the computer and watch the film on the screen. You can stop it, reverse it, put it in slow motion, and so on. And you can behave like a photographer in the street. You can grab that Cartier Bresson-inspired moment, and save it. . . . The computer gives you the power to shift everything around in the film. I can take a character from one scene, store the character in the attitude that I've selected, and then I can move that character into any of the other scenes.

(Burgin 1991: 8)

Another use of digital technologies, which strikes at historical certainties concerning photography, is the manner in which digital code can be used as a common denominator for effecting translations between the range of older and previously separate analogue media. In this way, digital technologies bring about a convergence of the still and moving image with sound. Such a convergence of previously discrete media (print, photography, film, video, recorded sound and speech) in new interactive audio-visual architectures has developed in CD-Rom and on-line forms of interactive multimedia.

What this basically enables is an unprecedented kind of editing, within and across previously distinct media, to build new kinds of audio-visual structures. In common with traditional film editing this involves the practice of selecting, cutting, combining, juxtaposing, and narrative reorganisation of material from diverse places and times. In this way, digital technology extends the producer's selecting and editing function (the choice of what to view and when), through mouse, keyboard or touch screen or sensors, to the consumer. This offer of *choice and non-linear* access to content, together with the user's ability to add to, or write into, the text has come to be described as 'interactivity'.

'Convergence' is again a striking feature of the form. In everyday life, the activities of reading a book, looking at still images in a magazine, watching a film, TV or videotape are temporally sequenced and spatially distributed; we are likely to do them in different places at different times, and each engages our attention differently. In using a multimedia programme these different modes of attention to a range of specific media are drawn together; they converge. If we add activities like listening to a lecture and asking questions at a tutorial to the above list, we can see how the multi-mode, distance-learning packages of institutions like the Open University seem to prefigure the educational use of interactive multimedia.

Convergence and interactivity signal some actual changes in the relationship between a viewer and an image or a sequence of images and text. Multimedia audiences or users cannot, for instance, be thought of as gazing distractedly, as 'delegating their look', as the TV viewer has been observed to do (Ellis 1991: 112). They do not experience sound and image as it weaves in and out of other domestic activities and relationships in the manner of TV viewing. Nor, in comparison to the 'viewing subject' of cinema, can they be thought of as being swept along by a narrative's tensions and resolutions; secretly aligning their own looking with that of the camera and the actors with which they identify (Mulvey 1981; Ellis, 1991). The replacement of the term 'viewer' with that of multimedia 'user' is intended to signify the way attention is differently engaged. Nothing 'happens' or proceeds without their initiation. Any sustained involvement requires concentration and motivation, whether the programme in question is a game, pornography, or an educational or database package.

The postmodern image

It was William Mitchell who made the connection between 'post-photography' and 'postmodernity' most explicitly when he stated that 'The tools of digital imaging are felicitously adapted to the diverse projects of our postmodern era' (Mitchell 1992: 7). This is because, argues Mitchell, the digital medium 'privileges fragmentation, indeterminacy, and heterogeneity' and 'emphasises process or performance' rather than 'a kind of objective truth' which has previously been assured by traditional photography's 'quasi-scientific procedure and closed, finished perfection'.

The 'felicitous' link that Mitchell sees between such images and 'our diverse postmodern projects' is largely a metaphorical one. In describing

7.14 Esther Parada, 2–3–4–D: Digital Revisions in Time and Space, 1991–1992, At the Margin

digital images with words like 'fragmentation', 'indeterminacy' and 'hetero-geneity', Mitchell echoes closely the language of postmodern social and cultural theory. Steven Best and Douglas Kellner, for example, characterise postmodern patterns of thought as rejecting 'modern assumptions of social coherence and notions of causality in favour of multiplicity, *plurality, fragmentation, and indeterminacy'* (Best and Kellner 1991: 4).

This analogy is a little slim; there being no inherent reason for a particular technology to always be used the same way. An instructive example came early in the application of digital technology to photography, in the CD-Rom 'I Photograph to Remember' (1993), in which the photographer Pedro Meyer uses the digital medium in a way that does not foreground its technical capacity for producing fragmentation or indeterminacy. On the contrary, he presents a narrative sequence of traditional photographs at high resolution, through which the viewer is able to move at a contemplative pace, reflecting upon each one and its relationship to a thoughtful and economic voiceover.

The point here is not that one of two competing forms or styles – that of 'fragmentation and indeterminacy' – is necessarily superior to the other – that of a supposed photographic unity – but that *neither* is the necessary outcome of the technologies employed. Both technologies can be used either way, given the intention and the skill to do so. The fact that they may be used in one way or another is a cultural and not a technological matter.

Digital deconstruction and theories of language

The artist Esther Parada has suggested that the application of the computer to photographic representation will result in more 'overt recognition and discussion' of the manipulation that is inherent in the practice (Ziff 1991: 132). In holding this view, she is clearly on similar ground to Martha Rosler (see above), in that they both choose to stress the manipulability of the photographic process. However, it is William Mitchell – whom we have met, so far, as the theorist of the difference between photographic and the digital image processes – who pursues this point furthest. In difficult language, he proposes that the emergence of digital imaging can be seen as a means to 'expose the aporias in photography's construction of the visual world, to deconstruct the very ideas of photographic objectivity and closure, and to resist what has become an increasingly sclerotic tradition' (Mitchell 1992: 8).

By this, Mitchell seems to mean two things. First, that a software application, such as Adobe Photoshop, can be an **heuristic** tool for *understanding* photographic representation. Within a few hours' use, such a program allows the user to run through many of the manipulations and conventions which are part of the practice of photography. Seen this way, digital image technology becomes a critical tool which can demonstrate in practice what has been argued in theory for some three decades: that photographic images are themselves special kinds of constructions. This 'deconstructive' project is itself fully in line with aspects of postmodern cultural practice which is frequently concerned with a self-conscious and playful use of language and style – whether visual, literary or architectural – or sets out to reveal their operation.

Mitchell proceeds from this statement to draw an analogy between digital imaging and some contemporary theories of language. He suggests that an analogy can be drawn between the open-endedness of the digitised image and **poststructuralist** theories of language and meaning. The emphasis in such theories is upon the polysemic nature of signs (their capacity to mean more than one fixed thing) and their indeterminacy (the way that language and sign systems are always 'in process' because they are being continually modified and nuanced as they are written and spoken in differing social contexts).

They never reach a final destination of fixed, settled meaning; that is, any kind of 'closure'. Mitchell suggests that we should understand digital imaging in this way. He proposes that, in the realm of visual images, digital technology is deconstructing the singular, fixed images of photography (their objectivity and closure). In this process, we are released from the grips of a worn-out and ailing photographic tradition and its outmoded mission.

Here, Mitchell appears to be drawing upon the philosopher **Jacques Derrida**'s ideas about the nature of language and meaning. More recently, the photographic historian and theorist Geoffrey Batchen has also found these theories of language and meaning useful when reflecting upon the supposed difference between analogue and digital images. In fact, he uses similar

JACQUES DERRIDA (1930–) French post-structuralist philosopher and Paris-based professor, born in Algeria. He is centrally concerned with the deconstruction of texts, particularly literature. His focus is on the fluidity of language, the unfixity of meaning, and on play between words. Key works include *Of Grammatology* (1967), *Writing and Difference* (1967) and *The Truth in Painting* (1978)

'Derridean' ideas to suggest that photography is itself a digital process. As we saw earlier in this chapter, photographs may be special kinds of signs; that is, indexical signs (signs which are caused by the objects they represent) or, as Batchen puts it, they are 'inscribed by the very objects to which they refer' (Batchen 1997: 215), but they are nevertheless signs. In a reworking of structuralist theories, one of Derrida's propositions about the nature of linguistic signs is that they are unstable. Any particular sign has meaning because it has a relation of difference to other signs; another way of saying this is that its meaning derives from what it is not; any sign entails others, and is always referring beyond itself to others which are not present.

Whenever a sign brings something to mind or calls up its presence, it therefore relies on something that is absent. Batchen argues that if we think of photographs in such poststructuralist semiotic terms we will override our preoccupation with the photograph's special indexical status (its 'analogical stability') and we are returned once more to see how a photograph's meaning arises from an unstable, relational play of signs. Batchen concludes that this is tantamount to recognising that photography itself is a digital process; it signifies through a system of signs playing across a field of presences and absences, positives and negatives, '0's and '1's.[3]

To return to Mitchell's suggestive analogies between modernism, photography, postmodern theories of language and digital imaging. Whilst he draws on a number of useful insights in making them, they must be criticised on a number of grounds. First, as was pointed out above, they are based on a very selective view of photography and a rather predetermined view of digital imaging. He cites the work of Paul Strand and Edward Weston, whom he sees as two modernist heroes of photography, and whose work he sees as exemplifying the aesthetic characteristics of photography (Mitchell 1992: 6–9). This hardly does justice to the range and variety of photographies which have been practised for a century and a half. It does, however, allow him to juxtapose a kind of stereotypical icon of photography – an image of the carefully framed and finely resolved photographic print – with another image: the pixelled, layered, montaged, and possibly interactive, digital image. Second, Mitchell largely ignores the many historical and social continuities of use to which the photograph and the digital image is put. Third, Mitchell's arguments tend to sail very close to a kind of **technological determinism**, a way of seeing technology as an autonomous force having definite outcomes which are independent of the culture which conceived and developed them, and of the uses to which they are put.

Finally, it has also been argued that behind Mitchell's proclamation of a digital revolution in image culture, there is a deeper sense in which he believes that there is a logical and progressive, technological evolution at work in the replacement of the camera by the computer (Robins 1995).

3 For his account of this argument and also his ideas about the different relation that photographic and digital images have to time, see GEOFFREY BATCHEN (1997) **Burning with Desire**, Cambridge, MA: The MIT Press, pp. 207–216. In making the argument that photography is 'a digital process', Batchen references the work of Jacques Derrida (1976) *Of Grammatology*, trans. Gayatri Chakravorty Spivak (Baltimore, MD: The Johns Hopkins University Press). Derrida's work is difficult and an approach to it may be made through the chapter on poststructuralism in J. Sturrock (1986) *Structuralism*, Fontana, and the chapter on Derrida in J. Sturrock (ed.) (1979) *Structuralism and Since: from Levi-Strauss to Derrida*, Oxford: Oxford University Press.

The limits of critical thought about post-photography

Robins accepts Mitchell's claim that 'The "image revolution" is significant in terms of a further and massive expansion of vision and visual techniques, allowing us to see new things and to see in new ways' (Robins 1995: 35). This involves a 'logic of development which is about a shift from a perceptual approach to images (seen as quotations from appearances), to one more concerned with the relation of imaging to conceptualisation' (Robins *ibid.*). In short, 'post-photography' displaces chemical photography's basis in the representation of appearances with a more sophisticated way of knowing; one that is based upon theories, algorithms and data. These are now used to simulate or to image *concepts about* objects and processes. In an age when our ideas about science, fact, truth and reality have become increasingly complex and problematic, 'post-photography' turns out to be a continuation, on a higher plane, of just one historical aspect of photography. This is the positivist project to collect facts, to measure and to record as a means of gaining objective knowledge of the world. Seen this way, talk of digital images as revolutionary becomes 'hype'; they are simply a more sophisticated technology which continues to be harnessed to the task of 'getting at the real truth' (Robins 1995).

We have seen a number of times in this chapter how much thinking about photography and digital imaging tends to work through constructing binary oppositions between them. Robins warns of similar problems in the 'technological progressivism' which he detects in this emerging discourse on 'post-photography'. This is because it constructs a false polarisation between past and future, between photography and digital culture, and unthinkingly conflates new technology with good technology:

> From such a deterministic perspective, it is no longer relevant to take seriously the virtues of photographic culture, nor is it meaningful to question the virtues of post-photographic culture. Should we not be challenging this affirmative logic? Is not the whole process more complex?
>
> (Robins 1995: 33)

This new 'post-photographic' discourse tends to limit the breadth of the ways in which we have been used to thinking about the culture of images. Our sense of the complexity and imaginative richness of images and visual culture is reduced to the terms of rational logic and progressive development. There is a danger that this discourse ignores other ways of thinking about images and their relation to the world: their emotional and subversive power, the awkward questions they can pose, and the alternative worlds they can help us imagine.

343

SUMMARY

A great deal of what has been considered in this chapter suggests that developments in digital image technology build upon the forms, uses and practices of photographic culture. In turn they are accelerating many of the cultural processes in which photography has been involved and are in the process of transforming others. We have even seen how it is possible to challenge the usually accepted opposition between photography's indexical or analogue signs and digital code. Yet, at the same time, a good deal of the critical attention given to photography in an age of electronic imaging is preoccupied with exploring – whether to deplore (Ritchin) or to celebrate (Mitchell) – the idea of radical difference and an historical watershed in visual culture.

There is clearly a real tension here, one which may be characteristic of moments of such change involving 'genuinely new technologies' (Williams 1974), and the different locations and levels on which change is experienced. Many a darkroom and enlarger has been replaced with an Apple Mac or a PC, a range of peripheral technologies, and the rapid acquisition of the 'know-how' to use them. Courses in photography have added multimedia and digital imaging to their curricula. The everyday landscape of 'photographic' images – on TV, at the cinema, and in magazines and newspapers – changes in both subtle and sensational ways, and these changes to traditional media have been joined by new media forms: the domestic PC running multimedia CD-Roms or accessing websites on-line, for entertainment, education, publicity and communication.

For some, in particular a generation of photographers trained before the mid-1980s, these changes may have been experienced on a scale which can be likened to that which photography brought about for the portrait painters of the early nineteenth century (Freund 1980), although such a comparison has to be qualified in at least two ways. First, digital technology impacted upon a photographic practice which had already been changed by analogue electronic and video technologies. Second, digital technology arrived in a technologically sophisticated world which cannot be directly likened to the nineteenth-century impact of photography on a handmade image culture.

It is at the level of ideas and critical responses to these changes that the tension seems to be greatest. Thinking through the implications of technological change and conceiving of ways in which it may be creatively used is not simply an abstract and academic task. It needs to be undertaken in close relationship to the practical use of the new image technologies as their possibilities are explored. This is producing new concepts and frameworks of understanding, just as other genuinely new media and communications technologies have done in the past. Yet, there is a clear danger that premature generalisations and simplifications are likely to be rife – and mystifying – if the historical and cultural context of technological change is not taken fully into account.

BIBLIOGRAPHY

KEY TEXTS

Benjamin, W. (1970) 'The Work of Art in the Age of Mechanical Reproduction' in H. Arendt
(ed.) *Illuminations,* London: Fontana (originally published in 1936)

Binkley, T. (1993) 'Refiguring Culture' in P. Hayward and T. Wollen (eds) *Future Visions; New
Technologies of the Screen,* London: BFI

Darley, A. (1990) 'From Abstraction to Simulation: Notes on the History of Computer Imaging'
in P. Hayward (ed.) *Culture, Technology, and Creativity in the Late Twentieth Century',*
London: John Libbey and Co Ltd

—— (1991) 'Big Screen, Little Screen: The Archaeology of Technology', *Ten-8,* 2(2) *Digital
Dialogues*

Lister, M. (ed.) (1995a) *The Photographic Image in Digital Culture*, London and New York:
Routledge

Mitchell, W.J. (1992) *The Reconfigured Eye: Visual Truth in the Post-photographic Era,*
Cambridge, MA: The MIT Press

Nichols, B. (1988) 'The Work of Culture in the Age of Cybernetic Systems', *Screen* 29(1), Winter

Ritchen, F. (1990a) *In Our Own Image: The Coming Revolution in Photography*, New York:
Aperture

—— (1990b) 'Photojournalism in the Age of Computers' in C. Squiers (ed.) *The Critical
Image*, Seattle: Bay Press, pp. 28–37

Robins, K. (1991) 'Into the Image: Visual Technologies and Vision Cultures' in P. Wombell (ed.)
PhotoVideo, London: Rivers Oram Press

—— (1995) 'Will Images Move Us Still?' in M. Lister (ed.) *The Photographic Image in Digital
Culture*, London and New York: Routledge

Rosler, M. (1991) 'Image Simulations, Computer Manipulations: Some Considerations', *Ten-8*
2(2), *Digital Dialogues*

Williams, R. (1974) *Television, Technology and Cultural Form*, London: Fontana

Willis, A-M. (1990) 'Digitisation and the Living Death of Photography' in P. Hayward (ed.)
Culture, Technology, and Creativity in the Late Twentieth Century, London: John Libbey
and Co Ltd.

Wombell, P. (ed.) (1991) *PhotoVideo: Photography in the Age of the Computer,* London:
Rivers Oram Press

OTHER REFERENCES

Axelmunden, V.H. *et al.* (eds) (1997) 'Photography after Photography: Memory and
Representation in the Digital Age', GB Arts International

Barthes, R. (1977a) 'The Photographic Message' in S. Heath (ed.) *Image, Music, Text*, London:
Fontana

—— (1977b) 'The Rhetoric of the Image' in S. Heath (ed.) *Image, Music, Text*, London: Fontana

Batchen, G. (1997) *Burning With Desire*, Cambridge, MA: The MIT Press

Becker, K. (1991) 'To Control our Image: Photojournalists Meeting New Technology' in
P. Wombell (ed.) *PhotoVideo*, London: Rivers Oram Press

Benjamin, W. (1970) 'Some Motifs in Baudelaire' in H. Arendt (ed.) *Illuminations,* London:
Fontana

Best, S. and Kellner, D. (1991) *Postmodern Theory: Critical Interrogations*, London: Macmillan

Boddy, W. (1994) 'Archeologies of Electronic Vision and the Gendered Spectator', *Screen* 35(2):
105–122

Bode, S. and Wombell, P. (1991) 'Introduction: In a New Light' in P. Wombell (ed.) *PhotoVideo:
Photography in the Age of the Computer*, London: Rivers Oram Press

Buck–Morss, S. (1991) *The Dialectics of Seeing; Walter Benjamin and the Arcades Project,* Cambridge, MA: The MIT Press

Burgin, V. (1991) 'Realising the Reverie' *Ten/8* 2(2), *Digital Dialogues*

Crary, J. (1993) *Techniques of the Observer: On Vision and Modernity in the Nineteenth Century,* Cambridge, MA: The MIT Press

Davis, S. (1995) 'Welcome Home Big Brother', *Wired* Magazine, May

Debord, G. (1970) *The Society of the Spectacle,* Detroit: Black and Red

Dewdney, A. and Boyd, F. (1995) 'Television, Computers, Technology and Cultural Form' in M. Lister (ed.) *The Photographic Image in Digital Culture,* London and New York: Routledge

Druckery, T. (1991) 'Deadly Representations or Apocalypse Now', *Ten/8* 2(2): 16–27, *Digital Dialogues*

Ellis, J. (1991) *Visible Fictions: Cinema, Television, Video,* London and New York: Routledge

Freund, Gisele (1980) *Photography and Society,* London: Gordon Fraser

Graham, B. (1995) 'The Panic Button (In Which our Heroine Goes Back to the Future of Pornography)' in M. Lister (ed.) *The Photographic Image in Digital Culture,* London and New York: Routledge

Green, D. (1984) 'Classified Subjects', *Ten/8* 14: 30–37

Grundberg, A. (1986) 'Veins of Resemblance', in P. Holland, J. Spence and S. Watney (eds) *Photography/Politics: Two,* London: Comedia

—— (1990) 'Photography in the Age of Electronic Simulation' in *Crisis of the Real,* New York: Aperture

Haddon, L. (1993) 'Interactive Games' in P. Hayward and T. Wollen (eds) *Future Visions: New Technologies of the Screen,* London: BFI

Hall, S. (1988) 'The Work of Art in The Electronic Age', *Block* 14

Harvey, D. (1989) *The Condition of Postmodernity,* Cambridge, MA: Blackwell

Harvie, C. *et al.* (1970) *Industrialisation and Culture 1830–1914,* London: Macmillan/The Open University Press

Hayward, P. (1993) 'Situating Cyberspace: The Popularisation of Virtual Reality' in P. Hayward and T. Walker (eds) *Future Visions: New Technologies of the Screen,* London: BFI

Heim, M. (1995) 'The Design of Virtual Reality' in Mike Featherstone and Roger Burrows (eds) *Cyberspace, Cyberbodies, Cyberpunk: Cultures of Technological Embodiment,* London, California and New Delhi: Sage

Jameson, F. (1984) 'Postmodernism or the Cultural Logic of Late Capitalism', *New Left Review* 146, July/August

—— (1993) 'Postmodernism and Consumer Society' in A. Gray and J. McGuigan (eds) *Studying Culture,* London, New York, Melbourne and Auckland: Edward Arnold

Jukes, P. (1992) 'The Work of Art in the Domain of Digital Production', *New Statesman and Society,* 17 July: 40–41

Kember, S. (1995) 'Medicine's New Vision' in M. Lister (ed.) *The Photographic Image in Digital Culture,* London and New York: Routledge

Lister, M. (1995b) 'Introductory Essay' in M. Lister (ed.) *The Photographic Image in Digital Culture,* London and New York: Routledge

Lury, C. (1992) 'Popular Culture and the Mass Media' in R. Bocock and K. Thompson (eds) *Social and Cultural Forms of Modernity,* Cambridge: Polity Press

McGrath, R. (1984) 'Medical Police', *Ten/8* 14: 13–18

Makela, Tapio (1997) 'Photography, Post-Photography', *Creative Camera,* April/May

Malina, R.F. (1990) 'Digital Image – Digital Cinema: The Work of Art in the Age of Post-mechanical Reproduction', *Leonardo,* Supplemental Issue: 33–38

Marvin, C. (1988) *When Old Technologies Were New,* New York: Oxford University Press

Maynard, P. (1997) *The Engine of Visualisation: Thinking Through Photography,* New York: Cornell University Press

Mulvey, L. (1981) 'Visual Pleasure and Narrative Cinema' in T. Bennett *et al.* (eds) *Popular Television and Film,* London: BFI/OU (originally published in 1975)

Nead, L. (1992) *The Female Nude: Art, Obscenity and Sexuality*, London and New York: Routledge

Neale, S. (1985) *Cinema and Technology: Images, Sound, Colour*, London: Macmillan

Piper, K. (1991) 'Fortress Europe: Tagging the Other' in P. Wombell (ed.) *PhotoVideo: Photography in the Age of the Computer*, London: Rivers Oram Press

Punt, M. (1995) 'The Elephant, the Spaceship and the White Cockatoo: An Archaeology of Digital Photography' in M. Lister (ed.) *The Photographic Image in Digital Culture*, London and New York: Routledge

Ride, P. (1997) 'Photography and Digital Art', *Creative Camera*, April/May

Slater, D.R. (1991) 'Consuming Kodak' in J. Spence and P. Holland (eds) *Family Snaps: The Meanings of Domestic Photography*, London: Virago Press

—— (1995) 'Domestic Photography and Digital Culture' in M. Lister (ed.) *The Photographic Image in Digital Culture*, London and New York: Routledge

Snyder, J. (1980) 'Picturing Vision', *Critical Enquiry* 6, Spring: 499–526

Snyder, J. and Allen, N.W. (1975) 'Photography, Vision, and Representation', *Critical Enquiry* 2, Autumn: 143–169

Stafford, B.M. (1991) *Body Criticism, Imaging the Unseen in Enlightenment, Art and Medicine*, Cambridge, MA: The MIT Press

Tagg, J. (1988) *The Burden of Representation: Essays on Photographies and Histories*, London: Macmillan

Virilio, P. (1989) *War and Cinema*, London: Verso

Virilio, P., Baudrillard, J. and Hall, S. (1988) 'The Work of Art in the Electronic Age', *Block* 14

Walker, I. (1995) 'Desert Stones or Faith in Facts' in M. Lister (ed.) *The Photographic Image in Digital Culture*, London and New York: Routledge

Williams, R. (1974) *Television, Technology and Cultural Form,* London: Fontana

Ziff, T. (1991) 'Taking New Ideas Back to the Old World' in P. Wombell (ed.) *PhotoVideo: Photography in the Age of the Computer,* London: Rivers Oram Press

Glossary

Key terms

aesthetic Pertaining to perception by the senses, and, by extension, to the appreciation or criticism of beauty, or of art. Thus 'aesthetics' references the criteria whereby we judge a work of art. Such criteria primarily include formal conventions (composition, tonal balance, and so on). Aesthetic philosophy is concerned with systems of principles for the appreciation of the beautiful, including the beautiful in art.

analogue A form of representation, such as a painting, a chemical photograph or video tape, in which the image is composed of a continuous variation of tone, light or some other signal. Similarly, a gramophone record is an analogue medium for reproducing sound or music. Analogue representation is based upon an unsegmented code while a digital medium is based upon a segmented one in which information is divided into discrete elements. The hands of a traditional (analogue) clock which continuously sweep its face, in contrast to a digital clock which announces each second in isolation, is a common example of the difference.

art In this book we distinguish between 'Art', referring to 'high art' and related gallery and funding institutions, and 'art' as creative skill.

autographic A generic term applied to all of those processes – drawing and painting being the main ones – in which images are made by the action and coordination of the eye and hand, and without mechanical or electronic intervention. Autographic images are authored wholly by physical and intellectual skill, or as a general field of (artistic) practices.

carnivalesque A concept developed by the Russian theorist Bakhtin to describe the taste for crude laughter, bad taste, excessiveness (particularly of bodily functions) and offensiveness. It celebrates a temporary liberation from recognised rules and hierarchies and is tolerated because, once people have been allowed to let off steam, those norms can be re-established.

code Used here in the **semiotic** sense to refer to the way in which signs are systematically organised to create meaning – the Morse code is one simple example. Cultural codes determine

the meanings conveyed by various cultural practices, say, the way people dress or eat their meals; photographic codes control the way meanings are conveyed in a photograph – for example, the details that give a news photograph its sense of authenticity, or a wedding photograph the right sort of dignity. In chapter 3 the discussion of Jo Spence's work elaborates on the use of photographic codes. Cultural codes are centrally examined in chapter 4.
See **semiotics**

commodity   Something which is bought and sold. The most commonly understood forms of commodity are goods which have been manufactured for the marketplace, but within capitalism other things have also been commodified. Natural resources and human labour have also been metamorphosed into commodities.

commodity culture   A term increasingly used to describe the culture of industrial capitalism. Within today's culture everything, even the water we drink, has become a product to be bought and sold in the marketplace. Commodity culture also infers the naturalisation of this system to the extent that we cannot imagine another way of living.

construction   This refers to the creating or forging of images and artefacts. In photography this particularly draws attention to the deliberate building of an image, rather than its taking from actuality, through **staging**, **fabrication**, **montage** and **image-text**. The term also reminds us of Soviet Constructivism, which emphasised the role of Art in the building of a new social order and used industrial elements, putting them together as work. It also draws upon theories of **deconstruction**.

deconstruction   A radical poststructuralist theory, centred upon the work of French literary theorist, Jacques Derrida, which investigates the complexity and, ultimately indeterminable, play of meaning in texts. Derrida's focus is literary, but the analysis may be extended to the visual.

discourse   The circulation of an idea or set of ideas. Photography is one of the many media – including newspapers, books, conversation, television programmes, and so on – which constitute contemporary discourses.
See **ideology**.

epistemological   A branch of philosophy concerned to establish by what means knowledge is derived. It is concerned with questions such as what it is possible to know and how reliable is knowledge. In the present context, questions can be asked about what kind of knowledge images provide, and how they do it.

fantasies   The term 'fantasy' usually refers to stories, daydreams and other fictions. It is sometimes distinguished from 'phantasy', which is a more technical term from **psychoanalysis** referring to **unconscious** processes. This book draws on both meanings, especially when discussing writers and photographers influenced by psychoanalytic thought.
See **psychoanalysis**, **unconscious**

fetishism   The substitution of a part for the whole; or use of a thing to stand in for powerful but repressed forces. In Freudian theory fetishism refers to the displacement and disavowal of sexuality. Fascination or desire are simultaneously denied, and indulged through looking at an object or image which stands in for that which is forbidden. Thus a photographic image of a fragment of a woman's body may stand in for woman as object of sexual desire.
See **objectification**, **psychoanalysis**, **voyeurism**

Formalism   The prioritisation of concern with form rather than content. Focus on composition and on the material nature of any specific medium.

gaze This has become a familiar term to describe a particular way of looking at, perceiving and understanding the world. It was brought into currency by writers on cinema, concerned to analyse the response of the audience as voyeurs of the action on the screen. The voyeuristic gaze is used to describe the way in which men often look at women, as well as the way in which Western tourists look at the non-Western world. More recently, discussions have focused on the implications of a 'female gaze'.

hegemony Dominance maintained through the continuous negotiation of consent by those in power in respect of their right to rule. Such consent is underpinned by the possibility of coercion. See **ideology**

heuristic An educational strategy in which students (or researchers) are trained to find things out for themselves.

historicisation Used (in chapter 7) to refer to the process by which events or other phenomena are given a place in an historical narrative. Photography may be defined by the position that it occupies in a larger historical schema or an unfolding over time of technologies and practices.

identity A person's identity is their sense of self and the different contexts within which that selfhood is constructed. It can never be given one simple, coherent description. For example, the national identity into which one is born may well clash with the cultural identity of the community in which one chooses to live; or a gay identity, based on sexuality, may clash with a religious identity based on strict rules governing sexual behaviour.

ideology This term is commonly used in two differing but interconnected ways. In this book it is used primarily to refer to a system of bodies of ideas which may be abstract, but which arise from a particular set of class interests. The term is also commonly used to refer to ideas which are illusory, whose purpose is to mask social and economic relations which actually obtain. For instance, the idea that children need their mother at home (which was common in the 1950s) masked the economic relations of patriarchy whereby married women were rendered financially dependent upon their husbands.

index One of three kinds of sign defined by American semiotician, C.S. Peirce. The indexical sign is based in cause and effect, for example, the footprint in wet sand indicates or traces a recent presence. The other two types of sign are the iconic (that which is based in resemblance), and the symbolic, or sign proper (that which is entirely conventional). See **semiotics**

mimetic representation Based upon imitation, upon showing rather than telling, a concept central to traditional post-Renaissance art theory. See **representation**

modernism In everyday terms 'modern' is often used to refer to contemporary design, media or forms of social organisation (as in 'the modern family'). But 'modern' also frequently refers to the emphasis upon modernisation from the mid-nineteenth century onwards, and, more particularly, to Modern movements in art and design from the turn of the twentieth century. It is essentially a relative concept (modern by contrast with . . .); its precise usage depends upon particular contexts. In this book we distinguish between three terms: modernism, sets of progressive ideas in which the modern is emphasised and welcomed; and *modernity*, social, technological and cultural developments. The term '*Modernism*' is used in chapter 6 to refer to particular emphasis on form and materiality in modern art. Throughout the book a distinction is made between the modern, and the postmodern or contemporary. See **postmodern**

objectification It is often argued that photography objectifies people by turning them into things or objects to be looked at thereby disempowering them.
See **voyeurism**

ontological Ontology is a branch of philosophy. It concerns the study of how things exist and the nature of various kinds of existence. It involves the logical investigation of the different ways in which things of different types (physical objects, numbers, abstract concepts, etc.) are thought to exist.

the Other A concept used within **psychoanalysis** and **identity** theory, and within post-colonial theory, to signify ways in which members of dominant groups derive a sense of self-location partly through defining other groups as different or 'Other'. Thus, within patriarchy, the male is taken as the norm, and woman as 'Other'; that is, not male. Similarly, in racist ideologies, whiteness is taken for granted, therefore blackness is seen as Other.
See **identity**, **psychoanalysis**

phenomenology A philosophical movement founded by Edmund Husserl in the early twentieth century in which the focus is on perception and consciousness, upon what the senses and the mind notice.

polysemic A property of signs is that they can have many meanings, depending on their context and the interests of their readers. Hence the frequent use of captions, or words within the image, to help anchor meaning.

positivism As is implied in the roots of the term itself, positivism stresses that which is definite or positive, i.e. factually based. Positivism, with its associated emphasis upon logical deduction and empirical research methods, including the social survey, is associated with the Victorian period in Britain, although its roots lie in earlier, eighteenth-century philosophy.

postmodern Literally 'after the modern', the postmodern represents a critique of the limitations of modernism with its emphasis upon progress and, in the case of the Arts, upon the materiality of the medium of communication. Philosophically, postmodernism has been defined as marking the collapse of certainty, a loss of faith in explanatory systems, and a sense of dislocation consequent on the global nature of communication systems and the loss of a clear relation between signs and their referents.

poststructuralist At its most simple, this means 'after Structuralism', also implying critical thinking that contests and goes beyond Structuralist theory and method, rejecting the idea that all meaning is fundamentally systematic. In this book it is used to refer to a group of theories which stress the way that the human 'self' and the meaning made of the world is constructed through the languages (including visual languages) which we use. Poststructuralist thinking challenges the idea that there is a fixed and stable human subject who can have certain knowledge.

See **identity**, **structuralism**

private and public spheres We lead our lives within two distinct modes, a 'private' sphere, which is made up of personal and kinship relations and domestic life, and a 'public' sphere, made up of economic relations, work, money-making and politics. The 'private' sphere tends to be controlled by moral and emotional constraints, the 'public' sphere by public laws and regulations. This distinction, although contested by feminist writers, underlies the way the terms 'private' and 'public' are used in this book, especially in chapter 3.

psychoanalysis The therapeutic method established by Sigmund Freud, which involves seeking access to traumatic experiences held in the **unconscious** mind.
See **repression**, **unconscious**

representation This refers to ways in which individuals, groups or ideas are depicted. Although this seems obvious, the use of the term usually signals acknowledgement that images are never 'innocent', but always have their own history, cultural contexts and specificity, and therefore carry **ideological** implications.

repression Unpleasant or unwelcome thoughts, emotions, sensations are 'repressed' when they are forced into the **unconscious**. The phrase 'the return of the repressed' means that such emotions surface into the conscious world in different form.
See **psychoanalysis**, **unconscious**

reproduction The production by machine of many identical copies. The process of mass production when applied, through photography, print technology, and electronic recording to the copying of visual images or music. As this process has become increasingly sophisticated, the reproduction of original works of art has reached a stage where the reproduction is, for almost all intents and purposes, as good as the original. Where it does not, and cannot, replace the original autographic work is in bearing the traces and marks of its maker. Such originals have been spoken of as having an 'aura' (Benjamin) due to our sense of their being unique and of having a history. There are, broadly, two schools of thought about the impact of reproduction on original images. One deplores the 'cheapening' of unique originals through reproduction; the other celebrates the process as a way of democratising visual and aural culture. Whatever the case, photography is a technology which has reproducibility built in. A negative is produced precisely to be able to make infinite numbers of prints, each, in principle, being identical. The phenomenon of the 'artist' photographer's proof, or 'original' print, is therefore an ironic twist and an example of the political economy triumphing over technological determinations. The digital technology now reproduces the photograph.

scopophilia The human drive to look or observe; in Freudian theory the fundamental instinct leading to **voyeurism**.
See **fetishism**, **voyeurism**

semiology see **semiotics**

semiotics The science of signs, first proposed in 1916 by linguist Ferdinand de Saussure, but developed in particular in the work of Roland Barthes (France) and C.S. Peirce (USA). Semiotics – also referred to as semiology – is premised upon the contention that all human communication is founded in an assemblage of signs – verbal, aural and visual – which is essentially systematic. Such sign systems are viewed as largely – or entirely – conventional; that is, consequent not upon 'natural' relations between words or images and that to which they refer, but upon arbitrary relations established through cultural convention. The sign proper has two aspects, signifier and signified. The signifier is the material manifestation, the word, or pictorial elements. The signified is the associated mental concept; that is, conventionally associated with the specific signifier. While separable for analytic purposes, in practice the signifier and the signified always go together.
See **code**

social and economic history History may be written in many ways. Economic history deals with changes in work patterns and the ways in which human societies have sustained themselves. Social history deals with the organisation of societies – marriage, education, child-rearing and the like. A history of photography is normally seen as part of art history or, more broadly, of cultural history. In chapter 3 it is suggested that we can understand personal photography better if we consider it within a social and economic context. Chapter 4 takes the social and the economic as the primary context for understanding commercial uses of photography.

straight photography Emphasis upon direct documentary typical of the Modern period in American photography.

structuralism Twentieth-century theoretical movement within which stress is laid upon analysis of objects, cultural artefacts and communication processes, in terms of systems of relations rather than as entities in themselves.

technological determinism This refers to the proposition that technological invention alone determines new cultural formations. The notion has been criticised primarily on the grounds that new technologies arise from research enterprises driven largely by economic imperatives and perceived social or political needs. Technological developments may be seen as an effect of cultural desires as well as a major influence within cultural change.

teleology Arguments and explanations in which the nature of something is explained by the purpose or 'end' which it appears to have. In this view photography, and then cinema, may be understood as being caused by a human desire to achieve ever more comprehensive illusions of reality and are seen as striving towards a future achievement.

unconscious In **psychoanalysis**, that which is **repressed** from the individual's conscious awareness yet gives rise to impulses which influence our behaviour. Freud insisted that human action always derives from mental processes of which we cannot be aware.
See **repression**, **psychoanalysis**

voyeurism Sexual stimulation obtained through looking. In photography voyeurism refers to the image as spectacle used for the gratification of the (hitherto construed as male, heterosexual) spectator.
See **fetishism**, **objectification**, **psychoanalysis**

For a comprehensive definition and discussion of *technical* terms in photography see:
Baldwin, G. (1991) *Looking at Photographs: A Guide to Technical Terms*, California: The Paul Getty Museum and London: British Museum Press.

For fuller discussion of various contributions to twentieth-century debates, including Barthes, Benjamin, Foucault and Freud see:
Lechte, John (1994) *Fifty Key Contemporary Thinkers*, London: Routledge.

Photography archives

Work by many photographers, historical and contemporary, is kept under proper conservation conditions in specific archives (or collections). Researching images – perhaps for an extended essay or dissertation – may lead you to want to look at original prints. Here we list some key archives which may be of help to you. However, you should always phone, fax or e-mail in advance to check that the work that interests you is held there and to make a viewing appointment.

KEY PUBLIC ARCHIVES IN BRITAIN

National Museum of Photography, Film and Television, Pictureville, Prince's View, Bradford, West Yorkshire BD5 0TR Tel: 01274 727488

National Portrait Gallery, Charing Cross Road, London WC1 Tel: 0171 306 0055. For photographic portraiture archives and exhibitions

Royal Photographic Society, The Octagon, 46 Milsom Street, Bath BA1 1DN Tel: 01225 462841[1]

Scottish National Portrait Gallery, 1 Queen Street, Edinburgh Tel: 0131 556 8921. For portraiture archives

Victoria and Albert Museum, South Kensington, London SW7 Tel: 0171 938 8500. Holds the National Collection of the Art of Photography

OTHER ARCHIVES

Barnado's Photographic and Film Archive, Tanners Lane, Barkingside, Ilford, Essex IG6 1QG Tel: 0181 550 8822 x345

The Documentary Photography Archive, c/o 7 Towncroft Lane, Heaton, Bolton BL1 5EW Tel: 0161 247 1765

IRIS, Women's Photography Archive, Staffordshire University Tel: 01782 294721

Jo Spence Memorial Archive, 152 Upper Street, London N1 1RA Tel: 0171 359 9064

National Sound Archive, British Library Tel: 0171 412 7440. Interviews with contemporary photographers

1 At the time of finalising this edition, Autumn 1999, the RPS was seeking to move – destination not determined

Many organisations, including newspapers and commercial companies, maintain their own archives. However, access to these may be limited, by appointment only or based on payment of search fees. Among the foremost such collections in Britain are:

Hulton Getty Picture Collection, Unique House, 21–31 Woodfield Road, London W9 2BA. Archives include *Picture Post, Express, Evening Standard*
Mary Evans Picture Library, 59 Tranquil Vale, London SE3 0BS Tel: 0181 318 0034. Includes the Fawcett Library (women's rights)

Most city libraries include photography in their local history collections. Sometimes this covers major bodies of work; for example, Edinburgh City Libraries house a large collection of calotypes by Hill and Adamson.

ARCHIVES IN THE USA

International Museum of Photography and Film, George Eastman House, 900 East Avenue, Rochester, New York 14607–2298 Tel: (716) 271 3361. Work by over 10,000 photographers
New York Public Library Photography Collection, 42nd Street at Fifth Avenue, New York, NY 10018 Tel: (212) 930 0837. Work by over 2000 photographers

Collections with holdings of over 1000 photographers
Art Institute of Chicago, Michigan Avenue at Adams Street, Chicago, IL 60603 Tel: (312) 443 3600
Center for Creative Photography, University of Arizona, Tucson, AZ 85721 Tel: (602) 6212211
Colorado Historical Society, Denver, Colorado. Tel: (303) 866 3682. Holds 500,000 photographic images
Harry Ransom Humanities Research Center, University of Texas at Austin, PO Drawer 7219, Austin, TX 78713 Tel: (512) 471 8944. Houses five million photographs
Getty Center for the History of Art and the Humanities, Santa Monica, California. Tel: (310) 458 9811. Archive of 1.5 million images
Library of Congress, Prints and Photographs Division, Washington DC 20540–4840 Tel: (202) 707 5000. Over fifteen million prints and photographs including early daguerreotypes
Marriott Library (Manuscripts Division), University of Utah, Salt Lake City Tel: (801) 581 7200
Metropolitan Museum of Art, New York (Department of Photographs), Fifth Avenue at 82nd Street, New York NY 10028 Tel: (212) 879 5500
Museum of Fine Arts, 1001 Bissonnet Street, Houston, Texas TX 77005 Tel: (713) 639 7300
Museum of Modern Art, 11 West 53rd Street, New York, NY 10019 Tel: (212) 708 9400. Has a large gallery devoted to permanent collections where vintage prints of the great photographers are housed. Contemporary photographs are also held
Museum of New Mexico (photographic archives), Santa Fé, NM 87504–2087. Tel: (505) 827 4793
Mystic Seaport Museum, Mystic, Connecticut. Nation's foremost maritime museum. Tel: (860) 572 5388
National Museum of American History, Smithsonian Institute, 14th Street and Constitution Ave, NW, Washington DC 20560 Tel: (202) 357 3176
New Orleans Museum of Art, 1 Collins Diboll Circle, City Park, New Orleans, LA 70124 Tel: (504) 488 2631
San Francisco Museum of Modern Art, 151 Third Street, San Francisco, CA 94103 Tel: (415) 357 4000
University of New Mexico, Albuquerque, NM 87131 Tel: (505) 277 0111
Visual Studies Workshop, Rochester, New York State. Tel: (716) 442 8676

(Most of the above archives have websites which also give fax and telephone numbers (or use directory enquiries).)

For smaller archives, and for listings of photographers included in the collections listed above, see Andrew H. Eskind (ed.) (1996) *Index to American Photographic Collections*, compiled at the

International Museum of Photography at George Eastman House, Rochester, 3rd edn. New York: G.K. Hall & Co.

See also *USA Photography Guide* (1995 2nd edn, Tucson/Munich: Nazraeli Press) for details of galleries, publishers, associations, museums and collections, courses.

ARCHIVES ELSEWHERE (ENGLISH-LANGUAGE-BASED)

Australia
Collections of photography are held at:
Art Gallery of New South Wales, Domain, Sydney, NSW Tel: (2) 9225 1700
LaTrobe Library, State Library of Victoria, 328 Swanston Street, Melbourne, Victoria 3000 Tel: (3) 669 9888
Mitchell Library, State Library of New South Wales (major photography collection), Macquarie Street, Sydney, NSW 2000 Tel: (2) 9273 1414
National Gallery of Australia, POB 1150, Canberra, ACT 2601 Tel: (2) 6240 6411 (art collection including photography)
National Gallery of Victoria, 180 St Kilda Road, Melbourne, Victoria Tel: 9208 0222
National Library, Canberra. Tel: (612) 6262 1111
Queensland Art Gallery, South Brisbane, Queensland 4101 Tel: (7) 3840 7303

Canada
Canadian Museum of Contemporary Photography, Ottawa, Ontario. Tel: (613) 990 8257. Over 158,000 images by Canadian photographers.
National Gallery of Canada, 380 Sussex Drive, Ottawa, Ontario K1N 9N4 Tel: (613) 901985. An international collection of over 17,000 photographs ranging from early photography to the contemporary

(For listing of Canadian archives see *Guide to Canadian Photographic Archives*, 1984, Ottawa: Public Archives of Canada.)

Africa
Benususan Museum of Photography, Africana Museum, Public Library, Market Square, Johannesburg 2001. Historical collection, with particular reference to South Africa. Tel: (2711) 833 5624

New Zealand
Alexander Turnbull Library, POB 12349, Wellington 6000 Tel: (4) 474 3000. Some 846,000 photographs.
Auckland Museum, Private Bag 92018, Auckland 1 Tel: (9) 309 0443. Contemporary collection of Robin Morrison photographs.
National Archives, 10 Mulgrave Street, Wellington Tel: (4) 499 5595. Over 200,000 photographs.

(For listings of all major and regional photograph collections in New Zealand see Directory of New Zealand Photograph Collections, 1992, available from The National Library Shop, POB 1467, Wellington Tel. (4) 474 3056 (Joan McCraken).)

Note: for other European archives see H. Evans and M. Evans (compilers) (1992) *Picture Researcher's Handbook: An International Guide to Picture Sources and How to Use Them*, London: Chapman and Hall. See also *European Photography Guide 6*, Gottingen: European Photography 1997.

KEY BRITISH MAGAZINES AND JOURNALS

Autograph, The Association of Black Photographers (founded 1988), quarterly.

British Journal of Photography, London (founded 1854), weekly. Focus on commercial photography.

Camerawork, London (until 1985). Concerned with social and political issues.

Creative Camera, London, published six times a year. Contemporary gallery-based photography.

History of Photography, Oxford (academic journal), quarterly, 1977– .

Portfolio, Portfolio Gallery, Edinburgh, published twice yearly.

Ten/8, Birmingham (until 1992; titled *Ten.8* in the two final issues).

KEY NORTH AMERICAN MAGAZINES AND JOURNALS

Afterimage, Visual Studies Workshop, Rochester, NY. Issues in photography and video.

Aperture New York/San Francisco, quarterly since 1952. Themed issues and portfolios.

Blackflash, The Photographers Gallery, Saskatoon, Saskatchewan, Canada. Three yearly. Journal of photo-based and electronic-art production.

Border Crossings; Winnipeg, Manitoba, quarterly, An interdisciplinary arts review featuring articles, book reviews, artist profiles, and interviews covering the full range of the contemporary arts in Canada and internationally.

Canadian Art, Toronto, Ontario, quarterly. Visual arts in Canada. Includes critical profiles of new artists and established art world figures.

CV Photo, Montreal, Quebec, quarterly. Richly illustrated magazine, photographic work, essays.

October, The MIT Press, Cambridge, MA, quarterly since 1976. Academic journal: art, criticism, theory and history.

Parachute, Montreal, quarterly. Contemporary art including photography. Bilingual.

Visual Anthropology Review, published by the American Anthropological Association. Debates on documentary and anthropology.

OTHER MAGAZINES AND JOURNALS

published in English or with translation

Camera Austria, contemporary photography. Quarterly.

European Photography, Gottingen, Germany, founded 1980. Twice yearly.

Flash Art International, European Art magazine, founded 1980. Six issues a year.

Katalog, Denmark. Quarterly journal of photography and video, founded 1988.

NZ Journal of Photography, New Zealand Centre for Photography, POB 27–344, Wellington, articles about NZ photography and portfolios of images. Quarterly.

Photofile, Australian Centre for Photography, Sydney, founded 1983. Thrice yearly.

PhotoVision, Spain, founded 1981. Twice yearly.

(See *European Photography Guide 6* (Gottingen: European Photography, 1997) for listings of magazines by country and language of publication.)

WEBSITES

Dealing with photography and digital media. You should also use keyword searches to ensure you find the most up-to-date sites.

ADAM
www.adam.ac.uk
The Art, Design, Architecture & Media Information Gateway is a searchable catalogue of Internet resources internationally selected and catalogued by professional librarians in UK Higher Education.

ADA'WEB
http://www.adaweb.com
A website which aims to provide contemporary artists (visual artists, as well as composers, movie directors, architects, choreographers, etc.) with a station from which they can engage in a dialogue with users of the internet.

ARTEC
http://www.artec.org.uk
Artec is a leading arts and technology centre based in London. It is the host for the Channel site. Carries out digital media training, houses arts residencies and commissions network projects.

CAFE SOCIETY
http://www.pulsemag.demon.co.uk/
The Cafe Society is an open forum for the promotion, debate and exhibition of photography and electronic images through the internet and alternative gallery venues in the cities of Hull and Amsterdam.

CHANNEL
http://www.channel.org.uk/interface/start.html
Channel shows new artists' work and experimental projects. It aims to test the possibilities of digital arts practice and to cut across traditional media boundaries and spaces.

COPIOUS ART LINKS
(Center for Advanced Study in Postcontemporary Art).
http://rampages.onramp.net/~dnewman/artlinks.htm#.
An extensive list of websites concerning the practice and theory of visual art within a broad and critical cultural context.

CTHEORY
http://www.ctheory.org/
Ctheory is an international journal of theory, technology and culture. Articles, interviews and key book reviews in contemporary discourse are published weekly as well as theorisations of major 'event-scenes' in the mediascape.

THE CRITICAL EYE
http://www.thecriticaleye.com/
online 'zine concerned with photography criticism, each edition focusing on a different movement/topic, e.g. 'The Urban Landscape', 'Current Trends In Digital Representation', 'Multiculturalism', 'Deconstructing The Gaze', 'Modernism', etc.

INTERFACE
http://www.cgrg.ohio-state.edu/interface/
An academic journal of art and technology.

IRIS – Women Photographers
http://www.staffs.ac.uk/ariadne
Features images, writing and information on women photographers.

LEONARDO – Electronic Almanac
http://mitpress.mit.edu/e-journals/LEA/home.html
Leonardo Electronic Almanac (LEA). An electronic journal dedicated to providing a forum for those
who are interested in the convergence of art, science and technology. Includes: profiles of media
arts facilities and projects; profiles of artists using new media; feature articles comprised of
theoretical and technical perspectives; an on-line gallery exhibiting new media art.

LIPSERVICE
http://www.spelthorne.ac.uk/pm/lip/lipserv.htm
Magazine of London Independent Photography. The on-line presence of the London Independent
Photography Group. Aims to promote independent photography, critical debate on photography,
organizes exhibitions, etc.

MUTE
http://www.metamute.com/
On-line version of the London-based journal of digital art and media critique.

PHOTOGRAPHY IN NEW YORK
www.photography-guide.com/
National and international listings of art photography exhibitions and events.

PHOTOMETRO MAGAZINE
http://www.photometro.com/
On-line photography 'zine.

SCREENING THE PAST
http://www.latrobe.edu.au/www/screeningthepast/index.html
An international electronic journal of visual media and history. Covers photography, film, television
and multimedia.

TRANS
http://www.echonyc.com/~trans/
Particularly concerned with the relationship of text to images. Contains essays, reviews, etc. on a
broad range of media.

ZONEZERO
http://www.zonezero.com/
ZoneZero is dedicated to photography and its journey from the analogue to digital world. It aims
to carry an ongoing debate on all the issues surrounding the 'representation of reality' and other
subjects relevant to the transition from analogue to digital image-making. It aims to promote an
understanding of where, in the context of the digital age, the tradition of the 'still image' is
headed. Carries extensive on-line exhibitions of photography. Has a special interest in Latin
American work.

Bibliography

Ades, Dawn (1974) *Dada and Surrealism*, London: Thames and Hudson

Agee, J. and Evans, W. (1939) *Let Us Now Praise Famous Men*, New York: Random House

Alexander, S. (1998) 'Photographic Institutions and Practices' in Michel Frizot *A New History of Photography*, Cologne: Konemann

Alloula, Malek (1987) *The Colonial Harem*, Manchester: Manchester University Press

Alloway, Lawrence (1966) 'The Development of British Pop' in Lucy R. Lippart (ed.) *Pop Art*, London: Thames and Hudson

Arnason, H.H. (1988) *A History of Modern Art*, London: Thames and Hudson, third edition (updated and revised to include photography)

Arts Council (1972) *From Today Painting is Dead*, London: Arts Council

—— (1975) *The Real Thing, An Anthology of British Photographers 1840–1950*, London: Arts Council

—— (1979) *Three Perspectives on Photography*, London: Arts Council

—— (1987) *Independent Photography and Photography in Education*, London: Arts Council

—— (1991) *Shocks to the System*, London: The South Bank Centre

Axelmunden, V.H. *et al.* (eds) (1997) 'Photography after Photography: Memory and Representation in the Digital Age', GB Arts International

Bacher, Fred (1992) 'The Popular Condition: Fear and Clothing in LA', *The Humanist*, September/October

Back, L. and Quaade, V. (1993) 'Dream Utopias, Nightmare Realities: Imagining Race and Culture within the World of Benetton', *Third Text* 22

Badger, Gerry and Benton-Harris, John (eds) (1989) *Through the Looking Glass,* London: Barbican Art Gallery

Bailey, David (1988) 'Re-thinking Black Representations', *Ten/8* 31

—— (1989) 'People of the World' in P. Wombell (ed.) *The Globe: Representing the World*, York: Impressions Gallery

Bailey, David and Hall, Stuart (eds) (1992) *Ten/8* 2(3), *Critical Decade*

Baker, Lindsay (1991) 'Taking Advertising to its Limit', *The Times*, 22 July, p. 29

Bakhtin, Mikhail (1984) *Rabelais and His World*, Bloomington: Indiana University Press

Barrett, M. and McIntosh, M. (1982) *The Anti-Social Family*, London: Verso

Barthes, Roland (1957) 'The Face of Garbo', in *Mythologies*, London: Granada, 1973

—— (1973) *Mythologies*, London: Granada (first published 1957), republished in London by Grafton Books, 1986

—— (1977a) 'The Photographic Message' in S. Heath (ed.) *Image, Music, Text*, London: Fontana

—— (1977b) 'The Rhetoric of the Image', 'The Third Meaning' and 'The Photographic Message' iin S. Heath (ed.) *Image, Music Text*, London: Fontana

—— (1981) *Camera Lucida*, New York: Hill and Wang, republished in London by Fontana, 1984

Batchen, Geoffrey (1990) 'Burning with Desire: The Birth and Death of Photography', *Afterimage*, January

—— (1997) *Burning With Desire*, Cambridge, MA: The MIT Press

Bate, David (1993) 'Photography and the Colonial Vision', *Third Text* 22

Baudelaire, Charles (1859) 'The Salon of 1859', reprinted in P.E. Charvet (ed.) (1992) *Baudelaire, Selected Writings on Art and Artists*, Harmondsworth: Penguin

Bazin, André (1967) 'The Ontology of the Photograph' in *What is Cinema?* Volume 1, Berkeley, Los Angeles, and London: University of California Press

Becker, K. (1991) 'To Control our Image: Photojournalists Meeting New Technology' in P. Wombell (ed.) *PhotoVideo: Photography in the Age of the Computer*, London: Rivers Oram Press

Bede, C. (1855) *Photographic Pleasures*, London

Beloff, Halla (1985) *Camera Culture*, Oxford: Blackwell

Belussi, Fiorenza (1987) *Benetton: Information Technology in Production and Distribution: A Case Study of the Innovative Potential of Traditional Sectors*, SPRU, University of Sussex

Benetton (1993) *Global Vision: United Colors of Benetton*, Tokyo: Robundo

Benjamin, Walter (1931) 'A Small History of Photography' in (1979) *One Way Street*, London: New Left Books. Also published as (1972) 'A Short History of Photography', *Screen* 13(1)

—— (1938) 'The Paris of the Second Empire in Baudelaire', in *Charles Baudelaire: A Lyric Poet in the Era of High Capitalism*, London: Verso, 1985

—— (1970a) 'The Work of Art in an Age of Mechanical Reproduction' in Hannah Arendt (ed.) *Illuminations*, London: Fontana. Revised edition 1992. Originally published in *Zeitschrift fur Sozialforchung* 5(1), 1936

—— (1970b) 'Some Motifs in Baudelaire' in Hannah Arendt (ed.) *Illuminations*, London: Fontana

—— (1992) 'Unpacking My Library' in *Illuminations*, London: Jonathan Cape, 1970; Fontana, 1973/1992. Originally published in *Literarische Welt*, 1931

Benson, S.H. (n.d.) *Some Examples of Benson Advertising*, S.H. Benson Firm

Berger, John (1972a) *Ways of Seeing*, Harmondsworth: Penguin

—— (1972b) 'The Political Uses of Photomontage' in *Selected Essays and Articles, The Look of Things*, Harmondsworth: Penguin

Bernstein, B. (1971) *Class, Codes and Control*, Vol. 1, *Theoretical Studies Towards a Sociology of Language*, London: Routledge & Kegan Paul

Best, S. and Keller, D. (1991) *Postmodern Theory: Critical Interrogations*, London: Macmillan

Bezencenet, Stevie (1982a) 'What is a History of Photography?', *Creative Camera* 208, April

—— (1982b) 'Thinking Photography', *Creative Camera* 215, November

Bhabha, H. (1990) 'Novel Metropolis', *New Statesman and Society*, 9 February

Binkley, T. (1993) 'Refiguring Culture' in P. Hayward and T. Wollen (eds) *Future Visions: New Technologies of the Screen*, London: BFI

Bishton, D. and Rearden, J. (eds) (1984) Black Image – Staying On *Ten/8* 16

Boddy, W. (1994) 'Archaeologies of Electronic Vision and the Gendered Spectator', *Screen* 35(2): 105–122

Bode, S. and Wombell, P. (1991) 'Introduction: In a New Light' in P. Wombell (ed.) *PhotoVideo: Photography in the Age of the Computer*, London: Rivers Oram Press

Boffin, T. and Fraser, J. (1991) *Stolen Glances: Lesbians Take Photographs*, London: Pandora Press

Bolton, Richard (ed.) (1989) *The Contest of Meaning*, Cambridge, MA: The MIT Press

Bourdieu, P. (1965/1990) *Photography: A Middle Brow Art*, London: Polity Press

Braden, Su (1978) *Artists and People*, London: Routledge & Kegan Paul

Brandt, Bill (1961) *Perspective of Nudes*, London: The Bodley Head

Braun, Marta (1992) *Picturing Time: The Work of Etienne-Jules Marey (1830–1904)*, Chicago, IL: University of Chicago Press

Breton, André (1978) *What is Surrealism? Selected Writings* in F. Rosement (ed. and introduction), London: Pluto Press

Bright, Deborah (1990) 'Of Mother Nature and Marlboro Men: An Inquiry into the Cultural Meanings of Landscape Photography' in Richard Boston (ed.) *The Contest of Meaning*, Cambridge, MA: The MIT Press

—— (ed.) (1998) *The Passionate Camera: Photography and Bodies of Desire*, London and New York: Routledge

Brookes, Rosetta (1992) 'Fashion Photography' in J. Ash and E. Wilson (eds) *Chic Thrills: A Fashion Reader*, London: Pandora

Brown, Beverley (1981) 'A Feminist Interest in Pornography: Some Modest Proposals' in Parveen Adams and Elizabeth Cowie (1990) *The Woman in Question*, London and New York: Verso

Buck-Morse, S. (1991) *The Dialectics of Seeing: Walter Benjamin and the Arcades Project*, Cambridge, MA: The MIT Press

Burgin, Victor (ed.) (1982) *Thinking Photography*, London: Macmillan

—— (1983) 'Photography, Phantasy, Function' in *Thinking Photography*, London: Macmillan

—— (1986) 'Re-Reading Camera Lucida' in *The End of Art Theory: Criticism and Postmodernity*, London: Macmillan

—— (1991) 'Realising the Reverie', *Ten/8* 2(2), Digital Dialogues

Butler, Susan (1989) *Shifting Focus*, Bristol/London: Arnolfini/Serpentine

Butt, Gavin (1998) *Men on the Threshold: The Making and Unmaking of the Sexual Subject in American Art 1948–1965*, Unpublished Ph.D., University of Leeds

Carlebach, M.L. (1992) *The Origins of Photojournalism in America*, Washington DC: Smithsonian Institute

Carr, E.H. (1964) *What is History?*, Harmondsworth: Penguin

Cartier-Bresson, H. (1952) *The Decisive Moment*, New York: Simon and Schuster

Cartwright, Lisa (1995) *Screening the Body: Tracing Medicine's Visual Culture*, Minneapolis and London: University of Minnesota Press

Chadwick, Whitney (1985) *Women Artists and the Surrealist Movement*, London: Thames and Hudson

—— (1998) *Mirror Images: Women, Surrealism and Self-Representation*, Cambridge, MA: The MIT Press

Chambers, Eddie (1999) 'D-Max: An Introduction' in *Run Through the Jungle*, Annotations 5, London: INIVA

Chanan, M. (1996) *The Dream That Kicks*, London: Routledge

Chester, Gail and Dickey, Julienne (eds) (1988) *Feminism and Censorship: The Current Debate*, Bridport, Dorset: Prism Press

Christian, J. (1990) 'Paul Sandby and the Military Survey of Scotland' in N. Alfrey and J. Daniels (eds) *Mapping the Landscape*, University of Nottingham

Clarke, Graham (1997) *The Photograph*, Oxford: Oxford University Press

Clark, Kenneth (1956) *The Nude*, Harmondsworth: Penguin, 1960

Coe, B. (1989) 'Roll Film Revolution' in C. Ford (ed.) *The Story of Popular Photography*, Bradford: Century Hutchinson Ltd/National Museum of Photography, Film and Television

Coe, B. and Gates, P. (1977) *The Snapshot Photograph. The Rise of Popular Photography 1888–1939*, London: Ash and Grant

Coke, Van Deren (1972) *The Painter and the Photograph*, New Mexico: University of New Mexico Press

Coleman, A.D. (1979) *Light Readings*, New York: Oxford University Press

Cooper, Emmanuel (1990) *Fully Exposed: The Male Nude in Photography*, London: Unwin Hyman

Corner, John and Harvey, Sylvia (1990) 'Heritage in Britain', *Ten/8* 36

—— (eds) (1991) *Enterprise and Heritage*, London: Routledge

Craik, Jennifer (1994) 'Soft Focus: Techniques of Fashion Photography' in *The Face of Fashion*, London: Routledge

Crary, Jonathan (1990) *Techniques of the Observer: On Vision and Modernity in the Nineteenth Century*, Cambridge, MA: The MIT Press

Crawley, G. (1989) 'Colour Comes to All' in C. Ford (ed.) *The Story of Popular Photography*, Bradford: Century Hutchinson Ltd/National Museum of Photography, Film and Television

Crimp, Douglas (1995) *On the Museum's Ruins*, Cambridge, MA: The MIT Press

Crimp, Douglas and Rolston, Adam (1990) *AIDS Demo/Graphics*, Seattle: Bay Press

Csikszentmihalyi, M. and Rochberg-Halton, E. (1992) *The Meaning of Things: Domestic Symbols and the Self*, Cambridge: Cambridge University Press

Darley, A. (1990) 'From Abstraction to Simulation: Notes on the History of Computer Imaging' in P. Hayward (ed.) *Culture, Technology, and Creativity in the Late Twentieth Century*, London: John Libbey and Co Ltd

—— (1991) 'Big Screen, Little Screen: The Archaeology of Technology', *Ten/8* 2(2), Digital Dialogues

Davidoff, L. and Hall, C. (1976) 'The Charmed Circle of Home' in J. Mitchell and A. Oakley (eds) *The Rights and Wrongs of Women*, Harmondsworth: Penguin

Davis, S. (1995) 'Welcome Home Big Brother', *Wired* Magazine, May

Debord, G. (1970) *The Society of the Spectacle*, Detroit: Black and Red

Delpire, Robert and Frizot, Michel (1989) *Histoire de Voir*, Paris: Photo Poche

Dentith, Simon (1995) *Bakhtinian Thought: An Introductory Reader*, London: Routledge

Devlin, Polly (1979) *Vogue Book of Fashion Photography*, London: Condé Nast

Dewdney, A. (1991) 'More Than Black and White: The Extended and Shared Family Album' in J. Spence and P. Holland (eds) *Family Snaps: The Meanings of Domestic Photography*, London: Virago

Dewdney, A. and Boyd, F. (1995) 'Television, Computers, Technology and Cultural Form' in M. Lister (ed.) *The Photographic Image in Digital Culture*, London and New York: Routledge

Drake, M. and Finnegan, R. (eds) (1994) *Studying Family and Community History: 19th and 20th Centuries*, Vol. 4, *Sources and Methods: A Handbook*, Cambridge: Cambridge University Press/Open University

Druckery, T. (1991) 'Deadly Representations or Apocalypse Now', *Ten/8* 2(2): 16–27, Digital Dialogues

Dubin, Steven C. (1992) *Arresting Images: Impolitic Art and Uncivil Actions*, London and New York: Routledge

Dworkin, Andrea (1981) *Pornography: Men Possessing Women*, London: The Women's Press

Eastlake, Lady Elizabeth (1857) 'Photography', *Quarterly Review*, April, reprinted in Beaumont Newhall (ed.) (1980) *Photography: Essays and Images*, London: Secker and Warburg

Edwards, Elizabeth (ed.) (1992) *Photography and Anthropology 1860–1920*, New Haven, CT: Yale University Press

Edwards, Steve (1989) 'The Snapshooters of History', *Ten/8* 32

Elias, Norbert (1994) *The Civilising Process: Vol 1, History of Manners*, Oxford: Blackwell

Ellis, J. (1991) *Visible Fictions: Cinema, Television, Video*, London and New York: Routledge

Enos, Katherine (1997/1998) 'Crash & Pornography Culture', www.pomegranates.com

Evans, C. and Thornton, M. (1989) *Women and Fashion: A New Look*, London: Quartet

Evans, Jessica (ed.) (1997) *The Camerawork Essays*, London: Rivers Oram Press

Ewing, William (1991) 'Perfect Surface' in *The Idealising Vision: The Art of Fashion Photography*, New York: Aperture

—— (1994) *The Body*, London: Thames and Hudson

—— (1996) *Inside Information: Imaging the Human Body*, London: Thames and Hudson

Falk, Pasi (1997) 'The Benetton–Toscani Effect – Testing the Limits of Conventional Advertising' in Mica Nava, Andrew Blake, Iain MacRury and Barry Richards (eds) *Buy this Book*, London: Routledge

Felman, S. and Laub, D. (1992) *Testimony: Crises of Witnessing in Literature, Psychoanalysis and History*, London: Routledge

Ferguson, Russell (1992) 'A Box of Tools: Theory and Practice' in R. Ferguson *et al.* (eds) *Discourses: Conversations in Postmodernism, Art and Culture*, Cambridge, MA: The MIT Press

Fisher, Andrea (1987) *Let Us Now Praise Famous Women*, London: Pandora

Ford, C. (1989) *The Story of Popular Photography*, Bradford: Century Hutchinson Ltd/National Museum of Photography, Film and Television

Foster, Hal (1993) *Compulsive Beauty*, Cambridge, MA, and London: The MIT Press, Chapters 4 and 5

—— (1996) 'Obscene, Abject, Traumatic', *October* 78, Autumn

Frank, R. (1959) *The Americans*, New York: Grove Press

Freedman, Jim (1990) 'Bringing it all Back Home: A Commentary on *Into the Heart of Africa*', *Museum Quarterly*, February

Freud, Sigmund (1905) 'Three Essays on Sexuality', in Vol. 7 of Freud (1953–1964) *Standard Edition of the Complete Works*, trans. James Strachey, London: Hogarth Press

Freund, Gisele (1980) *Photography and Society*, London: Gordon Fraser

Frizot, Michel (ed.) (1998) *A New History of Photography*, Cologne: Konemann (originally published in French, 1994)

Gabriel, T. (1995) *The Intolerable Gift*, unpublished conference paper, London: BFI

Galassi, Peter (1981) *Before Photography*, New York: MOMA

—— (1995) *American Photography 1890–1965*, New York: MOMA

Gamman, Lorraine and Makinen, Merja (1994) *Female Fetishism: A New Look*, London: Lawrence and Wishart

Gasser, Martin (1992) 'Histories of Photography 1839–1939', *History of Photography* 16(1), Spring

Geraghty, C. (1991) *Women and Soap Opera: A Study of Prime Time Soaps*, Cambridge: Polity Press

Gernsheim, Alison (1981) *Victorian and Edwardian Fashion, A Photographic Survey*, New York: Dover (originally published 1963, revised edition)

Gernsheim, Helmut and Gernsheim, Alison (1965) *A Concise History of Photography*, London: Thames and Hudson

—— (1969) *The History of Photography from the Earliest Use of the Camera Obscura in the Eleventh Century up to 1914*, 2 vols, London and New York: McGraw-Hill (first edition, 1955)

Gidal, T.N. (1973) *Modern Photojournalism*, New York: Macmillan

Goddard, Angela (1998) *The Language of Advertising: Written Texts*, London: Routledge

Godfrey, Tony (1998) *Conceptual Art*, London: Phaidon

Goffman, Erving (1979) *Gender Advertisements*, London: Macmillan

Goldberg, Vicki (ed.) (1981) *Photography in Print*, Albuquerque: University of New Mexico

Goldman, Robert (1992) *Reading Ads Socially*, London: Routledge

Graham, B. (1995) 'The Panic Button (In Which our Heroine Goes Back to the Future of Pornography)' in M. Lister (ed.) *The Photographic Image in Digital Culture*, London and New York: Routledge

Graham, Judith (1989) 'Benetton "Colors" the Race Issue', *Advertising Age*

Graham-Brown, Sarah (1988) *Images of Women: The Portrayal of Women in Photography of the Middle East 1860–1950*, London: Quartet Books

Gray, Camilla (1962) *The Russian Experiment in Art*, London: Thames and Hudson

Green, D. (1994) 'Classified Subjects', *Ten/8* 14: 30–37

Green, Jonathan (1984) 'The Painter as Photographer', *American Photography*, New York: Harry N. Abrams

Greenberg, Clement (1939) 'Avant-Garde and Kitsch', in *Art and Culture*, Boston, MA: Beacon Press, 1961. Reprinted in C. Harrison and P. Wood (eds) (1992) *Art in Theory 1900–1990*, Oxford: Blackwell

—— (1961) 'Modernist Painting' reprinted in F. Frascina and J. Harris (eds) (1992) *Art in Modern Culture*, London: Phaidon

—— (1991) 'Four Photographers', first published 1964, reprinted in *History of Photography* 15(2), Summer

Green-Lewis, Jennifer (1996) *Framing the Victorians, Photography and the Culture of Realism*, Ithaca and London: Cornell University Press

Grey, C. (1991) 'Theories of Relativity' in J. Spence and P. Holland (eds) *Family Snaps: The Meanings of Domestic Photography*, London: Virago

Griffiths, P.J. (1971) *Vietnam Inc.*, New York: Macmillan

Grundberg, Andy (1986) 'Veins of Resemblance' in P. Holland, J. Spence and S. Watney (eds) *Photography/Politics: Two*, London: Comedia

—— (1990a) 'On the Dissecting Table' in Carol Squiers *The Critical Image*, London: Lawrence and Wishart

—— (1990b) 'Photography in the Age of Electronic Simulation' in *Crisis of the Real*, New York: Aperture

Gupta, Sunil (1986) 'Northern Media, Southern Lives' in Photography Workshop (ed.) *Photography/Politics: Two*, London: Comedia

—— (1990) 'Photography, Sexuality and Cultural Difference', *Camerawork Quarterly* 17(3)

—— (ed.) (1993) *Disrupted Borders: An Intervention in Definitions of Boundaries*, London: Rivers Oram Press

Haddon, L. (1993) 'Interactive Games' in P. Hayward and T. Wollen (eds) *Future Visions: New Technologies of the Screen*, London: BFI

Hall, C. (1979) 'Early Formation of Victorian Domestic Ideology' in S. Burman (ed.) *Fit Work for Women*, London: Croom Helm

Hall, Stuart (1972) 'The Social Eye of *Picture Post*', *Cultural Studies* 2, CCCS, Birmingham

—— (1988) 'The Work of Art in The Electronic Age', *Block* 14

—— (1991) 'Reconstruction Work: Images of Post-War Black Settlement' in J. Spence and P. Holland (eds) *Family Snaps: The Meanings of Domestic Photography*, London: Virago

—— (1993) 'Encoding/Decoding' in S. Durring (ed.) *The Cultural Studies Reader*, London: Routledge (first published 1980)

—— (ed.) (1997) *Representation, Cultural Representations and Signifying Practices*, London: Sage/Open University

Hannavy, J. (1975) *Roger Fenton of Crimble Hall*, London: Gordon Fraser

Hardy, B. (1977) 'Bert Hardy', *Camerawork* 8

Harker, Margaret F. (1979) *The Linked Ring: The Secession Movement in Photography in Britain 1892–1910*, London: Heinemann

—— (1988) *Henry Peach Robinson*, Oxford and New York: Blackwell

Harrison, Charles and Wood, Paul (1993) 'Modernity and Modernism Reconsidered', Chapter 3 of Paul Wood, Francis Frascina, Jonathan Harris and Charles Harrison *Modernism in Dispute*, London: Yale University Press/Open University Press

Harrison, Martin (1991) *Appearances: Fashion Photography Since 1945*, London: V&A

Harvey, D. (1989) *The Condition of Postmodernity*, Cambridge, MA: Blackwell

Harvie, C. *et al.* (1970) *Industrialisation and Culture 1830–1914*, London: Macmillan and the Open University Press

Haworth-Booth, Mark (ed.) (1975) *The Land: Twentieth Century Landscape Photographs*, selected by Bill Brandt, London: Gordon Fraser Gallery

—— (ed.) (1988) *British Photography: Towards a Bigger Picture*, New York: Aperture

—— (1992) *River Scene, France*, Los Angeles, CA: J. Paul Getty Museum

—— (1997) *Photography: An Independent Art*, London: V&A Publications

Hayward, P. (1993) 'Situating Cyberspace: The Popularisation of Virtual Reality' in P. Hayward and T. Walker (eds) *Future Visions: New Technologies of the Screen*, London: BFI

Heiferman, Marvin (1989) 'Everywhere, All the Time, for Everybody' in Marvin Heiferman and Lisa Phillips (eds) *Image World*, New York: Whitney Museum of Art

Heron, Liz and Williams, Val (1996) *Illuminations: Women Writing on Photography from the 1850s to the Present*, London and New York: I.B. Tauris

Hershkowitz, R. (1980) *The British Photographer Abroad: The First Thirty Years*, London: Robert Hershkowitz Ltd

Hewison, Robert (1987) *The Heritage Industry*, London: Methuen

Higonnet, A. (1998) *Pictures of Innocence: The History and Crisis of Ideal Childhood*, London: Thames and Hudson

Hiley, M. (1983) *Seeing Through Photographs*, London: Gordon Frazer

Hill, Paul and Cooper, Thomas (1992) *Dialogue with Photography*, Manchester: Cornerhouse Publications

Hirsch, J. (1981) *Family Photography: Context, Meaning and Effect*, New York: Oxford University Press

Hirsch, M. (1997) *Family Frames: Photography, Narrative and Postmemory*, Cambridge, MA: Harvard University Press

Hoggart, Richard (1957) *The Uses of Literacy*, Harmondsworth: Penguin, 1959

Holland, P. (1991) 'The Old Order of Things Changed' in J. Spence and P. Holland (eds) *Family Snaps: The Meanings of Domestic Photography*, London: Virago

—— (1992) *What is a Child?*, London: Virago

—— (1997) 'Press Photography' in A. Briggs and P. Cobley (eds) *Introduction to Media*, London: Longman

Holland, P. and Dewdney, A. (eds) (1992) *The Child, Seen but Not Heard?*, Bristol: Watershed Media Centre. Exhibition catalogue and introduction

Holmes, Oliver Wendell (1859) 'The Stereoscope and the Stereograph', *Atlantic Monthly* 3, reprinted in B. Newhall (ed.) (1980) *Photography: Essays and Images*, London: Secker and Warburg

Horne, Donald (1984) *The Great Museum: The Re-presentation of History*, London: Verso

Howard, F. (1853) 'Photography Applied to Fine Art', *Journal of the Photographic Society*, London

Hudson, D. (1972) *Munby, Man of Two Worlds*, London: John Murray

Hurley, Jack (1972) *Portrait of a Decade: Roy Stryker and the Development of Documentary Photography in the Thirties*, Baton Rouge: Louisiana State University Press

Hutchison, Robert (1982) *The Politics of the Arts Council*, London: Sinclair Browne

Iles, Chrissie and Roberts, Russell (eds) (1997) *In Visible Light*, Oxford: Museum of Modern Art

Isherwood, C. (1939) *Goodbye to Berlin*, Harmondsworth: Penguin Books

Isherwood, S. (1988) *The Family Album*, London: Broadcasting Support Services

Jameson, Fredric (1984) 'Postmodernism or the Cultural Logic of Late Capitalism', *New Left Review* 146, July/August

—— (1991) *Postmodernism, Or, the Cultural Logic of Late Capitalism*, London: Verso

—— (1993) 'Postmodernism and Consumer Society' in A. Gray and J. McGuigan (eds) *Studying Culture*, London, New York, Melbourne and Auckland: Edward Arnold

Jameson, S. (1937) 'Writing in Revolt', *Fact* 4

Jay, Martin (1993) *Downcast Eyes: The Denigration of Vision in Twentieth Century French Thought*, San Francisco: University of California Press

Jeffrey, Ian (1981) *Photography, A Concise History*, London: Thames and Hudson

—— (1982) 'Some Sacred Sites', *Creative Camera* 215, November

—— (1991) 'Morality, Darkness and Light: The Metropolis in Pictures' in Martin Caiger-Smith *Site Work*, London: The Photographers' Gallery

Jhally, Sut (1990) *Codes of Advertising*, London: Routledge

Jukes, P. (1992) 'The Work of Art in the Domain of Digital Production', *New Statesman and Society*, 17 July: 40–41

Kalogeraki, K. (1991) 'My Father's Land' in J. Spence and P. Holland (eds) *Family Snaps: The Meanings of Domestic Photography*, London: Virago

Kelly, A. (1979) 'Feminism and Photography' in P. Hill, A. Kelly and J. Tagg *Three Perspectives on Photography*, London: ACGB

Kelly, Mary (1981) 'Reviewing Modernist Criticism', *Screen* 22(3)

Kember, S. (1995a) 'Medicine's New Vision' in M. Lister (ed.) *The Photographic Image in Digital Culture*, London and New York: Routledge

—— (1995b) 'Surveillance, Technology and Crime: The James Bulger Case' in M. Lister (ed.) *The Photographic Image in Digital Culture*, London: Routledge

Kendrick, Walter (1987) *The Secret Museum: Pornography in Modern Culture*, New York: Viking, republished in 1996 by the University of California Press

Kenyon, D. (1992) *Inside Amateur Photography*, London: Batsford

Kern, Stephen (1983) *The Culture of Time and Space 1800–1918*, Cambridge, MA: The MIT Press

Kipnis, Laura (1992) '(Male) Desire and (Female) Disgust: Reading Hustler' in Lawrence Grossberg *et al.* (eds) *Cultural Studies*, London and New York: Routledge

Kotz, Liz (1998) 'Aesthetics of Intimacy' in Deborah Bright (ed.) *The Passionate Camera: Photography and Bodies of Desire*, London and New York: Routledge

Kozloff, Max (1979) *Photography and Fascination*, USA New Hampshire: Addison House

—— (1987) *The Privileged Eye*, Albuquerque: University of New Mexico Press

Kracauer, Siegfried (1960) 'Photography', Chapter 1 of *Theory of Film*, Oxford: Museum of Modern Art

Krauss, Rosalind (1981) 'A Note on Photography and the Simulacral', *October*, Winter, reprinted in Carol Squiers (ed.) (1991) *The Critical Image*, Seattle: Bay Press/London: Lawrence and Wishart

—— (1986) *The Originality of the Avant-Garde and Other Modernist Myths*, Cambridge, MA: The MIT Press

Krauss, Rosalind and Livingston, Jane (1986) *L'Amour Fou*, London: Arts Council of Great Britain

Kruger, Barbara (1983) *We Won't Play Nature to your Culture*, London: Institute of Contemporary Arts

—— (1990) *Love for Sale: The Words and Pictures of Barbara Kruger*, New York: Harry N. Abrams, Inc

Kuenzli, Rudolf E. (1991) 'Surrealism and Misogyny' in Mary Ann Caws, Rudolf Kuenzli and Owen Raaberg *Surrealism and Women*, Cambridge, MA: The MIT Press

Kuhn, A. (1991) 'Remembrance' in J. Spence and P. Holland (eds) *Family Snaps: The Meanings of Domestic Photography*, London: Virago

—— (1995) *Family Secrets: Acts of Memory and Imagination*, London: Verso

Lalvani, Suren (1996) *Photography, Vision, and the Production of Modern Bodies*, Albany: State University of New York

Lamagny, Jean-Claude and Rouille, André (1987) *A History of Photography*, Cambridge: Cambridge University Press

Lange, Dorothea (1960) 'The Assignment I'll Never Forget' in Beaumont Newhall (ed.) (1980) *Photography: Essays and Images*, London: Secker and Warburg

Lavin, Maud (1993) *Cut with the Kitchen Knife: The Weimar Photomontages of Hannah Hoch*, New Haven, CT: Yale University Press

Leiss, W., Kline, S. and Jhally, S. (1986) *Social Communication in Advertising*, Toronto: Methuen

Lewinski, J. (1978) *The Camera at War*, London: W.H. Allen

Lewis, B. and Harding, D. (eds) (1992) *Kept in a Shoebox: The Experience of Popular Photography*, Bradford: Yorkshire Art Circus/National Museum of Photography, Film and Television

Linkman, A. (1993) *The Victorians: Photographic Portraits*, London: Tauris Parke Books

Linkman, A. and Warhurst, C. (1982) *Family Albums*, Manchester: Manchester Polytechnic. A fully illustrated exhibition catalogue with an introduction

Lipton, Eunice (1980) 'The Laundress in Nineteenth Century French Culture', *Art History*, Vol. 3, No. 3, pp. 215–313, abridged version in Francis Frascina and Charles Harrison (1983) *Modern Art and Modernism: A Critical Anthology*, HarperCollins

Lister, M. (ed.) (1995a) *The Photographic Image in Digital Culture*, London and New York: Routledge

—— (1995b) 'Introductory Essay' in M. Lister (ed.) *The Photographic Image in Digital Culture*, London and New York: Routledge

Lloyd, J. (1985) 'Old Photographs, Vanished Peoples and Stolen Potatoes', *Art Monthly* 83, February

Lovell, Terry (1980) *Pictures of Reality*, ch. 5.3, London: BFI

Lury, C. (1992) 'Popular Culture and the Mass Media' in R. Bocock and K. Thompson (eds) *Social and Cultural Forms of Modernity*, Cambridge: Polity Press

Lyons, Nathan (1966) *Photographers on Photography*, Englewood Cliffs, NJ: Prentice Hall

McCauley, Elizabeth Anne (1994) *Industrial Madness: Commercial Photography in Paris 1848–1871*, New Haven, CT, and London: Yale University Press

Macdonald, G. (1979) *Camera: A Victorian Eyewitness*, London: Batsford; based on a Granada television series

McGrath, R. (1984) 'Medical Police', *Ten/8* 14: 13–18

Magli, Patrizia (1989) 'The Face and the Soul' in M. Feher *et al.* (eds) *Zone 4: Fragments for a History of the Human Body, Part Two*, Cambridge, MA: Zone/The MIT Press

Makela, Tapio (1997) 'Photography, Post-Photography', *Creative Camera*, April/May

Malina, R.F. (1990) 'Digital Image – Digital Cinema: The Work of Art in the Age of Post-mechanical Reproduction', *Leonardo*, Supplemental Issue: 33–38

Mann, S. (1992) *Immediate Family*, London: Phaidon

Martin, R. (1991) 'Unwind the Ties That Bind' in J. Spence and P. Holland (eds) *Family Snaps: The Meanings of Domestic Photography*, London: Virago

Marvin, C. (1988) *When Old Technologies Were New*, New York: Oxford University Press

Mavor, C. (1996) *Pleasures Taken: Performances of Sexuality and Loss in Victorian Photographs*, London: I.B. Taurus

Mayhew, H. (1861) *London Labour and the London Poor*, reprinted 1967, London: Frank Cass

Mayle, Peter (1983) *Thirsty Work: Ten Years of Heineken Advertising*, London: Macmillan

Maynard, P. (1997) *The Engine of Visualisation: Thinking Through Photography*, New York: Cornell University Press

Mayne, R. (1986) *The Street Photographs of Roger Mayne*, London: V&A Museum

Mellencamp, Patricia (1992) *High Anxiety: Catastrophe, Scandal, Age and Comedy*, Bloomington: Indiana University Press

Metz, Christian (1985) 'Photography and Fetish', *October* 34, Autumn

Meyer, Moe (ed.) (1994) *The Politics and Poetics of Camp*, London: Routledge

Minto, C.S. (1970) *Victorian and Edwardian Scotland from Old Photographs*, London: Batsford

Mitchell, W.J. (1992) *The Reconfigured Eye: Visual Truth in the Post-photographic Era*, Cambridge, MA: The MIT Press

Mitter, Swasti (1986) 'Flexibility and Control: The Case of Benetton' in *Common Fate Common Bond; Women in the Global Economy*, London: Pluto

Moholy-Nagy, László (1967) *Painting, Photography, Film*, London: Lund Humphries

Montoussamy-Ashe, Jeanne (1985) *Viewfinders: Black Women Photographers*, New York: Dodd, Mead

Morris, Roderick C. (1992) 'The Best Possible Taste', *Spectator*, 15 February

Mulvey, Laura (1981) 'Visual Pleasure and Narrative Cinema' in T. Bennett *et al*. (eds) *Popular Television and Film*, London: BFI/OU. Originally published in 1975, also in Mulvey, L. (1989) *Visual and Other Pleasures*, London: Macmillan

Musello, C. (1979) 'Family Photography' in J. Wagner (ed.) *Images of Information*, London: Sage

Myers, Kathy (1986) *Understains: Sense and Seduction in Advertising*, London: Comedia

—— (1990) 'Selling Green' in C. Squiers (ed.) *The Critical Image: Essays on Contemporary Photography*, Seattle: Bay Press

Nairne, Sandy (1987) *State of the Art, Ideas and Images in the 1980s*, London: Chatto & Windus

Nead, L. (1992) *The Female Nude: Art, Obscenity and Sexuality*, London and New York: Routledge

Neale, S. (1985) *Cinema and Technology: Images, Sound, Colour*, London: Macmillan

Newhall, Beaumont (1982) *The History of Photography*, New York: MOMA, fifth edition, revised and enlarged (first edition 1937)

Nichols, Bill (1981) *Image and Ideology*, Bloomington: University of Indiana Press

—— (1988) 'The Work of Culture in the Age of Cybernetic Systems', *Screen* 29(1), Winter

Nochlin, Linda (1978) *Realism*, Harmondsworth: Penguin

Nye, David (1985) *Image Worlds: Corporate Identities at General Electric 1890–1930*, Cambridge, MA: The MIT Press

Ohrn, Karen Becker (1980) *Dorothea Lange and the Documentary Tradition*, Baton Rouge: Louisiana State University Press

Olalquiaga, Celeste (1992) *Megalopolis: Contemporary Cultural Sensibilities*, Minneapolis: University of Minnesota Press

O'Reilly, John (1998) 'Death is Probably the Last Pornographic Issue Left', *Guardian*, 2 February

Parr, M. (1995) *Small World: A Global Photographic Project, 1987–1994*, Stockport: Dewi Lewis Publishing

Parr, M. and Stasiak, J. (1986) *'The Actual Boot': The Photographic Post-card Boom 1900–1920*, Bradford: A.H. Jolly (Editorial) Ltd/National Museum of Photography, Film and Television. Exhibition catalogue and introduction

Penlake, R. (1899) *Home Portraits for Amateur Photographers*, London

Penn, Irving (1974) *Worlds in a Small Room*, London: Studio Vista

Phaidon (1997) *The Photography Book*, London: Phaidon

Phillips, Christopher (ed.) (1989) *Photography in the Modern Era: European Documents and Critical Writings 1913–1940*, New York: MOMA

Phizacklea, Annie (1990) 'The Benetton Model' in *Unpackaging the Fashion Industry: Gender, Racism and Class in Production*, London: Routledge

Piper, K. (1991) 'Fortress Europe: Tagging the Other' in P. Wombell (ed.) *PhotoVideo: Photography in the Age of the Computer*, London: Rivers Oram Press

Pollock, Griselda (1977) 'What's Wrong with "Images of Women"?', reprinted in R. Parker and G. Pollock (eds) (1987) *Framing Feminism*, London: Pandora Press

—— (1990) 'Missing Women – Re-Thinking Early Thoughts on Images of Women' in C. Squiers (ed.) *The Critical Image: Essays on Contemporary Photography*, Seattle: Bay Press

Posner, Jill (1982) *Spray it Loud*, London: Routledge

Powell, R. (1985) *Photography and the Making of History: Brunel's Kingdom*, Bristol: Watershed Media Centre

Price, D. (1983) 'Photographing the Poor and the Working Class', *Framework* 22(22), Autumn

Price, Mary (1994) *The Photograph: A Strange, Confined Space*, Stanford, CA: Stanford University Press

Prochaska, David (1991) 'Fantasia of the Phototheque: French Postcard Views of Senegal', *African Arts*, October

Pryce, W.T.R. (1994) 'Photographs and Picture Postcards' in M. Drake and R. Finnegan (eds)
    Studying Family and Community History: 19th and 20th Centuries, Cambridge:
    Cambridge University Press/Open University
Pultz, John (1995a) *The Body and the Lens: Photography 1839 to the Present*, New York:
    Harry N. Abrams, Inc
—— (1995b) *Photography and the Body*, London: Weidenfeld & Nicolson
Punt, Michael (1995) 'The Elephant, the Spaceship and the White Cockatoo: An Archaeology of
    Digital Photography' in M. Lister (ed.) *The Photographic Image in Digital Culture*, London
    and New York: Routledge
Quartermaine, P. (1992) 'Johannes Lindt: Photographer of Australia and New Guinea' in
    M. Gidley (ed.) *Representing Others: White Views of Indigenous Peoples*, Exeter:
    University of Exeter Press
Rabinowitz, Paula (1984) *They Must be Represented: The Politics of Documentary*, London:
    Verso
Ray-Jones, T. (1974) *A Day Off: An English Journal*, London: Thames and Hudson
Richards, Thomas (1990) *Commodity Culture in Victorian Britain*, London: Verso
Ride, P. (1997) 'Photography and Digital Art', *Creative Camera*, April/May
Riis, J.A. (1918) *The Making of an American*, New York: Macmillan
Ritchen, F. (1990a) *In Our Own Image: The Coming Revolution in Photography*, New York:
    Aperture
—— (1990b) 'Photojournalism in the Age of Computers' in C. Squiers (ed.) *The Critical
    Image*, Seattle: Bay Press, pp. 28–37
Roberts, John (1993) *Renegotiations: Class, Modernity and Photography*, Norwich: Norwich
    Gallery, Norfolk Institute of Art and Design
—— (ed.) (1997) *The Impossible Document: Photography and Conceptual Art in Britain
    1966–1976*, London: Camerawords
—— (1998) *The Art of Interruption: Realism, Photography and the Everyday*, Manchester:
    Manchester University Press
Robertson, G., Mash, M., Tickner, L., Bird, J., Curtis, B. and Putnam, T. (eds) (1994) *Travellers'
    Tales: Narratives of Home and Displacement*, London: Routledge
Robins, Corinne (1984) *The Pluralist Era: American Art 1968–1981*, New York: Harper & Row
Robins, K. (1991) 'Into the Image: Visual Technologies and Vision Cultures' in P. Wombell (ed.)
    PhotoVideo: Photography in the Age of the Computer, London: Rivers Oram Press
—— (1995) 'Will Images Move Us Still?' in M. Lister (ed.) *The Photographic Image in Digital
    Culture*, London and New York: Routledge
Rodchenko, Alexander (1928) 'Against the Synthetic Portrait, for the Snapshot', published in the
    Moscow journal *Novy LEF: New Left Front of the Arts* in C. Phillips (ed.) (1989)
    Photography in the Modern Era: European Documents and Critical Writings 1913–1940,
    New York: MOMA
Rodgerson, Gillian and Wilson, Elizabeth (eds) (1991) *Pornography and Feminism: The Case
    Against Censorship*, London: Lawrence and Wishart
Rogers, Brett (ed.) (1994) *Documentary Dilemmas: Aspects of British Documentary
    Photography 1983–1993*, London: British Council
Rosenblum, Naomi (1994) *A History of Women Photographers*, New York, London, and Paris:
    Abbeville Press
—— (1997) *A World History of Photography*, New York, London, and Paris: Abbeville Press
    (previous editions, 1984, 1989)
Rosler, Martha (1989) 'In, Around and Afterthoughts (on Documentary Photography)'
    in Richard Bolton (ed.) *The Contest of Meaning: Critical Histories of Photography*,
    Cambridge, MA: The MIT Press
—— (1991) 'Image Simulations, Computer Manipulations, Some Considerations', *Ten-8* 2(2),
    Digital Dialogues
Rowland, Anna (1990) *The Bauhaus Source Book*, Chapter 6, 'Graphics', Oxford: Phaidon

Ruby, Jay (1995) *Secure the Shadow: Photography and Death in America*, Cambridge, MA, and London: The MIT Press

Ryan, James R. (1997) *Picturing Empire: Photography and the Visualisation of the British Empire*, London: Reaktion Books

Said, Edward (1985) *Orientalism*, London: Penguin (first published 1978)

Savan, Leslie (1990) 'Logo-rrhea', *Voice*, 24 November, New York

Scharf, Aron (1974) *Art and Photography*, Harmondsworth: Pelican, revised edition

Schildkrout, Enid (1991) 'The Spectacle of Africa Through the Lens of Herbert Lang', *African Arts*, October

Segal, Lynne and Macintosh, Mary (eds) (1992) *Sex Exposed: Sexuality and the Pornography Debate*, London: Virago

Sekula, Allan (1978) 'Dismantling Modernism, Reinventing Documentary (Notes on the Politics of Representation)' in J. Liebling (ed.) *Photography: Current Perspectives*, Rochester, New York: Light Impressions Co

Sherman, Cindy (1986) 'The Archive and the Body', *October* 39, reprinted in Richard Bolton (ed.) (1989) *The Contest of Meaning: Critical Histories of Photography*, Cambridge, MA: The MIT Press

—— (1991) 'Reading an Archive' in Brian Wallis and Marcia Tucker (eds) *Blasted Allegories*, Cambridge, MA: The MIT Press

—— (1997) *Retrospective*, London: Thames and Hudson

Slater, D.R. (1983) 'Marketing Mass Photography' in H. Davis and P. Walton (eds) *Language, Image, Media*, Oxford: Blackwell

—— (1991) 'Consuming Kodak' in J. Spence and P. Holland (eds) *Family Snaps: The Meanings of Domestic Photography*, London: Virago

—— (1995a) 'Photography and Modern Vision: The Spectacle of "Natural Magic"' in C. Jenks (ed.) *Visual Culture*, London: Routledge

—— (1995b) 'Domestic Photography and Digital Culture' in M. Lister (ed.) *The Photographic Image in Digital Culture*, London and New York: Routledge

Snyder, Joel (1980) 'Picturing Vision', *Critical Enquiry* 6, Spring: 499–526

—— (1994) 'Territorial Photography' in W.J.T. Mitchell (ed.) *Landscape and Power*, London: University of Chicago Press

Snyder, J. and Allen, N.W. (1975) 'Photography, Vision, and Representation', *Critical Enquiry* 2, Autumn: 143–169

Solanke, A. (1991) 'Complex Not Confused' in J. Spence and P. Holland (eds) *Family Snaps: The Meanings of Domestic Photography*, London: Virago

Soloman, J. (1995) 'Interrogating the Holiday Snap' in J. Spence and J. Soloman *What Can a Woman do with a Camera?*, London: Scarlet Press

Solomon-Godeau, Abigail (1991a) *Photography at the Dock: Essays on Photographic History, Institutions and Practices*, Minneapolis: University of Minnesota Press

—— (1991b) 'Who is Speaking Thus?' in *Photography at the Dock: Essays on Photographic History, Institutions and Practices*, Minneapolis: University of Minnesota Press

—— (1991c) 'Reconsidering Erotic Photography: Notes for a Project of Historical Salvage' in *Photography in the Dock*, Minneapolis: University of Minnesota Press

Sontag, Susan (1979) *On Photography*, Harmondsworth: Penguin

Spence, J. (1987) *Putting Myself in the Picture*, London: Macmillan

—— (1991) 'Soap, Family Album Work . . . and Hope' in J. Spence and P. Holland (eds) *Family Snaps: The Meanings of Domestic Photography*, London: Virago

—— (1995) *Cultural Sniping*, London: Routledge

Spence, J. and Holland, P. (eds) (1991) *Family Snaps: The Meanings of Domestic Photography*, London: Virago

Spence, J. and Soloman, J. (eds) (1995) *What Can a Woman do with a Camera?*, London: Scarlet Press

Spender, H. (1978) 'Humphrey Spender: M. O. Photographer', *Camerawork* 11

Squiers, Carol (ed.) (1990) *The Critical Image*, London: Lawrence and Wishart

—— (1992) 'The Corporate Year in Pictures' in R. Bolton (ed.) *The Contest of Meaning: Critical Histories of Photography*, Cambridge, MA: The MIT Press

Stafford, B.M. (1991) *Body Criticism, Imaging the Unseen in Enlightenment, Art and Medicine*, Cambridge, MA: The MIT Press

Stallabrass, J. (1997) 'Sebastiano Salgado and Fine Art Photojournalism', *New Left Review* 223

Stallybrass, Peter and White, Allon (1986) *The Politics and Poetics of Transgression*, Ithaca and New York: Cornell University Press

Stanley, J. (1991) 'Well, Who'd Want an Old Picture of me at Work?' in J. Spence and P. Holland (eds) *Family Snaps: The Meanings of Domestic Photography*, London: Virago

Steele-Perkins, Chris (ed.) (1980) *About 70 Photographs*, London: Arts Council of Great Britain

Stein, S. (1981) 'The Composite Photographic Image and the Composition of Consumer Ideology', *Art Journal*, Spring

—— (1983) 'Making Connections with the Camera: Photography and Social Mobility in the Career of Jacob Riis', *Afterimage* 10(10)

—— (1992) 'The Graphic Ordering of Desire: Modernisation of a Middle-Class Women's Magazine 1919–1939' in R. Bolton (ed.) *The Contest of Meaning: Critical Histories of Photography*, Cambridge, MA: The MIT Press

Stokes, Philip (1992) 'The Family Photograph Album: So Great a Cloud of Witnesses' in Graham Clarke (ed.) *The Portrait in Photography*, London: Reaktion Books

Stott, W. (1973) *Documentary Expression and Thirties America*, London: Oxford University Press

Strand, Paul (1917) 'Photography', *Camera Work* 49/50, reprinted in B. Newhall (1982) *The History of Photography*, New York: MOMA

—— (1980) *Photography: Essays and Images*, London: Secker and Warburg

Stryker, Roy (1979) in Peninah R. Petruck (ed.) *The Camera Viewed: Writings on Twentieth-Century Photography*, New York: E.P. Dutton

Sullivan, Constance (ed.) (1990) *Women Photographers*, London: Virago

Szarkowski, John (1989) *Photography Until Now*, New York: MOMA

Tagg, John (1988) *The Burden of Representation: Essays on Photographies and Histories*, London: Macmillan

Taylor, John (1994) *A Dream of England: Landscape, Photography and the Tourist's Imagination*, Manchester: Manchester University Press

Taylor, Mark C. (1997) *Hiding*, Chicago, IL, and London: University of Chicago Press

Thomas, Alan (1978) *The Expanding Eye: Photography and the Nineteenth Century Mind*, London: Croom Helm

Thomas, Deborah Willis (1985) *Black Photographers 1840–1940: An Illustrated Bio-Bibliography*, New York: Garland

Thompson, F.M.L. (ed.) (1990) *The Cambridge Social History of Britain 1750–1850*, Vol. 2, *People and Their Environment*, Cambridge: Cambridge University Press

Thomson, J. (1877) *Street Life in London*, n.p.n.

Townsend, Chris (1998) *Vile Bodies: Photography and the Crisis of Looking*, Munich and New York: Prestel-Verlag and Channel Four Television Corporation

Trachtenberg, A. (1982) *The Incorporation of America*, New York: Hill and Wang

—— (1989) *Reading American Photographs*, New York: Hill and Wang

Treuherz, J. (1987) *Hard Times: Social Realism in Victorian Art*, London: Lund Humphries

Tucker, Anne (1973) *The Woman's Eye*, New York: Knopf

—— (1984) 'Photographic Facts and Thirties America' in David Featherstone (ed.) *Observations: Essays on Documentary Photography*, Carmel, CA: Friends of Photography

Turner, Peter (1987) *History of Photography*, London: Hamlyn

Urry, J. (1990) *The Tourist Gaze: Leisure and Travel in Contemporary Societies*, London: Sage

Vance, Carole S. (1990) 'The Meese Commission' in Carol Squiers (ed.) *The Critical Image: Essays on Contemporary Photography*, Seattle: Bay Press

Virilio, P. (1989) *War and Cinema*, London: Verso

Virilio, P., Baudrillard, J. and Hall, S. (1988) 'The Work of Art in the Electronic Age', *Block* 14

Walker, I. (1995) 'Desert Stones or Faith in Facts' in M. Lister (ed.) *The Photographic Image in Digital Culture*, London and New York: Routledge

Walkerdine, V. (1991) 'Behind the Painted Smile' in J. Spence and P. Holland (eds) *Family Snaps: The Meanings of Domestic Photography*, London: Virago

Warner, M. (1992) 'Women in the Victorian Family Album', *Creative Camera*, May

Warner Marien, Mary (1988) 'Another History of Photography', *Afterimage*, October: 4–5

—— (1991) 'Toward a New Prehistory of Photography' in Daniel P. Younger (ed.) *Multiple Views*, Albuquerque: University of New Mexico Press

—— (1997) *Photography and Its Critics, A Cultural History, 1839–1900*, Cambridge and New York: Cambridge University Press

Watney, S. (1991) 'Ordinary Boys' in J. Spence and P. Holland (eds) *Family Snaps: The Meanings of Domestic Photography*, London: Virago

Watriss, Wendy and Zamora, Lois (eds) (1998) *Image and Memory: Photographs from Latin America 1866–1994*, Austin: University of Texas Press

Weaver, Mike (1982) *Photography as Fine Art*, London: Thames and Hudson

—— (1986) *The Photographic Art*, London: Herbert

—— (1989a) *The Art of Photography*, London: Royal Academy of Arts/New Haven, CT: Yale University Press

—— (1989b) *British Photography in the Nineteenth Century: The Fine Art Tradition*, Cambridge: Cambridge University Press

Weernink, Wim (1979) *La Lancia: 70 Years of Excellence*, London: Motor Racing Publications

Wells, Liz (ed.) (1992) 'Judith Williamson, Decoding Advertisements' in *Reading into Cultural Studies*, London: Routledge

—— (ed.) (1994) *Viewfindings, Women Photographers: 'Landscape' and Environment*, Tiverton, Devon: Available Light

Werge, J. (1890) *The Evolution of Photography*, London

Wilkinson, Helen (1997) ' "The New Heraldry": Stock Photography, Visual Literacy and Advertising in 1930s Britain', *Journal of Design History*, 10(1)

Willett, John (1978) *The New Sobriety, Art and Politics in the Weimar Period*, London: Thames and Hudson

Williams, Linda (1995) 'Corporealized Observers: Visual Pornographies and the Carnal Density of Vision' in Patrice Petro *Fugitive Images*, Bloomington: Indiana University Press

Williams, Raymond (1974) *Television, Technology and Cultural Form*, London: Fontana

—— (1976) *Keywords*, London: Fontana

—— (1979) 'The Arts Council', *Political Quarterly*, Spring

—— (1980) 'Advertising the Magic System' in *Problems in Materialism and Culture*, London: Verso

—— (1989) 'When Was Modernism' in *The Politics of Modernism*, London: Verso

Williams, Val (1986) *Women Photographers. The Other Observers, 1900 to the Present*, London: Virago (revised edition 1991, *The Other Observers. Women Photographers from 1900 to the Present*)

—— (1994) *Who's Looking at the Family?*, London: Barbican Art Gallery. Exhibition catalogue and introduction

—— (1998) *Look at Me: Fashion and Photography in Britain, 1960 to the Present*, London: British Council

Williamson, Judith (1978) *Decoding Advertisements: Ideology and Meaning in Advertising*, London: Marion Boyars

—— (1979) 'Great History that Photographs Mislaid' in Photography Workshop (ed.) *Photography/Politics: One*, London: Comedia

Willis, A-M. (1990) 'Digitisation and the Living Death of Photography' in P. Hayward (ed.) *Culture, Technology, and Creativity in the Late Twentieth Century*, London: John Libbey and Co Ltd

Winship, Janice (1987a) 'Handling Sex' in R. Betterton (ed.) *Looking On: Images of Femininity in the Visual Arts and Media*, London: Pandora

—— (1987b) *Inside Women's Magazines*, London: Pandora

Wollen, Peter (1978) 'Photography and Aesthetics', *Screen* 19(4), Winter, reprinted in *Readings and Writings*, London: Verso and New Left Books, 1982

Wombell, P. (1991) *PhotoVideo: Photography in the Age of the Computer*, London: Rivers Oram Press

Ziff, T. (1991) 'Taking New Ideas Back to the Old World' in P. Wombell (ed.) *PhotoVideo: Photography in the Age of the Computer*, London: Rivers Oram Press

Index

Note: Page references in bold indicate photographs, those in italics indicate condensed biographies.